Slaves Tell Tales

Slaves Tell Tales

AND OTHER EPISODES IN THE POLITICS OF
POPULAR CULTURE IN ANCIENT GREECE

Sara Forsdyke

PRINCETON UNIVERSITY PRESS   PRINCETON AND OXFORD

Published by Princeton University Press, 41 William Street,
Princeton, New Jersey 08540
In the United Kingdom: Princeton University Press, 6 Oxford Street,
Woodstock, Oxfordshire OX20 1TW

press.princeton.edu

Jacket art: Cup: Aesop and the fox, Moscioni Collection n.8601. Courtesy of the
American Academy in Rome, Photographic Archive.

Library of Congress Cataloging-in-Publication Data

Forsdyke, Sara, 1967–
    Slaves tell tales : and other episodes in the politics of popular culture in ancient
Greece / Sara Forsdyke.
        p. cm.
    Includes bibliographical references and index.
    ISBN 978-0-691-14005-6 (hardcover : acid-free paper) 1. Greek literature—History
and criticism. 2. Popular culture—Greece—History—To 146 B.C. 3. Oral tradition—
Greece—History—To 1500. 4. Literature and society—Greece—History—To 146 B.C.
5. Greece—Politics and government—To 146 B.C. I. Title.
    PA3009.F67   2012
    880.9′358—dc23   2011044725

British Library Cataloging-in-Publication Data is available

This book has been composed in Sabon

Printed on acid-free paper. ∞

Printed in the United States of America

10 9 8 7 6 5 4 3 2 1

For my parents,
Patricia and Donald Forsdyke, with love and gratitude

———————————————————————————————————————

Contents

Figures

Acknowledgments

I STARTED WORKING on this project in 2003 and have benefited greatly from the comments and advice of my colleagues in the Department of Classical Studies at the University of Michigan. In particular, Ruth Scodel has frequently put her wide knowledge of Greek literature at my disposal and provided many helpful comments on my work. Perhaps even more important, she has offered practical and moral support as I have tried to juggle the competing demands of work and family.

My interest in Greek history continues to thrive because of the stimulus of mentors and friends far and wide. In particular, the opportunity to share ideas annually with the Midwestern Consortium of Ancient Greek Historians and Political Theorists has been a great privilege. Included in this group are Ben Akrigg, Greg Anderson, Ryan Balot, Matthew Christ, Judith Fletcher, Sara Monoson, Kurt Raaflaub, Eric Robinson, Arlene Saxonhouse, Bernd Steinbock, Bob Wallace, and Victoria Wohl. Josine Blok, Paul Cartledge, and Robin Osborne kindly gave me opportunities to present portions of this work before helpful audiences. Peter Hunt, Nino Luraghi, and Robin Osborne have generously read portions of this work in draft. None of these, of course, are responsible for any remaining errors of fact or judgment, but I thank them heartily for their constructive comments and disagreements. Leslie Kurke shared an early version of her book on Aesop, and stimulated me to think about Aesop from a literary angle. Finally, Josiah Ober continues to be an inspiring role model for me as I move into the middle phase of my career. His scholarship and his mentorship have been invaluable and I strive (however imperfectly) to follow his example as I guide my own students toward productive professional lives.

Hearty thanks also go to the editorial and production staff at Princeton University Press, including Julia Livingston, Sara Lerner, and especially Rob Tempio. It has been a great pleasure to work with such a group of highly professional yet friendly publishers. Karen Verde provided skillful copyediting, and improved my style in numerous places.

I gratefully acknowledge the support of the Humanities Institute at the University of Michigan which provided me with a year of uninterrupted research time in 2005–6.

Some of the material in chapter 3 appears also as part of "Peer-Polity Interaction and Cultural Competition in Sixth Century Greece," in N. Fisher and H.van Wees, eds., *Competition in the Ancient World*, Classical Press of Wales, Swansea, 2011, pp. 147–74. Chapters 4 and 5 previously appeared as articles in the *Journal of Hellenic Studies* ("Revelry and Riot in Archaic Megara: Democratic Disorder or Ritual Reversal?" 125 (2005): 73–92, Cambridge University Press) and *Past and Present* ("Street Theater and Popular Justice in Ancient Greece: Shaming, Stoning and Starving Offenders Inside and Outside the Courts," *Past and Present* 201 (2008): 3–50, Oxford University Press). I have revised these articles to reflect my most recent research, and expanded them to include parts that had to be cut from the original journal versions. Finally, I have modified these articles in order to make them more accessible to a general audience. For permission to reprint this material, I thank the Society for the Promotion of Hellenic Studies and Oxford University Press.

Last but not least, thanks go to my family: my husband, Finn, and our children, Thomas and Sophie. All three are an endless source of joy and happiness. While writing this book, I have shared many wonderful moments with my extended family, including my parents-in-law, Oddbjørg and Einer Larsen, my sisters, Ruth Forsdyke, Polly Seegert, and Charlotte Forsdyke, my sister-in-law, Helena Larsen, and brothers-in-law, Allan Jensen and Per Larsen. I thank them all for the good times together. I dedicate this book to my parents, Patricia and Donald Forsdyke, who gave me a wonderful start in life and then let me fly free.

Abbreviations_____

Abbreviations for ancient authors and works follow the standard list in the *Oxford Classical Dictionary* (OCD), third edition, ed. S. Hornblower and A. Spawforth, 1996. In addition, the following abbreviations are used for standard modern editions of ancient Greek literature and documentary sources.

DK	H. Diels and W. Kranz, *Fragmente der Vorsokratiker*, 6th ed., 1952.
FGrHist	F. Jacoby, ed., *Die Fragmente der Griechischen Historiker*. Leiden, 1923–69.
IG	*Inscriptiones Graecae*
Kassel–Austin	R. Kassel and C. Austin, eds., *Poetae Comici Graeci*. Berlin, 1983–
West	M. L. West, *Iambi et Elegi Graeci*. Oxford, 1971.

Figure 1.
Map of Greece.

INTRODUCTION

1

Peasants, Politics, and Popular Culture

> A lot of grassroots history is like the trace of the
> ancient plough. It might seem gone for good with
> the men who ploughed the field many centuries
> ago. But every aerial-photographer knows that,
> in a certain light, and seen at a certain angle, the
> shadows of long-forgotten ridge and furrow can
> still be seen.
> —E. J. Hobsbawm[1]

THIS BOOK ATTEMPTS to understand the ways that ordinary farmers, craftsmen, and slaves in ancient Greece made sense of their world and their place in it. Unlike the wealthy elites, who produced written texts illustrating their worldviews, the ordinary people of ancient Greece left little or nothing from which their experiences and perspectives can be recovered. Like the "trace of the ancient plough," the culture of these groups is largely lost since it existed in "living" forms such as festivals and oral storytelling. Yet when seen from the right angle, the surviving evidence can reveal traces of this lost culture. This study is an attempt to excavate popular forms of culture that lie barely discernable beneath the surface of ancient Greek literature.

Yet this book is not simply an antiquarian inquiry into some curious cultural relics, but an attempt to show that forms of popular culture were vital to the practice of politics in ancient Greek communities. While the intimate linkage between popular culture and politics is not surprising to historians of other time periods, it has received less attention by historians of ancient Greece. The remarkable sophistication of the ancient Greek city-state, and especially of the classical Athenian democracy, has seduced historians into believing that the formal institutions, rather than informal social practices, were the primary locus of politics.

By contrast, I argue that diverse forms of popular culture such as festival revelry, oral storytelling, and the spontaneous collective punishment of social offenders were crucial aspects of ancient politics. Drawing on the approaches of historians of other pre-modern societies, as well as the interpretations of social scientists who study modern peasant cultures, I show that these and other forms of popular culture were sites of vital political discourses and practices that, at different times and places, operated alongside, within, and sometimes even in opposition to the formal institutions of the Greek city-state.

Although I make some strong claims about the importance of popular culture in the classical Athenian democracy, I also draw material from a variety of different ancient Greek city-states. By looking broadly at popular culture throughout Greece, this book puts Athens in perspective and shows, contrary to much modern scholarship, that Athens had more in common with other city-states (e.g., Sparta), and indeed pre-modern and modern peasant societies in general, than is currently recognized.

The Comparative Method: A Problem-Oriented Approach

Each essay in this collection begins with a question. Why did slave-owners on the island of Chios establish a hero-cult for a runaway slave? Why did the ruler of Sicyon name the tribal divisions of his city after lowly animals such as pigs, asses, and swine? Why did the poor citizens of Megara invade the houses of the rich and abuse them verbally and physically? Why were adulteresses in Aeolian Cyme mounted on a donkey and paraded around the town? I suggest that the answers to these questions reveal something fundamental about ancient Greek civilization, namely the centrality of popular culture to the political discourses and practices of the Greek city-state.

Yet in order to arrive at this answer, I reach far beyond the confines of Greek history to examine, for example, images of the grotesque body in popular culture of the Middle Ages, slave tales of trickster animals in the antebellum South, or the ways that landlords and peasants in contemporary Malaysia engage in an ideological struggle to define the terms of their mutual dependence. I draw from this comparative material in part because so much of the evidence for the ancient Greek past—particularly the everyday life of ordinary citizens and slaves—has been lost. By comparing ancient Greece to other historical societies, we can sometimes recognize similarities and patterns that help illuminate the relatively scanty evidence for popular culture in ancient Greece.[2]

There are great risks, of course, in using comparisons in this way. Critics will be quick to charge me with intellectual dilettantism—picking and choosing superficial points of similarity between societies while ignoring fundamental differences of social structure and historical context.[3] In response, it is important to emphasize that I am not claiming *identity* of either social structures or causal relations between various social and political phenomena in different historical periods. Rather, the comparative evidence is used in one of two ways. First, it is used to support and in some cases provide texture (allow for "thick description") of cultural practices that are only hinted at in outline in the ancient evidence. For example, the social context of an ancient Greek song in which a group of boys appear to threaten a wealthy landowner if he does not give them food and drink can be illuminated by comparison with similar, potentially violent rituals of hospitality between rich and poor in Early Modern Europe.

Second, the comparative evidence is used to construct general models by which the ancient evidence might be understood.[4] For example, patterns of riot and protest in Early Modern Europe can provide the framework for understanding some of the ways in which ordinary citizens in ancient Greece negotiated their relations with those more powerful than themselves. In the latter case, the applicability of the early modern evidence is based not on a single point of comparison—the fact of riot—but rather on a pattern of elements that is evident in both cultures, for example, a concurrence of economic distress among ordinary citizens and extra-institutional, ritualized forms of collective action. I claim neither that the causes of economic distress were identical, nor that the social structures of the ancient Greek city-state and Early Modern Europe were the same. And, as we shall see, the rituals of protest took different forms in different historical societies. English peasants made cacophonic music before the houses of the wealthy, while French journeymen engaged in ritualized forms of cat torture as a mode of protest against exploitation. In ancient Greece, youths sang songs outside the houses of the wealthy and demanded lavish fare. On occasion, these rituals of hospitality resulted in assaults on wealthy landowners' property and even their families.

While acknowledging the cultural specificity of each historical society as well as their differences of social structure, economy, and political regime, I nevertheless argue for a common pattern, namely the tendency of ordinary citizens and peasants to use ritualized forms of popular culture as a medium for expressing discontent. Through the use of such general comparisons, I hope not only to shed light on some hitherto neglected features of Greek civilization, but also to add some case studies from ancient Greece to the available pool of empirical examples through which historians can understand the dynamics of pre-modern societies.

Whereas this study places considerable emphasis on such patterns of similarity between ancient Greece and other societies, I do not intend to obscure the historical specificities of each civilization. My emphasis on similarities is in part a reaction to the tendency of ancient historians to stress the exceptionality of ancient Greece (a term which usually refers to the Athenian democracy).[5] Certainly ancient Greece was a distinctive society with its own cultural traditions, social structures, and historical trajectories. Yet these differences should not lead us to think that ancient Greece was unique in every aspect. A central argument of this book is that by recognizing certain parallels in non-elite worldviews between ancient Greece and other periods of history, we can recover a largely overlooked terrain of the political life of ancient Greek communities.

Popular Culture: How to Recover It?

While this book is aimed in part at ancient historians, I also hope to pique the interest of historians of popular culture in other time periods. Despite the deficiencies of our sources in some regards, ancient Greece provides rich historical material that can illuminate some fundamental problems relating to the study of non-elite culture. I have already touched upon the first such problem, namely the methodological issue of how to recover the culture of ordinary people of the past. This question arises from the obvious fact that the mass of farmers, craftsmen, and slaves left little in the way of material remains, let alone written texts. How then can we confidently reconstruct the ways that they viewed and experienced the world? How can we know the fears, hopes, and fantasies of the mass of laboring humanity in past ages?

On the surface, the difficulties of recovering the culture of the masses might seem to be less severe for historians of ancient Greece. After all, ancient Athens was a democracy during its "Golden Age" (fifth and fourth centuries BCE) and hence the cultural achievements of this period were at least in part a product of the people—the ordinary citizens who farmed the fields, attended festivals, and voted in the political assembly. Yet this view is problematic for several reasons. First, Athens was unique in the degree of involvement of the masses in the institutions of the state. Most ancient Greek states were oligarchies, and, although there were other democracies, these were less radically egalitarian than Athens. If we want to understand the culture of ordinary people throughout the Greek world, we cannot look to Athens as representative. Second, even among historians of Athenian democracy, there is a vigorous debate about the degree to which the surviving evidence reflects a genuinely non-elite perspective. For example, scholars have noted that most surviving speeches given in the political assembly and law courts were by politicians from wealthy Athenian families and that elite values feature in the arguments made by these speakers.[6] Other scholars have argued, conversely, that elite speakers were compelled to appeal to the beliefs of the mass of ordinary citizens in their audience and that therefore the surviving speeches reflect non-elite or democratic culture.[7] Regardless of one's position in this debate, it is an undeniable fact that all the literature that survives from ancient Greece was written by wealthy elites. How then, can we be sure that any surviving text reflects a non-elite world view?

By comparison, historians of the early modern period have the "chapbook," a cheap printed book, as evidence of the popular culture of their period.[8] These scholars can also reasonably rely on the collections of oral tales gathered by folklorists in the nineteenth century.[9] Similarly, historians of slavery in the modern era have oral and written testimony that has allowed them to reconstruct aspects of the culture of, for example, slaves in the antebellum South.[10] By contrast, no popular books or recordings of oral tales survive from ancient Greece.[11] Ancient popular culture has been lost—at least in its direct form—to later researchers.

The qualifying phrase, *at least in its direct form*, is a crucial point. Some elements of popular culture survive as refracted through the writings of elites.[12] Occasionally, elite writers mention elements of popular culture in the course of pursuing other agendas. For example, Plato and Aristotle provide evidence for popular festivity even as they construct an ideologically motivated argument connecting festivity with social disorder and democracy. By stripping away this ideological bias and by analyzing the Greek evidence in relation to popular festivity in other cultures, one can recover something of its significance for non-elites in ancient Greece.[13]

There are two other ways in which Greek popular culture has entered the surviving literary record. First there are literary genres that bear a clear genetic relation to popular non-literary forms. Most important among these genres are iambic poetry, comedy, satire, and the novel.[14] These literary genres often preserve clearly identifiable popular themes (especially reversals of normal relations, obscenity, and grotesque imagery) even if we cannot take for granted that these elements are exact copies of their popular versions.

Second, there are those genres that—though not derived from popular forms—nevertheless draw material from them. For example, Herodotus makes use of folktales, fables, and proverbs in his *Histories*.[15] More broadly speaking, the theme of the downfall of the mighty in Greek tragedy may owe something to the reversals or leveling of hierarchical relations in both popular ritual and storytelling. Plato's representation of Socrates in his philosophical dialogues similarly seems to bear some relation to the popular grotesque (as Bakhtin has called it) both in his personal appearance and in his penchant for using analogies drawn from the world of ordinary laborers.[16] Again, however, we cannot assume that these appropriations are direct reflections of popular culture and can therefore be simply lifted from elite texts unproblematically.

What are we to do, then, with these diverse and indirect remains of popular culture? How can we move responsibly from surviving literature to popular culture? The problem is not new, even for historians of popular culture in later periods. Peter Burke has described the popular culture of Early Modern Europe as "An Elusive Quarry" and spends several chapters of his book dealing with the problem of recovering a culture that was largely oral and articulated in "living" forms such as festivals.[17] Even Bakhtin's brilliant discussion of the popular culture of the Middle Ages has come under severe criticism for its acceptance of Rabelais's comic novels *Gargantua* and *Pantagruel* as a direct source for peasant culture in sixteenth-century France. Most notably, the literary scholars Stallybrass and White have challenged Bakhtin's attempt to understand popular culture through the lens of a literary text.[18]

The arguments of these scholars are worth considering. Stallybrass and White propose that there are no separate domains, such as authorship and popular festivity, but rather each "are constructed in interconnection with each other."[19] Using the example of Ben Jonson's play *Bartholomew Fair*, they write: "there can be no question of understanding the play either as a homology of the 'real' Bartholomew Fair, or as a mere thematic pillaging of popular custom by an aloof and appropriative high culture."[20] According to these scholars, sites and domains of discourse emerge out of an "historical complex of competing domains and languages each carrying different values and kinds of power."[21]

The idea that popular culture is not a monolithic entity, neatly separated from other realms of non-literary and literary expression has been one of the major theoretical breakthroughs of recent scholarship.[22] Historians of popular culture in such diverse periods as Early Modern Europe and twentieth-century America now agree that "popular"/non-elite and "official"/elite culture must be studied in relation to one another. As Natalie Davis puts it,

> [T]he hegemonic model of late medieval and early modern "official" cultures (whether of clerics or of kings) that suppressed "popular" cultures for their own ends has been modified to allow for some exchange of motifs and circulation of images across boundaries of learning and power.[23]

The recognition of the hybrid nature of mass and elite cultures presents both a challenge and an opportunity. On the one hand, popular culture is an inextricable blend of popular and elite elements. Furthermore, we only have direct access to the composite forms of culture that survive in literary texts written by elites. On the other hand, the very fact that popular culture has infiltrated or been appropriated into elite literary texts means that some aspects of the "living" culture of non-elites have survived (albeit in mediated ways) to be studied by scholars. The trick is to recognize these appropriations and to decode what these images and themes would have signified to non-elite audiences. Below, I outline the main points of my approach to these methodological problems in relation to ancient Greek popular culture. In the chapters that follow, I present some concrete examples of how this methodology can reveal the hidden landscape of popular culture that lies below the surface of Greek literature.

The way that we approach Greek literature as a source for popular culture depends in part on whether it was written for an audience of fellow elites (e.g., philosophy and historiography) or for performance before a mixed audience of elites and non-elites (e.g., tragedy and comedy). Literature written for elite audiences often draws on popular themes. Yet, as Stallybrass and White argue, we cannot speak simply of "appropriation" or "transference" of elements of popular culture to elite contexts. Rather, elements of popular culture are recreated for their new contexts in ways that make use of popular forms, but also adapt them to their own agendas. While we need to take seriously how these popular elements have been put to new uses in their surviving literary contexts, nevertheless, we can often identify elements that do not quite fit the narrative or ideological context of the surviving literary text. I suggest that these incongruous elements reflect earlier instantiations of popular themes which have been only imperfectly adapted to their new contexts. In other words, elite appropriations leave traces—vestiges—of earlier popular performances. While it must be recognized that these "popular performances" were themselves a hybrid mix of elements drawn from both high and low culture, these vestiges nevertheless can provide insight into the themes and meanings of popular culture.[24]

A different methodology is appropriate for Greek literature that was composed for a mixed audience of elites and non-elites. Tragedy and comedy, for example, were performed at publicly funded festivals.[25] When popular forms such as the folktale, fable, or proverb appear in dramatic plays, therefore, we might entertain the possibility that elites and non-elites understood them differently. In particular, by thinking about what these tales and proverbs might mean from the perspective of ordinary farmers, craftsmen, and even slaves, we may be able to understand the uses of these cultural forms among non-elites.

It should be emphasized that the performance context for some ancient literature is not well known. Was iambic poetry, for example, performed at public festivals or at elite drinking parties?[26] Furthermore, some ancient Greek literature, though aimed primarily at elites, may have been read aloud by slaves to their masters. In this latter case, we cannot assume that this literature reached elite ears alone, or that slaves understood the text in the same way as their masters.[27] By thinking about our surviving texts from both elite and non-elite perspectives, in other words, we can see how the same story could have very different meanings for these different audiences.

We are aided, finally, in the task of identifying popular meanings of ancient Greek literature by the work of scholars of popular culture in better-documented eras, especially the medieval and early modern periods. By comparing the themes of popular culture in these periods with those of elite texts from ancient Greece, it is often possible to identify imagery and symbolism that would have resonated particularly strongly for non-elite audiences. By following the lead, then, of scholars of the popular culture of the Middle Ages, the Early Modern period, and even of slave and peasant societies of the modern era, we are put on the track of the imaginary of the ordinary Greek citizen and slave.

A brief example may help illustrate these methodologies. Greek literature frequently uses the language of food consumption and images of grotesque bodies to characterize bad leaders of the civic community. For example, in Homer's *Iliad*, Achilles calls Agamemnon a "king who devours his people."[28] Similarly, the poet Hesiod addresses some village leaders as "gift-eaters."[29] The poet Alcaeus not only accuses his political rival, Pittacus, of "gobbling up the city" but abuses him by calling him "pot-bellied," "big-bellied," and "one who eats secretly by night."[30] Whereas in these Greek texts, this language is put in the mouths of elite speakers—or, in the case of Hesiod, at least a reasonably prosperous farmer—comparison with the use of such imagery in other historical periods suggests that these texts are drawing on a rich set of metaphors used popularly to describe the exploitation of the poor by the rich.[31]

As scholars of Early Modern Europe have observed, the culture of peasants is often characterized by bodily images, and frequently draws its "themes, motifs and patterns from hunger."[32] Contemporary peasant societies provide even more striking parallels with these Greek expressions. In Malaysian peasant speech, to collect interest is "to eat interest," to take bribes is "to eat bribes," and to exploit another is "to eat their sweat."[33] As James Scott comments, "[h]ere the peasantry's historical preoccupation with food and the accusation of ... cannibalism are joined together in a powerful, suggestive metaphor."[34] The pattern is the same in other South East Asian countries. In a striking parallel with Alcaeus' claim that his political rival, Pittacus, "gobbles up the city," an official in pre-colonial Burma was called the "eater" of a district.[35]

These parallels suggest that the elite writers of Greek literature and the elite characters within these texts have appropriated metaphors commonly used by non-elites *to critique elites*. The paradox of elite appropriation of non-elite critiques of elites not only reveals that some of the rich texture of Greek literature is drawn from non-literary culture, but also that non-elite culture was highly politicized. This point leads to the second major historical theme addressed in this book, the relation between popular culture and politics.

Popular Culture and Politics

The relation between culture and politics is a topic that lies at the intersection of the disciplines of anthropology, history, and political science.[36] A central debate in these fields has been whether the mass of ordinary laborers are capable of developing their own political culture or whether they are dominated both culturally and politically by elites. While some cultural historians (e.g., Bakhtin) have constructed celebratory narratives of the ways that "the People" resisted elite authority, others, including major political theorists such as Marx, Gramsci, and Althusser, have conceptualized the lower classes as the passive pawns of a dominant ideology. Both poles in this debate have been subjected to substantive criticism. For example, Bakhtin's concept of a sphere of unofficial culture that subverts official ideology not only artificially separates "official" and "unofficial," culture, but seems to reflect conditions in Stalinist Soviet Union rather than the popular culture of the Middle Ages. On the other hand, Marxists and neo-Marxists like Gramsci and Althusser have been criticized for conceptualizing the masses as the passive consumers of elite cultural constructions, especially those that justified the conditions of elite domination. Critics of this school of thought point out that this view leaves "no room for autonomous action by the people" or for their "reflexive understanding of the structure in which they are embedded and the possibility of their doing something about it."[37]

Recent scholarship has found a middle ground between the two positions outlined above. These scholars have proposed a more nuanced model of pragmatic interaction between high and low, official and unofficial culture in which each side deploys cultural symbols in order to maximize gains for itself in ways that acknowledge the constraints of material conditions and the realities of the balance of power. Rather than viewing "official" culture and "popular" culture as distinct spheres, moreover, these interpretations argue that there was much overlap and interaction. For example, the British Marxist historian of the French Revolution, George Rudé, describes popular ideology as "a mixture, a fusion of two elements, of which only one is the peculiar property of the 'popular' classes and the other is superimposed by a process of transmission and adoption from outside."[38]

Rudé distinguishes between the "inherent" or "traditional" beliefs of the people and the "derived" element that comes from the educated elite (the

liberal aristocracy and the bourgeoisie). Among the inherent beliefs of the
people, Rudé counts the notions of a right to land and to a fair price for
bread. In contrast to these rather limited and "backward-looking" views,
popular ideology also absorbs from intellectuals more "forward-looking"
political concepts such as individual liberty, the social contract, and the
"Rights of Man." Despite his emphasis on the importance of acknowledging the beliefs of ordinary peasants for understanding popular protest, Rudé ultimately argues that without leaders from the outside versed
in the more sophisticated political ideologies of the times, popular protest
was not able to change the status quo.[39]

The work of George Rudé and other British Marxist historians like
Eric Hobsbawm and E. P. Thompson has done much to further our understanding of the culture of the masses and its role in protest.[40] In essence,
these scholars have shown how peasants mobilized their own modest
cultural and material resources, sometimes in highly sophisticated ways, to
secure their basic well-being. These studies have demonstrated that while
peasant movements were unable to overthrow the system, they nevertheless played an important role in resisting greater exploitation. Peasants
did so by constructing and reinforcing an ideology of reciprocity between
rich and poor—Thompson's so-called moral economy. Far from being a
passive class, thoroughly brainwashed by a dominant ideology that ob-
scured the realities of their condition, these scholars have shown that
subordinate groups operated in active and pragmatic ways to improve
the conditions of their existence.

Other scholars from different national and political traditions have
further elaborated our picture of non-elite worldviews. In France, historians working from the *Annales* school have mined local archives to show
the ways that the environmental and material conditions of peasants
influenced their worldviews (mentalités).[41] Foremost among these are
the well-known works of E. Le Roy Ladurie, whose studies of peasants
of Languedoc have forever enriched our understanding of the details of
everyday life in fourteenth-century France.[42] Other historians, such as
Carlo Ginzburg and David Sabean, have produced micro-histories of particular individuals or villages that illuminate wider peasant perspectives
in early modern Italy and Germany respectively.[43]

In the 1960s and 1970s, American scholars turned to anthropology
and borrowed models to show how peasant culture not only partook of
"rites of reversal," but deployed these in ways that articulated their visions of the world and occasionally challenged the status quo. Particularly important among the scholarship evincing the "anthropological
turn" in historical studies is the work of Natalie Zemon Davis, who examined various aspects of early modern French society in light of Victor
Turner's theories of ritual reversal.[44] Davis argued that periods of popu-

lar festivity and protest in sixteenth- and seventeenth-century France were not simply occasions when the peasants "let off steam" only to be more firmly put back in their subordinate social positions once the festival was over (Turner's so-called safety valve theory). Rather, Davis suggested that for the mass of peasants, women, and children who participated, these rites helped articulate a common identity and even presented them with new possibilities for restructuring social relations. Similarly Robert Darnton, inspired in large part by the cultural anthropology of Clifford Geertz, showed how relatively powerless apprentice printers in seventeenth-century Paris could thumb their noses at those above them through sophisticated manipulation of certain cultural symbols (cats) in both popular and elite culture.[45]

Davis's work helped to inspire a whole field of work in the late 1970s and 1980s on popular culture, especially as manifested in the "public life" of towns and villages. Parades, processions, and festivals became the center of analysis in the work of historians of medieval and Early Modern Europe.[46] For these scholars, public ritual was a site of complex negotiation of cultural symbols that articulated, and at times contested, the norms by which the community was ordered. Historians, anthropologists, and political scientists of the modern era soon joined in the trend and produced analyses of power as articulated through forms of public spectacle.[47] While some of this work has been reflected in studies of ancient Greece—especially the interest in processions—not enough has been done to examine how civic forms of ritual appropriate and blend popular and elite cultural traditions in complex ways.[48] One of the aims of this study is to show that while scholars naturally focus on the institutionalized forms of these rituals, much of the political work performed by these rituals takes place through their informal manifestations in the villages and towns of ancient Greece.

Another group of historians working on Indian history has also challenged Marxist views of the inertia of the peasantry.[49] Drawing inspiration from Gramsci's acknowledgment of the raw energy and turbulence of the peasantry, these scholars have argued that subordinate classes do indeed have an autonomous sphere of thought and action. During the 1980s, these scholars produced a series of publications entitled *Subaltern Studies*, by which they endeavored to re-inscribe the lower classes into the political history of colonial India. Central to the mission of these studies was to show that the mass of laboring people did have a particular form of political consciousness, as evidenced by their formation of peasant movements and rebellions.

Historians of slavery in the antebellum South have similarly challenged the idea that slaves were subject to false consciousness and were the helpless victims of unequal distribution of resources and the hegemonic ideas of the ruling class. Historians such as Eugene Genovese and Lawrence Levine, for example, have argued that slaves were well aware of the conditions of their oppression but were realistic about their chances of emancipation. Rather than risk almost certain death through violent revolution, these groups chose lesser paths of resistance, including working slowly, breaking tools, and generally thwarting the will of their masters. Some slaves, of course, used the system of rewards to gain emancipation from their masters. But what these scholars show most strikingly is the ways that slaves used the cultural tools around them (for example, African cultural traditions and Christianity) to shape a vision of the world that strengthened their sense of identity and helped them go on under conditions of enormous adversity.

Similarly, James Scott has examined the ways that peasants in contemporary South East Asia engaged in everyday forms of resistance that helped them struggle against the changes to their way of life brought about by the introduction of modern machinery and techniques of irrigation and fertilization (the "Green Revolution" of the 1960s and '70s).[50] Far from being passive in the face of increasing economic hardship, peasants used every means at their disposal to defend their way of life, including machine-breaking, strategic work strikes, and moral censure of the rich. Scott shows how even everyday language was a site for ideological contestation between rich and poor. For example, whereas wealthy landowners described the rice given to workers who had helped with the harvest as a "bonus," the workers themselves considered it part of their expected "payment" for labor. For the workers, the rice was a customary right, whereas the landowners "wish[ed] to maximize the discretionary character of the benefit ... because it [was] precisely this aspect of their power that yield[ed] the greatest social control."[51]

Scott's focus on language as a means of resistance is important for the present study and is worth expanding upon. Scott presents a typology of peasant speech based on both his ethnographic study of a Malaysian village and his wide reading of comparative history and political theory. According to Scott, peasant speech falls into three categories. First there is the "public transcript," namely, the ways peasants speak in the presence of their superiors. In such forms of speech, peasants assume a stance of deference and willing submission to authority. Scott argues that to focus on this realm (often the most accessible, especially for historical studies) is to miss out on a wide range of speech that takes place either among peasants themselves in the absence of their social superiors (the "hidden transcript") or in public, but in coded forms which mask their subversive content. Included in the latter are all sorts of informal speech, including jokes, riddles, proverbs, fables, and folktales—in short, popular culture. By reading popular culture as a form of coded speech with a political meaning for subordinate groups, Scott opens a new terrain for the study of the politics of ancient Greek popular culture. In chapter 2, I pursue this approach by examining the many fables, proverbs, and folktales preserved in Greek literature. I argue that many do not fit well in their surviving literary context, and can be better understood when re-contextualized as a form of coded peasant speech.

This brief survey of historical scholarship on peasants and politics gives an indication of the major influences on this book. Yet I also hope that this book will make its own contribution to the ongoing debate about peasants, politics, and popular culture. One advantage, for example, of studying the relation between popular culture and politics in an ancient society such as classical Greece is that it demonstrates that the kinds of conflicts between wealthy landowners and peasants that historians of later periods attribute to specific events (such as the enclosure of common lands or the introduction of combine harvesters) in fact go much further back in time. Indeed, I suggest that the conflict between rich and poor in ancient Greece followed patterns of exploitation and resistance very similar to later periods of history. Whereas scholars such as James Scott imply that in an "older agrarian order" there was a balanced reciprocity between rich and poor that had only recently been threatened by new practices, my studies demonstrate that the poor have always had to struggle to enforce this norm. The idea of an earlier era in which rich and poor engaged in uncontested mutual reciprocity is a myth constructed by the poor as part of their ongoing attempts to secure their livelihood.

On the other side, the rich have always introduced new practices in their attempts to increase profits. Double-cropping, modern machinery, and changes in the ways loans are contracted can be genuinely new, but they are only the most recent weapons in the timeless drive of the rich to get richer. In other words, my argument is that rich and poor have engaged in an ideological and practical struggle that followed similar patterns from ancient Greek to modern times. Certainly, there have been moments of crisis in which patterns of conflict become particularly clear, but there has never been a time when the rich were wholly constrained by "traditional" values, or where the poor lived in contented interdependence with the rich. Not in ancient Athens, not in pre-industrial Europe, not in contemporary South East Asia.

The studies of popular culture surveyed above have had relatively little impact on the study of ancient Greece. Indeed, Kostas Vlassopoulos's recent critique of the practice of Greek history emphasizes that ancient historians need to engage much more systematically with developments in other fields of history.[52] Vlassopoulos calls on historians to use comparative methods and specifically mentions the movement known as "history from below" as well as the Subaltern Studies movement. With a few notable exceptions, historians of ancient Greece have focused on the city-state (*polis*), its political institutions, and the cultural artifacts it produced (e.g., temples, tragedies).[53] Yet historians of other periods are increasingly dispensing with the nation as a focus of analysis. Transnational or global history is becoming more mainstream, and this shift in focus has allowed for new objects of study that cross geographic and temporal boundaries.[54] Ancient Greece has much to offer these broader historical debates, and I hope that this book is a step in that direction.

Key Arguments

At this point, it may be useful to summarize some of the key assumptions and arguments of the book. Following this overview, I provide a more detailed discussion of the economy, social structure, and political institutions of the Greek city-state in comparison with those of later societies discussed in this book. In addition, the final section of the chapter emphasizes the heterogeneous character of "the People" and the multiple ways that this category can be subdivided (e.g., men and women, craftsmen and farmers, free and slave). By recognizing the diverse identities and subdivisions of non-elites, I attempt to avoid oversimplification of the worldviews of the many groups who contributed to the production of popular culture.

1. Farmers, craftsmen, and slaves in ancient Greece participated in a rich and vibrant culture that is only indirectly attested in the surviving evidence. This culture consisted of both discourses (e.g., oral storytelling) and practices (e.g., festival ritual and various forms of popular justice).

2. Popular culture is political. The key political functions of the popular discourses and practices examined in this book include the articulation of non-elite worldviews and the negotiation of relations between powerful and weak, both the rich and the poor, as well as masters and slaves.

3. Popular culture existed alongside the formal institutions and official civic discourses of the Greek city-state, and played a vital political role in the regulation and reproduction of the social order.[55]

4. Major methodological difficulties face the historian who attempts to recover the culture of farmers, craftsmen and slaves in ancient Greece. Direct evidence (material or textual) is largely lacking. For this reason, indirect methods must be used.

5. The method of this book is to examine Greek literature for traces of popular culture. We cannot, of course, assume that the

themes, imagery, and symbolism of Greek literature—even those genres performed before popular audiences—are direct copies of these elements as they existed in non-elite contexts. Rather, Greek literature is a complex blend of elite literary culture and the "living" and largely oral culture of non-elites. The hybrid nature of Greek literature does, however, mean that elements of popular culture are not completely lost to modern scholars.

6. Several complementary methods for detecting and reconstructing the indirect remains of popular culture in Greek literature are possible:

   a. For texts written for elite audiences (e.g., philosophy, historiography), the identification of elements that do not fit the narrative or ideological context.

   b. For texts written for mixed audiences of elites and non-elites (e.g., tragedy, comedy, iambic poetry), the consideration of what a given theme or image might mean from a non-elite perspective.

   c. Comparison of the themes and imagery of Greek literature with those of the culture of peasants and slaves in better documented eras. In this book, I make particular use of comparative examples drawn from medieval and early modern Europe, the antebellum South and contemporary South East Asia. These comparisons in no way are intended to elide crucial differences of historical context, social structure, and culture. Despite these differences, however, significant patterns remain that help the historian of ancient Greek popular culture make better sense of the evidence.

7. The methods outlined above reveal certain central themes and images of non-elite culture in ancient Greece, particularly the reversal of normal relations, images of the grotesque body, and obscene humor.

8. These themes and images played a vital role in affirming certain elements of non-elite worldviews and normative outlook. The norms emphasized in this book include the following:

   a. Those lower down on the social order (ordinary farmers, craftsmen, and slaves) have a right to the basic means of survival including, most importantly, land and food.

   b. The greed of the powerful threatens the well-being of the weak and undermines the stability of the social order.

   c. The powerful have an obligation to ensure the basic well-being of the weak.

9. While non-elite discourses and practices seldom overturned the social order, they nevertheless played a vital role in affirming

non-elite collective identity and values. These articulations were
the means by which subordinate groups resisted the ever constant threat of further exploitation.

10. While the phrases "popular culture" and "non-elite worldviews"
may suggest that free Greek farmers, craftsmen, and their (often)
non-Greek slaves shared a common culture and worldview, it is
important to recognize that popular culture in ancient Greece
was not a monolithic entity. Rather, popular culture was a dynamic and ever-changing field of speech and action in which various groups participated to varying degrees over time. In some
instances, the interests of free citizens and slaves did, in fact,
converge. On such occasions, these groups participated in a
common set of practices and discourses that articulated a common worldview. In other instances, we can isolate particular
practices and discourses that were distinctively the province of
free citizens or of slaves. Recognition of the parallels and fissures between these two groups among others (outlined in the
next section) allows us to appreciate the fluidity and flexibility
of popular culture in ancient Greece.

It should be emphasized that this book is not an extended, comprehen-
sive treatment of all aspects of popular culture and politics in the ancient
Greek city-state. Rather, it presents a series of case studies, connected by
a common purpose—to uncover some of the ways that non-elite groups
conceptualized the world, regulated and reproduced the social order, and
interacted with those in positions of authority above them.

Economy, Society, and Politics in Ancient Greece

Since this book draws on comparative examples to illuminate the ancient
Greek evidence for popular culture, it is important at the outset to acknowledge the ways that ancient Greece was a distinctive society with its
own cultural traditions, social structure, and political systems. What follows, therefore, is a brief sketch of the economy, society, and political
structures of ancient Greece that highlights points of similarity and difference with the other historical periods discussed comparatively in this
book. This survey will also illustrate the heterogeneous character of "non-
elites" in ancient Greece. Indeed, it is important to recognize that the
people who participated in popular culture were themselves made up of
diverse groups whose worldviews sometimes overlapped and sometimes
diverged. This overview, therefore, will outline the different ways of dividing "the People" (for example, by class, status, and gender) in order to

avoid oversimplification of the complex identities of those who contributed to the production of popular culture in ancient Greece.[56]

It is widely agreed that Ancient Greece was an agrarian society. While
in some city-states (e.g., Athens), a significant percentage of the citizen
population was engaged in manufacturing and trade, in most city-states
the vast majority of the population would have been farmers.[57] Yet beyond the broad consensus on this point lies a host of fiercely debated questions. Did all citizens have relatively equal plots of land, or were there
significant inequalities? Was ancient farming geared at self-sufficiency, or
was there considerable production for market exchange? Was agriculture
dependent on slave labor? These are notoriously difficult questions to
answer given the available evidence. As Lin Foxhall writes: "ancient 'peasants' are like post holes—you can see the places where they ought to have
been, but frequently the evidence for their existence is only indirect."[58]

Despite the methodological difficulties, scholars have begun to frame
the general structural features that characterized ancient Greek society
and its economy. First of all, despite the much-vaunted principles of self-
sufficiency and equality in our literary sources, it is clear that there were
significant inequalities of landownership in all Greek states, including
egalitarian Sparta and democratic Athens.[59] For example, a recent study
of landownership in classical Athens suggests that the richest 5 percent of
the population controlled 32 percent of the land.[60] Second, it is clear that
the wealthy were producing agricultural and other goods for the market
on a large scale.[61] Grains, oil, wine, and a whole host of other agricultural
products flowed within and beyond Greece through well-established trade
networks. In addition, by the fifth century, wealth was being generated
through ownership of skilled slaves, and we hear of numerous prominent individuals in Athens whose income was derived in whole or in part
through the manufacture of such goods as leather, lamps, and couches.[62]
Some wealthy slave-owners even rented out their slaves to mine operators,
thereby generating a steady return on their investment in human capital.[63]

The wealthy elites used the profits from these enterprises to support
their leisured lifestyles and pay for the various community services through
which they legitimized their superior social and political status. Not only
did these men provide the political and military leadership for the Greek
city-states, including democratic Athens, but they frequently organized and
financed festivals, feasts, and other communal activities. In some states,
such as Athens, the obligation of the wealthy to use some of their profits
toward communal ends became institutionalized (see below). In other
states, this norm was enforced through informal, yet powerful, communal expectations.

The land of the wealthy was farmed either by slave labor (e.g., in Athens, Chios, Corinth, Megara, Aegina) or by serf-like populations (e.g., in

Sparta, Thessaly, Crete). The extent of the use of slaves in agriculture in classical Greece has been a major point of debate in recent scholarship. The emerging consensus seems to be that, at least for classical Athens, slaves were widely used in agriculture as well as in manufacturing and trading enterprises.[64] This acknowledgment of the centrality of slavery to the Athenian economy led Moses Finley to classify classical Athens as one of five historical slave societies, the others being Roman Italy from the second century BCE to the second century CE, and Brazil, the Caribbean, and the American South in the eighteenth and nineteenth centuries.[65]

The classification of Athens and Rome as slave societies, moreover, has allowed for much recent fruitful comparison of ancient and modern slavery.[66] For example, it is frequently noted that the distribution of slaves in classical Greece and in the American South was similar. In both societies, only a few very rich families owned more than fifty slaves, while most slaves worked in groups of fewer than twenty.[67] By contrast, Roman estates (*latifundia*) and sugar plantations in the Caribbean employed large groups of hundreds of slaves. The similarities and differences between these ancient and modern slave societies have been used to explain a wide variety of features of Greek civilization, including the relative frequency of rebellion among Sparta's serf-like population (the helots) in contrast to the absence of revolt in chattel-slave owning states like Athens.[68] The present study accepts the legitimacy and utility of comparison between ancient and modern slavery, and builds on this earlier work. In particular, in chapter 2, I draw on the work of scholars of slave culture in the antebellum South to illuminate and explain some strategies of resistance by slaves in ancient Greece.

With the exception of states like Sparta that conquered a large indigenous population and compelled it to produce food for them, most citizens of ancient Greek city-states farmed their own land with the help of their families and possibly a slave or two.[69] These citizens farmed land of varying sizes and fertility. Some would have enough to produce a modest surplus that could be used to engage in market trade, while others would have been capable only of bare subsistence. The proportions of moderately prosperous to poor farmers are impossible to determine due to the paucity of evidence for all but the wealthiest farmers. As Lin Foxhall puts it: "It seems likely that the social order of Greek poleis was not sharply divided into simple groups of 'rich' and 'poor' or 'large estates' and 'small estates.' However the fragmentary nature of our sources means that we cannot determine with any accuracy the composition of this spectrum."[70]

One key difference between the agrarian societies of ancient Greece and the peasants of early modern Europe, however, is that ancient Greek farmers were fully enfranchised citizens. In classical Athens, most significantly, ordinary farmers and craftsmen exercised political power over themselves in the world's first direct democracy. Democratic regimes existed in a number of other ancient Greek city-states, moreover, although these were neither as stable as the Athenian democracy, nor as well-documented.[71] Even in oligarchies like Sparta, Corinth, and Chios, however, ordinary citizens had access to some of the political institutions of the state, especially the popular assembly, but also in some cases, a popular council.[72] Unlike peasants in early modern Europe, therefore, and unlike their own slaves and serf-like populations, Greek farmers and craftsmen were not subject to the political control of outside groups.

In many ways (but not all), this distinction in juridical status between free Greek farmers and their slaves and serfs was a crucial factor in ancient Greek society and culture. The political institutions of the Greek state worked to enforce sharp distinctions between free citizen and slave, and the ideological superstructure, including much of the literary production, also reinforced these distinctions. Free citizens could participate in the political and legal processes, and were considered to have the mental and physical attributes suited to these activities. Slaves, conversely, had no political or legal rights and were believed to have bodies designed for physical labor. In contrast to the rational and self-directing citizens, slaves were thought to have mental faculties appropriate for following the commands of others. While the bodies of free citizens were inviolable, the bodies of slaves could be beaten, tortured, and abused at will. Finally, it was considered appropriate for citizens to perform labor for themselves and their family, while servile labor was conceptualized as work for the benefit of others.[73]

Despite the strength of these political, legal, and ideological distinctions, there is considerable evidence that the differences between free and slave were not always apparent in everyday life.[74] As we have seen, slaves worked side-by-side with citizen-farmers in the fields. Furthermore, in the construction of civic buildings and other urban crafts, slave and free workers performed similar tasks for equivalent wages.[75] Some slaves were allowed to keep a portion of their earnings and even lived apart from their masters.[76] Banking slaves, for example, or those employed as agents in the trading enterprises of elites, could live relatively autonomously and sometimes accumulated considerable wealth.[77] Even certain publicly owned slaves, such as the one employed by the state to test the purity of silver coinage, are known to have enjoyed personal autonomy and material prosperity.[78]

In warfare, recent work has shown that slaves not only fought in battles alongside their masters, but also rowed in the fleet side-by-side with free citizens and hired mercenaries.[79] The ideological construction whereby citizens were defined as those who fought in defense of the community had to be insisted upon in the face of considerable overlap between slave and free, on the one hand, and non-citizen and citizen, on the other. Briefly stated, in some important spheres of life in the ancient city, notably economic production and military service, there seems to be considerable overlap between the activities of the free farmer, craftsman, or soldier and the slave, despite the strenuous construction of ideological distinctions between them. In addition, given that there was no obvious physical difference like skin color between free and slave as there was in the American South, it was significantly easier for a slave to pass himself off as a citizen in daily interactions.

One might expect that Greek citizens distinguished themselves from slaves through dress and behavior. Yet, at least in classical Athens, these means of distinguishing two statuses do not seem to have been rigorously observed.[80] Notoriously, one ancient observer complained that one could not tell the difference between slaves and citizens on the streets of Athens.[81]

> There exists the most lack of restraint among slaves and non-citizen residents at Athens, and it is not possible to strike [these groups] there nor will a slave get out of the way for you. I will tell you the reason for this local custom. For if the law allowed a slave or non-citizen resident or freedman to be struck by a free man, then many times someone would strike an Athenian citizen thinking him to be a slave. For the people there dress no better than the slaves and metics and are no better in appearance.

While this view is clearly exaggerated, coming as it does from a critic of Athenian democracy, it must contain a grain of plausibility in order to be an effective complaint. Moreover, it is a charge that it is echoed in other critical sources.[82] In all likelihood, the evidentiary basis of these claims about the freedom and comfortable lifestyles of slaves in Athens was the skilled slaves who were allowed to keep a portion of their earnings and lived apart from their masters. Although this group of privileged slaves is clearly not representative of slave experience as a whole, it does suggest that in everyday life, the distinction between the two statuses was not always vividly apparent.

Just as the political and ideological distinctions between ancient Greek citizens and their slaves might be less relevant in the realm of everyday life, so the juridical differences between ancient Greek farmers and early modern and modern peasants can obscure certain similarities in their lived experience of the world. First, the fundamental fact of life for both Greek citizen-farmers and peasants in more recent eras is that they have to labor for a living. Unlike the members of the few prosperous families, the lives of the majority of Greek citizens and their slaves were determined by the labor cycles of the agricultural year.[83] The fact of continual agricultural

Figure 2.
The Land of Cockayne, 1566, by Pieter Brueghel the Elder. Note the houses
roofed with pancakes, the plump, leisured peasants, and the roast pig with a
knife stuck in its back, conveniently ready for carving. Alte Pinakothek, Munich.
Image © Bayer&Mitko/ARTOTHEK.

labor conditions much of the worldview of these groups and provides an
important point of contact with other agrarian societies, both pre-modern
and modern.

   One simple example helps to illustrate this fact. A notable feature of the
popular culture of peasants in early modern Europe is the fantasy of a
world in which the earth freely gives up nourishment without the need
for human labor (fig. 2). Such utopias crop up frequently in Greek literature and, as I argue in chapter 2, they derive from precisely the same fact
of life that drove pre-modern peasants to this fantasy: the unavoidable
reality of bone-wearying agricultural toil for the vast majority of ordinary
Greeks.

   For the (probably) large numbers of families who had only enough
land to feed their families and no more, fluctuations in crop yield from
year to year made their livelihood precarious.[84] A second point of contact, therefore, between ancient Greece and other agricultural societies
is that their lives were colored, and for some, wholly determined, by the
need to secure their livelihood not only against a recalcitrant landscape,
but in the face of changes in the availability of labor due to the family life

cycle. A major benefit of comparative research in this area has been to illuminate the strategies by which ancient Greek subsistence farmers managed these risks.[85] One such strategy underlies many of the cultural phenomena examined in this book, namely the creation and maintenance of links of reciprocity between ordinary farmers and the wealthier landowners in their communities.

These two facts—the need for continual labor and the difficulties of building a livelihood out of the soil—are the fundamental conditions, I suggest, that shape the worldviews not only of ancient Greek farmers and their slaves but also of agricultural laborers in different times and places. Therefore, although there is legitimate resistance among ancient historians to the use of the word "peasant" to describe ancient Greek citizen-farmers, I suggest that there remain some important similarities of everyday life and worldview between ordinary farmers and slaves in ancient Greece on the one hand, and peasants in early modern Europe and modern East Asia, on the other.[86] As Paul Cartledge puts it: "Provided 'peasant' retains its etymological sense of 'countryman,' and does not necessarily connote political subordination or subjection, the term is in my view a helpful one, since it points to the fact that most ancient Greeks lived in and off the country and that ... the Greek economy was unalterably rural and agricultural at its base."[87]

A second characteristic of the peasantry in more recent periods of history, however, is also broadly inapplicable to ancient Greek citizen-farmers, although again it offers certain points of contact. It is generally true of peasant societies in Early Modern Europe and modern East Asia that "the surplus extracted from peasant producers supports other social strata."[88] In contrast to this feature of early modern and modern peasant societies, the wealthier strata in classical Athens and several other major ancient slave-owning states (e.g., Chios) extracted surplus not from the toil of poor citizen-farmers, but through slave labor. Medieval serfs and early modern peasants, by contrast, "support(ed) the upper strata through the payment of rents, a share of the crop, or labor services."[89]

Yet behind this basic distinction between free citizen-farmers in ancient Greece and peasants in later periods of history lie some similarities. First of all, even if Greek citizen-farmers were not *formally* subject either politically or economically (as serfs or tenants) to wealthy landlords, "*in practice, however, they were only too likely to be exploited.*"[90] Evidence for this assertion comes from a variety of sources. First, there is widespread evidence for indebtedness among the poor to their wealthier neighbors.[91] This fact is particularly well attested for the archaic period in states like Athens and Megara, where elite leaders were forced by widespread popular unrest to enact measures relieving the peasantry from their debts.[92] As I discuss in chapter 4, these measures, known as the "Release from Burdens" in Athens, and the "Return of Interest" in Megara, seem to have checked some of the most egregious cases of exploitation of the poor by the rich. Yet it is apparent that these measures did not end the unequal distribution of resources or the tensions that arose from this imbalance.

The evidence for class tensions in Greek city-states, both democratic and oligarchic, is plentiful.[93] There is no need to provide an extensive catalogue of instances of civil strife between rich and poor, as the examples have been thoroughly studied.[94] Yet a few illustrative examples show that in many cases the same factors that fueled peasant revolts in early modern Europe and modern South East Asia—namely, for access to land and debt relief—also drove ordinary Greek citizens to rebellion. An instigating event for the gruesome civil war that broke out on the island of Corcyra in 428, for example, was a legal indictment against five of the richest citizens by one Peithias, the "leader of the people."[95] In the ensuing strife, oligarchs were killed not simply for their opposition to democracy, but "by their debtors because of the money they owed."[96] In 412, the people on the island of Samos rebelled against the elites, who were also known as "those who hold the land." After killing or expelling some six hundred of these landowners, the masses distributed the land and property of these men among themselves.[97]

An anecdote deriving probably from the middle of the fourth century BCE further elaborates this pattern of indebtedness leading to violent rebellion of the poor:

> Theocles and Thrasonides in Corinth and Praxis in Mytilene valued property but little and displayed magnanimity seeing their fellow citizens in a state of poverty while they themselves were affluent. They also advised others to lighten the burden of poverty for those in need. And after they did not succeed in convincing the others, they themselves remitted the debts owed to them, and thus gained not only money but life itself. For those whose debts were not remitted, attacked their creditors, and, wielding the arms of rage, and proffering the most reasonable claim, that of irresistible necessity, slew their creditors.[98]

A parallel for the enlightened practice of the Corinthian and Mytilenian individuals memorialized in this anecdote can be found in classical Athens. The rich Athenian politician Cimon is said to have opened up his estates for all comers and allowed anyone who liked to come and pick fruit or other produce.[99] Cimon's generosity, as that of the Corinthian and Mytilinean individuals above, is remarkable precisely because it was the exception. The unspoken norm was that the rich either ignored the needs of the poor, or did the very minimum required to secure the social peace. The poor in turn strove within the limits of their power to obligate the rich to help the poor. It is no coincidence that conservatives like Plato report that the standard slogans of democrats were for a redistribution of the land and a cancellation of debts, i.e., "the classic slogans of oppressed peasantries" throughout history.[100]

The centrality of land and debt relief to popular unrest in ancient Greece puts ancient Greek rural laborers in alignment with peasantries in other times and places. Even if ancient Greek citizen-farmers were not generally subject to rents and taxation, the experience of strong tensions between a small group of large landowners and a large group of small landowners was similar. As Lin Foxhall observes, even if the distribution of land was relatively egalitarian when judged by the standards of Rome or by a modern perspective, the ancient Greeks themselves may still have perceived great inequalities of wealth and engaged in class warfare to defend their interests.[101] The essays that follow trace some of the ways that ancient Greeks responded to and managed this tension, not only through violence, but on a day-to-day basis through a politics of resistance.

The existence of strong class tensions between rich and poor citizens in the ancient Greek city-states points to an area of overlap between the lived experience of ordinary citizen-farmers and their slaves. If, as I have suggested above, free Greek citizens labored with insufficient land and often became obligated to richer citizens through debt, then their lived experience of the world would have shared some similarities with that of their slaves, despite differences in juridical status. Just as slaves toiled on the land and resented the easy living of those whose wealth depended on their labor, so ordinary citizens were angered by the disproportionate share of the land controlled by the wealthy, and suffered from the humiliation and hardship of being dependent on these same men for loans and other forms of support in times of need.

Evidence for a common class position and worldview among ordinary Greek citizen-farmers and their slaves can be found in the instances of civil unrest in which slaves and ordinary citizens fought together against the wealthy landowners. For example, in the civil war in Corcyra in 428, both democrats and oligarchs offered freedom to the slaves if they fought on their side. The majority of slaves, however, supported the democrats.[102] Similarly, when the Chian oligarchs rebelled from the Athenian empire in 412, they faced opposition not only from the Athenians (who had established a base in Chian territory), but also from their own slaves. According to Thucydides, most of the Chian slaves deserted to the Athenians at their base in Chian territory and "did the most harm [to the Chian oligarchs] due to their knowledge of the land."[103] Earlier in the fifth century, finally, a civil war erupted in Syracuse in which the mass of ordinary citizens and the slaves fought together against the "landowners."[104]

What these examples suggest is the ability of slaves to organize themselves and even channel their collective actions toward common goals,
some of which they might share with other groups in society. The fact
that both sides offered freedom to the slaves in the Corcyrean example
shows that the slaves were not simply motivated by personal interest, but
by politics. Moreover, despite differences in origin, language, and location
in the countryside, slaves on Corcyra, Chios, and at Syracuse apparently
acted collectively against elite landowners.[105] Even more strikingly, despite differences in juridical status, slaves fought alongside the ordinary
free farmers and craftsmen who formed the bulk of the democratic faction
in these civil wars.[106] As Alain Bresson comments in regard to rebellion
of slaves on Chios, there was clearly "un rapport entre population libre et
population non-libre."[107]

These examples of collaboration between ordinary Greek citizens and
their slaves do not, of course, completely negate the evidence for tensions
between free citizens (rich and poor) and their slaves. Despite the absence
of full-scale slave rebellion, moreover, there is considerable evidence that
slaves in ancient Greece resisted their masters (rich or poor) through lower
risk modes of opposition such as are attested for other slave-owning
societies, namely, "malingering, complaints, tool-breaking, mistreatment
of draught animals and livestock, work slowdowns, theft, fantasy folklore, flight and, at moments of extreme duress, acts of violence toward
masters."[108]

The flight of individual slaves, for example, was a common occurrence
in Greek city-states. Comedy depicts flight as a typical behavior of slaves,
and the chore of tracking down a runaway slave is represented as a mundane fact of life in Greek literature.[109] The reception of runaway slaves
from one city by another could even be a *casus belli* in some circumstances.[110] More unusual but still significant are those occasions when
slaves took advantage of the disruptions of civil war to escape their masters en masse. For example, when the Spartans established a base in Athenian territory in 413 BCE, twenty thousand Athenian slaves took the opportunity to flee.[111] In such cases, we must imagine that slaves belonging
to all classes of Athenian citizens, not just those owned by the wealthy,
were among those who preferred to escape slavery than remain with their
owners.

As already noted, ancient Greece follows the general pattern of slave
societies in which full-scale slave rebellion is rare due to the inherent difficulties and dangers of organizing revolt. Ancient Sparta provides some-
what of an exception in that it experienced relatively frequent rebellions
of their enslaved serf population (the helots).[112] Most scholars cite two
factors to explain the absence of full-scale rebellion among slaves in classical Athens and other ancient Greek slave-owning states. First, there was

considerable ethnic heterogeneity among the slaves who came from a variety of cultures including Thrace, the Black Sea region, Lydia and Caria in Asia Minor. These diverse origins, according to scholars, prevented slaves from forming a common identity or even speaking to one another. Second, it is believed, the employment of slaves in a wide variety of occupations limited their opportunities to mix with one another and prevented them from developing a common class perspective.[113]

Yet the example of coordinated flight among slaves just mentioned suggests that slaves had developed effective channels of communication. Furthermore, the examples of collaboration between slaves and ordinary Greek citizens cited above strengthen the case for considering slaves as quite capable of communicating among themselves and organizing themselves politically. In what language did slaves of diverse ethnic origins communicate with one another? In all likelihood, slaves communicated in Greek or a pidgin form of Greek, as well as in their native languages in those places where significant concentrations of slaves of a certain ethnicity were to be found.[114] It is obvious that most slaves needed to be able to speak Greek, and many even to read and write it, in order to be useful to their Greek masters.[115] Indeed, there are numerous examples from ancient Greece of slaves who were fully literate in Greek and served as accountants, secretaries, and teachers for private individuals, business enterprises, and even the state.[116]

It is likely, moreover, that slaves in Greece became Hellenized fairly rapidly and therefore that Hellenic culture could facilitate the development of a collective identity among them. It is not hard to see that slaves who worked alongside their Greek masters and lived in their houses would acquire elements of Greek culture. For example, in Euripides' play *Ion*, the chorus of slave girls belonging to Creusa say that they have heard the stories of Heracles and Iolaus while weaving.[117] The tombstones of non-Greeks (including slaves and ex-slaves) in Athens, moreover, show that many adopted Greek forms of self-representation, despite their non-Greek origins.[118] In some cases, the dedication on a tombstone reveals mistakes in written Greek, suggesting a grasp of Greek that was perhaps adequate for daily communication, but still imperfect in written form.[119]

Interestingly, sometimes Greek-style funerary monuments and epitaphs were accompanied by a parallel inscription in the native language of the deceased.[120] Similarly, scholars have noted that many non-Greeks adopted names that blended Greek and non-Greek elements.[121] These facts suggest that slaves maintained some sense of their ethnic origins despite considerable assimilation to the culture of their masters. It is likely, therefore, that slaves had contacts with members of their land of origin, something that must not have been hard to do in cosmopolitan cities like classical

Athens, where a sizeable number of foreigners were either resident or temporary visitors.[122]

Finally, the evidence of slave names shows that there were concentrations of particular ethnicities in Athens, and therefore such slaves might have had opportunities to communicate in their native language and maintain ties to their native culture. The frequency of generic slave names associated with certain ethnicities indicates that certain ethnic groups, such as Thracians, were well represented among slaves, even if we cannot always be sure that a specific slave actually was of the ethnicity that his name suggested. Slaves in Athens are frequently called Thraitta, or "Thracian women," Lydos, or "Lydian man," Syros, or "Syrian man."[123] Manes, one of the most common slave names, seems to be associated with Phyrgian ethnicity.[124] It appears, moreover, that slaves of certain ethnicities were concentrated in particular sectors of the economy. Phrygians, for example, seem to be overrepresented among mining slaves, and Phoenecian slaves appear frequently among banking and slaves engaged in trade.[125]

It is likely that these ethnic groups found occasions to speak in their native tongues and even maintained their own associations. The Thracian cult of Bendis is perhaps the best known foreign cult in Athens, and it is likely that it served as a focal point for Thracian culture for both free and slave.[126] We can imagine similar meeting points for different ethnic groups, much like the Plataeans, who, after the destruction of their city by the Spartans in 427, met monthly at the cheese market.[127] Ancient slaves seem to have enjoyed considerable freedom of movement, as indeed was necessary if they were to be useful to their masters.[128] It is very likely that all but the most oppressed slaves, therefore, found the opportunity to gather and communicate with one another, as the examples of their joint actions (flight, rebellion) discussed above suggest.

If we return now from this extended discussion of slaves and slave culture to the free Greek citizens, it must be stressed that just as the slave population was internally differentiated by (for example) ethnicity, occupation, and levels of literacy in Greek, so the citizen population was internally diverse. I have already pointed out that ordinary Greek citizen-farmers possessed land of varying sizes and fertility and therefore enjoyed levels of wealth varying from bare subsistence to moderate prosperity. It is important to stress, moreover, that not all free citizens were farmers. In some city-states, the non-agricultural segment of the economy was considerable, and many ordinary citizens were engaged in manufacturing and trade.[129] Alain Bresson has estimated that in classical Athens, less than half the population consisted of farmers and that ordinary citizens were as likely to be craftsmen or traders as farmers.[130] This estimate corresponds with some of our more qualitative evidence, such as Xenophon's much quoted claim that the political assembly of Athenian citizens was composed of "fullers, cobblers, carpenters, blacksmiths, farmers, and traders."[131]

When we speak of popular culture in Athens and many other city-states, therefore, we are speaking of the culture not just of farmers and their slaves, but also of free and slave craftsmen and traders. There are in fact some indications of the perspective of these latter groups in our sources of popular culture. For example, in the common "peasant" fantasy of a world in which nature spontaneously produces food, the obsolescence of the crafts is envisioned alongside that of agricultural toil:

> What need will we have any longer for your plows, yokemakers, sicklemakers, or smiths, or for sowing or staking? Rivers of black broth, gushing abundantly with rich sprinkle-bread and cakes of Achillean barley, will flow of their own accord through the crossroads from Wealth's springs, ready for us to scoop some up.[132]

For large commercial cities like Athens and Corinth, then, we must assume that the culture of the working classes was not wholly agricultural in outlook, but also shared something of the worldviews of artisans and traders. The incorporation of the crafts in the fantasy of a world without toil illustrates the flexibility of popular culture and its ability to absorb the perspectives of different groups within a common cultural form. Recognition of the hybrid nature of the working classes in states like Athens, therefore, does not weaken the argument for (at least in some contexts) a unified popular culture in which all groups could partake.

In some city-states, most famously classical Athens, successful revolutions against elite rule resulted in the establishment of relatively stable democracies. The success of the Athenian democracy, I shall argue, rested in part on its remarkably thorough incorporation of non-elite normative outlooks and practices into the ideologies and institutional structures of the state. Indeed, classical Athens institutionalized some of the customary mechanisms for redistributing the resources of the wealthy toward the poor through the creation of formal civic duties ("liturgies") to be performed by the rich for the benefit of the wider community.[133] These duties included the obligation to fund a festival through which the poor not only were entertained at the expense of the rich, but were provided with meat, wine, and other foodstuffs as part of the communal feast. As I argue in the chapters that follow, these formal institutions were only one form of a wide array of social mechanisms by which the obligations of the rich toward the poor were enforced.[134]

Much of the evidence for these practices must be gleaned from casual references or indirect sources. Elite leaders in classical Athens, for example, not only brag of their performance of formal civic obligations such as financing a warship or the production of a tragedy, but also occasionally mention informal acts of magnanimity such as paying for the ransom of a poor citizen captured by the enemy in war, or supplying the dowry for the daughter of a poor citizen.[135] In a few cases, we even have fragments of public monuments praising elites for their benefactions in relation to "the crops" of the village.[136] This indirect and fragmentary evidence is only the tip of the iceberg in the sense that regular informal loans and subsidies between rich and poor were probably vital not only to the survival of many small farmers, but also to the bond that held the community together.[137] Despite the wide array of formal and informal mechanisms for redistributing wealth, however, Athenian literary texts reveal that constant ideological struggle between wealthy elites and the mass of ordinary citizens was a prominent feature of Athenian collective life.[138]

A further complication of the major dividing lines in Greek society between rich and poor and between free citizens and their slaves was the existence of a substantial group of free non-citizens. As usual, we know more about these non-citizens in Athens than in any other Greek community. Some were ex-slaves who had been granted or managed to purchase their freedom. In comparison with Rome, these seem to be very few in number. The majority were free Greeks who had left their natal community and immigrated to a new polis, hence their title, *metoikoi* (metics), or "those who have changed their residence." Under exceptional circumstances, these immigrants could be granted citizenship, but in most cases they remained free non-citizens in their new communities.[139] This group was generally very active in commerce and manufacturing, and we know of particular individuals at Athens who became quite wealthy. On the other hand, metics had no political rights, could not own land, and were required to pay a special tax and be represented by a citizen if they came into legal difficulties.[140]

Once again, however, the political and legal distinctions are not the whole story. Metics served alongside citizens as garrison soldiers and rowers in the Athenian navy.[141] We also hear of metics freely participating in the highest social, political, and intellectual circles at Athens.[142] Citizens, moreover, frequently patronized, socialized with, and sometimes cohabited with free non-citizen women.[143] It is likely that the strict legal rules for citizenship (citizen parents on both sides) were in practice frequently bent to admit the illegitimate offspring of these liaisons. If we believe traditions about the great statesman Pericles, then he not only relied on the metic Aspasia for his political policies, but had his children by her admitted to citizenship.[144] This is not the only noted case of such disregard of legal rules, and we may wonder how many other cases, associated with less famous individuals, have gone unnoticed in the historical record.[145]

In addition to these legal distinctions and their complications in everyday life, we might surmise that the divisions between free and slave or between citizen and non-citizen were blurred by occupational differences. Rural laborers, whether free or unfree, citizen or metic, might sometimes have more in common with one another than with urban artisans, bankers, and traders. The one banking slave about whom we know a fair amount seems to have identified very strongly with the citizen population, since the benefactions he made to the state resulted in a grant of citizenship to his family.[146] While this case is admittedly an exception, it does suggest that we should not assume that slaves always aligned themselves ideologically with other slaves against their masters. Conversely, we might question whether citizens always provided a united front in keeping slaves in check. The evidence presented above suggests not only that certain subdivisions of the citizenry (oligarchs and democrats) might seek the support of slaves against their fellow citizens, but that individual citizens might favor certain highly skilled slaves over their fellow citizens in employment and in society.[147] In contrast to the American South, where slaves were sharply marked off from the free by their skin color and where even non-slaveholding whites formed militias to hunt down runaway slaves, in ancient Greece the lines between free and slave were often blurred and could apparently sometimes be overridden.

Perhaps the most important distinction that complicated strong class and status divisions in ancient Greece is that of gender. All women, whether citizen or not, were treated like non-citizens and slaves insofar as they were denied full political rights and were considered, like slaves and children, to lack the rational capacities required for self-rule.[148] Yet despite this dominant ideology and the formal limitations on women's public roles, there is considerable evidence that women created a culture of their own, asserted their opinions, and participated in the social and political lives of their communities.[149] As has often been noted, the important roles granted to women in civic cult stand as a potent symbol of their actual importance to the community.[150] Myth and ritual put women at the center of the civic imagination and it is likely that ancient Greek women asserted their power in ways that were not only influential but occasionally even upset the official ideologies of the state.[151]

The point of this overview of ancient Greek social structure is to show that it was composed of a myriad of overlapping social groups, and that different dividing lines could come to the fore in different contexts. In the political assembly, the divisions between citizen and non-citizen, male and female were dominant. In the law courts, male citizens were marked off from free non-citizen metics and citizen women insofar as the latter two groups need a male citizen to represent them in court. Yet these three groups may be considered similarly privileged, in contrast to slaves who had no legal rights at all, and indeed whose (often valuable) testimony had to be extracted under torture.[152] Yet even in legal contexts, divisions between citizen and non-citizen, free and slave, male and female could also be elided. As I demonstrate in chapter 5, even in classical Athens, women, and possibly metics and slaves, participated not only in extra-judicial punishment of social offenders but also in formal legal procedures when they formed the crowd of onlookers who observed the physical humiliation of offenders in court and participated by heckling.

It is precisely by looking beyond the formal institutions and laws to the informal social practices that we can best see how the "official" divisions of society were elided in everyday life. Far from reifying the fluid and overlapping divisions of Greek society, then, this study demonstrates the ways that formally distinct groups (e.g., free male citizens, free female citizens, and slaves) came together in certain spheres of life and jointly constructed, and often contested, the principles upon which collective life was made possible.

Part One

DISCOURSES

2

Slaves Tell Tales: The Culture of Subordinate Groups in Ancient Greece

NYMPHODORUS OF SYRACUSE, an itinerant ethnographer who lived in the third century BCE, recorded the following marvelous story about a bandit-slave on Chios:[1]

> The slaves of the Chians ran away from them and set out for the mountains. Gathering together in great numbers, they damaged the countryside of the Chians; for the island is rough and full of forests. The Chians themselves tell the story:
>
> A little before our own time, a certain slave, after running away, made his home in the mountains. Since he was courageous and successful in military affairs, he led the fugitive slaves as a king leads an army. The Chians set out in arms against him many times but they were unable to accomplish anything. When Drimakos (for this was the runaway slave's name) observed the Chians perishing in vain, he said to them, "For you, Chian masters, the trouble from your slaves is never going to end. How could it when it happens in accordance with an oracle and a god ordained it? But if you make a treaty with me and permit us to live in peace, I will be the initiator of many good things for you."
>
> And so the Chians made a treaty with him and an armistice for a certain period of time. Drimakos then prepared weights and measures and his own personal seal. He showed these to the Chians and said "Whatever I take from any of you, I will take using these weights and measures. And after I have taken sufficient things, I will close up your storehouses with this seal and leave them alone. And I shall examine those of your slaves who run away and if they seem to me to have run away because they suffered something intolerable, I will keep them with me. But if they have no justification, I will send them back to their masters."
>
> The remaining slaves, seeing that the Chians gladly accepted this arrangement, ran away much less often since they feared the judgment of Drimakos. And even the runaway slaves who were with him were much more afraid of him than of their own masters. They

did everything he required, obeying him as they would a military commander. For he punished those who were disobedient and he did not allow anyone to plunder a field or do any other harm without his permission. And on festival days, after marching forth from the fields, he used to take wine and unblemished sacrificial victims, except what the masters voluntarily gave. And if he discovered anyone plotting against him or laying an ambush, he punished him.

Later—for the city announced that it would give a lot of money to anyone who caught Drimakos or brought in his head—this Drimakos, being now quite old, summoned his boyfriend to a certain place and said to him: "I have loved you especially of all people and you are a child, a son and everything else to me. I have lived long enough, but you are young and in the flower of life. What then is the point? You must become good and noble! Since the city of the Chians is offering a lot of money to the one who kills me and they promise to grant the killer freedom, you must cut off my head and bring it to Chios and, after taking the money from the city, live prosperously."

Although the youth protested, Drimakos persuaded him to do this. And so the youth, after cutting off Drimakos' head, took from the Chians the reward that had been announced. After burying the body of the runaway slave, the youth went back to his native land. And the Chians once again were wronged and robbed by their slaves. Recalling the reasonableness of the dead man, they established a shrine in the countryside, and named it after the Kindly Hero. And even today runaway slaves bring him first fruits of everything that they steal. And they say also that Drimakos appears to many of the Chians in their sleep and warns them of the plots of their slaves. And those Chians to whom he appears, go to the site of his hero shrine and sacrifice to him.

Nymphodorus reports these things.[2]

This wonderful tale cannot be accepted as an accurate account of historical events on Chios. Even if Nymphodorus had not introduced his narrative as "a story (*muthos*)" told by the Chians, its fictive character is evident in the numerous conventional and dramatic features of its style and plot. For example, the opening of the story ("A little before our time …") places the events vaguely in the past, a typical technique of oral storytelling that both separates the extraordinary events of the tale from present times, and simultaneously suggests that there was once a time when such things could happen. So typically English fairytales begin "Once upon a time …" and French ones similarly: "Il était une fois …" In some traditions, the connection between the indefinite past and the wondrous events recounted is developed extravagantly, as in the beginning of one English oral tale:

> Once upon a time—a very good time it was—when pigs were swine and dogs ate lime and monkeys chewed tobacco, when houses were thatched with pancakes, streets paved with plum puddings and roasted pigs ran up and down the streets with knives and forks in their backs, crying "Come and eat me!"[3]

We will return to pancake-roofed houses and pigs with knives in their backs shortly. For the moment, we simply note that the chronological vagueness of the opening of our story is one of several other features of the style that indicate that it once circulated as a folktale. Indeed, despite the relatively straightforward narration of the plot (typical of oral story-telling), there are little poetic touches that suggest the work of a master raconteur. Drimakos' leadership skills, for example, are signaled not only through direct narration of his exploits, but also through effective use of simile: "he led the fugitive slaves, as a king leads an army"; his men "obeyed him, as they would a military commander." Another bandit tale that we will consider shortly balances the same direct narration with rhetorical flourishes, for example in the use of the figure of speech known as *polyptoton* (the repetition of a word in different grammatical forms in the same sentence): "Although he was pursued by many men, and although [the emperor] Severus eagerly followed his trail, *he was never really seen when seen, never found when found, never caught when caught.*"[4]

The most important feature of our tale that reveals its fictive nature is the idealization of the leading character. Drimakos is uncannily successful in battle against the Chians. Try as they might, the Chians are unable to defeat him.[5] Drimakos is not only brave in battle, but he is also clever, eloquent, disciplined, just, and self-sacrificing. Our admiration for Drimakos grows as the narrative illustrates each of these remarkable personal qualities in turn. The story culminates in the poignant scene in which Drimakos persuades his lover to cut off his head so that the young slave can gain his freedom. It is possible that this ending represents a fictive inversion of a less admirable historical truth, namely that slave leaders are usually betrayed by one of their fellow slaves.[6] The hero Drimakos—far from being secretly betrayed by his closest friends—*requires* his companion to betray him. Drimakos dies in order to save his lover from slavery. What more moving ending for the story of a courageous slave could be devised than this?

The conclusion that the story of Drimakos is fiction does not mean, of course, that it has no historical value. As we learned many decades ago from anthropologists, and more recently from cultural historians, the stories that people tell can reveal much about the way they perceive the world. Already at the beginning of the twentieth century, Wolf Aly chastised scholars of his time for dismissing Greek folktales as trivial entertainment: "These stories, which we have unjustly banished as fit for children, reveal all the hopes and fears of Mankind."[7] Less grandly, Robert Darnton has analyzed French folktales to show how they express French peasants' perception of the world as a "cruel and capricious place." Constant labor, hunger, and oppression by the rich are the background against which the action of these tales is played out. These conditions, as Darnton eloquently points out, provide the context for the development of one of the central themes of many French folktales, namely, the fantasy of overcoming one's adversaries and escaping poverty. In these tales, the poor peasant or his surrogate (Puss in Boots, Tom Thumb, Petit Jean) manages to rise above his circumstances and defeat those more powerful than himself through luck, supernatural intervention, or cunning intelligence. In contrast to the German versions of these universal tale-types, French versions emphasize the overcoming of one's adversaries through human cleverness, rather than supernatural forces.

James Scott, a political scientist, has taken Darnton's study one step further to argue that the stories told by peasants, slaves, and other disempowered groups are a form of political resistance. Scott's idea is that subordinate groups use stories to create a cultural space for themselves that is separate from that of dominant groups. By telling stories, these groups are able to imagine a world where power relations are different. While these fantasies of "the world turned upside down" are seldom realized, their retelling serves as a medium for group cohesion and facilitates lower-level resistance to power.

This idea that stories are a form of resistance among subordinate groups provides a possible interpretation of the social context for the telling of the story of Drimakos. As mentioned in chapter 1, Scott's model posits three forms of peasant speech, each of which has a different performance context. According to Scott, when peasants speak in the presence of their superiors, they adopt a pretense of willing subordination that affirms the social order and the ideology of the dominant class. Scott labels this form of speech the *public transcript*. Diametrically opposed to the public transcript is the *hidden transcript*, namely the ways that peasants speak among themselves when their masters are absent. In this form of speech, peasants openly express their opposition to current conditions and articulate their desire to gain revenge on their superiors.

Most interesting for our purposes is Scott's third mode of peasant speech, one

> that lies strategically between the first two. This is a politics of disguise and anonymity that takes place in public view but is designed

to have a double meaning or to shield the identity of the actors. Rumor, gossip, folktales, jokes, songs, rituals, codes and euphemisms —a good part of the folk culture of subordinate groups—fits this description.[8]

Scott offers the Brer Rabbit stories of slaves and trickster tales more generally as examples, and writes:

> At one level these are nothing but innocent stories about animals; at another level they appear to celebrate the cunning wiles and vengeful spirit of the weak as they triumph over the strong.[9]

In making this argument, Scott builds on the work of scholars of African American culture. Lawrence Levine, in particular, has argued that slave stories about tricksters—both animal and human—played a crucial role in providing psychological release and vicarious revenge for African American slaves against their masters: "Brer Rabbit's victories became the victories of the slave."[10] Like Darnton, Levine acknowledges that the trickster figure is not unique to slave culture, yet shows that there are definite patterns to the ways that this group deploys this stock character. While the stories of white Americans tended to endow their heroes with supernatural physical prowess, slave tales "were more obsessed with manipulating the strong and reversing the normal structure of power and prestige."[11] Levine also recognizes the key role that the fictive character of the stories plays in shielding this realm of group self-expression from repression:

> By ascribing actions to semi-mythical actors, Negroes were able to overcome the external and internal censorship that their hostile surroundings imposed on them. The white master could believe that the rabbit stories his slaves told were mere figments of a childish imagination, that they were primarily humorous anecdotes depicting the "roaring comedy of animal life." Blacks knew better. The trickster's exploits, which overturned the neat hierarchy of the world in which he was forced to live, became their exploits; the justice he achieved, their justice; the strategies he employed, their strategies. From his adventures they obtained relief; from his triumphs they learned hope.[12]

The story of Drimakos, a slave-hero who repeatedly defeats the free men of Chios and even dictates terms to them, seems—at first glance—to be just the sort of tale that slaves might delight in telling among themselves. As we have seen, Drimakos is invincible and possesses all the virtues of a fictive heroic character. When he dies, it is as an old man, and on his own terms. It is not difficult to imagine this story as a focal point of slave hopes, fantasies, and group pride on ancient Chios.

Yet despite the attractiveness of interpreting this story as a tale that originated and circulated among slaves, there are two major problems with this approach. First, we cannot be certain that our story derives from slaves. In fact, Nymphodorus states that "the Chians" tell the story, and this would imply that he heard it from free Chian citizens, not the non-Greek foreign slaves who served them.[13] Second, and perhaps more important, several features of the story do not fit well with the interpretation of this story as a "slave tale." Why, for example, does Drimakos interrogate runaway slaves and send some back to their masters? Why does Drimakos punish slaves who plunder Chian farms without his permission? In short, why is Drimakos—if he is a fiction of the slave imagination—so restrained when he could have exacted so much more from his former oppressors? By comparison, Brer Rabbit shows much less compunction—and indeed considerable brutality—in taking vengeance on his stronger opponent. In one tale, Brer Rabbit scalds Fox by pouring a pot of boiling peas over him. In another tale, he entices Fox into the hollow of a tree by promising a treat of melted honey. Brer Rabbit then sets the tree on fire and burns Fox to death.[14]

Once we begin along this line of inquiry, a myriad of details appear to contradict the simple reading of the story as a slave fantasy of a world turned upside down. If Drimakos is a slave hero, then he is a strikingly non-revolutionary one. We are told, for example, that slaves ran away *less*, not more often, since they were more afraid of Drimakos than their own masters.[15] The Chian masters seem to have appreciated the beneficial effect of Drimakos' rebellion only after Drimakos' death, when they are said to have set up a hero shrine in his honor. And apparently the dead slave showed his gratitude in return: he warned Chian masters of threats against them from their slaves. At the end of the story we are left with the paradoxical image of the free Chians worshipping a dead slave. Drimakos, it seems, is a slave-hero that the free Chians not only can tolerate, but even celebrate.

Unlike Darnton (who studied eighteenth-century French peasants), Levine (who studied North American slavery), and Scott (who studied contemporary South East Asian peasants), we do not have direct evidence for the performance context of the story of Drimakos. We must use the story itself to determine the group among whom the story circulated and to whom it was meaningful. But, as we have seen, the story is full of contrasting elements, some which appear to represent a slave perspective, others which relate to the worldview of the Chian masters. On the one hand, Drimakos' role as leading character in the story and his heroism would seem to be primarily a product of a slave imagination.[16] The story reads, in many ways, like Darnton's French folktales or Levine's trickster figures, insofar as the hero outwits his more powerful adversaries. We may conjecture that the primary significance of Drimakos for slaves was the hope or fantasy that the powerless could overcome the strong. This interpretation is implicit in the claim that slaves themselves sacrificed the first fruits of what they stole at the hero's shrine. It seems that slaves also could celebrate the dead slave.

On the other hand, as a story of the triumph of the "little guy," the hero of our tale does not end up much better off than before. In contrast to the peasant hero in French folktales who sometimes becomes rich and marries a princess, Drimakos takes only what he needs and lives the life of an outlaw.[17] At the end of the story, he manages to save one individual from slavery, but only at the cost of his own life. The exchange of one body for another hardly represents a big win.[18] This is far from a fantastic vision of a new world order where slaves are on top.[19] Most contradictory, in this regard, is the clear indication that, as a result of Drimakos' actions, slaves ran away *less* often than before. It turns out that the bandit-slave is good for the slave system!

If Drimakos is not the idealized trickster figure of French folktale or of African American animal tales, then perhaps a better parallel can be found in the *human* tricksters of African American slave tales. These tricksters, as Levine notes, are often constrained in the rewards they can obtain through their cunning.[20] Whereas animal heroes can vent their anger and desire for revenge, slave tales featuring human tricksters typically mute the revolutionary implications of their message by using their cunning merely to improve temporarily their material conditions—for example by successfully stealing a pig or chicken. Like some French peasant tales in which the trickster is rewarded with a good meal, rather than a princess or kingdom, the slave trickster fills his belly without threatening the system.[21] Despite the modest nature of the rewards, nevertheless the emphasis in both these tale types—at least for peasants and slaves who told them—is the triumph of the weak over the strong, a theme which serves as a proxy for their own desire for release from oppression.

An even closer parallel to the Drimakos tale, however, can be found in the English folk-hero Robin Hood.[22] Many features of the Robin Hood legend correspond to the story of Drimakos. Robin Hood is courageous, clever, disciplined, and just. More significantly, Robin Hood robs only to restore what rightly belongs to the poor, not to overturn the social order. Indeed Drimakos, like Robin, fits the type of the "social bandit," as Eric Hobsbawm once labeled this phenomenon: a robber whose actions aim at rectifying injustices in the community.[23] Hobsbawm's description of the actions of social bandits could be applied without much modification to Drimakos:

Insofar as bandits have a "programme," it is the defense or restoration of the traditional order of things "as it should be" (which in traditional societies means as it is believed to have been in some real or mythical past). They right wrongs, they correct and avenge cases of injustice, and in doing so apply a more general criterion of just and fair relations between men in general, and especially between the rich and poor, the strong and the weak. This is a modest aim, which leaves the rich to exploit the poor (but no more than is traditionally accepted as "fair"), the strong to oppress the weak (but within the limits of what is equitable, and mindful of their social and moral duties). It demands not that there should be no more lords, or even that lords should not be expected to take their serfs' women, but only that when they did, they should not shirk the obligation to give their bastards an education. In this way social bandits are reformers, not revolutionaries.[24]

Several scholars have convincingly criticized Hobsbawm's acceptance of the social bandit as an actual historical figure, and have instead argued that it is largely an ideological construction. In real life, bandits were violent men who operated between the interstices of state authority. By plundering villages and farms and sometimes killing innocent people, bandits typically harmed, rather than helped, the peasantry.[25]

If bandits were in reality violent, anti-social men, why did they become the object of heroic songs and legends? Even more important for our inquiry is the question of what function the figure of the bandit played in the literary traditions that are our sources for these legends? This later question is the focus of Brent Shaw's brilliant study of banditry in the Roman Empire.[26] Shaw argues that, although the figure of the bandit "existed in popular belief, imagination and [oral] communication," it was preserved in elite literary traditions because it served an important function for the ruling class itself. Specifically, the bandit was useful for "contrasting just and unjust ideals of power."[27] Appearing frequently in the context of the usurpation of power by an emperor whose legitimacy was suspect, the bandit was a kind of "imperator manqué," "a symbol of what the emperor should be."[28] The representation of the bandit as just, fairdealing, and restrained, then, plays an important role in the construction of ideals of leadership among the Roman elite. Implicit in Shaw's discussion is the idea (drawn from symbolic anthropology) that socially marginal figures (criminals, outlaws, and even women) are symbolically powerful. Meaning in these tales is often articulated by inversion or role reversal between what is central/powerful and what is marginal/weak.[29]

Shaw concludes that legends of bandits "serve the purposes of both popular and upper-class concerns."[30] On the one hand, such legends appeal to a deep-seated—but not revolutionary—desire for social justice among the common people. As Shaw puts it, the figure of the bandit

> is a powerful image of fearsomely compelling dimensions generated by people who desired that some such man could be found. They desperately wanted a savior from the present networks of power in which they were enmeshed, a man who could rescue them from their oppression and who could provide for a genuinely just social order, a paradise.[31]

On the other hand, as Shaw stresses, the bandit plays a key role in the articulation of norms of imperial rule. The ambiguity of the figure of the bandit in Roman culture is best illustrated in Shaw's discussion of the tale of the bandit Bulla Felix.[32] As we shall see, Bulla shares some striking features with Drimakos, and his legend can help us understand the contradictory elements of the tale of Drimakos.

Bulla Felix was the leader of a band of six hundred men who plundered Italy for two years around the year 205 CE. Like Drimakos and Robin Hood, Bulla is reported to have been singularly successful. His legendary luck in evading capture is memorably articulated by the Roman historian Dio, as we have already noted: "he was never seen when seen, never found when found, never caught when caught."[33] And, like Drimakos, his name echoes his fortune, "Bulla the Lucky (Felix)." Even more striking is his reputation for fair dealing. As Shaw notes, he confiscated only part of what he captured and detained skilled artisans for only as long as he needed them. On releasing these craftsmen, he even went so far as to grant them a parting gift.

The justice and generosity of Bulla, as well as his role in the construction of norms of legitimacy, are strikingly demonstrated in an episode in which the bandit captures, through a clever deception, the centurion responsible for tracking down his gang. Bulla then sets up a mock court for a trial. Bulla himself appears dressed as a Roman magistrate and calls before him the centurion, whose head had been shaven like a slave. Bulla proclaims his "sentence": "Carry this message back to your masters: let them feed their slaves so that they might not be compelled to turn to a life of banditry."[34]

Shaw rightly perceives that this episode presents a fictive role reversal between legitimate authority—the centurion turned slave—and illegitimate outlaw—the bandit turned Roman magistrate. Shaw emphasizes the function of this contrast in articulating ideals of leadership among the Roman elite. Yet he also acknowledges the ambiguity of the story in that it also appears to address non-elite concerns. Indeed, Shaw locates the origins of bandit stories generally in "popular" aspirations for justice. Shaw never addresses exactly who is embraced by the term "popular," yet he nevertheless provides an important model for interpreting bandit stories as ambiguous and multi-vocal fictions that effectively address the concerns of both elite and non-elite audiences. This model can be applied to the story of Drimakos, and helps to explain some of the fundamental paradoxes in that tale. Comparison of the two bandit stories together, furthermore, will illuminate the role of bandit stories in "popular" culture, and specifically the ways non-elite groups (both free citizens and slaves) might have understood the story. Scholars, like Shaw, rightly focus on the meanings of these tales for the elite Romans who wrote them down. But they have not sufficiently addressed their significance for non-elites.

Before we undertake this latter task, it is perhaps worth noting that Shaw's interpretation of the bandit as an ambiguous figure in the Roman imagination can be paralleled with recent scholarship on Robin Hood. Scholars have long struggled to identify the exact connotations of the term "yeoman" that is frequently applied to Robin Hood. According to some scholars, the word signified a free peasant, and thus Robin was a representative of peasant ideology. Other scholars have noted that, by the fifteenth century, the term came to mean a member of an intermediate class between peasantry and gentry, including craftsmen and tradesmen. Yet still others have argued that a yeoman was a household office and that therefore the legends of Robin Hood were "nurtured in the halls of castles and manor, and were not for peasant ears."[35]

In contrast to all of these interpretations, Richard Almond and A. J. Pollard have recently suggested that Robin Hood would have been identified by fifteenth-century audiences as a particular type of yeoman, a forester, whose status lay between peasantry and gentry. For these scholars, it is precisely the intermediate status of Robin Hood that makes him a flexible, ambivalent figure who can address the concerns of both peasantry and gentry. Almond and Pollard suggest that the surviving tales reflect "the common stock of stories as told to different audiences in different tones." Some of the tales reflect an orientation toward landed gentry. In these versions, Robin and his men display considerable respect for aristocratic status. Other tales, however, reflect a popular comic tradition, for instance, by parodying aristocratic rituals such as hunting. The most important point, then, is that—whatever the origins of the Robin Hood legend—by the fifteenth century, Robin "is already all things to all men."[36]

The figure of the bandit in Roman culture and early modern English society, therefore, is an ambiguous symbol whose precise ideological content could be adapted according to performance context to address the needs of different groups in society. The paradoxes in the Drimakos legend can be similarly understood in this way. The version as we have it seems to preserve in some details an original subversive slave tale (a celebratory "slaves-on-top" narrative), heavily overlain by the elite slave-holders' credo: treat your slaves humanely and they will not rebel.

What Shaw, on the one hand, and Almond and Pollard, on the other, do not address, however, is exactly how these competing versions come together and coexist in the same story. Why—if what we have is an elite version—are so many potentially subversive elements allowed to remain? On the other hand, if this is a peasant/slave tale, why does the story allow so many intrusions of elite ideology? Almond and Pollard solve this problem by positing different versions performed for different audiences. Shaw, by contrast, assumes that what we have is an elite version that somehow manages to ignore the revolutionary implications of depicting a bandit punishing a centurion. What these scholars do not explain, in short, is how these conflicting elements function together, as they clearly do in the story of Drimakos, Bulla Felix, and—to the extent "yeoman" is an ambiguous term—in the legend of Robin Hood.

To put the problem anther way, why do elites make use of a popular tale? Why are elites not content with their own heroes, figures such as Lucius Quinctius Cincinnatus (fig. 3), who served as consul and dictator and was legendary for his virtue and simplicity? Why, in other words, did elites need slave heroes?[37] Why appropriate a tale with so many potentially subversive meanings? Why are these elements not stamped out completely? Why, in short, do we get a blending of these diverse traditions and not a complete re-writing of the tale to fit one particular ideology or audience? What is the social context in which this mixing takes place and why?

I suggest that the answer to these questions is that these stories play a role not just in articulating the distinctive ideology of *separate groups* but in mediating tensions *between* groups. That is, these tales are important cultural devices through which elites and non-elites (both peasants and slaves) worked out a way of living together. Bandit legends then are not just stories adapted at different times to different audiences, but actually a common cultural product of diverse groups, heard by all groups, if not simultaneously, at least within the same political community. These stories are a cultural meeting place through which the principles of mutual accommodation are worked out.

In the second half of this chapter, I will suggest that the tale of Drimakos provides a clue to how this cultural negotiation of political differences works. I will furthermore draw on comparative historical evidence—especially the evidence of more recent slave societies—to show the importance of such cultural mechanisms both in ameliorating the conditions of subordinate groups *and* in preserving the social order by which elites continued to dominate. My interpretation, like those of Levine, Darnton,

Figure 3.
Statue of Cincinnatus, by Eleftherious and Mercene
Karkadoulias, Cincinnati, OH. Cincinnatus is depicted
at the moment when he gave up the powers of dictator
(symbolized by the bundle of rods, or *fasces*) and
returned to private life as an ordinary farmer (symbolized by the plow). Reproduced with the permission of
the University of Cincinnati Libraries. Source: The
Architecture and Urban Planning Collection, University
of Cincinnati Libraries Digital Collections.

and Scott, grants to slaves an active role in this process, and shows how
these tales function not simply to provide psychological release but to
negotiate better treatment in the very real conditions of slavery.

In making this argument, I do not deny that slaves and peasants, as
well as elites themselves, had their own separate cultural traditions. They
certainly did. The legend of Cincinnatus, for example, was perhaps one
such elite tradition.[38] In regard to subordinate groups, Scott has labeled

these separate traditions the hidden transcript. As always, the problem is that this hidden transcript is visible only as traces underneath the elite traditions that were written down and survive as our principal sources. Despite this difficulty, in the next section, I discuss some common themes from the hidden transcript of non-elites as background to exploring in more depth how the Drimakos story represents the fusion of this hidden transcript with the official ideology (public transcript) of elites. Isolation, to the degree possible, of common themes of popular traditions, will help us appreciate the ways that bandit tales—and the story of Drimakos in particular—have adapted to the elite traditions and ideologies (and vice versa) in order to advance a realistic non-elite agenda.

Slave and Peasant Worldviews: The Hidden Transcript

The practical and theoretical problems facing an historian of the culture of subordinate groups have already been highlighted in chapter 1. There I outlined a method for circumventing these obstacles in relation to ancient Greek popular culture. In this section, I use some concrete examples to illustrate the utility of the methods proposed in chapter 1. More important for the argument of this chapter, the discussion that follows provides some concrete examples of the worldviews of ordinary citizens and slaves in ancient Greece. The examples will illustrate the overlap between principal themes of ancient Greek popular culture and the story of Drimakos.

Broadly speaking, the themes of Greek popular culture fall into three general categories, each of which is discussed in turn below:

1. Role Reversal or the "World Upside Down" (WUD)
2. Fantasies of Magical Abundance or "The Reign of Kronos"
3. Animal Fables or Pessimistic Worldviews and the Dream of Revenge

Role Reversal and the "World Upside Down"

The theme of the reversal of the natural order, where land animals change places with fish, and dolphins take to the mountains and trees, appears in some of the earliest literary texts from ancient Greece. For example, the seventh-century poet Archilochus and the fifth-century historian Herodotus make use of this theme in high-blown literary and rhetorical analogies. In Herodotus' *Histories*, for example, an ambassador from Corinth uses the image to convince the Spartans of the folly of their plan to overthrow the Athenian democracy: "The sky will be below the earth and the earth will be up above the sky, and men will inhabit the sea and fishes the land, since you Spartans are preparing to overthrow democracy and install tyrants in cities."[39] The ambassador's use of the image of the world upside down suggests that it was usually employed to express something unexpected, something that should not happen if things are as they ought to be. In other words, the analogy reinforces the status quo through the absurdity of the image of the world upside down.[40] But was the image always used this way? Or, to put it another way, was this the meaning of the image for all social groups?

One cannot help noticing the similarity of this image to the theme of the "World Upside Down" in popular culture in Early Modern Europe where "mice ate cats, children spanked parents, the hare snared the hunter, and fish flew in the air" (fig. 4).[41] According to one scholar, this image was an effective form of popular resistance precisely because of its ambivalence. Specifically, it masked "the dangerous, vindictive, anarchic" with the 'childish'" and thus served as an effective vehicle for expression of resistance without provoking repression by the authorities.[42] Was popular culture similarly the original social context of the "fish in the sky" theme in Greek literature? Did subordinate groups in ancient Greece use this image to express their resistance to those above them by imagining—in a veiled way—a world in which relations were reversed? It is obviously impossible to prove this speculation in any definitive way. On the other hand, two arguments may be made in favor of this interpretation.

First, analogies with the sub-human or animal world are a key part of traditions about the slave Aesop and his fables. I argue below that the Aesopic tradition represents an accumulation of popular traditions in which slaves and non-elite citizens imagined a reversal of relations between themselves and those more powerful than themselves.[43] Of course, as we have it, the Aesopic tradition has been incorporated into the traditions of the dominant class.[44] But originally, I will suggest, the figure of Aesop might have served to articulate non-elite hopes, strengthen non-elite group cohesion, and ultimately encourage non-elites in their daily struggle against those more powerful than themselves.[45] For example, in traditions about the life of Aesop, he is depicted as constantly outwitting his master. Furthermore, as we shall see shortly, the main theme in at least some "Aesopic" fables is the revenge of the weak upon the strong.[46] Analogies with animals or inanimate objects, I shall argue, are especially well suited to obscuring the subversive content of some non-elite forms of culture.

Second, it is notable that the iambic poetry of Archilochus, in whom the image of the reversal of the natural order first appears, has strong connections with popular culture, particularly the obscene and abusive speech that characterized the cultic worship of Dionysus and Demeter.[47]

Figure 4.
The World Turned Upside Down. London, 1647. Note the fish in the sky, the mouse chasing the cat, the hare chasing the fox, the wheelbarrow pushing the man, and the cart pulling the horse. © The British Library Board, 11626.d.27. All rights reserved.

Since the iambic poem in which this image appears is fragmentary, it is difficult to tell exactly how Archilochus employs the image. It may be significant, however, that, according to a scholiast, it concerned a father hoping for a marriage for his ugly daughter, and in this context he seems to be saying "anything can happen":

> There is nothing now you can't expect, nothing's against the odds,
> there are no miracles, now Zeus the father of the gods
> has turned noonday into night and hidden the bright sun
> out of the sky, so clammy dread came over everyone.
> From now on all is credible, and like enough to be:
> let none of you now be surprised at anything you see,
> not even if land animals switch to where dolphins roam,
> and the salt sea and the crashing waves become their chosen
>   home,
> while dolphins take a fancy to the mountains and the trees.
> Indeed, already we observe that Archeanactides,
> the ... the son of ...
> has entered wedlock ...
> ... but my daughter ...
>
>   (fr.122; trans. West)

In this example, in contrast to the Herodotean usage, the image seems to be employed in service of an argument that something unexpected *could* happen, since anything might happen, just as day once turned into night during an eclipse. It is just possible that this usage is closer to a popular vision or dream that things might be different, that customary relations might be reversed. If this is indeed the case, then we can see how this popular image of a world upside down is appropriated and its meaning inverted in later literary renditions. In the case of the ambassador's speech, ironically, its inverted use—the idea that something *should not* happen, rather than the popular idea that something *could* happen—is used in support of a pro-democracy/anti-tyranny argument.[48] If, as I have argued elsewhere, the ambassador's speech has been shaped by Athenian democratic ideology, then the Herodotean passage is a fascinating example of the appropriation and adaptation of popular culture by the Athenian democracy.[49]

Be this as it may, this example possibly illustrates one way in which an element of popular culture has become integrated into literary culture. One reason why the image has been able to be absorbed so easily into official or dominant traditions is its flexibility, indeed its essential ambiguity. Like the WUD images in the early modern period, it can be read two ways—as an affirmation of the status quo—"fishes in the sky are clearly ridiculous and impossible"—or as a veiled threat of revolution and revenge—"it just might happen." As D. Kunzle puts it:

> The essential ambivalence of WUD permits, according to circum-stances, those satisfied with the existing or traditional social order to see the theme as a mockery of the idea of changing that order around, and at the same time, those dissatisfied with that order to see the theme as mocking it in its present, perverted state. But the discontented have yet another alternative: to see WUD as a promise of revenge and a vindication of just desires.[50]

Greek examples of the theme of WUD are similarly ambiguous, cloaking a hoped-for reversal in human relations behind the apparently impossible vision of a reversal of the natural world order.[51]

Fantasies of Magical Abundance: The Reign of Kronos, the Land of Cockaigne, and the Big Rock Candy Mountain

The similarity between the ancient theme of "fishes in the sky" and popu-lar versions of the World Upside Down in Early Modern Europe puts us on the track of another possible element of Greek popular culture that survives in Greek literature. Here I am referring to the concept of the Reign of Kronos (Roman Saturn) where the earth freely gives up plentiful food without any labor by men. The most complete version of this theme survives in the *Works and Days* by the seventh-century poet Hesiod, al-though echoes of it can be found in Homer and later Greek literature.[52]

> First the immortal gods who dwell on Olympus made
> A golden race of articulate men
> Who lived in the time of Kronos, when he was King on Olympus.
> They lived like the gods, having a carefree heart
> Without toil or suffering[53] and wretched old age never settled
>   upon them,
> But always the same in feet and hands,
> they delighted in festivities,[54] far from all evils.
> And they passed away as if succumbing to sleep.
> And they possessed everything good. The wheat-bearing fields of
>   their own accord provided plentiful harvest. And, at peace
>   willingly, they dwelled in possession of the best things.[55]

Whatever we make of Hesiod's own social status, the literary influences on his poetry, and his performance context, we can at least say that the kind of utopia envisioned in this part of his poem shares something with

popular images of a life without toil in early modern culture.[56] Peter
Burke has observed that a special genre of work-song sung by journeymen in early modern Europe enumerated a kind of fantasy workweek in
which no work is performed.[57] One Hungarian example, provided by
Burke, goes like this:

> Sunday I drink wine
> Monday I do no work
> Tuesday it is good to lie down,
> Wednesday, to get up again.
> Thursday to recover
> Friday to reckon up
> Hey! Saturday to ask
> What work have we to do?[58]

As in the Hesiodic utopia, in this work song the primary theme is a life
without work. This emphasis, of course, makes most sense from the perspective of those who must constantly work to survive, namely the laboring classes.

The most important Early Modern parallel, however, for the Hesiodic
Golden Age is the theme of the so-called Land of Cockaigne. In this imaginary land, "houses were thatched with pancakes, brooks ran with milk,
and there were roast pigs running about with knives conveniently stuck
in their backs" (fig. 2).[59] As a variant of the WUD theme, in this image of
reversal of the natural order of things, there is not only no toil, but most
important there is a plentiful abundance of rich foods which offer themselves up without any human labor. The popularity of this theme among
peasants and craftsmen is perhaps best illustrated by its evocation in an
English broadside ballad called "An Invitation to Lubberland" which was
first printed in 1685 (text box 1). This ballad in turn is thought to have
inspired one of the most famous American folk songs, "Big Rock Candy
Mountain" (text box 2).[60] In these popular songs, the hills are made of
candy, "the streets are paved with pudding-pies," and the rivers run with
wine, among other marvels.

Besides the clear evidence for the popular character of this theme in
medieval, early modern, and modern periods, the positive character of
this image of the world upside down would seem to arise naturally among
those who thought that a reversal of the way things are would be bound
to make things better. In Hesiod, indeed, there is a clear contrast between
the idyllic Age of Kronos and contemporary times as represented in the
poem:

> Now is the generation of iron. Nor do men cease
> from toil and suffering by day and perishing by night.[61]

Text Box 1

Some of the lyrics to *Invitation to Lubberland*, an English broadside ballad, first printed in 1685.

> The rivers run with claret fine,
> The brooks with rich canary,
> The ponds with other sorts of wine,
> To make your hearts full merry:
> Nay, more than this, you may behold,
> The fountains flow with brandy,
> The rocks are like refined gold,
> The hills are sugar candy.
> There's nothing there but holy-days
> With music out of measure;
> Who can forbear to speak the praise
> Of such a land of pleasure?
> There may you lead a lazy life,
> Free from all kind of labour:
> And he that is without a wife,
> May borrow of his neighbour.

While the image of the reign of Kronos is appropriated and adapted to a
variety of literary traditions and ideological contexts, the basic contrast
between continuous toil and carefree plenty would seem to be a product
of the imagination of non-elite culture.[62] As Paul Cartledge puts it: "[T]he
invention of utopias of instant plenitude in which the fruits of the earth
were available constantly on tap without human labour clearly spoke to
a profound and widely popular Greek yearning for freedom from agricultural toil."[63]

It is noteworthy, in this regard, that this theme frequently appears in
comedy, a genre with strong connections to popular culture. In addition
to the surviving Aristophanic comedies that feature a fantasy of magical
abundance, social justice, and peace (e.g., *Wealth, Birds, Peace*), many
lost comedies apparently rhapsodized about the idea of a life without
work in which the earth freely gave up abundant food and drink.[64] In
Telecleides' comedy "The Amphictyons," for example, a divine character
(presumably Kronos himself) says:

> Well, I'll describe the sort of life I provided mortals with in the old
> days.

Text Box 2

Lyrics to the song, *Big Rock Candy Mountain*, believed to be a hobo song, and recorded in 1928 by Harry McClintock.

> One evening as the sun went down and the jungle fire was
>   burning,
> Down the track came a hobo hiking and he said boys I'm
>   not turning,
> I'm headin' for a land that's far away beside the crystal
>   fountains
> So come with me we'll go and see the Big Rock Candy
>   Mountains
> In the Big Rock Candy Mountains there's a land that's fair
>   and bright
> Where the handouts grow on bushes and you sleep out every
>   night
> Where the boxcars are all empty and the sun shines every
>   day
> On the birds and the bees and the cigarette trees
> Where the lemonade springs where the bluebird sings
> In the Big Rock Candy Mountains
> In the Big Rock Candy Mountains all the cops have wooden
>   legs
> And the bulldogs all have rubber teeth and the hens lay soft
>   boiled eggs
> The farmers' trees are full of fruit and the barns are full of
>   hay
> Oh, I'm bound to go where there ain't no snow
> Where the rain don't fall and the wind don't blow
> In the Big Rock Candy Mountains
> In the Big Rock Candy Mountains you never change your
>   socks
> And the little streams of alcohol come a-trickling down the
>   rocks
> The brakemen have to tip their hats and the railroad bulls
>   are blind
> There's a lake of stew and of whiskey too
> You can paddle all around 'em in a big canoe
> In the Big Rock Candy Mountains
> In the Big Rock Candy Mountains the jails are made of tin

> And you can walk right out again as soon as you are in
> There ain't no short handled shovels, no axes saws or picks
> I'm a goin to stay where you sleep all day
> Where they hung the jerk that invented work
> In the Big Rock Candy Mountains
> I'll see you all this coming fall in the Big Rock Candy
>   Mountains

Peace, first of all, was as readily available as washing-water.
The earth didn't produce fear or diseases. Instead,
    what they needed appeared spontaneously,
because every torrent-gully flowed with wine, and
    barley-cakes fought with loaves of bread
around people's mouths, begging them to gulp down
the whitest ones, if they would be so kind. The fish
    would come home,
roast themselves, and serve themselves up on the
    tables.
A river of broth flowed next to their couches, rolling
    along warm chunks of meat;
and streams of sauce were there for anyone who
    wanted some,
so there wasn't any reason to resent a man for soaking
    his mouthful until it was soft and gulping it down.
There were ... sprinkled with seasonings in little dishes.
Roast thrushes accompanied by milk-cakes flew down their
    throats;
the unbaked cakes jostled against one another around
    their jaws, producing an uproar;
and the children played knucklebones with slices
    of sow's womb and meat-trimmings.
People were fat back then—as big as the Giants![65]

Interestingly, these comic passages are preserved in Athenaeus in the same
section of his dialogue in which he records the story of the bandit-slave
Drimakos. We will return to the significance of this conjunction at the
end of this chapter. What is important to note now is that the speaker in
Athenaeus' dialogue cites these comic utopias in support of the argument
that in primitive times no use was made of slaves. For the speaker, then,
the free and abundant availability of food is closely connected with the

idea that there was no need of labor, especially slave labor. This idea is most explicitly brought out in a quotation from Crates' comedy "Wild Animals":

> SPEAKER A: So no one's going to own a male or female slave, and an old man's going to do all his work alone?
> SPEAKER B: Certainly not; I'll make everything capable of moving itself.
> A: How's this going to help them?
> B: All the household equipment will come of its own accord, whenever someone shouts "Table! Set yourself beside me!
> Get yourself ready without any help! Knead, my little grain sack! Pour some wine, ladle! Where's the cup? Go wash yourself!
> Get up on the table, barley-cake! The cookpot should already have been pouring out the beets.
> Fish! Get over here!" "But I'm not roasted on the other side yet!" "Then turn yourself over, baste yourself, and sprinkle on some salt!"[66]

A fragment of Pherecrates' *Persians* similarly emphasizes the connection between the lack of need for labor—this time perhaps free peasant and slave labor—and the plentiful abundance of food:

> What need will we have any longer for your plows, yokemakers, sicklemakers, or smiths, or for sowing or staking?
> Rivers of black broth, gushing abundantly with rich
>   sprinkle-bread
> and cakes of Achillean barley, will flow of their own accord
>   through
> the crossroads from Wealth's springs, ready for us to scoop some
>   up.
> Zeus will rain ... wine, dumping it over the roof-tiles like a
>   bathman;
> Streams of grape-clusters will pour down from the roofs, accompanied by
> cakes stuffed with cheese, as well as hot pea-soup and lily
>   porridge-cakes;
> and the trees in the mountains will shed not leaves, but roasted
> kid-meat sausages, soft baby squid, and stewed thrushes.[67]

In contrast to the vision of a magical world of plenty lie the harsh realities of life that were also frequently depicted in popular traditions and myths. Hesiod's version of the myth of Prometheus and Pandora, for example, reflects a bleak perspective on human life: toil, poverty, and disease are the immutable facts of mortal existence, and hope is its only sustaining force.[68] Like French folktales in which the stark conditions of peasant life are the context in which the folk hero cleverly outwits his superiors and gains wealth and happiness, the harrowing facts of life for the poor and the weak are the background against which the magical abundance of the Reign of Kronos is imagined.

The argument that this vision of plenty is a product of the laboring classes does not exclude the fact that the wealthy slave-owning classes also took pleasure in them. Indeed, the ritual articulation of these myths— the Festival of Kronos in Greece and the Festival of Saturn in Roman society—featured masters and slaves feasting together.[69] As many scholars have pointed out, slavery was a burden even for masters, and even they could enjoy liberation from the pressures created by the social hierarchy.[70] Kathleen McCarthy has brilliantly argued, furthermore, that the theme of role reversal between masters and slaves in Roman comedy provided relief even for free Roman masters from the highly hierarchical structure of Roman society.[71] In sum, the argument for the centrality of these myths to slave culture does not eliminate the possibility of their appropriation and adaptation by elites. The survival of these themes in Greek and Roman comedy attests to the appeal and adaptability of these themes to elite needs.

Despite these concessions, we must not lose sight of the primary appeal of these images to those who must labor for a living. Indeed, the very fact that the idea of a reign of Kronos/Saturn is ritually articulated in a slave festival is a key indicator of its origins among, or at least its central importance to, the oppressed. I will return to this point at the end of this chapter.

Animal Fables: A Pessimistic Worldview and the Dream of Revenge

The theme of the world as a harsh and unforgiving place is perhaps most directly articulated in animal fables, a cultural form with clear popular roots. As we shall see, most surviving animal fables depict a world of natural hierarchies in which the strong dominate over the weak. This theme, which ostensibly naturalizes and justifies the domination of the weak by the strong, is, on closer inspection, frequently articulated from the perspective of the oppressed. This is to say that fables represent the difficult circumstances of the weak and demonstrate the futility of attempts to change the world.[72] Yet within this perspective, fables often simultaneously inculcate strategies for managing relations with the powerful in ways that optimize gains for the weak. In a significant number of fables, moreover, as well as in stories about the inventor of fables (the slave Aesop), another, more revolutionary, perspective is evident. These latter fables and folktales suggest that the weak will ultimately gain revenge on their oppressors, either through their own cunning or through divine intervention.

Before turning to the fables to show how they illustrate these themes, it is necessary to say something about the nature of the ancient Greek fable and its relation to ancient Greek popular culture. Although several scholars have recognized the basis of the fable in the culture of peasants and slaves, others have denied this connection.[73] Niklas Holzberg, for example, has written, "What the figure of Aesop definitely does not personify is the common people's spirit of rebellion against oppressive rule."[74] Holzberg's objection (and that of most of the opponents to the idea of fables as popular culture) is based on the observation that the surviving Greek fables display a wide variety of ideological positions and are therefore not the product of one particular social group.[75]

It is certainly true that the surviving Greek fables articulate diverse worldviews. Yet this diversity can be accounted for both by the nature of our sources, and by the very function of animal fables as a form of disguised speech in which the meaning for certain groups is hidden beneath a narrative surface that is inoffensive to those who benefit from the status quo. It is obvious that our elite literary sources would be most likely to appropriate those fables that had ostensible value in reinforcing domination of the strong, despite (as I shall argue below) the primary role of Greek fables in articulating the worldview of the weak. The combination of elite selective tendencies and the dissimulating nature of the fable have contributed to the ideological diversity of surviving fable collections.

One way of side-stepping the selective bias of our sources is to focus on the earliest preserved fables from Greece. Though these early fables often survive in fragmentary or allusive form, I suggest that they are better guides to the role of the fable in ancient Greece than the more complete and extensive collections of the Hellenistic and Roman periods. The latter, chronologically later, compilations represent appropriations designed to serve the needs of elite orators and their audiences. As such, they present a selection of fables that appeal to the moral and ideological principles of a wide audience, especially those of free citizens, and often those of the ruling powers. Fables in surviving late collections, therefore, tend to articulate general moral principles and often reinforce the status quo.

By contrast, the earliest Greek fables survive primarily (but not exclusively) in literature with strong connections to popular culture (e.g., iambic poetry, comedy). Consideration of these early fables in isolation from their surviving context in Greek literature, moreover, allows us to think about their potential meanings in non-literary, non-elite contexts. Attention to elements of the fables that are inconsistent or in conflict with their literary appropriations, furthermore, reveals clues to their meaning for non-elites. These methods reveal that the primary themes of early Greek fables relate to the worldviews of subordinate groups. Specifically, early Greek fables articulate the wretched conditions of the weak, the dream of revenge upon the strong, and offer practical advice for managing relations with the powerful.

More significant even than the presence of these themes is the fact that it was precisely in the time of these early Greek fables (eighth to fifth centuries BCE) that the genre gradually became associated with a Thracian slave named Aesop living on the Greek island of Samos.[76] What is striking is that, in Greek traditions, a slave is credited with inventing the fable.[77] In the Near East (from which the Greeks are believed to have adopted the genre), fables had no particular connection with slaves. In Greece, by contrast,

> [i]n the fifth century, probably in Samos, the legend of a repulsive ugly and worthless looking slave … was developed into a fully-fledged novella in which the slave was a shrewd and witty fellow, given to impressing points on his superiors by means of apt parables. Once given this starting-point, the Greek instinct to attach anonymous compositions or achievements to any appropriate individual ensured that Aesop would attract fables. Many fables which had hitherto had no fixed context became fables that Aesop had told on some occasion or other. By Aristophanes' time the Αἰσωπικὸν γελοῖον [Aesopic funny tale] is a recognizable category of story, and there is apparently a book in which the inquisitive may read about Aesop's life and death, and his wit and wisdom. But the circulation of fables is still predominantly oral.[78]

This reconstruction is as convincing as one can hope for given the scanty evidence.[79] Yet an obvious question arises from this scenario. Why, in Greece, did the fable become attached to a slave? Why was the slave Aesop considered an "appropriate individual" for the fable in Greece?

The Near Eastern prototype from which much of the legend of Aesop is derived, namely the sage Ahikar, was a vizier to the Assyrian king. A vizier is a high-ranking official in the royal hierarchy and a close advisor to the king. He is in no way equal in status to the deformed slave Aesop. The move from sage to a slave in the Greek tradition, therefore, requires some explanation.[80] Niklas Holzberg, in his study of the ancient fable, does briefly address the question of why the Greek inventor of fables is figured as a slave, and posits an obvious answer. Holzberg suggests that, since the fable came to Greece through Near Eastern wisdom literature,

> who better to tell such fables than the natives of the Near East now living in Greece, for example, educated citizens from the towns of

Asia Minor who had been carried off as slaves? Perhaps in the end there really is some historical truth behind the legendary *logopoios* [storyteller] Aesop who lived in bondage on Samos.[81]

Holzberg's idea, then, is that actual slaves from the Near East may have brought the fable to Greece, and that is why the fictional (or real?) tradition of the slave Aesop developed in Greece.[82]

Whether or not Holzberg is correct, however, it is highly significant that fables came to be *imagined* as the product of a slave. Fifth-century Greeks believed that the fable was invented by a slave, whether or not this is historically accurate. Something about the fable—either its actual popularity among their slaves, or the content of these early fables—caused the Greeks to associate it with a slave. I suggest that both of these factors led the Greeks to attribute the fable to the ugly and misshapen but devastatingly clever slave named Aesop (fig. 5). From then on, it was an easy step to elaborate a biography for this real or imagined slave author. What Odysseus was to the free Greek imagination, so Aesop was for slave culture. Aesop, following the pattern of the fables themselves, became the slaves' trickster, a cunning hero who triumphs not over Cyclopes, Sirens, and Scyllas, but over a human master. As we shall see, the biography of Aesop had important ideological functions for masters too.

Unfortunately, the fifth-century versions of the story of Aesop do not survive. A late version of the tale dating to the second century CE, however, probably retains the basic story line of earlier versions, despite the obvious intrusion of later concerns (especially the philosophical and ideological agendas of the movement known as the Second Sophistic), and the relative (though not complete) absence of fables themselves.[83] In this late version (known as the anonymous "Life of Aesop"), Aesop constantly outwits his master, but does not wreak brutal revenge on his oppressor, as some animal tricksters do. Instead, Aesop uses his cunning to improve the conditions of his slavery, just as do the human tricksters of Afro-American slave tales. I shall argue in the final part of this chapter that the second-century "Life of Aesop," like the story of the bandit slave Drimakos, represents a compromise between the fantasy of all-out revenge envisioned in animal fables and the practical need to negotiate better treatment in the very real and inescapable conditions of slavery. As such, the "Life of Aesop" blends slave traditions celebrating the slave-hero with the dominant ideology of the free Greeks, namely, the necessity and naturalness of slavery.

It should be emphasized that I am not suggesting that the fable was unique to slave culture.[84] Indeed, its appearance in a wide variety of ancient genres, as well as the great range of moral and ideological messages it is made to impart, show that it is an extremely flexible cultural form

Figure 5.
Aesop (?) talking to a fox. Attic red-figure cup, attributed to the Painter of Bolognia, c. 450 BCE. Museo Gregoriano, Vatican. Photo courtesy of the American Academy in Rome, Photographic Archive.

that—like the image of the World Upside Down—was found to be useful to many different social classes and groups in the ancient world.[85] What I am suggesting is that the animal fable, with its imagery taken from the natural world, was a medium ideally suited for disguising the expression of the rawest desires of slaves for revenge upon their masters. Slaves readily recognized and exploited the suitability of the fable to the politics of disguise. Let us see how this is the case by examining several fables in particular.[86]

One of the earliest fables surviving in the Greek tradition is the "Fox and the Eagle."[87] Archilochus' poem is fragmentary, but later prose collections provide a more complete version of the fable:

An eagle and a fox became friends and decided to live near each other, thinking that their friendship would be strengthened by cohabitation. And so the eagle flew up into a very tall tree and made its nest, while the fox went into a thicket that lay beneath and gave birth. One day, when the fox had gone out to forage, the eagle, at a loss for food, flew down into the thicket and seizing the cubs dined on them along with its nestlings. The fox, upon returning and realizing what had been done, was more distressed by the inability to exact vengeance than by the death of its cubs, since as a land animal it was unable to pursue one that had wings. Therefore, standing far away, it cursed its enemy, the only thing left for the powerless and weak. And it happened that the eagle soon paid the penalty for its sacrilege against friendship. Some people were sacrificing a goat in the countryside and the eagle flying down carried off from the altar a burning entrail. When it had been brought to the nest, a strong gust of wind kindled a bright flame from the thin and aged straw. Because of this the nestlings were set on fire and since they were not yet capable of flight they fell to the ground. The fox ran up within sight of the eagle and devoured them all.[88]

We should, of course, be wary of assuming that this late version was identical to that circulating in Archilochus' time. Yet certain elements seem to be fundamental to both versions: the Eagle and Fox make an agreement, the Eagle breaks the agreement, the Fox is unable to avenge itself because of its weakness relative to the Eagle, and finally the Fox gains revenge on the Eagle through divine assistance.

Archilochus uses the fable to express his anger with Lycambes over a broken marriage agreement.[89] Archilochus compares himself to the Fox and suggests that he will get revenge for this act of betrayal. While these aspects of Archilochus' appropriation of the fable fit the poetic context, one element stands out as incongruous: eagles and foxes are species that are naturally at odds with one another. They inhabit different spheres and prey on one another. Much of the effectiveness of this fable, and many other fables, lies in the application to human affairs of this innate hostility between species. A central point of the fable is that, while these two animals are temporarily able to get along with one another, eventually nature wins out, and they revert to their inborn tendencies.[90]

The incongruity of the theme of the natural hostility between species with Archilochus' poetic usage of the fable should prompt us to think of contexts in which this theme would be more appropriate. Given the connection between fables and slaves already posited, it is worth asking what the fable might mean to a slave audience. From the slave perspective on the world, the idea of the natural hostility between species is strikingly relevant. Though master and slave can live together, their interests are ultimately at odds, and mutual animosity is their natural state. The plot of this particular fable is also more relevant to slaves than to the literary scenario of Archilochus' poem (we do not know, at least from the surviving fragments, in what sense Lycambes was more powerful than the poet). When interpreted from a slave perspective, the fable seems to express both their inability to avenge injustices done against them (like their enslavement) and their hopes for divine vengeance.

This idea that, although the weak may not be able to exact revenge for the wrongs done against them by the powerful, the gods will punish evildoers in the end, was evidently featured prominently in Archolochus' version of the fable. In one surviving fragment of the poem, for example, the fox prays to Zeus to observe and punish the Eagle for his crime:

> Zeus, father Zeus, yours is the rule in heaven,
> you oversee men's deeds,
> wicked and lawful,
> and both the violence and the justice of beasts are your concern.[91]

Shortly after this prayer, divine punishment follows by means of a spark of fire from the burning entrails of a goat that the eagle had snatched from a sacrificial altar. As a consequence of this theft, the eagle's nest is set on fire and the nestlings fall into the jaws of the fox waiting below. While the idea that wrongdoing would be punished was important to enforcing justice among all social groups in Greece, this particular version of this generic idea stresses the imbalance of power and the inability of the weaker party to exact vengeance on his own. Such a version is tailored to the interests of the weak in that it both expresses their frustration at their own helplessness and articulates the belief—necessary to their endurance of their condition—that in the end they would gain vengeance on their oppressors.

A parallel for the importance of the concept of divine justice for subordinate groups may be found in the belief of African American slaves that, despite their situation, god was looking out for them. Indeed, slaves in the antebellum South believed, just as the Israelites had before them, that they were God's chosen people. As Genovese and Levine have shown, slaves in the American South were not passively converted to Christianity, but actively adapted Christianity to their own needs.[92] While the slaves dismissed and rejected those parts of the scripture that inculcated obedience to their masters (e.g., the Letters of Paul), they enthusiastically celebrated, in their sermons and spirituals, other parts of Christian doctrine that concerned the release of God's chosen people from bondage, or the coming of the Kingdom of God. In short, throughout their long period of oppression, African American slaves remained confident that they would be emancipated by the hand of God. When liberation finally came, moreover, they were convinced that the victory of the North in the Civil War was God's doing.[93] We may similarly imagine that slaves in Greece adapted the concepts of Greek religion—in particular the idea of the justice of the gods—to their own needs, and that animal fables were one vehicle through which they articulated their belief that the gods would ultimately punish their masters for the wrongs done against slaves.[94]

A similar example of the use of religion as a tool of social control of the rich by the poor can be found in the folk beliefs of contemporary Malaysian peasants. According to James Scott, Malaysian peasants believed that the failure of the rich to ensure the well-being of the poor would be punished not only by Allah in the next world, but also in the present life through accidents and illnesses. When Scott questioned the good health of a wealthy villager who was also renowned for his tight-fistedness, a peasant pointed to the back trouble of the rich man, and his wife's fall down some steps, as evidence of divine punishment for his lack of generosity.[95]

Returning to the Greek world, we may conclude that the fable of the Eagle and the Fox expresses three complementary themes, each with particular significance for slave communities:

1. There is a natural and inevitable hostility between animal species (just as between master and slave),
2. The weak are unable to avenge themselves directly for the injustices committed against them by the strong (just as slaves are helpless before their masters).
3. The gods ultimately will ensure that justice is upheld, and thereby the weak will gain revenge on the strong (just as the gods will ultimately avenge slaves).

It is interesting to note, further, that although Fox is helped by the gods, it is he himself who ultimately exacts bloody revenge. When the fire from the sacrifice sets the nest on fire, the eagle's nestlings tumble down and are devoured by Fox. Presumably this vivid image of tit-for-tat violence contributed to the psychological relief that such fables granted to slaves. As we shall see from many other early Greek fables, the depiction of the violent revenge of the weak is a prominent theme. Like Brer Rabbit, but unlike Drimakos and Aesop himself, Fox exacts a brutal punishment on his more powerful opponents. He is able to do so, in part, because the figure of the rebellious slave is hidden safely behind this innocent animal figure.

The bloody revenge of the weak upon the strong, as well as the idea of natural hostility between species, is particularly strikingly articulated in another well-known early fable. This fable is preserved in Aeschylus' tragedy *Agamemnon*, and concerns a man who reared a lion cub in his house. At first the cub was docile, playing with the children and delighting their parents by lying tamely in their arms. Since the cub had been taken away from his mother while still a defenseless pup, he at first fawned on his owners in order to get food for his belly. When the cub became a lion, however, he reverted to his innate nature, paying back his human parents for his upbringing by devouring the members of the household in a blood-bath of killing.

In Aeschylus' play, the fable is deployed as an analogy to the initially alluring but ultimately destructive Helen. More broadly, the play uses the fable to illustrate how one unjust act begets another (Paris' abduction of Helen results in the destruction of Troy, Agamemnon's sacrifice of Iphigenia prompts Clytemnestra's murder of Agamemnon, which in turn leads to Orestes' vengeance on Clytemnestra).[96] Yet several elements of the fable do not fit well with this literary use, and suggest other possible meanings. For example, while Helen is like the lion cub in that she is abducted and taken into a foreign home, she is not like the lion cub in that she herself is not transformed from harmless plaything to destructive beast. She does not herself exact revenge on her abductor—that is the role of her former husband Menelaus and the Greek army. A better analogy for Helen's story would be one in which the mother lion came to the man's house to recapture her cub and wreak vengeance on those who wronged her.

But what happens when we think about the meaning of this fable for slaves? Slaves are uprooted from their native land and placed in a foreign home. Slaves fawn before their masters in order to gain food and shelter. Following through with the analogy, the fable would then suggest that slaves will revert to their natural hostility toward their masters when given the chance. As told among slaves, this fable expresses both the awful necessity to please one's oppressor and the dream of wreaking bloody revenge.[97] Most slaves, of course, were constrained to act perpetually like the cub and never got the opportunity to avenge themselves on their masters. Nevertheless, the fable allowed slaves to imagine (in disguised speech) bloody revenge and thereby encourage them in their more restrained modes of everyday resistance (theft, malingering, and, more rarely, flight). On very rare occasions, slaves might even be driven to act out the fable—as did a slave belonging to a city prefect in Rome who murdered his owner.[98] The factors militating against this extreme behavior are clear not only from its rarity in the historical record, but also from the measures taken by masters to prevent this sort of retaliation. In Rome, the law stated that all of the household slaves were to be executed for failing to reveal the conspiracy against their master. In the case of the city prefect just mentioned, this meant that some four hundred household slaves were put to death.

The struggle of the weak to gain justice from the strong is the central theme of another early Greek fable: The Eagle and the Dung Beetle.[99] In Aristophanes' comedy, *Peace*, the main character Trygaios explicitly states that he got the idea of flying up to the gods on a dung beetle from the stories of Aesop. According to Arisophanes' *Wasps*, and the anonymous *Life of Aesop*, moreover, Aesop used this fable to warn the people of Delphi not to harm him, after they accused him of stealing a libation bowl.[100] In this fable, a lowly dung beetle gets revenge on the mighty eagle who had wronged him. The beetle avenged himself by finding the eagle's nest and rolling out the eggs so that they fell and broke. When the eagle sought refuge in the lap of Zeus, to whom the Eagle is consecrated, the beetle flew up to Zeus and dropped a pellet of dung in his lap. Zeus jumped up to shake off the dung pellet and caused the eggs to fall, smashing to the ground once again.

In this fable, the lowly but clever dung beetle outwits not only the mighty Eagle but also his divine protector, Zeus. Here cunning intelligence, rather than divine will, ensures the victory of the weak over the strong.[101] This fable exhibits a similar character to French folktales with its emphasis on human intelligence, rather than divine action, as the weapon of the weak. The main point of the fable, however, like that of the other two just considered, is the revenge of the weak on the powerful. This theme is most clearly evident in the pairing of the Eagle, grandest of the birds, with the humble dung beetle. Aristophanes underlines this imbalance of powers and the theme of revenge in his short allusion to the fable in his *Peace*. When Trygaios' daughter questions whether a smelly creature such as a dung beetle could really fly up to the gods, Trygaios responds: "He [the dung beetle] came because of an old grudge against the eagle and, by rolling out the eggs, he avenged himself."[102] The theme of the revenge of the weak upon the powerful, moreover, is the reason why Aesop is made to use this fable in his warning to the people of Delphi. Aesop, although a mere slave who looked more like "a turnip" than a person, suggests that he is capable of avenging any misdeeds done against him by the people of Delphi, despite the latter's close relationship to the gods.[103]

A similar articulation of the theme of the triumph of the weak over the strong is evident in a fable alluded to in a satyr play by the fifth-century playwright Achaeus. Although this play survives only in fragments, a few lines of iambic trimeter mention a version of what may be the most famous Greek fable of all time: the fable of the Tortoise and the Hare. Achaeus' version, however, featured an eagle and a tortoise, as is clear from the preserved quotation from the play: "the rapid one was even caught by the weak ones, then, just as the eagle by the tortoise in a short time."[104] It is perhaps significant that in Achaeus' version, it is the weak, not the slow, that are contrasted with the fast, thus partially revealing perhaps the real conflict at the heart of the fable: that between the weak and the strong (or, more explicitly, between slaves and their masters).

It is interesting to observe that Homer seems to model his tale of the love of Ares and Aphrodite on the central idea of this fable. When Aphrodite's husband, the lame blacksmith Hephaestus, learns of the liaison between his wife and the mighty war god, he devises a mechanical cage that falls down and traps the unsuspecting lovers as they lie in bed. When the gods gather around the bed and mock the lovers, they comment among themselves: "Evil deeds do not prosper. Indeed, the slow one has surpassed the quick, since Hephaistos, who is slow and lame, has caught with his craft, Ares, who is the swiftest of the Gods who dwell on Olympus."[105] Since Ares is known for his strength, but not particularly for his speed, it seems that Homer has deliberately adapted the words of the mocking gods to echo the fable. Ironically, Ares' strength is perhaps more in line with the reality allegorized in the fable itself. For slaves, the fable signified their hopes and fantasies of revenge on their masters. The modern scholars who claim that there are no fables in the Homeric epics have neglected such indirect reflections of fables.[106]

Let us turn now to the most famous, and also most problematic, early Greek fable, the Hawk and the Nightingale.[107] Hesiod explicitly labels this fable an *ainos*, a form of allegorical or riddling speech whereby one thing is said by means of another. This term is one of the three usual terms used to designate the animal fable.[108] Hesiod uses the fable of the Hawk and the Nightingale to illustrate the injustice of kings (Hawks), who prey on those weaker than themselves such as Hesiod himself (Nightingales). Yet Hesiod's use of the fable is problematic, as has often been noted. While the message in Hesiod's poem is that Justice will prevail in the end, the fable seems to convey the opposite message: the weak can only struggle in vain against the powerful. In Hesiod's version of the fable, the Hawk, holding the lamenting Nightingale in his talons, says:

> Blessed one, why do you cry aloud? One much stronger holds you
>   now.
> You will go wherever I take you, even though you are a singer.
> I will make you my supper, if I wish, or I will set you aside.
> Foolish is he who wishes to struggle against those who are
>   stronger.
> He will be deprived of victory, and, in addition to these shameful
>   things,
> will suffer baneful things.[109]

Martin West observes that "what we miss [in the fable] is the subjection of the bad bird by another higher power," which is what we get in Archilochus' fable of the Eagle and the Fox (discussed above).[110] Since the fable seems to convey the opposite message to the one that Hesiod aims to inculcate, West observes that Hesiod seems "to negate the parallelism of animal and man which is fundamental to the genus of the fable."[111] Hesiod's use of the fable as a negative exemplum for the behavior of men is especially clear in the later verses: "Fish and beast and winged birds eat one another because there is no justice among them, but Zeus gave men justice, which is better by far."[112] Thus, for Hesiod, the fable illustrates the differences, not the similarities, between beasts and men.[113]

Yet if we remove the fable from the context of Hesiod's poem, and think about what it might mean for subordinate groups, there are other possible interpretations that do not negate the parallelism between men and beasts.[114] Most important, the fable seems to express the dire conditions of the weak when faced with the superior resources of the strong. Indeed, the Hawk's pronouncement of the meaning of the fable focuses on the consequences for the weak of irrational attempts to escape their situation of oppression: "Foolish is the one who wants to contend against the strong. For he is deprived of the victory and suffers baneful things in addition to his humiliation." While the overt message of the fable seems to be that the strong will always dominate the weak and therefore resistance is futile, the meaning for subordinate groups may be more subtle than this: it expresses the pitiless injustice of the strong and represents the miserable helplessness of the weak.[115] In this sense, the fable of the Hawk and the Nightingale articulates a message directly opposite to the fantasy of revenge expressed in the two fables discussed above. Yet slaves in ancient Greece, like their counterparts in the American South, felt both sentiments, and the fable was a suitable vehicle for expressing both their most fantastic hopes *and* their practical understanding of the miserable realities of their situation.[116]

A fable mentioned by Aristotle conveys the same theme of realism in relations between weak and strong.[117] According to this fable, some hares made speeches in an assembly of animals about how they should all be equal. In response, the lions asked "Where are your claws and teeth?" This fable, like those of the Hawk and the Nightingale and Eagle and the Fox, gives a realistic assessment of the imbalance of power between different species and impresses on its audience the role of force in determining relations between them.[118] Central to these fables is the idea that one cannot change the innate nature of animal species. Interestingly, this is a theme that occurs frequently in proverbs, a popular form closely related to the fable.[119] Whereas we, in the modern Anglo-American tradition, might say "a leopard cannot change his spots," the ancient Greeks employed similar animal proverbs, such as "You will never make a crab walk straight" or "You will never make the prickly hedgehog smooth."[120] These popular sayings (note they survive for us in comedy) are structured as "impossibilities" (*adunata*), and are sometimes incorporated into speech to deny the possibility of something happening, as in "X will not happen before a wolf marries a sheep."[121]

The theme of innate character and natural hostilities between species is of course a generalizable moral dictum that encourages distrust and caution in all human relations. Yet the deployment of similar themes in fables in which such distrust and caution are encouraged in the weaker party suggests that these animal proverbs may similarly be expressions of slave values. After all, it was particularly important for slaves to be on their guard, given their vulnerable position relative to their masters. As such, these themes in fables and proverbs inculcated lessons among slaves about how to deal with their superiors. This message is in fact consistent with the moral message of the tales and proverbs of African American slaves. As Levine shows, slave tales did not always feature a fantasy of triumph over the strong, but often taught slaves strategies for coping with their masters. For example, slave tales sometimes "underlined the dangers of acting rashly and striking out blindly, as Brer Rabbit did when he assaulted the tar-baby. They point out the futility of believing in the sincerity of the strong, as Brer Pig did when he allowed Fox to enter his house."[122]

Not all fables are so dire in tone and practical in message. A more playful spirit seems to be at work in the fable of the Fox and the Monkey. This fable was told by Archilochus, but the poem survives only in fragmentary form. These fragments are sufficient, however, for us to see that Archilochus' version follows that preserved in later prose traditions. The fable went like this: an assembly of animals elected a monkey king because of his dancing. A fox, jealous of the monkey, lured him into a trap by pretending to offer some meat to the new King. When the monkey was caught in the trap and his bottom was exposed, the fox ridiculed him for his appearance, which was unbecoming of a king: "Oh monkey, you are king with a backside like that?" Following our previous practice of imagining what such a fable might mean for slaves, we might conjecture that this fable captures the disdain that slaves might feel toward their masters. By demonstrating that social superiority does not correspond with intellectual superiority, the fable enacts a role reversal between the high and the low that contrasts with the objective conditions of slave existence. It is not hard to see how slaves might delight in telling and retelling a story that demonstrated the gap between social appearances and real worth. It is this theme that runs throughout the later *Life of Aesop*, as we shall see.

A further set of early Greek fables seems designed to inculcate advice for relations between slaves and masters and among slaves themselves in relation to their masters. Aristotle cites the seventh-century poet Stesichorus for a fable concerning the Horse, the Stag, and the Man:

> A horse occupied a meadow all by himself. When a stag came along
> and destroyed the pasture, the horse wanted revenge. He called on
> a man to help punish the stag. The man consented on the condition
> that the horse submit to the bit and allow him to mount him carry-
> ing javelins. The horse agreed and allowed the man to mount him.
> But instead of being avenged, the horse himself became a slave to
> the man.[123]

According to Aristotle, Stesichorus related this fable to the people of Himera, who had chosen a certain Phalaris as dictator and were about to
grant him a bodyguard.[124] We are not told precisely the circumstances
under which the people of Himera chose to take these actions, but the
fable seems to suggest that it was in order to avenge themselves against
their external enemies. Presumably Phalaris was a strong military leader,
or the people of Himera believed that authoritarian rule might improve
their military success. In sum, Stesichorus uses the fable to suggest that
the people of Himera are paying a high, indeed unacceptable, price for
their victory over their political enemies: their political freedom.

But what if we consider this fable in relation not to political freedom,
but to personal freedom? What might the fable mean for slaves? If we
imagine this fable being told among slaves, it seems to suggest that conflicts between slaves should not be resolved by deepening the enslavement
of one party. In the fable, of course, the horse is initially free, and it is only
when he enlists the aid of man that he becomes enslaved. Yet as applied
metaphorically to relations among slaves, this scenario could relate to
relative degrees of enslavement—the horse with the bit in his mouth stands
for the ultimate degree of degrading subservience.[125] The fable warns
slaves not to let their own rivalries and hostilities drive them to accepting
more degrading terms of slavery. More generally, the central message of
the fable, that freedom is the ultimate good, is at least as well suited to the
situation of slaves as it is to the political context in which it is applied by
Stesichorus.

An even more direct articulation of the central value of personal freedom can be found in the fable of the Wolf and the Dog. A fragment of
Archilochus preserves one line of this fable which is known more fully
from later versions.[126] A hungry wolf admires a well-fed dog until he
notices that the dog's neck had been worn bare. When he learns that the
dog had to wear a collar, the wolf realized that his free but poor condition
was better than the apparently luxurious life of the dog. This fable underlines the desirability of freedom through a vivid symbol of the degrading
condition of the slave: the worn neck of the dog. Just as real slaves' bodies
bore the marks of their enslavement, so the dog's apparently comfortable
life comes at a high price: his physical submission to a master.[127]

Aristotle records another fable that seems to offer more cynical advice to slaves about relations with masters:

> A fox while crossing a river was driven into a ravine. Unable to get out, she suffered for a long time as many fleas took hold of her. A hedgehog then wandered by and when she saw the fox, she took pity on him. The hedgehog asked if he could remove the fleas, but the fox refused. When asked the reason, the fox replied: "These ones are already full of me and draw little blood. But if you remove these, others will come that are hungry and will drink up my remaining blood."[128]

Aristotle attributes this fable to Aesop, who is said to have used this fable as part of his defense in Samos of a demagogue at his trial on a capital charge. According to Aristotle, Aesop advised the Samians not to put to death the demagogue because he had already become wealthy and therefore would not continue to drain the public coffers. A replacement politician, by contrast, would once again steal the public funds.

Like the fable of the Horse, Stag, and the Man discussed above, this fable is deployed by Aristotle as a metaphor for political relations. Aristotle's usage, however, is a rhetorical appropriation designed for the ears of the free citizens of an ancient Greek city-state. If we disembed the fable from its Aristotelian context, we can begin to think about what it might signify for slaves. In this latter context, the fable seems to advise slaves to endure those who exploit them rather than to attempt to get rid of them. New masters will only inflict further damage. Attempts to become fully free will only lead to new suffering. This cynical and depressing perspective is in tune with some of the other fables that depict master-slave relations in realistic but dire terms.

The Public Transcript: Elites and the Dominant Ideology

Let us turn now to the slaveholders' perspective. It is necessary to set out the main lines of the dominant ideology before analyzing the ways that the tale of the bandit slave Drimakos interweaves the hidden transcript of slaves with the public transcript of elites. No long explication of slaveholders' views is necessary, since the central tenets of this worldview are readily apparent in the texts that survive.[129] Briefly stated, the key points of the ideology of the free Greek slaveholders were:

- slaves are less than human; they lack rationality; their bodies are made so as to serve as tools that can be used by free men
- slaves benefit from being dependent on their masters

The *locus classicus* for this ideology is the notorious passage in Aristotle's *Politics* in which the theory of natural slavery is expounded.[130] Though the passage has been subject to much debate in modern scholarship, it is clear that it both naturalizes slavery and finds moral justification of slavery in the paternalistic model: masters "take care" of their slaves in return for service.[131] Certainly slaveholders in later eras, including the antebellum South, frequently resorted to Aristotle's arguments in defense of slavery.[132] Even Stoic philosophers, such as Seneca, who recognized that slaves were human, did not question the existence of slavery. Seneca's compromise was to advocate the humane treatment of slaves in order that they would cease to resist their situation.[133]

All this is very familiar. What is worth emphasizing, however, is that the slaveholders' perspective is precisely the ideological context of our source for the Drimakos story, namely the elite Greek intellectual of the Roman empire, Athenaeus.[134] In order to see how this is so, it is useful to outline the structure and key themes of the section of Athenaeus' immense dialogue, *The Learned Banqueters*, in which Drimakos' story is narrated.[135] As we shall see, the story of Drimakos is told as one of many examples drawn from Greek traditions to illustrate the answer to a question posed by one of the guests at this dinner, namely, did people have slaves in the old days?[136] The Drimakos story is also, however, deployed as an illustration of the problems arising from societies, such as contemporary Roman society, with many slaves. This argument in turn is part of a larger discourse that asserts the natural and moral rightness of slavery ("slavery is good for slaves") but also warns its readers of the corrupting effect of certain types of slavery on Roman society. By placing the story of Drimakos in this larger framework, we will see exactly how elite Roman slaveholders (such as those that formed Athenaeus' audience) found meaning in the story of a bandit-slave.

After some opening banter between Athenaeus and his companion Timocrates, Athenaeus launches into an account of a conversation that took place at a dinner attended by some learned men, or sophists.[137] First he sets the scene, noting that slaves brought on "an enormous quantity of fish from the sea and lake, on silver platters, so that we marveled at the luxury as well as the wealth displayed; for our host had brought everything but the Nereids."[138] This setting is important for the dialogue that follows since it illustrates one of the key themes, namely, the corrupting effects of contemporary wealth and luxury on Roman values.[139]

After a lengthy diatribe on the extortionist tactics of fishmongers, one of the guests, Ulpian, asks a set of "thorny" questions, the answers to which are expounded at even greater length for the rest of the book. The questions include whether the earlier generations used silver vessels at their dinner parties, whether the word for platter is a Greek noun, whether in the past "some men owned a large number of slaves just as men do now," and whether the Greek word for frying pan is spelled both with a long eta and with an alpha.[140] The answers to these questions range from a very short reply about the Greek words, to a longer response about Greek silver vessels, to an even longer response about the slavish types (*parasites*) and flatterers that hang about the wealthy hoping for tidbits from the table. It is never explicitly stated why the topic of parasites comes up, but it becomes clear that silverware, parasites, and flatterers are all connected to the general theme of the decadence of Roman dining compared to that of the ancients.[141] The question of slaves is postponed until later in the dialogue.

The negative judgment on Roman decadence is clear not only from the many explicit condemnatory remarks, but also from the extreme nature of some of the acts described.[142] According to one anecdote, some flatterers lean close to their patrons after the latter had broken wind and inquire where such delicate perfumes could be purchased.[143] Even more grotesque are the flatterers who presented their faces to be spat upon by their patron, and "as they licked the spittle, or even his vomit, they declared that it was sweeter than honey."[144] These anecdotes are followed by others illustrating excessive luxury and the degrading flattery. For example, there is the king who is fanned by pigeons. This marvel was arranged by smearing the king with a type of Syrian perfume to which the birds were attracted. Slaves were then deployed to shoo away the pigeons just as they were about to land on the body of the king, thereby making the birds fan the king with their wings as they fluttered away. In another example, female flatterers are condemned for using their bodies to create a human ladder for their mistress to mount into her carts.[145] As one speaker sums up, flattery degrades both the flatterer and the one who is flattered. He then recounts how Demetrius Poliorcetes recognized the corrupting effects of flattery on both parties when he chastised the Athenians for assimilating him to a god and declared that "not a single Athenian of his time had shown himself great and fine in soul."[146]

After this long tirade, there is a break in the dialogue as Atheneaeus reminds the audience that the setting of this critique of luxury is itself extremely decadent: "there appeared before us a crowd of servants bringing things to eat." This contextual detail is immediately set in contrast to a tale of admirable self-sufficiency: when a certain Thamneus arrived home with guests and found nothing prepared, he himself ground the grain and prepared the meal. This anecdote emphasizes the contrast between past and present mores and serves as a segue to the last of Ulpian's questions: whether the ancients had as many slaves as men do now.[147] In response, one of the diners suggests that they should all recite what they have read about slaves.[148] The discussion of slavery is then undertaken partly as a competitive display of learning, but more importantly, as a contribution to the overarching theme of the moral decline of the Romans from ancient times.

From the myriad of ancient authorities cited by the diners on the question of slavery, two main arguments emerge. Succintly put, the first claim is that the numbers of slaves have grown exponentially since ancient times and that this growth is both a symptom and a cause of the lamentable moral decline of contemporary Roman society. The absence of slavery in the mythical past is supported by numerous examples, not least through citations of the comic versions of the Reign of Kronos discussed above. General Lucullus' conquest of King Mithridates and his importation of Eastern luxury back to Rome are cited as the beginning of the end of the good old Roman culture. Traditional Roman moderation and virtue are exemplified by the great Roman generals of the past such as Scipio and Caesar, who each had only a few slaves. This argument comes close to recognizing what modern scholars have come to call the "poison" of slavery, that is, the harmful effects of slavery on both masters and slaves.[149]

The second argument is almost in direct conflict with the first. At the very least it takes a much more pragmatic attitude toward slavery. Briefly put, the second argument goes like this: slavery is an inescapable facet of human communities and, when managed properly, is beneficial to both slave and master. The starting point for this second argument is the familiar claim that slaves lack rationality and therefore benefit by being ruled by their more capable betters. This argument is supported by numerous examples of communities giving themselves over as slaves to others on fixed conditions. The Thessalian Penestae, for example, "gave themselves up as slaves to the Thessalians according to a stipulation by which the latter were neither to carry them out of the country nor put them to death, while they themselves were to till the land for the Thessalians and render them contributions due."[150] Numerous other examples of this arrangement are cited approvingly, including the Spartan Helots, Cretan Clerotae, and the Heracleotean Mariandynians. One authority is even cited as claiming that the Thessalian Penestae "were better off than their own masters"![151]

In contrast to these positive examples of a mutually beneficial relationship between masters and slaves, other examples show the negative consequences of the mismanagement of this relationship. Abuse of this sort arises, according to the argument, principally from the fact that slaves are now commonly purchased rather than acquired through conquest. The Chians are then blamed for being the first to make use of bought slaves. The story of Drimakos is then cited as an example of the disastrous consequences of this innovation.[152] Not only did the Chians suffer from the revolt led by Drimakos, but much later on (in 86 BCE) they were enslaved by Mithridates and handed over by him to their own slaves. The speaker concludes, "so truly did the gods punish the Chians for being the first to use purchased slaves."[153]

In sum, the story of Drimakos is deployed in a moralizing argument about the proper treatment of slaves. That this argument is presented more in the masters' interest of preserving the system of slavery than out of a concern for the slaves themselves is made quite clear from the quotation from Plato's *Laws* that immediately precedes the narration of the story of Drimakos:

> We must treat them properly, not merely for their own sakes, but even more out of respect to ourselves, and so never do violence to them. One must punish one's slaves according to their deserts, not admonishing them as one would freemen and so making them conceited; practically every address to a slave should be a command, and one should on no account joke with them in any way, whether they are females or males. This is the kind of conduct toward slaves which many persons adopt, thus very foolishly, by making them conceited, rendering life more difficult for them in serving, and for their masters in ruling.[154]

Following this passage, the story of Drimakos is then recounted as a negative example in a twofold argument describing the enormous growth in numbers of slaves in Roman society and deploring the consequent degradation of the master-slave relationship. More particularly, the story of Drimakos serves as an admonitory tale to Roman slaveholders that aims to instruct them in managing their relationship with their slaves in such a way that the system of slavery, and hence their interests, will not be threatened. Athenaeus therefore deploys the story of Drimakos as a building block in the construction of the dominant ideology of elites: slavery is both natural and good.

But, as I pointed out at the beginning of this chapter, the story of Drimakos is not so simple. Indeed, Drimakos possesses many remarkable, even heroic, qualities that belie the convenient fiction that slaves are irrational beings that need masters to guide their labor. How are we to explain these elements in a story that is deployed to buttress the slave system? In the final part of the chapter, I will explain the coexistence of these contradictory elements as the product of cultural negotiation through which masters and subordinate groups worked out a *modus vivendi* that ensured both that the system of slavery endured and the basic well-being of slaves was protected. Far from being an invention of subordinate or dominant groups in isolation, I suggest that the story of Drimakos is a common cultural product worked out by both parties under the pressures created by the system of slavery. While the brute reality of slavery left

little scope for slaves to exert pressure on their masters, I suggest that
stories such as that of Drimakos were one device through which non-
elites actively negotiated for an improvement in their conditions.

Discursive Negotiation and Mutual Accommodation

This lengthy survey of popular themes and elite ideology has attempted
to show that it is possible to isolate distinct traditions in the ancient
sources. Slaves and other subordinate groups articulated their hopes and
desires through visions of the natural order turned upside down, through
animal tales in which the weaker outwitted the stronger, and through
fantasies of a world in which no labor was required but food and drink
flowed freely from the recesses of the earth. Masters, on the other hand,
articulated their belief in the naturalness and justice of slavery by telling
tales of groups who "willingly" submitted to their superiors and thereby
improved their own conditions of life.

It should be clear now that the story of Drimakos shares something
of both traditions. On the one hand, the narrative reads as a celebratory
slaves-on-top/world-upside-down tale insofar as Drimakos and his fol-
lowers defeat their more powerful masters and dictate terms to them. On
the other hand, the tale avoids the full implications of a successful slave
rebellion by representing the slaves as driven only by the goal of securing their basic well-being and not by the desire to overthrow the slave
system.

The coexistence of two distinct worldviews in the story of Drimakos,
I suggest, needs some explanation. Why can the story of Drimakos be
read as a slaves-on-top/WUD narrative, on the one hand, and an affirmation of the immutability of the slave system, on the other? It is not enough
to say that different versions of the story were told to different audiences,
since elements from both ideologies are tightly interwoven into the narrative plot of the story. The hero Drimakos cannot simply be taken out of
the story when it is recounted before an audience of slaveholders. Nor,
when the story is recounted among slaves, can Drimakos' restraint in
plundering his former masters' lands be easily erased since these elements
are key to his characterization as a just and fair-dealing leader. It seems
clear that the story that we have is the outcome of repeated retellings by
both slaveholders and subordinate groups and that the story is a collective
product of both groups. We need to explain, therefore, how and, more
important, *why* this collective cultural co-production takes place.

The story of Drimakos provides a unique clue to the context in which
such cultural negotiation might take place, namely, the hero shrine.[155] We
are told at the end of the story that the Chians, "reminded of the fairness

of the dead slave, set up a hero shrine in the countryside and gave it the name of the Kindly Hero."[156] According to the story, both slaves and free Chians made offerings to the hero. Runaway slaves dedicated a portion of everything they stole to the hero, while Chian masters sacrificed to the hero whenever he appeared to them in their sleep and warned them of the plots of their slaves. It seems that both groups came together in worshipping the hero. Is it possible that this cult was the physical context of the negotiation of a modus vivendi between slaves and masters that we see articulated in the story of Drimakos? That is to say, did the dead hero symbolize in action (common cult) and speech (shared oral tradition) the mutual accommodation between masters and slaves in Chios? The cult of Drimakos then becomes the physical embodiment of the terms of agreement between masters and slaves, namely that slaves shall have sufficient livelihood (symbolized by the food and other items stolen by runaway slaves under the hero's patronage) and that masters shall not suffer rebellion from their slaves (symbolized by the warnings of the hero of plots against the masters).[157]

What I am suggesting is that the cult of the hero and the story of Drimakos represent the physical and symbolic manifestation of a "contract" worked out over generations by which masters and slaves managed to live together. This interpretation is compatible with the role of hero-cults in other regions of Greece. It would be wrong, of course, to suggest that hero-cults had a single function, and indeed modern scholars have come up with a variety of different explanations for them.[158] Yet one consistent feature of the hero-cult appears to be its role in uniting a diverse community under a common cultural symbol. Thus the proliferation of hero-cults in the eighth century has been associated with the need for the newly formed city-states to root themselves in the mythological past and forge a common collective identity.[159] A similar burst of cultic worship of heroes in the sixth century has been interpreted as a symptom of the need to overcome divisive competition between elite families, each with their own ancestral family heroes.[160] Finally, the increased importance of the hero Theseus in late sixth century Athens, as well as the replacement of Ionian tribal divisions with new divisions named after local Athenian heroes, seem to be mechanisms designed to overcome elite status distinctions and unite the Athenian people within the newly created democracy.[161]

Like hero shrines in many other parts of Greece, then, the cult of Drimakos presumably played an important role in unifying the Chian community. Unlike most modern scholarly interpretations of hero-cult, however, my interpretation of the cult of Drimakos puts slaves in the foreground and suggests that it was particularly tensions between slaves and masters that were the focus of the integrating functions of this hero-cult.[162] Furthermore, unlike most hero-cults, in the case of this Chian one, we not only know who came together to celebrate it, but also the meaning of the cult for different groups. We have this information because the ethnographer Nymphodorus, during a visit to Chios, probably asked the Chians about a monument in their countryside. In response, the Chians told him the story of Drimakos.

The story of Drimakos is therefore in part an aetiology, or explanation of the origins, of a shrine in the Chian countryside.[163] Like Herodotus before him, and Pausanias after him, Nymphodorus probably collected many of his stories from oral informants who either offered up information about their culture or were prompted to do so by the inquisitive ethnographer. Often these stories centered on a physical monument and served to explain how it came to be there.[164] Frequently these explanatory stories had little to do with the actual historical origins of the monument, but were devised by later generations seeking to explain something about which they no longer had accurate knowledge. It is noteworthy in this regard that the shrine of Drimakos is dedicated to the Kindly Hero, a generic title, compatible with many different stories.[165] Most shrines in the Greek countryside are nameless, but insofar as we know the names of those to whom they were dedicated, they were usually mythological figures like Oedipus, the Seven Against Thebes or Menelaus and Helen (fig. 6).[166] It is possible that the story of Drimakos became attached to a shrine that originally belonged to a different mythological figure or even a god.[167]

While I have suggested that the figure of Drimakos symbolized a common recognition of the mutual accommodation of slaves and masters in Chios, it would be wrong to deny that each side also cultivated its own more group-centered meanings of the cult. For slaves, the figure of Drimakos might have stood as a symbol of their superiority over their masters, or even of their desire for revenge for the many abuses committed against them. By contrast, masters may have worshipped Drimakos as a guarantee of their own personal safety from possible retribution from their slaves, and, more abstractly, as a symbol of the ultimate security of the slave system.

This explanation of *how* these disparate groups came together in cult does not explain *why* they did so. Why in particular would slaves accept this arrangement which evidently caters better to the masters' interest than that of the slaves? The answer to this question lies in the vastly inferior position that slaves found themselves in compared to the masters. In short, slaves had no choice but to accept the status quo. What they could do was work to ameliorate the conditions of their slavery, and comparative evidence from other slave and peasant societies suggests that this is exactly the strategy that these groups took. I suggest that the story of Drimakos, and its material counterpart in cult, represents the discur-

Figure 6.
Shrine thought to be dedicated to the hero Menelaus at Sparta. Hero shrines
like this one are found scattered throughout the Greek landscape, and often
have no inscription identifying the recipient of the cult. Photo by Ian Moyer.

sive articulation of an historical strategy for slave survival, namely the
acceptance of slavery in return for the negotiation of better conditions.

Subordinate groups like to imagine a world upside down, or a complete reversal in power relations. In practice, however, these groups want
some security of basic well-being rather than total revolution whose outcome was uncertain and certainly potentially more threatening to their
marginal existence that to that of their superiors. As Eugene Genovese
emphasizes in his study of slave culture of the American South, slaves un-
questionably wanted freedom, but they were realistic about their chances
and strategized in ways that optimized their gains with least risk to an
already precarious existence.[168]

Perhaps the most striking manifestation of this strategy among historical slaves and peasants is the ways that they have resisted oppression not by
outright violence but engaging in what they deemed to be "fair" practices.
For example, E. P. Thompson has observed that peasants in eighteenth-
century England protested high food prices not by plundering granaries
but by mimicking, "sometimes with great precision," official procedures
for setting a fair price for corn.[169] As Thompson shows, when peasants felt

that grain was being withheld in order to raise prices, they marched out to farms, granaries, and mills, brought the grain to market themselves, and sold it at a price they deemed fair. In one example,

> [t]he Honiton lace-workers, in 1766, who, having taken corn from the farmers and sold it at the popular price in the market, brought back to the farmers not only the money but also the sacks.[170]

An earlier example of this pattern of popular protest occurs in fictive form in an episode in Rabelais's *Gargantua* known as "Cake Peddler's War."[171] In this affair, some bakers on their way to market refused to sell their fancy flat-cakes to some peasant farmers who accosted them along the way. Even though the peasants offered the going rate, they were rudely rebuffed by the cake-peddlers. The conflict soon escalated into a full-scale brawl in which the peasants—aided by some shepherds who happened to be nearby—got the best of it. The peasants then helped themselves to the flat-cakes. Rather than taking the cakes for free, however, the peasants "paid the going rate, adding a hundred walnuts and three basketfuls of ripe white grapes."[172]

Although the action of Drimakos is not exactly parallel—he does not pay (at least literally) the masters for the supplies he takes—I suggest that the symbolism of his action is the same. It represents a strategic move to improve the condition of the slaves by striking a bargain with the masters using procedures that the masters acknowledge as legitimate (weights, measures, seals), just as peasants in sixteenth-century France and eighteenth-century England sought a modicum of security using the ruling classes' own tools—monetary payment (along with payment in kind!) and official procedures for "setting the price."

Even more closely parallel to the Drimakos story are historical examples of treaties between runaway slaves and masters, particularly in Jamaica and Surinam.[173] These treaties grant the slaves "freedom and autonomy in return for a pledge of allegiance to the colonial regime, including the duty to return runaways and to defend the public order—that is to suppress slave rebellions."[174] Genovese, in his study of these servile revolts, concludes that the slaves "had a restorationist or isolationist, rather than a revolutionary" goal.[175] This conservative outlook can be recognized as a product of the same risk-diminishing strategies of resistance visible in the behavior of early modern peasants described above, and in Genovese's own analysis of slave culture in the American South. In all these cases, these subordinate groups accepted a system that they could not overturn, but only at the price of gaining certain minimum rights for themselves.

The same cultural logic is apparent in traditions about the slave Aesop, perhaps most directly in the following passage in the *Life of Aesop*.[176]

This passage occurs early on in the *Life*, when the philosopher Xanthos is on the verge of buying Aesop from the slave dealer.

> XANTHOS: I wish to buy you, but you won't try to run away will you?
>
> AESOP: If I wish to do this I will not make you my advisor [in this enterprise], as you [take] me as your advisor. But who determines whether I run away? You or me?
>
> XANTHOS: Clearly, you do.
>
> AESOP: No, you do.
>
> XANTHOS: Why do I?
>
> AESOP: If you are a good master, no one, fleeing the good goes to the bad, giving himself over to wandering and the expectation of hunger and fear. But if you are a bad master, I will not stay one hour with you, not even half an hour, not even a second.

Aesop's forthright outspokenness and direct assertion of his power over his own destiny is undisguised in this passage, yet it lies side by side with the narrative assumption that Aesop will remain and will depart only if his master breaks his side of the bargain by treating him badly. The same ambiguity underlies this entire Aesop tradition as runs through the Drimakos story. The tension between the slaves' need for humane treatment and the master's desire for the maintenance of the slave system is also apparent in the verdict that the bandit Bulla Felix announces to the centurion who had been assigned to capture him: "Carry this message back to your masters: let them feed their slaves so that they might not be compelled to turn to a life of banditry." In all these cases, the stories allow for direct assertion of slave superiority within a framework that reassures masters that slavery as a system is not in danger.

The "contract" worked out in these fictions is precisely the equilibrium reached by historical masters and slaves in the antebellum South. Genovese argues that the slaves managed to exploit the basic fact of slaveholder dependency on slave labor in order to transform the doctrine of slaves as absolute property into a doctrine of reciprocity, or paternalism. If the masters wanted unproblematic labor, then they had to provide a minimum of humane treatment to their slaves. Once the basic necessity that masters "take care" of their slaves was recognized, it was easier for the slaves to establish their basic human dignity and carve out a "living-space" or cultural sphere that was their own. As Genovese writes:

> The slave's acceptance of paternalism, therefore, signaled acceptance of an imposed white domination within which they drew their own lines, asserted rights, and preserved their self-respect.[177]

A good illustration of this slave strategy can be found in an episode in the *Life of Aesop*.[178] In this passage, Aesop consistently frustrates his master by doing exactly as his master says—no less or more. For example, when his master tells him to bring an oil flask to the bath, Aesop brings the flask but neglects to put oil in it. When reproached by his master, Aesop parrots his master: "You told me to bring the flask, but you did not mention oil. And you told me to do nothing more than what I was ordered since, if I didn't obey you, I would be whipped." Next, Aesop is told to go home and cook lentil for dinner for his master and his guests. This time the master takes care to specify in great detail how Aesop should perform this task: "Put the lentil in the pot, add water and put it on the hearth in the kitchen. Put on wood and light the fire. If it goes out, blow on it to restart it." Aesop goes home and puts one lentil in the pot, cooks it and serves it to his master. When the master asks where the rest of the lentils are, Aesop responds, "You said 'cook lentil,' not lentils. One is singular, the other is plural."

Now of course much of this dialogue is a parody of learned interest in precision of language, but there is more to it than this. When Xanthos finally cries out in exasperation that Aesop will drive him mad, Aesop says, "If you hadn't been so strict in setting down the rules, I would have served you much better." This ending, I suggest, spells out the central idea of the passage, namely, the need to give slaves a "living space." In essence the story illustrates how Aesop forces his master to recognize the humanity of slaves, and to grant them some freedom to use their human capacities for reason. In Aesop's victory, the very capacities denied to slaves by the ideology of the slaveholders are expressly and forcefully affirmed. In this way, the story furthers the agenda of slaves and destabilizes the dominant ideology of the ruling class even while ostensibly reinforcing that same ideology.

Keith Hopkins, in his excellent article on the *Life of Aesop*, recognizes the master's understanding of the story, that is, the central advice that the story offers to slaveholders: "The real lesson is that good service from a high quality slave cannot be based on explicit instructions, or fear or punishment. It has to be based on trust."[179] Yet this is only one side of the story. As the story was told among slaves, or as slaves read the story as entertainment to their masters, the lesson might have been different.[180] Slaves are on top. Slaves have superior cunning and intelligence compared to their masters. For slaves, the story acknowledges the humanity, dignity, and ultimately power of slaves to determine their own destiny.

Before we leave this discussion of the relation between the story and historical slave strategies of resistance, it is worth noting briefly a few other elements in the tale of Drimakos that have clear parallels in histori-

cal slave rebellions. First, and most obviously, the establishment of a maroon community of slaves—on a mountain or other fortified spot—is a
common strategy of slave rebellions, and one which Genovese—studying
rebellions in the Caribbean—has noted was a key factor in whether slave
revolts were successful or not.[181] Paul Cartledge has similarly observed
that the formation of such outposts by the enslaved laborers of Sparta
(*helots*) was an important factor in their relative success against their
masters.[182] One might also note that Drimakos claims divine sanction for
his revolt, a feature that he shares with other slave leaders, including
those of the slave rebellions in Sicily in the second century BCE, as well
as those of the Caribbean, as Brent Shaw has observed.[183]

But even if the story of Drimakos, like the story of the Roman bandit
Bulla Felix, is "full of credible [historical] details," this observation does
not change the fact that the tale as a whole is an ideologically motivated
fiction.[184] As we have learned from studies of oral tradition and social
memory, stories about the past are retold in the present, not in order to
keep an accurate record, but because they are meaningful (they articulate
norms, worldviews, ideals) to those who tell them.[185] The stories told by
the Chians to Nymphodorus of Syracuse when he visited sometime in the
third century BCE must have been ideologically meaningful to them (and
perhaps to several generations of slave-owners before them). What I have
tried to show in this chapter is that they were also meaningful to slaves.

Conclusion: Something to Do with Chios?

The fantasy of "slaves on top" that I have argued underlies the story of
Drimakos is also strikingly articulated in a proverb circulating already in
the time of Eupolis, a fifth-century Athenian comic poet. All of Eupolis'
comedies are lost, but one line from a comedy apparently contained the
following proverb: "A Chian has bought himself a master."[186] As we have
seen, proverbs are one of the genres linked by Scott with the disguised
speech of subordinate groups. Furthermore, there was a fluid relationship
between proverbs and fables in popular culture, and I have already suggested that the Aesopic fable played a key role in the culture of subordinate groups.[187] Finally, the genre of comedy in which this and many other
proverbs and fables are preserved has strong connections with popular
culture.[188] Is it possible that the story of Drimakos—or at least a story of
a slave who dominates his master on Chios—goes back as far as Eupolis'
time, that is the fifth century? Behind the cryptic proverb preserved in
Eupolis' comedy may lie a much more expansive slave tradition—already
apparently connected with slaves on Chios—that slaves (at least in fantasy)

could be on top. In short, there was something about the slaves on Chios that made them a fertile source of the popular imagination, even in Athens. In this conclusion, I want to speculate why this was so.

We may start by noting that slavery has a long history on Chios. Not only does Theopompus (a native Chian) claim that the Chians were the first to begin purchasing slaves, but we have independent epigraphical evidence for slaves going back to the fifth century.[189] In the late fifth century, Thucydides claimed that the Chians had the largest number of slaves apart from the Spartans.[190] The reason for the early and extensive use of slaves on Chios is to be found in its status as a relatively large and fertile island conveniently located to optimize on trade routes. Slave labor was the necessary ingredient to transform these natural endowments into wealth. By employing slaves on their lands, the Chians were able to produce surplus amounts of wine, figs, and other agricultural products that they then exported for profit.[191] Chios is known to have exported wine already in the Archaic period, and Chian merchants are attested at trading centers as widely spread as Al Mina, Egypt, Etruria, and the Black Sea.[192] At the time of the Ionian Revolt in 494 BC, the Chians raised the largest contingent, providing one hundred ships, one-third of the Ionian fleet combined.[193] Chios' naval strength was so great that they provided only ships and no tribute to the Greek alliance against the Persians known as the Delian League.[194] Thucydides, indeed, rhapsodized on Chian prosperity, noting that apart from the Spartans, the Chians were the most successful at combining wealth and prudence so that as their city became more powerful they also increased their own security.[195]

In his narrative of the Chian rebellion from the Athenian empire in 412 BC, Thucydides comments both on how well-cared for the fields of the Chians were when the Athenians ravaged them, as well as the negative consequences of Chian reliance on large numbers of slaves:

> Because of the large number of slaves, the Chians punished them harshly when they misbehaved. When the Athenian army invested the walls closely, many slaves right away deserted the Chians and went over to the Athenians. Moreover, because these slaves knew the Chian landscape well, they inflicted the most damage.[196]

The exploitation of the aid of the slaves by foreign invaders occurs throughout later Chian history.[197] For example, Iphicrates made use of Chian fears about their slaves in a clever trick of war in 389/8. According to Polyaenus, Iphicrates "spread a report at Mytilene, that he intended shortly to provide a number of shields, which would be sent to the slaves on Chios. The Chians believed this rumour, which made them afraid of a rebellion among their slaves. They immediately sent presents to Iphicrates, and entered into an alliance with Athens."[198] During a siege of Chios in

201, Philip V attempted to get the Chian slaves to revolt by promising them freedom and, more strikingly, marriage with their owners.[199] Finally, during the First Mithridatic War (89–85 BCE), a commander of Mithridates of Pontos captured the Chians and handed them over to their slaves on the condition that they settle in Colchis.[200] In response to the strategies of their opponents, Chian masters were sometimes compelled to offer their slaves freedom in return for their military assistance.[201] Although other states were similarly vulnerable because of the uncertain loyalty of their slaves, the size of the Chian slave population made the cooperation of the "enemy within" more crucial on Chios than anywhere else, excepting Sparta.[202]

In sum, the history of Chios shows that the Chians had a definite problem with their slaves, one that was well recognized outside Chios, and even exploited in times of war. Given this evidence for a large and relatively rebellious slave population on Chios, it is not surprising that Chian slaves and masters came up with a novel solution to stabilize their relations: a dual hero-cult and a corresponding aetiological legend through which slaves and masters enacted and articulated the terms of their mutual accommodation. If the efficacy of myth and ritual lies in its collapsing of the legendary past with the cultic present, as Kowalzig has recently reminded us, then it appears that the cult of Drimakos was ideally formulated to achieve this goal.[203] We must imagine that the practitioners of the cult in the time of Nymphodorus symbolically re-enacted through their joint participation in the cult the treaty which the legendary slave-hero negotiated with the Chian masters. On this reading the cult itself, rather than an actual treaty, is the primary means by which masters and slaves are drawn together into a common community. Cultic bonds, rather than political or legal ones, were the glue that tied the Chian masters to their slaves and vice versa.

In this sense, the cult of Drimakos can be compared to other communal rituals involving both slaves and their masters. In particular, the festival of the Kronia in Greece and the Saturnalia in Rome were occasions when slaves and masters came together in common worship, thereby temporarily removing or even reversing the social hierarchy.[204] The cult of Drimakos similarly symbolically enacts a removal or reversal of status relations between slaves and their masters. The symbolism of the cult of Drimakos, however, is even more dramatic than that of the Kronia/Saturnalia. While in the latter cults, masters merely feasted with or attended to their slaves, in the former, masters actually *worshipped a rebellious slave*. In this sense, while both cults played a similar role in integrating slaves and masters, the cult of Drimakos provides deeper insight into the fundamental nature of these cults as central to slave culture and as key to the active negotiation by slaves for better living conditions. Once we recognize the

essential role of the story of Drimakos in slave culture and in articulating relations between slaves and their masters, then we gain deeper understanding of the instigating role of slaves in the much more widespread
and probably older cult of Kronos/Saturn. Indeed, the popular origins of
the image of magical abundance that was the animating theme of these
latter festivals now finds further support in the cultic parallels with the
role of Drimakos' cult in slave culture.

Another parallel for the cult of Drimakos on Chios is the cult of the
hero Theseus at Athens.[205] According to our sources, slaves who were
treated with undue harshness could seek asylum in the precinct of the
hero. There the slave's claims would be heard, and, if considered justified,
the slave would be sold to a new master. Theseus, as a mythical hero of
Athens, is credited with a concern for the oppressed and therefore is a
fitting patron of runaway slaves. Apparently slaves appealed for asylum
quite frequently, since Athenian comedy coined a special term for "one
who spends time in the precinct of Theseus" (theseiotrips).[206] The choice
of a hero-cult as the place of refuge of slaves provides a striking parallel
with the hero-cult of Drimakos on Chios. As I have argued for the cult of
Drimakos, the rituals and the oral traditions of the cult of Theseus likely
represent a mutual accommodation between masters and slaves in ancient Athens. It is worth emphasizing once again, however, the crucial
distinction that on Chios, a slave, not a mythical hero, is the focus of the
worshipping community. Although the cult of Drimakos seems to share
some of the same functions as the festival of Kronos and the cult of Theseus at Athens, it is unique in the importance granted to the figure of a
slave. For this reason, the Chian cult seems to stand out as evidence of the
active role of slaves in the negotiation of master-slave relations.

The cultic solution to ongoing tensions between Chians and their
slaves seems to have been largely successful. Despite the evidence for the
desertion of slaves in times of war discussed above, Chios was a remarkably stable community and we hear of no major slave rebellions. As argued above, slaves probably accepted the slave system because they had
no choice. It was only in times of extreme external pressure like the siege
by the Athenians in 412 that the Chian slaves judged that the risks of
rebellion were worth the potential gain of freedom. For most of Chian
history, the slaves negotiated fair treatment and a "living space" through
their participation in the myth and rituals of the cult of Drimakos. It was
perhaps this living space granted to slaves in Chios that was the source
of the Athenian comic tradition that the Chians "had bought themselves
a master."[207]

What needs to be emphasized here is that both parties in the worshipping community formed by the cult of the hero had an *active role* in this
ongoing recreation of bonds. The slave community on Chios was an equal

partner with their Chian masters in this cult, and, if anything, had the upper hand. After all, the mediating heroic figure is a slave. As I have repeatedly stressed, the fact that the Chian masters worship a slave-hero is striking. Indeed, it is this odd feature in the legend of Drimakos that this chapter has tried to explain. The key, I suggest, is to recognize that a slave community, not just the free community of masters, lies behind this remarkable tale.

3

Pigs, Asses, and Swine: Obscenity and the Popular Imagination in Ancient Sicyon

When he was fighting a war against the Argives, Cleisthenes, [the tyrant of Sicyon], stopped the poetic recitations of the Homeric epics because Argos and the Argives were frequently mentioned. Furthermore, he was eager to remove the heroic shrine of Adrastus, son of Talaus, which was in the central marketplace of the people of Sicyon. Going to Delphi, he inquired of the oracle if he could remove Adrastus. The priestess gave the following oracular response to him: "Adrastus was king of the people of Sicyon, but you are a mere stone-thrower." Since the god did not permit him to do this deed, he went back home and devised a trick by which Adrastus might leave of his own accord.

When he thought he had discovered a way, he sent to Boeotian Thebes and said that he wished to escort [the hero] Melanippus, the son of Astacus, [to Sicyon]. The Thebans assented. Cleisthenes escorted Melanippus [to Sicyon] and appointed to him an enclosure in the town hall itself. In this way, Cleisthenes established the hero there in the most secure spot. Cleisthenes had escorted Melanippus [to Sicyon]—for it is necessary to explain this too—because he was most hateful to Adrastus, who had killed both his brother Mekisteus and his son-in-law Tydeus.

When [Cleisthenes] appointed the enclosure to him, he removed the sacrifices and feasts from [the cult] of Adrastus and gave them to [the cult] of Melanippus. The people of Sicyon had been accustomed to honor Adrastus very extravagantly. For Sicyon was the ancestral land of Polybus, and Adrastus was his grandson. When Polybus died without male offspring, he handed over the kingdom to Adrastus. The people of Sicyon honored Adrastus in many ways, but in particular they celebrated his sufferings with tragic choruses. In fact they did not honor Dionysus with choruses [as is customary elsewhere], but Adrastus. Cleisthenes restored the choruses to Dionysus and gave the rest of the sacrifices to Melanippus.

These are the things that were done [by Cleisthenes] to Adrastus. He also changed the Dorian tribal names to other names, so that the tribes not be the same for the people of Sicyon and the Argives. And in this act, he ridiculed the people of Sicyon very much. For by changing the endings of the words, he gave them the names of the sow, the ass and the piglet. To his own tribe, however, he gave a name reflecting his own leadership. His tribe, then, was called "Leaders of the People" and the others were called "Swinemen, Assmen and Pigmen." The people of Sicyon used these tribal names both during Cleisthenes' reign, and after his death for a further sixty years. After this, they discussed the issue among themselves and changed the names back to "Hyllatai, Pamphyloi and Dumanatai" [the old Dorian tribal names]. The fourth tribe they named after the son of Adrastus, Aigialeus. The members of this fourth tribe were therefore called the Aigialees." (Herodotus, *Histories* 5.67–68)

So the fifth-century historian Herodotus describes some very peculiar reforms allegedly made by Cleisthenes, a sixth-century tyrant of the city-state of Sicyon. The problematic nature of the insulting names of the tribal divisions has long been recognized.[1] Yet scholars have not questioned the other strange reforms attributed to the tyrant. Indeed, a great deal of scholarly ingenuity has been dedicated to rationalizing the tribes named after barnyard animals, but the rest of Herodotus' account has been accepted at face value. While scholars have argued that anti-tyrannical ideologies have most likely distorted what were originally unoffensive tribal names, no one has questioned Cleisthenes' bizarre attempts to expel the Argive hero Adrastus from Sicyon, or his ban on the performance of Homeric epic. In this chapter, I suggest that Herodotus' whole account of Cleisthenes is a satirical inversion of the historical facts and derives from fifth-century popular traditions that made use of a figure from the past to engage in a distinctive brand of "folk humor."

The concept of folk humor has been developed famously by Michael Bakhtin to describe the popular culture of the Middle Ages. The key characteristics of folk culture, according to Bakhtin, are images of the grotesque body, obscenity—both sexual and scatological—and the debasement of all that is high (e.g., official institutions, high culture), particularly by associating it with the "bodily lower stratum."[2] As I shall demonstrate, precisely this sort of popular humor runs through Herodotus' account of the reforms of Cleisthenes.[3] My aim in uncovering the influence of popular tradition on Herodotus' narrative, however, is not simply to show how it has distorted our evidence for earlier Greek history. Rather, I seek to understand the ways that popular traditions made use of the past to articulate a distinctive worldview. My aim, therefore, is not only deconstructive, but also reconstructive: I seek to recapture the ways that ordinary people—the mass of ordinary farmers, women, and even slaves—

created a cultural space in which they expressed their sense of themselves and the world around them. It is a tribute to the vitality and charm of folk culture that much of the "high" literature of antiquity—including Herodotus' *Histories*—has so thoroughly absorbed this popular element, thereby preserving (albeit in more or less distorted ways) the spirit of the mass of laboring humanity.[4] Historians and literary critics have largely either ignored the popular roots of much of classical literature, or failed to explore exactly what it can tell us about the ideals and aspirations of non-elites.

Once the full extent of influence of popular traditions on Herodotus' narrative is recognized, we can more easily observe the historical basis of Herodotus' account. The aim of the second half of the chapter is therefore also reconstructive. I argue that the very attribution of a series of cultic and tribal changes to a single colorful figure from the past is a typical feature of oral traditions. I suggest instead that these changes are better accounted for historically as the product of political and cultural interaction between city-states over the course of the Archaic period of Greek history (c. 750–500 BCE). In other words, these changes were not accomplished in one fell swoop by a single individual, but were enacted gradually over several centuries.

Popular Tradition and Cleisthenes of Sicyon

There are many features of Herodotus' narrative of Cleisthenes of Sicyon—not just the tribes named after lowly animals—that suggest the sort of ridicule of authorities and official power that is common in popular culture.[5] Indeed, the comic thrust of the whole narrative on Cleisthenes is the absurd ways that the tyrant pursued his hatred of the Argives. Yet this meaning is often lost on modern readers, hidden as it is behind a more obvious and serious anti-tyrannical perspective of Herodotus and his more "official" sources. On the surface the story conforms to a direct critique of tyranny, broadly acceptable to all fifth-century audiences, elite and nonelite alike. Yet just below the surface is a second level of meaning, not incompatible with anti-tyrannical political traditions, but with its own agenda quite distinct from straightforward political ideologies. In this sort of folk humor the key theme, as Bakhtin has taught us, is the degradation of all that is high—institutions, authorities, and high culture—not solely as a veiled critique of those above by those below, but more crucially as an expression of the dynamics of regeneration and renewal that is vital to the non-elite worldview. The meaning of the last part of this statement is best illustrated by example, and will become apparent in the analysis of Herodotus' narrative of Cleisthenes that follows.

Let us begin with the claim that Cleisthenes ended performances of Homer because the Argives and Argos were frequently mentioned. Herodotus' interpretation of Cleisthenes' action (and indeed, the action itself, as I shall argue later) is a patent absurdity, since it is based on a comically literal understanding of the term "Argives." The Greeks of Herodotus' time were familiar with Homer's use of the term Argives to designate the Greeks as a whole. Indeed, they knew that the frequent references to the Argives in the *Iliad* had no specific relation to Argos, except insofar as Agamemnon, the leader of the Greeks at Troy, was king there. Cleisthenes' ban on performances of Homer therefore is based on a ludicrous misreading of epic poetry. It is easy to see how a popular and official tradition might find amusement in representing the tyrant as stubbornly pursuing a policy based on woefully inadequate understanding of "high" culture.[6]

More subtly, the narrative itself relies on a satirical reading (or misreading) of high literature that can be compared to the travesties of official literature (for example, sacred texts) by popular traditions in the Middle Ages. As Bakhtin has shown, one of the three key manifestations of folk culture was the performance of comic verbal compositions that took the form of parodies of serious literature.[7] Parodies of Homeric epic have survived from antiquity and reflect the existence of this form of satire in ancient popular culture. Sometimes the parody consists in an exaggeration of high literary style, while at other times, humor is found through the juxtaposition of the high with the low.[8] For example, an heroic action may be performed by a lowly character. In the ancient parody of Homer's *Iliad* known as the *Batrachomyomachia*, frogs and mice are depicted in heroic combat. Conversely, base actions can be narrated in high epic style: in the ancient mock-epic poem, the *Margites*, the travails of an idiot are retold partly in epic meter.[9]

Cleisthenes' misreading of Homer, I suggest, is based on just such a comic travesty of epic. The degradation of the high style, in this example, is achieved by the debasement of its poetic style. In Homeric epic, the term "Argives" is used to designate the Greeks as a whole through the poetic figure of speech known as metonymy ("part for whole"). In Cleisthenes' misreading, by contrast, the term is reduced to a direct and unpoetic reference to the Argives of Cleisthenes' own time. The passage therefore achieves two sorts of degradation—a replacement of high poetic style with simple literalism and the representation of the great tyrant as an unlettered buffoon.

I will argue later in the chapter that this section of Herodotus' narrative is probably based on a comic inversion of what actually happened in sixth-century Sicyon. I will suggest that public performances of Homer were *introduced, not terminated*, in sixth-century Sicyon. As is typical of folk humor, popular tradition turned official actions upside down, subverting what was probably an official attempt to augment the cultural capital of Sicyon. By representing the tyrant as culturally backward, popular tradition turned the tyrant into an object of ridicule.

Let us turn to the next element in Herodotus' narrative: Cleisthenes' attempt to get rid of the hero-cult of Adrastus, an Argive hero and former Sicyonian king. As we shall see in the second half of the chapter, hero-cults were important features of the cultural and political landscape of sixth-century Greece. These heroes were powerful beings who needed to be appeased but could also provide supernatural protection for cities if they were properly worshipped. Cleisthenes' desire to expel the hero Adrastus from Sicyon, therefore, not only demonstrates blatant disrespect for the sacred status of heroes but potentially exposes the community to harm.

The narrative emphasizes the sacrilegious nature of Cleisthenes' desire to expel the hero by representing the tyrant as roundly rebuked by the Delphic oracle, which tells him that "Adrastus was king of Sicyon, but you are a mere stone-thrower (*leuster*)." The meaning of *leuster* is clearly derogatory, but its exact meaning has been the subject of scholarly debate, as I shall discuss shortly. What I want to emphasize now is that Herodotus' account of Cleisthenes' actions fits the pattern of a popular moral tale.[10] There are many forms of such morality tales, but the basic plot is that a powerful person who commits an unjust deed meets his just reward through the agency of the gods, chance, or the superior cunning of the weaker person against whom he transgresses. As we saw in chapter 2, the fables of Aesop contain many examples of this pattern, as do the stories told by subordinate groups throughout history. Following the lead of scholars of peasants and slaves in other historical eras, we may posit that morality tales of popular literature are a medium through which subordinate groups (e.g., slaves, ordinary farmers, and craftsmen) collectively imagined a different outcome from their interactions with their superiors. Such tales, therefore, represent a sphere of the culture of oppressed groups in which they articulated (often in disguised forms) their opposition to those above them.[11]

Cleisthenes' attempt to expel Adrastus is patterned according to a particular Greek variation on this theme: a powerful person about to contemplate an improper act consults the Delphic oracle and is told to refrain in pithy rebuke. A story told in another section of Herodotus' *Histories* represents one example of this variation on the theme.[12] According to this story, a rich Milesian once gave half his fortune for safekeeping to a Spartan named Glaucus who was renowned for his justice. Many years later, however, when the sons of the Milesian came to retrieve the money,

Glaucus claimed that he could not remember having been entrusted with it. After delaying for many months, Glaucus decided to consult the Delphic oracle as to whether he could keep the money entrusted to him. Glaucus is told that "Death awaits even one who has kept his oath. But Oath has a son, nameless, without hands and feet, but swift to pursue until he has seized and destroyed the race and house of the perjured one." After hearing this oracular response, Glaucus is deterred from his purpose. Yet the story does not end there. Glaucus is told by the priestess at Delphi that "to consult the god [about wrongdoing] and to do [wrong] amount to the same thing." Accordingly, Glaucus' family is destroyed "root and branch," even though Glaucus returned the money according to the oracle's advice.

Like Glaucus, the tyrant Cleisthenes conceives of a morally dubious action (the expulsion of a sacred hero), consults the oracle, and is told to refrain by the god. In Glaucus' case, the gods punish him for the mere impulse to injustice, despite his conformity to the god's prohibition. By contrast, Cleisthenes is deterred only momentarily, and immediately undertakes to find a way to side-step the god's injunction. The implication of the comparison of these two similarly patterned stories is that Cleisthenes is even more deserving of divine punishment than Glaucus.

In general, we may infer that stories patterned according to this type both critique the powerful for their illicit intentions and celebrate the gods by illustrating how the latter check the impious desires of the former.[13] Most interestingly for my purposes, the oracular rebuke of Cleisthenes involves a clever play on the active and passive meanings of the word *leuster* whose comic sense, as we shall see, relies on one of the central strategies of folk humor, namely, the degradation of the high. Let us see how this is so.

Scholars have long interpreted *leuster* as "stone-thrower" (from *lāas*, "a stone") in the sense of "mere skirmisher" with stones as opposed to the more honorable role of heavily armed soldier in a unit of the army. On this interpretation, the oracle makes a status distinction between the hero Adrastus as mythical king and the tyrant Cleisthenes as the lowliest of auxiliary troops.[14] By demoting the tyrant to the level of an impoverished stone-thrower, the oracle performs an overturning of status which, like the debasement of Homeric epic, is a typical trope of popular culture. As we have seen in chapter 2, popular storytelling frequently engaged in the fantasy of the overturning of the social order, and, as we shall see in subsequent chapters, rituals of popular festivity also articulated this basic pattern of reversing the social hierarchy, or bringing the high low.

Perhaps the best parallel for the demotion of Cleisthenes in ancient Greek popular culture is a work-song preserved in Plutarch's *Banquet of the Seven Sages*. According to Plutarch, the song was sung by a woman working a grindstone in a town on Lesbos, near the city of Mytilene, where Pittacus had ruled as a sort of constitutional dictator.

> Grind, mill, grind;
> Yes, for Pittacus used to grind
> King of Great Mytilene.[15]

While the song is preserved in a philosophical dialogue—a high literary form—the song probably derives from the oral culture of the masses. Indeed, the work-song, as scholars of slavery well know, is one of our best sources for the themes, images, and symbols of the laboring classes. And like other forms of popular culture, this ancient Greek work-song imagines an overturning of the social order in which the mighty are brought low. Indeed, the "uncrowning" of Cleisthenes and Pittacus are specific examples of a widespread and long-lasting theme in popular tradition in which the great figures of the past are cast in lowly occupations. We catch glimpses of this tradition in the second century CE satirist Lucian's work, *Descent to Hades*, and much more expansively in the popular traditions of the Middle Ages. For example, in Rabelais's evocation of the Underworld, all the great kings and tyrants of the past are depicted as toiling at lowly occupations.

> Alexander the Great [was] earning a miserable living by patching
>   old shoes.
> Xerxes was hawking mustard;
> Romulus was a salt-peddler;
> Numa an iron-monger;
> Tarquin a porter;
> Piso a peasant;
> Sulla a ferryman;
> Cyrus a cowherd;
> Themistocles a bottle-vendor;
> Epaminondas a mirror-maker;
> Brutus and Cassius surveyors;
> Demosthenes a vine-dresser;
> Cicero a stoker;
> Fabius a threader of rosary beads;
> Artaxerxes a rope-maker
> Aeneas a miller;
> Achilles a scurvy wretch;
> Agamemnon a pot-licker;
> Ulysses a mower;
> Nestor a gold-miner;
> Darius a caretaker of outhouses.[16]

The list goes on, but the point is clear: the high are brought low, just as the great tyrant Cleisthenes is imagined as reduced to a lowly skirmisher in the popular account of his rule that was Herodotus' source. While the main inspiration for Rabelais's list of downgraded rulers was the living popular culture of his own day, the fact that it also borrows from ancient literary traditions (e.g., Lucian's satire), which in turn probably borrow from ancient popular culture (as in the work-song), is a good example of the interplay between literary and popular traditions that I discussed in chapters 1 and 2.[17]

One of the fundamental insights of Bakhtin was that the demotion of the high by association with the low was not wholly negative.[18] Rather than simply parodying the high—officials, literature, or the institutions of the state—and thus critiquing them (though they did this too)—this form of popular culture was an exuberant celebration of life and death.[19] By debasing the high, popular culture evoked the life cycle by which death brings on new life. This theme in popular culture relates to a deeply positive understanding of the world in which death and destruction are followed by renewal and regeneration. The significance of this insight will become clearer as we consider other possible interpretations of the term *leuster*.

Daniel Ogden has recently proposed a new interpretation of the oracular rebuke of Cleisthenes.[20] Ogden suggests that the term *leuster* was associated with ancient Greek scapegoating rituals in which stones were thrown at scapegoats as they were driven out of the community.[21] Ogden's interpretation makes sense in the context since it associates Cleisthenes' planned action of expelling Adrastus with a ritual form of expulsion. Since scapegoating rituals were performed as a way of purifying and therefore renewing the community, it reinforces the idea of death and renewal that I suggested was inherent in Cleisthenes' depiction as a lowly stone-thrower.

Ogden argues that the meaning of the oracle would have been that Cleisthenes was attempting to expel Adrastus like one who expels a scapegoat: "Adrastus was king of Sicyon, but you are expelling him like a lowly scapegoat." The appropriateness of this analogy is clear from the fact that in Greek myth, kings were often the victims of scapegoating, while in actual ritual practice it was criminals and vagabonds who were chosen to fulfill this role.[22] The oracle exploits this dual association with scapegoats by emphasizing Adrastus' royal status and yet chastising Cleisthenes for treating him as a common beggar. The impiety of Cleisthenes' intended action is emphasized by the god's rebuke and, more humorously, by Adrastus' own name. As Ogden points out, "Adrastus" means "not running away" (from *a-drastos*) and therefore it is not surprising that he was "such an unaccommodating scapegoat."[23] Just as Cleisthenes' ban on performances of Homer revealed his comic misunderstanding of Homer's use of the term Argives, so here his attempt to expel Adrastus founders because of his failure to grasp the fact that Adrastus was immovable. In sum, this interpretation of the oracle highlights Cleisthenes' dimwitted nature, as well as the impiety and comic ineffectiveness of his actions.

Let us now return to the thread of Herodotus' narrative and continue our investigation into the ways that folk culture has shaped the story of the historical tyrant.

Cleisthenes is deterred by the oracle from his impious intention to expel Adrastus. Yet, following a pattern common to such morality tales, Cleisthenes is represented as foolishly trying to violate the spirit of the oracular advice. In one famous example of such a tale, the Samian tyrant, Polycrates, learns from a friend that the god is jealous of his prosperity. When his friend advises him to throw away his most prized possession in order to avoid the inevitable downfall that awaits those who enjoy un-limited success, Polycrates decides to throw a valuable signet ring into the sea. Later a fisherman catches an extraordinarily large fish and presents it to the king. The ring is found inside, proving that "no man can avoid his fate," however hard he might try.[24]

Like Polycrates, Cleisthenes will try to side-step the god's will, but will be unable to do so. Since the god prohibits Cleisthenes from expelling Adrastus, Cleisthenes contrives a scheme to get Adrastus to leave on his own accord. To this end, Cleisthenes set up a rival hero-cult to Adrastus' legendary Theban enemy Melanippus. The narrative describes Cleisthenes' scheme as a *mechane* ("contrivance, device"), language that recalls the theme of trickery prominent in popular traditions worldwide. Clever tricks make for good stories, as numerous tales from Herodotus attest. In Greek traditions, trickery is a flexible theme that can illustrate the cleverness of gods and heroes (Prometheus, Odysseus) or the wickedness of kings and tyrants (Polycrates, Peisistratus). The case of Cleisthenes cor-responds to the latter use of trickery, since it aims to subvert the will of the gods.[25]

To this end, Cleisthenes engaged in energetic—yet ultimately futile—efforts to make the hero Melanippus more important than Adrastus in the ritual calendar of Sicyon. First he established a shrine to Melanippus in the most central place of the city, "in the town hall itself." Next he transferred many cultic honors to Melanippus, including feasts and sac-rifices that had formerly been held in honor of Adrastus. Finally, Cleis-thenes cancelled the tragic choral dances formerly performed in honor of Adrastus and reassigned them to the god Dionysus.[26]

Despite all these efforts, however, it is clear that Adrastus retained a central place in the sacred landscape and cultic traditions of Sicyon. Herodotus himself tells us that Adrastus' shrine was still present in the marketplace of Sicyon in his own time. Even more significantly, Adrastus was a key figure in Sicyonian traditions about their kingship throughout antiquity, while Melanippus is absent.[27] The prominence of Adrastus in Sicyonian cult and oral traditions is a key fact in relation to which Herodotus' narrative of Cleisthenes' actions must be interpreted. Herodotus' audience was well aware of Adrastus' importance in the Greek mythical imagination, yet the narrative creates a negative portrait of the tyrant who engages in impious *and ineffective* actions to banish the Argive Adrastus from Sicyon. Cleisthenes is therefore something of a buffoon, since he is represented as striving so single-mindedly to diminish the cult of the city's most important hero, yet fifth-century Sicyonians continued to honor him as a king and hero. While it would be wrong to try to separate political from popular traditions in Herodotus' narrative, it should be recognized that Cleisthenes comes across *not just* as a negative political symbol, but also as *an impious and inept figure*, the kind in which popular traditions delight.

Turning finally to Cleisthenes' tribal reforms, we find the most obvious example of the influence of popular traditions on Herodotus' narrative. Herodotus suggests that the replacement of the Dorian tribes with four new tribes was designed not only to disassociate Sicyon from Argos but to "ridicule the Sicyonians." This representation of Cleisthenes' motives corresponds well with the fifth-century image of the tyrant abusing the community in order to promote his own power, and therefore is a clear sign that Herodotus' version derives from later anti-tyrannical traditions.[28] In the archaic period, however, tyrants were often popular leaders whose policies enhanced the cohesion and panhellenic stature of their communities.[29] Aristotle reports that Cleisthenes' family ruled for one hundred years and therefore endured the longest of all the tyrannical regimes.[30] Such remarkable stability suggests that the rule of the Cleisthenes' family, far from alienating the majority of their population, was in fact broadly acceptable.[31] A detail in Herodotus' account of the marriage of Cleisthenes' daughter Agariste (modeled on myths of the wooing of Helen) perhaps more reliably reflects the tyrant's treatment of his people. When the day arrived for the announcement of the successful suitor, "Cleisthenes sacrificed one hundred cattle and feasted both the suitors themselves *and all the Sicyonians*" (6.129).[32]

Several scholars have perceived that a popular tradition lies behind Herodotus' account of Cleisthenes' tribal reforms, but have not explained what makes it "popular" and, more important, what meanings the new tribal names had in terms of the values, worldview, and culture of the ordinary people among whom this story circulated.[33] Following Bakhtin's interpretation of folk humor, as well as the themes of the narrative as analyzed so far, we may conjecture that the popular flavor of this element of the story is due to its grotesque and obscene parody of the institutional reforms of the tyrant.

We do not have to look far for these elements. According to Herodotus, Cleisthenes replaced the earlier tribal names with names derived from the words for sow, pig, and ass. Yet as Victor Parker has observed, the derivation of Hyatai from *hus*, "sow," Choireatai from *choiros*, "piglet" and Oneatai from *onos*, "ass" is linguistically incorrect.[34] Rather, popular tradition has engaged in deliberate false etymologizing in order to associate Cleisthenes' tribes with animals. The collapsing of the distinction between the human and animal worlds is a central feature of folk culture, of course, visible not only in fables and proverbs but also in many other manifestations of popular culture.[35] More important, the animals from which the tribal names are falsely derived are precisely those that had grotesque and obscene connotations in Greek popular culture.[36]

The sow, most obviously, is an example of the grotesque body par excellence. Indeed, the sow is the first animal employed by Semonides in his notorious abusive satire on women (fr. 7).

> God made diverse the ways of womankind.
> One he created from a hairy sow;
> Everything in her house is defiled with filth
> And lies in a disorderly way on the floor,
> And she herself, unwashed, in dirty clothes,
> Becomes fat as she lies in excrement.[37]

While there has been much discussion of the precise relation of literary iambic to popular festivity, no one seriously doubts that it draws much of its content from the obscene speech (*aischrologia*) that was characteristic of the worship of Dionysus and Demeter in particular.[38] We may therefore conclude that the false derivation of a Sicyonian tribe from the word for sow drew on the grotesque and obscene connotations of this animal in popular culture. We might note in particular the grotesque bodily features of the sow—its shaggy hair, obesity, and predilection for filth and excrement.[39]

Turning to the other two tribal names, we should observe that pigs and asses also had obscene bodily connotations in popular culture. Pigs and piglets were well-known slang words for female genitalia.[40] Similarly, piglets were also associated with the cultic worship of Demeter, a primary locus of obscene speech in popular culture.[41] In the most widespread of festivals of Demeter, the Thesmophoria, for example, women placed piglets in pits in the ground and allowed them to rot before they presented them to the goddess by placing them on her altars.[42] Like the descent of Persephone to Hades told in the myth of Demeter itself, the burial of these piglets symbolized not only a paradoxical juxtaposition of death and life, but also the regeneration of human and agricultural fertility.[43] The connection between pigs, sexuality, and the popular conceptions of the regeneration and renewal of the world is then, in this example, particularly clear.

If we turn finally to the third tribe, it is striking that the ass (*onos*) was associated with excessive sexuality already from the seventh-century BCE onward. In Semonides' abusive poem on women, for example, a primary characteristic of the woman formed from the obstinate ass is her insatiable appetite for sex: "And likewise hungry for the act of love, she welcomes anyone who comes along."[44] As we have already noted, Semonides' iambic is a form associated with traditional obscene jesting and ribaldry (*aischrologia*) at festivals of Demeter and Dionysus. Indeed, Dionysus—the god of excessive sexuality par excellence—is frequently represented riding a donkey or an ass accompanied by ithyphallic satyrs in Greek art (figs. 7 and 8).[45] In these images, even the donkeys are depicted with oversized and erect phalluses, an invocation of the grotesque body. In some poleis, moreover, one form of popular justice against adulterers was to parade them in public mounted on an ass.[46] As Bakhtin observes, "the ass is one of the most ancient and lasting symbols of the bodily lower stratum."[47] By invoking in hyperbolic terms the lower bodily functions—often sexual or scatological—popular traditions draw on the themes of degradation and regeneration that, according to Bakhtin, are key features of folk humor and festivity.[48]

The debasement of Cleisthenes and his reforms through obscene humor is possibly paralleled in the popular work-song about Pittacus that we already discussed. As we noted above, the song partakes of the popular theme of the debasement of the high: the great leader Pittacus must grind his own grain, just as the tyrant Cleisthenes is cast as a lowly stone-thrower. More significantly for the present discussion, it is possible that in a popular context, the "grinding" done by Pittacus was understood metaphorically, not literally, as a reference to the tyrant's sexual voracity: "grind, mill, grind, just as Pittacus, great king of Mytilene, screws."[49] If this interpretation is correct, then the work-song parallels Herodotus' depiction of Cleisthenes' tribal reforms in the way it degrades the tyrant through obscene sexual humor. In both cases, the official "high" figures are brought low through association with coarse bodily functions.[50]

Like the image of the grotesque body of the scapegoat applied to Cleisthenes, the degradation of official institutions achieved by imputing obscene bodily meanings to Cleisthenes' new tribes not only satirizes the tyrant and his reforms, but articulates the principle of regeneration and renewal which is essential to the festive and utopian outlook of much of folk culture. As Bakhtin puts it, the theme of degradation followed by renewal "expresses the people's hopes of a happier future, of a more just

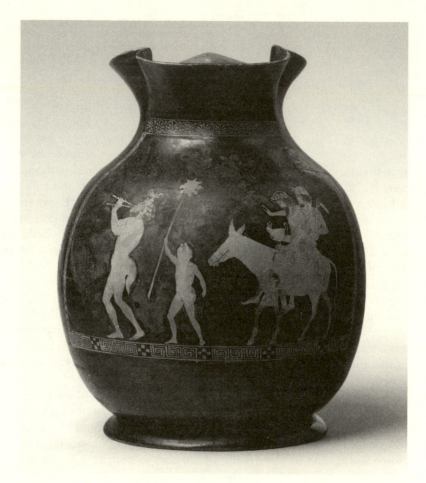

Figure 7.
Dionysus and Hephaestus mounted together on a donkey accompanied
by satyr. Greek terracotta jug, attributed to the Washing Painter (Attic,
Classical, c. 430–420 BCE). Metropolitan Museum of Art, New York,
Rogers Fund, 1908 (08.258.22).

social and economic order, of a new truth."[51] It is in this latter sense that
the people's comic version of the past articulates their distinctive worldview and serves as a medium for their group cohesion and identity.[52]

In sum, Herodotus' version of these events is not only colored by anti-
tyrannical traditions, but also deeply influenced by the themes of popular traditions. If the grotesque and obscene connotations of Cleisthenes'
tribal names are a product of popular parody, however, we still need to
ask what their "official" (historical) meaning was. Several scholars have

Figure 8.
Dionysus, followed by Hephaestus riding an ithyphallic donkey, and a satyr. Amphora of Panathenaic shape, AN1920.107, Bourgon Group, Ashmolean Museum, Oxford. Photo courtesy of the Ashmolean Museum, University of Oxford.

proposed non-insulting explanations of the tribal names. Lillian Jeffery and Victor Parker argue that the original connotation of the tribal names was topographical. Jeffery notes that Hya, Orneai, and Choireiai are all place-names attested elsewhere in Greece, and Parker observes that Plutarch mentions a war between Orneai and Sicyon.[53] It would not take much for a popular tradition to make a pun on this place name, deliberately corrupting Or- into On- and thereby ridiculing people from this place as Oneatai, i.e., "Ass-men."

Alternatively, Robin Osborne suggests that the new tribal names were based on parallels with other old ethnic groups such as Meropes, Dryopes, and Leleges (bee eaters, woodpeckers, storks) and that Cleisthenes' aim was to root the Sicyonians in the even more remote mythical past than such figures as Adrastus.[54] Van Wees, on the other hand, accepts the names as insulting, but argues that they were given to conquered people of Pellene and other surrounding towns, who were made serfs of the Sicyonians.[55]

Though these scholars differ in their explanations of Cleisthenes' new tribal names, and even on the question of whether the original sense of

the names was insulting or not, none of them question Herodotus' attribution of the changes to the tyrant Cleisthenes. Summing up then, scholars accept the three major points of Herodotus' narrative:

1. The Sicyonians originally had the same tribal divisions as Argos,
   namely those associated with "Dorian" ethnicity (the Hyllatai,
   Pamphyloi, and Dumanatai).
2. The tyrant Cleisthenes changed the Dorian tribal names to ones
   with animal-connotations which had
   a. non-insulting official meaning (Jeffery, Parker, Osborne) but
      were parodied in anti-tyranical popular traditions
   OR
   b. insulting connotations and were designed to denigrate
      i. those of Dorian ethnicity (Andrewes)
      OR
      ii. those neighboring peoples whom the Sicyonians conquered
         and enslaved (van Wees)
3. After the fall of the tyranny in 510 BCE—some sixty years after
   Cleisthenes' own death—the people of Sicyon changed their tribal
   names back to the original Dorian ones.

Several aspects of this reconstruction should give us pause. First, the see-
sawing back and forth in ethnic identity is unlikely, though not impossible, historically. Second, the thorough-going influence of popular humor
on the shape and content of Herodotus' narrative means that many elements of the story may have been adapted, or even invented, to fit the
subversive humor of Herodotus' popular sources. Finally, and perhaps
most important, much recent work on Dorian ethnicity and the other
major Greek ethnicity, Ionian, has shown that these identities do not reflect "original" biologically related racial groups. Rather, Dorian ethnic
identity is a cultural construct that was actively employed by various
communities over the course of the Archaic period in order to align themselves with or distinguish themselves from one another. In a process that
is now familiar from studies of nineteenth-century nationalism, archaic
Greek poleis cloaked these active and recent cultural constructions with
the legitimacy of ancient traditions, adapting or inventing myths that
projected their newly created ethnic identities far back in time.[56] This
new research should lead us to question whether the Sicyonians "originally" were of Dorian ethnicity and hence whether their Dorian tribal
names were in fact the original ones, as Herodotus' account claims.

I shall argue in the second half of the chapter that the tribal names attributed to Cleisthenes' reforms were in fact the original tribal names of
the Sicyonians and were based on place names. I suggest that Sicyonians

only changed to Dorian tribal names at the end of the sixth century when they wished to associate themselves more closely with other Peloponnesian states (particularly Sparta). Fifth-century popular traditions in Sicyon then accommodated this change by imputing obscene double meanings to the old tribal names, and attributing them to the malicious policies of their former tyrant.

Before we turn to this reconstruction, there is one final point to be made about the impact of oral tradition on Herodotus' account. As Rosalind Thomas has emphasized, oral traditions tend to cluster all social and political innovations around a single memorable figure from the actual or mythical past.[57] The process of simplification is well-recognized in the case of mythical and historical "culture heroes," including such figures as Prometheus, Hermes, the Seven Sages, and the archaic lawgivers.[58] In these cases, cultural innovations (e.g., the use of fire, writing, cultic practices) and political institutions (laws and even entire political systems) that were a product of long and complex historical processes are attributed to single "first inventors" (*prōtoi heuretai*). Quite often, a single figure is credited with a large number of inventions, laws, or political reforms that in fact were developed by numerous people over a long period of time.

Herodotus' narrative of Cleisthenes of Sicyon has not yet been viewed as a product of such simplification. Yet Cleisthenes was precisely the sort of colorful figure from the past around whom oral tradition would be likely to gather memories of historical developments. Indeed, Herodotus' own account of the competition staged by Cleisthenes for his daughter's hand in marriage is an excellent example of how oral traditions remember past events by clustering them around a single prominent figure from the past. Indeed, it might be surmised that it was this event (the year-long festivities surrounding the marriage of his daughter)—in addition to his Olympic and Pythian victories and his ostentatious building projects at Delphi (discussed below)—that projected Cleisthenes' fame across the Greek world and made him the focal point of a variety of different oral traditions. Not only has the story of the marriage competition been shaped by the panhellenic myth of the wooing of Helen, but other legendary figures have been incorporated into the story despite the chronological impossibility of their all having been present at an event c. 575.[59]

If the story of Cleisthenes' competition for the hand of Agariste is clearly a product of the clustering typical of oral traditions, why not consider the cultic and tribal reforms as similarly so shaped? In the second half of the chapter, I will demonstrate that detaching the reforms from the figure of Cleisthenes helps to resolve some of the problems—not least the allegedly insulting names of the new tribes—with Herodotus' narrative.

Cultic and Tribal Reforms in Sixth-Century Perspective: Peer-Polity Interaction

So far I have suggested that Herodotus' narrative about Cleisthenes' cultic reforms reflects popular traditions in which the tyrant is represented as dogmatically indulging his hatred of Argos in ridiculous and ultimately futile ways. Indeed, as I noted earlier, the cult of Adrastus continued to exist in the central marketplace of Sicyon in Herodotus' own time, despite Cleisthenes' alleged scheme to get rid of it by introducing a rival cult to the Theban hero Melanippus. So what are we to make of the story historically? We are left with two options. One option is the view that Cleisthenes' plan to diminish or get rid of Adrastus is an invention of the popular and political traditions that aimed to ridicule the tyrant and blacken his image. While this interpretation is possible, there is another more likely possibility.

It is more plausible to believe that, while popular and anti-tyrannical traditions have skewed the portrait of the tyrant, there were in fact some cultic changes in sixth-century Sicyon that Herodotus' account distantly reflects. On this reading, the cultic changes are not necessarily to be attributed to the tyrant himself, but rather to wider social and political forces affecting sixth-century poleis. The question becomes, then, why would the Sicyonian polis be interested in introducing a new hero-cult? Why, in addition, might Sicyonians at this time create or augment a festival in honor of Dionysus with tragic choruses? To answer these questions it helps to place these hypothetical changes at Sicyon in the context of cultic and festival developments in other sixth-century city-states.

The first thing to note is that the sixth century, like the eighth century before it, was a time when hero-cults were proliferating in Greece. For example, a cult of the hero Orestes, the son of Agamemnon, was established at Sparta, and the Argives set up a cult to the legendary heroes of the myth of the Seven Against Thebes. The introduction of a new hero-cult in Sicyon, therefore, seems to parallel developments in other city-states. The next question is why hero-cults were important at the time.

Numerous explanations have been offered for the role of hero-cult in the Greek polis. The most recent explanations note the utility of heroes as collective symbols with which the newly formed and rapidly developing city-states could root themselves in the mythological past and forge a common collective identity. In the case of the mid-sixth-century repatriation of the bones of Orestes to Sparta, for instance, Deborah Boedeker has suggested that Orestes served as a cultural symbol which linked "Sparta, but no contemporary Spartans, with its heroic past and thereby help[ed] dissipate competition for status among families that could otherwise have focused on their various ancestral heroes."[60] Jonathan Hall, by contrast, observes that certain heroes were claimed by multiple city-states, and therefore that "the function of the hero is not so much to serve as an exclusive and static emblem of a city's distinctive identity, but to articulate the dynamic relationships that might exist between several cities."[61] Using the example of the Argive cult to the Seven Against Thebes, Hall suggests that "the establishment of the [cult of the heroes] was intended to express both the centrality and the primacy of Argos within the Peloponnese as a whole."[62]

Hall's focus on competition between poleis for the "cultural capital" of mythological heroes certainly seems to fit the case of the heroes of the Seven Against Thebes. At Argos, as Pariente notes, no fewer than eight of the twenty-five heroic monuments mentioned by the travel-writer Pausanias (second century CE) have connections with the myth of the Seven, including a "house" of Adrastus, a sanctuary of Amphiaraos, and the graves of Amphiaraos' wife, Eriphyle, and Adrastos' father, Talaos.[63] Besides the existence of a cult of Adrastus at Sicyon, there were shrines to him at Megara and at Colonus in Attica, the territory of Athens.[64] The people of Megara claimed that Adrastus had died in their territory and the Athenians asserted that Adrastus sought their king Theseus' help in defeating the Thebans and retrieving the bodies.[65] The Athenians further explain that the bodies were buried at Eleusis and the second-century travel writer Pausanias identifies some prehistoric burials with the cult of the Seven Against Thebes.[66]

Athenian oratory from the fifth and fourth centuries reveals how the Athenians inserted themselves into various panhellenic myths (e.g., Amazons, Heraclidae, and Seven Against Thebes) in a way which not only reinforced a distinctive national tradition for themselves, but also rooted the newly powerful city into a much older and widespread mythological tradition. The speeches allegedly given by the leaders of two city-states, Tegea and Athens, before the battle of Plataea in 480 are excellent examples of how ancient Greek communities used the mythical past to compete for status in relation to one another.[67] In these speeches, each city-state contends for the most honored position in the battle line and justifies their claim through putative heroic actions in the past. The Athenians, for example, support their case by citing their virtuous actions in defense of the children of Heracles, who, according to myth, had been unjustly banished from the Peloponnesus by the tyrant Eurystheus. To further buttress their claim, they also recall their role in securing burial for the heroes of the myth of the Seven Against Thebes. According to the Athenians, as we have seen, these heroes were buried at Eleusis within Athenian territory.

The very existence of Adrastus in the genealogies of the kings of Argos and Sicyon (he was king of both places) is a wonderful example of what Jan Vansina and Jonathan Hall have called the "fissures" of traditions which reveal that considerable constructivism has taken place according to the needs of rival city-states.[68] Sicyonian tradition made Adrastus the adoptive heir of Polybus, a descendant of King Sicyon, the eponymous king of Sicyon, himself an immigrant from Athens.[69] The genealogy of the Sicyonian kings is, in fact, replete with abrupt breaks—kings who die with no descendants—which are then sutured over with imports from other regions. Men from Thessaly, Thebes, Athens, Argos fill the king list after the death of the last descendant of Aegialus, the first king of Sicyon who was probably invented to serve as an explanation for an early name of Sicyon, Aegialea. We will return to this early city name shortly. The point at the moment is that the king list may reflect—in a way impossible to unravel historically—the changing alliances and rivalries between Sicyon and other city-states over the centuries.

What do these interpretations suggest about the existence or introduction of hero-cults in sixth-century Sicyon? On Boedeker's model, the introduction of a cult of the Theban Melannipus could represent an attempt to create a civic symbol unconnected with any particular elite family in Sicyon. On this reading, we must assume that a particular prominent family claimed Adrastus as their ancestor, and that it was the prestige derived from this genealogical connection that the new civic hero was meant to override. The introduction of the Theban hero Melanippus then becomes a reaction to status competition among elites in Sicyon and an attempt to create a unifying civic symbol.

This interpretation is possible, but another one better fits with the observations made so far, namely the idea that Herodotus' narrative is a product of oral tradition and the evidence for multiple claims to Adrastus by rival city-states in the mid-sixth-century. I suggest that the introduction of a cult to Melanippus was an invention of anti-tyrannical tradition designed to ridicule the tyrant. While other city-states were eagerly asserting their claim to the prestige of the Seven Against Thebes, the tyrant is depicted as stubbornly championing the enemy (Melannipus was Theban, and fought against the Seven). Similarly, while other cities were busily enhancing civic festivals and performances of Homeric epic (e.g., at the Panathenaia at Athens), the tyrant banned such performances in Sicyon.

I suggest that historically it is more likely that the cult of Adrastus, not Melanippus, was *introduced* in Sicyon in the sixth century. I suggest that Sicyon, like Argos, Megara, and Athens, wanted a share of the prestige deriving from the myth of the Seven Against Thebes, and attempted to assert its status on a par with these city-states in part by creating a shrine to Adrastus. Rather than serving as a focus for a distinctive Sicyonian civic identity—how could it, given the claims that Argos and other city-states had on the hero?—the cult put Sicyon on a par with other leading city-states by positioning her competitively in the panhellenic cultural landscape. Thus the introduction of rival cults of Adrastus is, then, a form of "peer-polity" interaction, as Renfrew and Cherry have defined the term.[70] Much as the Greek city-states engaged in competitive temple-building ("my temple is bigger than your temple"), so these rival communities tried to show that they had a more intimate, or more significant, or at least *a role* in the panhellenic myth of the Seven Against Thebes.[71]

The cancellation of performances of Homeric epic and the transfer of tragic choruses from Adrastus' cult to Dionysiac cult are also explicable on the model of peer-polity interaction. I suggested above that Cleisthenes' ban on Homeric performances is probably a comic inversion of what actually happened, namely the introduction of public performances of Homer. If this argument is accepted, then developments in sixth-century Sicyon can again be related to developments in other cities, especially Athens.[72] Competitive public performances of Homer in Athens probably began in the early sixth century, when they become part of the expanded Panathenaic Games (c. 566).[73] Similarly, performances of tragic choruses seem to have begun in Athens in the later sixth century, as part of the expanded civic cult of Dionysus.[74] Both developments can be related to the general aim of increasing the stature of Athens within the Panhellenic world, though these expanded civic cults clearly also played an important role in enhancing civic unity and identity.[75]

It is likely that leaders of Sicyon were responding to these developments when they introduced public performances of Homer and enhanced their local cult of Dionysus with tragic performances. Herodotus' claim that the tragic choruses were transferred from the cult of Adrastus can then be understood as an invention of a popular tradition that distorted actual events in order to poke fun at the tyrant. While other city-states (including historical Sicyon) were augmenting their civic landscape with new hero-cults and expanded civic festivals, the backwards Cleisthenes was busy dismantling them. The very collapsing of these two, probably chronologically disparate, events (public performances of Homer in the early sixth century and tragic performances in the late sixth century), into the time of the tyrant is a nice example of the "telescoping" of the past that often takes place in oral traditions.[76]

Other evidence confirms that sixth-century Sicyon was striving for panhellenic status as a center of culture and great power. Cleisthenes' own victories at the Olympian and Pythian Games attest to his engagement in the circuit of athletic festivals, which granted panhellenic glory to the victors and their communities alike.[77] Even more significantly, Cleisthenes is said to have founded Pythian Games in Sicyon itself, a development that can be related to the foundation of other games around this time: the Nemean Games in 573, the Isthmian Games in 582, the Pythian Games in 586 or 582, and the expanded Panathenaic Games in 566.[78]

Another strategy for increasing the prestige of Sicyon was the construction of conspicuous monuments in panhellenic sanctuaries.[79] At Delphi, the people of Sicyon constructed a round building and a rectangular building known as the Monopteros.[80] The former building is not well preserved, but the latter is remarkable for its large sculptural panels evoking mythological scenes. While there is some debate about which myths are depicted, it is likely that there are scenes from Jason and the Argonauts, the sons of Zeus, Castor and Pollux, and their cattle-raid, Phrixus and the Ram, the Calydonian Bull, and the Rape of Europa.[81] Whatever the exact myths, it is clear that this building represents a tour-de-force of panhellenic cultural icons. By constructing this building in a prominent panhellenic sanctuary rather than at Sicyon itself, moreover, the Sicyonians assured that their cultural sophistication would be witnessed by the widest possible audience.[82] In short, it is clear that sixth-century Sicyon was striving to be recognized among the top rank of city-states in the Greek world.

Turning at last to the tribal names, I suggest similarly that Herodotus' narrative reflects, in a distorted way, events in sixth-century Sicyon. According to Herodotus, the people of Sicyon originally had Dorian tribal names. Cleisthenes, as we have seen, changed the names of the tribes, giving insulting animal names to most of the people, while naming his own tribe "Leaders of the People." The people of Sicyon retained these names for sixty years after the death of Cleisthenes. It was only c. 510, when Cleisthenes' descendant, the tyrant Aeschines, was overthrown, that the Sicyonians reverted back to their original tribal names.

As mentioned at the beginning of this chapter, recent work on Dorian and Ionian ethnic identities has shown that they do not reflect biological kinship in the prehistoric past, but rather were culturally constructed categories used strategically in the historical period to position communities alongside or against other communities. For example, the Athenians appear to have adopted Ionian ethnic identity and tribal divisions sometime between the eighth and the early sixth century. According to Robert Connor, this was a deliberate move by the Athenians to appropriate some of the cultural prestige of the cities of Ionia (the islands and coastal towns of modern Turkey) who were culturally more advanced than Athens at this time.[83] Only after the subjugation of Ionia to the Persians in the second half of the sixth century did the Athenians decide to replace their Ionian tribal divisions. According to this interpretation, the Athenian decision was a result not only of the declining prestige of Ionia, but also of the desire of the newly democratic Athens to shed the aristocratic associations of Ionian culture and politics. The Athenians therefore replaced the Ionian tribes with ten tribes named after local Athenian heroes.[84]

Connor's interpretation of Athenian ethnic strategies drew on earlier scholarship, particularly D. Roussel's book *Tribu et cité* (1976), and M. Sakellariou, *Between Memory and Oblivion* (1990), to set forth most clearly a "constructivist" view of Greek identities and tribal organization. Jonathan Hall developed these arguments much further in two books on Greek ethnicity.[85] Hall argues that Dorian and Ionian ethnic identities were adopted early in the archaic period by various cities as an active strategy for aligning themselves with and against other city-states. For example, though the Dorian ethnicity seems to originate at Argos, it was rapidly adopted by Sparta as it became the dominant power in the Peloponnesus. Christoph Ulf has made an even more radical claim that Sparta only adopted Dorian identity in the later sixth century as a response to the increasing importance of Athens and her appeals to Ionian ethnicity.[86] Though these scholars differ as to the details and exact timing, all agree that Dorian and Ionian ethnicities are constructions, adopted by various city-states during the course of the archaic period as an active strategy to ally with or oppose themselves to other city-states. More recently these findings have been extended to the fourth-century Peloponnesus where there was, in Nino Luraghi's formulation, an "ethnic revival" in the early fourth century.[87] Spartan hegemony and resistance to it, the emergence of Thebes, and the liberation of Messenia, for example, led to new political alignments that in turn were accompanied by the forging or adaptation of myths of ethnic origins.[88]

What does all this mean for the tribal changes in Sicyon? First of all, we may well wonder whether the claim that the Dorian tribes were the "original" tribes of Sicyon is historically accurate. Putting this suspicion together with the idea that Herodotus' attribution of the animal tribal names to Cleisthenes may have been an invention of anti-tyrannical popular tradition, we might propose that the "new" tribes were in fact the original tribal names of Sicyon and, as Jeffery and Parker propose, were based on place names.[89] As we have seen, Hya, Orneai, and Choireiai are all place names attested elsewhere in Greece, and Plutarch mentions a war between Orneai and Sicyon. It is noteworthy, moreover, that even when the people of Sicyon adopted the three Dorian tribes, they still needed one more tribe to accommodate all their people. This fourth tribe appears to retain one of the original tribal names, Aegialea, which appears to be based on the original place name for Sicyon, Aegialea, as noted above. This connection is further evidence, I suggest, that the original tribes were based on place names.

If it is accepted that the supposedly obscene names of the tribes were originally not obscene, and that they were the original tribal divisions of Sicyon, then it follows that Sicyon only adopted Dorian tribal names later in the sixth century, c. 510, when the Spartans overthrew the tyranny at Sicyon. This makes perfect sense since the Spartans identified themselves with Dorian ethnicity and it was a logical move for the Sicyonians to align themselves with this newly emerging power. After all, the Spartans had not only liberated the people of Sicyon from their tyranny at a time when tyranny had become unpopular, but more important, the Spartans had become the dominant power in the Peloponnesus at the time. Sicyon's power was apparently in decline then, and it would have been a strategic move to form an alliance with the major power of the moment.

As we have seen, fifth-century popular traditions accommodated the change in tribal names by imputing obscene double meanings to the old tribal names and attributing them to the malicious policies of their former tyrant. This move was facilitated not only by the anti-tyrannical ethos of the fifth century, but also by the genealogical connection between Cleisthenes of Sicyon and his grandson, the democratic reformer Cleisthenes of Athens. The latter was responsible for the tribal changes at Athens and it was an easy step for popular tradition both to associate the tyrant Cleisthenes with a change in tribal names, and to project the newly adopted Dorian identity of Sicyon farther back into the prehistoric past.

In a statement that has long been dismissed by scholars, Herodotus says that Cleisthenes of Athens copied his maternal grandfather, Cleisthenes of Sicyon, when he changed the Athenian tribal names.[90] If we down-date the tribal changes at Sicyon to 510, however, then they occurred only two years before the changes at Athens. The two sets of reforms therefore were indeed related to one another chronologically, as Herodotus claims, although not through the genealogical connection that he posits.

There remains one last thread to tie up. What are we to make of Herodotus' report that the tyrant Cleisthenes named his own tribe "Leaders of the People" (*Archelaoi*)? I suggest that this name represents a substitution by popular tradition of the original fourth tribe Aegialea.[91] By replacing the historical tribal name (Aegialea) with one that clearly represents the tyrant as self-aggrandizing at the expense of his people, popular traditions reinforced official anti-tyrannical ideologies of the fifth century.

Degradation, the Body, and Popular Discourse

This chapter has built on the arguments of the previous chapter to show how the mass of ordinary people in one city-state made use of the past to engage in a veiled critique of elite rule and to express a popular vision of the world in which life is renewed through the cycle of degradation and rebirth. Central to these popular discourses is humor, particularly the ridicule of the high through the association with the low. Cleisthenes becomes an object of popular humor in part through his representation as a lowly stone-thrower. His reforms, moreover, are playfully debased by association with animals symbolizing obscene and scatological bodily functions. Most important of all, this case study of one particular narrative shows not only how popular themes coexist with official civic traditions (anti-tyrannical ideologies) in our surviving literary sources, but that reversals of the high and the low are central to the discourses of non-elites in antiquity. While powerful elites (the natural rivals of the tyrant) are undoubtedly in part responsible for the construction of negative traditions about Cleisthenes of Sicyon, this chapter demonstrates that many of the themes of these traditions are drawn from popular culture and popular visions of the world. In the remaining chapters of this book, I show how the themes of popular culture outlined in this chapter (reversals of relations between high and low, images of the grotesque body and obscene speech) are present in the practices that structured non-elite life. As we shall see, festival ritual and informal modes of collective justice feature some of the same symbolism as the discourses examined in this chapter.

Part Two

PRACTICES

4

Revelry and Riot in Ancient Megara: Democratic Disorder or Ritual Reversal?

> Now what is the most familiar way of mobilizing
> the entire community? It is the village fiesta or its
> equivalent—the combination of collective ritual
> and collective entertainment.
> —E. J. Hobsbawm[1]

ACCORDING TO PLUTARCH, a number of shocking events took place in Megara in the sixth-century BCE. For example, the poor invaded the houses of the rich and demanded to be feasted sumptuously. If the poor did not receive the hospitality that they sought, they treated the rich with violence and insolence. At the same time, Plutarch reports, some sacred ambassadors from the Peloponnesus were attacked by a group of drunk Megarians. The revelers rolled the wagons of the ambassadors, with their wives and children inside, into a lake and drowned many of them. Finally, Plutarch mentions temple robbery as a further example of the outrages that took place during this time.[2]

Plutarch explains these incidents as the consequence of the insolence (*hubris*), licentiousness (*aselgeia*), lack of discipline (*akolasia*), and disorder (*ataxia*) which flourished under a democracy at Megara. Modern historians, surprisingly, have accepted Plutarch's analysis and have concluded that Megara was ruled by a democratic regime in the mid-sixth-century BCE. As Eric Robinson writes:

> Scholars have accepted early democracy in Megara more readily than elsewhere in Greece, if only because the evidence is difficult to dispute. A variety of literary sources combine to portray a radical and violently lawless popular regime in which the demos [People] used its supreme power to victimize the rich.[3]

This ready acceptance of early Megarian democracy, however, overlooks not only the ideological roots of Plutarch's description of Megarian democracy—namely fourth-century anti-democratic theory—but also the relation of the incidents of revelry and riot to rituals of social inversion. This chapter aims to rectify both these oversights by placing Plutarch and his anecdotes in their ideological and ritual contexts respectively.

In the first part of the chapter, I argue that consideration of the ideological position of Plutarch and his sources reveals that the connection between riotous behavior and democracy is a construction of anti-democratic thought and does not accurately reflect constitutional developments in Megara. In the second part of the chapter, I suggest that a better model for interpreting the incidents reported by Plutarch is customary rituals of social inversion and transgression. Drawing on comparative examples from the ancient world and Early Modern Europe, I show that popular revelry involving role reversal and the transgression of social norms was an important medium for the negotiation of relations between elites and masses in ancient Greece. I argue that such rituals provided temporary release from the constraints of the social hierarchy and served to articulate symbolically the obligation of the powerful to protect the weak.

The comparative historical examples show that such ritual reversals were usually non-revolutionary, but could turn violent in times of rapid social and economic change. I suggest that the violent episodes reported by Plutarch reflect the escalation of ritual revelry into real protest and riot in response to a crisis in economic relations between rich and poor in Megara. As the rich explored new opportunities for profit, the poor began to experience increasing hardship. In response, the poor became violent in their attempt to assert a "customary moral economy."[4] I suggest that elites in Megara prevented more far-reaching rebellion and political reform by enacting new measures for the economic relief of the poor. In particular we learn of the "Return of Interest" (*Palintokia*) legislation, whereby rich creditors were required to return the interest they had collected on their loans to the poor. While these measures provided immediate relief for the poor, they did not result in an overturning of the social and political order, let alone a democratic constitution in ancient Megara.

In the concluding section of the chapter, I address the broader historical question of why subordinate groups use ritual forms to express discontent with the social order. I also suggest that the case of ancient Greece offers some historical material that complements earlier historical scholarship on the causes and nature of conflict between rich and poor in agrarian societies. In particular, I argue that the case of ancient Megara illustrates that the struggle between rich and poor follows patterns similar to much later historical periods and therefore that the causes of this conflict and the characteristics of its expression are not unique to pre-industrial Europe. My case study from ancient Greece suggests that the outbreaks of violent protest in the ancient world and in Early Modern Europe were particularly vehement expressions of the ongoing, everyday struggle between rich and poor to improve the conditions of their existence. Central to the argument of this chapter and this book is the idea that informal cultural practices, not formal political institutions, were the primary venue for the negotiation of this conflict.

Disorder and Democracy: The Anti-Democratic Tradition

Modern scholars agree that Plutarch's anecdotes about early Megarian history are probably derived from Aristotle's lost *Constitution of the Megarians*.[5] Although scholars draw this conclusion partly on the basis of verbal parallels between Aristotle and Plutarch, they ignore the implications of these same verbal parallels for Plutarch's assessment of the nature of the Megarian regime. Specifically, the language that Plutarch and Aristotle use to describe the Megarian democracy has strong resonance with fifth- and fourth-century anti-democratic ideology, a fact which suggests that both authors drew on an ideological connection between democracy and disorder in their analysis of early Megarian history. That is to say, while the narratives of shocking events in early Megara probably derive from Megarian oral traditions, the connection between disorderly behavior and democracy is an inference drawn on the basis of anti-democratic theory.

I first demonstrate the strong connection between democracy and disorder in anti-democratic thought, and then show how Aristotle and Plutarch applied this association to the Megarian historical tradition.[6]

The historian Herodotus (fifth century BCE) provides our earliest evidence for systematic anti-democratic political theory. In a debate that Herodotus claims took place among some nobles in sixth-century BCE Persia, the weaknesses of democracy are described.[7] The principal criticism of democracy is that the insolence (*hubris*) of the undisciplined masses (*dēmou akolastou*) is no different from that of the tyrant.[8] According to this argument, the ignorance of the masses causes them to rush into affairs without thought, like a river in flood.[9] In this regard, the insolence of the masses is even more unbearable than that of the tyrant, who is at least capable of rational understanding of his actions.

> The tyrant, if he does something, he does it with forethought. But the masses are not capable of rational understanding. For how could they be capable of understanding, if they have neither been educated nor are naturally endowed with knowledge of the good? (3.81.2)

This anti-democratic argument culminates in the claim that nothing is more lacking in intelligence (*asunetōteron*) and more insolent (*hubristoteron*) than the useless crowd.[10]

This portrait of the rule of the people is echoed in the representation of the behavior of the Athenian masses by Herodotus' near contemporary, the historian Thucydides. For example, Thucydides depicts the Athenian people as ignorant about the facts of their own history, hasty and irrational in their decision-making, and quite savage (*agrioteron*) in their treatment of those who they suspect of anti-democratic sentiments.[11] Indeed, Thucydides' portrait of the Athenian people evokes characteristics usually associated with tyrannical rule, especially the paranoid suspicion of and brutality toward those elites who might threaten its rule.[12]

By the late fifth century, a standard set of terms began to emerge among critics of democracy as a way of conceptualizing the rule of the masses as opposed to that of the elite. A good starting point for appreciating this critical vocabulary is an anonymous treatise titled *Constitution of the Athenians*, whose author is sometimes referred to as the "Old Oligarch":

> The best sort is opposed to democracy in every land. For there is the least lack of restraint (*akolasia*) and injustice (*adikia*) in the best men, and the most trustworthiness in relation to useful affairs. Among the masses, however, there is the most ignorance (*amathia*), disorder (*ataxia*) and depravity (*poneria*).[13]

In this passage, the Old Oligarch reduces the anti-democratic tradition to five key terms: lack of restraint (*akolasia*), injustice (*adikia*), ignorance (*amathia*), disorder (*ataxia*), and depravity (*poneria*). Pseudo-Xenophon serves as a sort of intermediary between fifth-century critics of democracy, who stress the lack of intelligence and irrationality of the masses, and fourth-century authors, who highlight the demos' lack of restraint and propensity toward disorder. It is worth emphasizing, however, that these latter concepts are already present in Herodotus, since he uses the adjective *akolastos* to describe the masses, and his imagery of a river in flood evokes the idea of violent disorder.[14]

The key text for the concept of democratic lack of restraint (*akolasia*) in fourth-century anti-democratic thought is Book 8 of Plato's *Republic*. Here Plato explains how oligarchies can turn into democracies and argues that this happens when the rulers are more concerned with making money than with restraining indiscipline.[15] For Plato, the problem with democracy is that there is too much freedom, and—like Herodotus' tyrant—everyone can do whatever they like.[16] Under these circumstances, men give way to their desires. First they banish shame, self-control, moderation, and frugality from their souls, and welcome in turn insolence, anarchy, profligacy, and shamelessness.[17] Following an ironic allusion to Thucydides' account of the reversal of the evaluative content of words during times of civil war, and an equally ironic play on the democratic concept

of equality—each desire is equal, and no desire is deprived of its rights!—
Plato concludes that democracy is a pleasant (*hēdeia*), anarchic (*anarchos*), and variegated (*poikilē*) kind of political system, in which there is
neither order (*taxis*) nor compulsion (*anankē*).[18]

It is no coincidence that it is precisely from this passage that Plutarch
draws his description of the Megarian democracy: "Then, as Plato says,
the demagogues, serving as wine stewards, poured out too much unmixed
freedom (*akratos eleutheria*) and the Megarians were corrupted (*diaphtharentes*) and behaved outrageously (*aselgōs*) towards the rich."[19] Yet
Plutarch was not the first to discern the connection between social disorder and Megarian democracy. Aristotle had already perceived this association, as is evident from two passages in his *Politics*. The association
must have been developed more fully in his now lost *Constitution of the
Megarians*. It is noteworthy, however, that these passages come from Aristotle's discussion of the causes of changes in constitutions, and thus confirm that Aristotle was influenced in his analysis by Plato's similar discussion in Book 8 of the *Republic*.

> Democracies are overthrown when the wealthy feel contempt for
> the disorder (*ataxia*) and anarchy (*anarchia*). For example ... the democracy of the Megarians [was overthrown], when [the Megarians]
> had been defeated on account of their disorder (*ataxia*) and anarchy
> (*anarchia*). (1302b28–32)

> Democracies are overthrown most often through the licentiousness
> (*aselgeia*) of the leaders of the people. (1304b20–23)

Aristotle's use of the terms *ataxia* and *anarchia* and *aselgeia* (a synonym in this context for *hubris*) confirms that he drew on anti-democratic
ideology in his analysis of political change in early Megara. Yet it is
equally clear that Aristotle had a strong belief in the existence of an early
Megarian democracy, and it is likely that this belief was not simply based
on anecdotes of social disorder. We must ask, therefore, what was the
basis of Aristotle's belief? In other words, what in the Megarian historical
tradition, besides anecdotes of shocking behavior, gave proof of a democratic regime? Since Aristotle's comments on Megara in the *Politics* scarcely
run beyond the two quotations above, and since we no longer have the
Aristotelian *Constitution of the Megarians*, we must turn to Plutarch's
borrowings from Aristotle for the answer.

The only item in Plutarch's comments about the Megarian democracy
that goes beyond anecdotes of social disorder is a piece of legislation, the
"Return of Interest," or *Palintokia*. It is in fact thanks to the obscurity
of this latter term that we have Plutarch's first disquisition on Megara in
his treatise entitled *Greek Questions*.[20] In this work, Plutarch sets out to

explain certain obscure Greek terms whose meaning was no longer understood in his own time (second century CE). Plutarch begins his discussion of Megara with the following prompt: "What was the *Palintokia*?" Plutarch goes on to explain that the *Palintokia* was a decree passed at Megara under the democracy by which the poor received back the interest they had given to their creditors. Plutarch views this legislation as the culmination of the outrageous behavior of the poor toward the rich during the time of the democracy at Megara. Consideration of fourth-century conceptions of the origins of Athenian democracy, however, suggests that this piece of legislation was the starting point for Aristotle's belief in an archaic Megarian democracy, and that the other incidents of shocking behavior were simply taken as further evidence of this fact.

The most obvious basis for Aristotle's association between the *Palintokia* and democracy is Athenian beliefs about the sixth-century Athenian legislator Solon. In the fourth century, Solon was credited not only with legislation similar to *Palintokia*—namely the "Lifting of Burdens" or *Seisachtheia*—but also with the foundation of the Athenian democracy itself. Indeed, as Mogens Hansen has argued, although fifth-century Athenians correctly understood that their democracy was founded under the leadership of Cleisthenes, by the fourth century, "the accepted view was that Kleisthenes, after the expulsion of the tyrants, had only restored the democracy instituted by Solon."[21] One cause of this shift from Cleisthenes to Solon as founder of the democracy was the late fifth-century conflict between oligarchs and democrats over what was the "ancestral constitution."[22] The important point for our purposes is that in fourth-century Athens, Solon's measures for the relief of the poor were part and parcel of the conception of Solon as founder of the democracy.

Aristotle himself is prominent among the sources for this understanding of the origins of Athenian democracy.[23] Indeed, Aristotle highlights Solon's measures for the relief of the poor in his account of the Athenian constitution, and also credits Solon with far-reaching democratic reforms.[24] For Aristotle, Solon's first actions on being appointed arbitrator of the social conflict between rich and poor in sixth-century Athens were the ban on debt-slavery and the cancellation of debts.[25] These measures became known as the "Lifting of the Burdens" (*Seisachtheia*). Like the term *Palintokia*, the term *Seisachtheia* seems to preserve a genuine piece of early Athenian legislation. Yet Aristotle (and other fourth-century sources) credit Solon with many further, more historically questionable reforms. These reforms reflect the fourth-century conception of Solon as founder of the democracy and include the introduction of a council of four hundred drawn from each of the four tribal divisions of the people, the selection of magistrates by lot from candidates elected from the tribes, and the establishment of popular courts in which the masses sat in judgment of

their social superiors.[26] Solon is even credited by Aristotle with the intro-
duction of the provision for appeals to the Areopagus Council (*eisange-lia*) against those who attempt to overthrow the democracy, *even though the democracy had not yet been founded!*[27]

Given this evidence for Aristotle's view of the association between
Solon's legislation for debt relief and his alleged democratic reforms, it
is easy to see how he might have inferred the existence of democracy in
archaic Megara from evidence for similar measures for debt relief in
Megara.[28] However, whereas Aristotle based his account of Solon's democratic reforms both on the *Seisachtheia* and traditions regarding specific
constitutional reforms, his case for archaic Megarian democracy seems to
have been based solely on the *Palintokia* and accounts of social disorder.[29] In both cases, however, the historical basis for the re-imagining of
these sixth-century city-states as democracies was legislation providing
debt relief for the poor. Oddly, modern historians have agreed with the
equation between debt-relief and democracy in Megara, whereas they
make no such equation in the case of Athens.[30] This contradiction is dou-
bly odd because Solon's debt relief was much more dramatic than that
which took place in Megara. Solon cancelled debts altogether, whereas in
Megara only the interest was cancelled. Comparative examples from the
early modern period, however, suggest that there is no necessary relation
between democracy and economic measures for the relief of the poor.
Indeed, as I shall discuss in the final part of this chapter, elites often propose such measures in order to prevent further social unrest that might
lead to democratic political reform.

If early economic legislation was the historical kernel upon which traditions of sixth-century democracy were based, the association between
democracy and disorder in anti-democratic ideology enabled its further
elaboration in the case of Megara.[31] As we have seen, Plato theorized that
democracies are brought about by lack of restraint (*akolasia*). Similarly,
Plato reasons that democracies are overthrown when insolence (*hubris*)
and anarchy (*anarchia*) are not checked. Aristotle applies this causal sequence to his analysis of political change in archaic Megara since he attributes the overthrow of the archaic Megarian democracy to licentiousness
(*aselgeia*) and disorder (*ataxia*). We must still ask why Aristotle applied
the democracy-disorder model to Megara in particular. The answer, once
again, can be found in Plutarch, who recounts anecdotes of outrageous,
undisciplined behavior of the Megarians. Presumably these anecdotes are
derived, via Aristotle, from genuine Megarian oral traditions, where they
were preserved at least partly because of their shocking content. We may
assume that Aristotle connected the evidence for the *Palintokia* with the
accounts of revelry and riot in archaic Megara to produce his analysis of
early Megarian political development.

But if the *Palintokia* and social disorder in archaic Megara are not related to democracy, what was the context in which they occurred? In the
next section of this chapter, I suggest that part of the answer may be found
by analyzing the relationship between festival revelry and riot in times of
rapid social and economic change.

Festival Revelry in Ancient and Early Modern Europe

Social anthropologists and cultural historians have long recognized that
festival revelry frequently involves the temporary breakdown or even inversion of social hierarchies and norms. The Saturnalia in Rome and Carnival in Early Modern Europe are the best known examples, but there is
a whole array of more minor festivals both in the ancient world and in
pre-modern Europe which involve similar inversions.[32] In this section, I
argue that Plutarch's anecdotes about Megara relate to three forms of such
festival revelry:

1. the feasting of social inferiors by social superiors, sometimes involving the license to abuse the latter verbally or physically;
2. the license to break customary norms of behavior (cross dress-
   ing, public drunkenness, openly sexual/ribald behavior, reversal
   of roles between genders or "women on top");
3. license to break the law with impunity (e.g., robbery, assault,
   and other crimes normally regulated by law).

It should be emphasized that these categories are neither comprehen-
sive nor mutually exclusive, and represent a simplification of a very complex nexus of rituals. Historical examples of festival revelry, as we shall
see, often combine these and other forms of social inversion. In what
follows, I pick out the features of festival revelry that correspond to the
anecdotes about Megara.

Plutarch's account of how the Megarian poor invaded the houses of
the rich and demanded to be feasted lavishly relates to similar social rituals known most fully from the Saturnalia in ancient Rome and Christmas
or New Year festivals in Early Modern Europe. The Saturnalia was held
on the seventeenth of December and involved public feasts, revelry, and
the breakdown of social hierarchy.

The Roman historian Livy (59 BCE–17 CE) provides an account of
the Saturnalia of 217 BCE. Livy mentions a feast for the god (*lectister-
nium*) held in the temple of Saturn as well as a public feast.[33] Elsewhere
in his history, he describes the first feast for the gods ever held in Rome. In
addition to the couches (*lecti*) spread for the gods in the temples, the rite
was also celebrated in private houses in the following way:

Throughout the whole city, doors stood ajar, everything was left out
in the open to be shared by anyone who wished, and they say that
all visitors—whether known or unknown—were welcomed hospi-
tably, while people exchanged friendly and courteous words with
their enemies, setting aside their quarrels and disputes. Prisoners
too were freed from their chains for those days; and afterwards they
felt scruples about imprisoning those whom the gods had helped in
this way.[34]

In addition to holding open house for all, the most prominent feature of
the private celebration of the Saturnalia according to our sources was the
feasting of slaves by their masters.[35]

Similar festivals involving both the holding of open house and the
feasting of social inferiors by their superiors existed in Greece, as H. S.
Versnel has demonstrated. At the festival of Kronos in Attica and elsewhere in Greece, slaves were feasted by their masters. As the second century BCE Roman poet Accius wrote:

Most of the Greeks, and the Athenians above all, hold rites in honor
of Saturn. They call these rites the Kronia, and they celebrate the
day by holding feasts (*epulis*) in the towns and throughout the countryside. And with great revelry (*laeti*) they serve their own slaves.
This same custom has been passed on to us from there, so that here
also slaves feast with their masters.[36]

Similarly, Athenaeus, a Greek who wrote during the second century AD,
mentions a number of Saturnalia-like festivals throughout Greece:

At a festival of Hermes on Crete, the slaves feast while their masters
act as servants. At Troezen, the slaves play knucklebones with the
citizens and the masters host their slaves.[37]

After commenting on a similar Babylonian festival in which it was customary for masters to be ruled by their slaves, Athenaeus goes on to relate that at a festival to Zeus Pelorius held in the northern Greek region
of Thessaly, a sacrifice and feast were held to which all were welcomed.
Not only did foreigners attend, but slaves reclined at the banquet and
were waited upon by their masters. Even prisoners were set free and (Athenaeus implies) were allowed to feast alongside the others.[38]

Earlier in his work, Athenaeus mentions similar events at a festival of
Kronos in Alexandria and at the Spartan festival of Hyacinthus.

At the festival of Kronos the Alexandrians put loaves of bread in
Kronos' temple for anyone who wishes to eat.[39]

On the middle day of the Spartan festival of Hyacinthus, a great
varied throng of people gathers, and the whole city delights in the

spectacle of parades, music and dance. They also sacrifice many victims and the citizens feast all their acquaintances and their own slaves.[40]

As Versnel has observed, this aspect of the Kronia/Saturnalia complex of festivals involves a conception of the era of these gods as a golden age, that is, a time of peace, prosperity, and plenty in which men feasted and reveled together without conflict or social distinctions.[41]

Despite the similarity of these rituals to the events in Megara, however, it is important to observe that Plutarch suggests that the Megarian events involved not simply the breakdown of social categories and the feasting of the poor by the rich, but also the use of force, if the demands of the poor for lavish fare were not met. Plutarch claims that the rich were treated with violence (*pros bian*) and insult (*meth' hubreōs*) by the poor. Verbal and physical abuse of authorities, however, is a well-known feature of the festival revelry in the early modern period and is part of the accepted suspension or reversal of social hierarchies and norms.[42] Although verbal abuse is only weakly attested for the ancient Saturnalia/ Kronia festivals, it is relatively well attested for a number of other ancient festivals, notably festivals of Dionysus and Demeter. At the festivals of these gods, the shouting of abusive and obscene remarks (*aischrologia*) was a prominent feature of the ritual.[43] Physical abuse of superiors by inferiors, moreover, is attested for a festival in Kydonia on Crete. During this festival, the serfs lorded it in the city while the citizens stayed outside. If any citizen dared to enter the city during the festival, the serfs were permitted to whip them.[44]

The best parallel for the verbal and physical abuse of the rich by the poor in Plutarch's anecdotes about Megara, however, can be found in a related set of rituals in which groups of young men visit the houses of the rich and demand hospitality. In Greece, these rituals are known through the fortunate survival of songs that young men sang as they approached the doors of the rich.[45] The most famous example of this ritual song bears a striking resemblance to Plutarch's anecdote about Megara, and similarly attests to the possibility of violence if the demands of the poor were not met. The song is known as the Swallow Song, since it took place in the spring when the swallow appeared.[46]

Bring fruit and cake from your rich house and offer it to us, and a cup of wine and a basket of cheese. The swallow does not disdain even wheaten bread or pulse bread. Shall we go, or are we to get something? If you give us something, we will go, but if you do not we shall not let you be; we shall carry away your door or lintel, or your wife sitting inside. She is small; we shall carry her easily. But if

you give us something, let it be something big. Open, open the door
to the swallow; for we are not old men but children.[47]

Another song, the *Eiresione*, was named after the bough of olive wreathed
with wool that children on the Greek island of Samos carried around as
they made their calls at the doors of the rich. As the song attests, the
bough represented prosperity, and was brought by the boys to the house
in return for gifts. At Athens, the bough was left at the house to which it
was brought and was set up at the door so that prosperity might last
throughout the year. The bough is attested in several plays of Aristophanes,
and a sculptural representation further attests to the common occurrence
of this rite.[48]

> We take recourse to the house of a man of great means,
> Who has great resources and makes great noise, ever prosperous.
> Open of your own accord, doors, for Wealth will enter
> In plenty, and with Wealth, flourishing Cheer
> And welcome Peace. May the grain jars all be full,
> And the mound of dough ever top the kneading trough.
> Now [give us] beautiful barley meal laced with sesame ...
> I'll return, I'll return each year, like the swallow.
> I stand at the porch, feet stripped, so bring something quickly.
> For Apollo's sake, lady, give us something!
> If you will, well and good: if not, we won't wait about,
> We didn't come here to make our homes with you.[49]

Another form of this ritual is attested by the Crow Song, named after the
crow that the revelers carried:

> Kind friends give a handful of barley to the Crow, Apollo's daugh-
> ter, or a plate of wheat, a loaf of bread maybe, or a half-obol, or
> whatever you please. Give to the Crow, good sirs, something of what
> each of you has on hand. She will accept a lump of rock-salt; yes,
> she likes very much to feast on that. Who gives salt now will give
> honeycomb another day. Slave, push back the door! Abundance has
> heard us, and a maid brings figs for the Crow. Ye gods, may the girl
> prove to be blameless in every way, and may she find a husband rich
> and famous; I hope she may lay a son in the arms of her old father,
> and a girl baby on the lap of her mother—her own offspring to be
> nurtured as a wife for one of her kinsmen. As for me, wherever my
> feet carry me, I go in turn and sing at the door with tuneful muse,
> whether one gives or does not give more than I ask ... Nay good men
> hand out some of the wealth which your pantry hoards. Give, mas-
> ter, and you too, lady bride, give! It is the custom to give a handful

to the Crow when she begs. That is the refrain I sing. Give something, and it will be enough.[50]

Evidence of similar rituals from Early Modern Europe not only confirms the customary right of the poor to demand hospitality from the rich, but also the violence that could ensue if their demands were not met. One of the more amusing examples of this ritual is "Molly-Dancing" which was still performed in East Anglia, England during the first half of the twentieth century.[51] This wintertime street performance involved agricultural workers, dressed up in women's clothing and with blackened faces, performing parodies of social dances in exchange for largesse. According to Elaine Bradtke, the revelers "could be destructive, drunk and disreputable in appearance."[52] Although there were set times of year for the rite (often Boxing Day and Plough Monday), Molly dancers went out more frequently in periods of poor weather or famine in response to need.[53]

A striking example of the violence that could result from failure to give largesse may be found in the rituals of Plough Monday in England. On this day, gangs of young men went round the village threatening to plow up the property of home and business owners who did not give them money.[54] In some cases, the men actually followed through with their threat:

> The great event of the day was when they came before some house which bore signs that the owner was well-to-do in the world, and nothing was given to them. Bessy rattled his box, and the ploughmen danced, while the country lads blew the bullocks' horns, or shouted with all their might; but if there was still no sign, no coming-forth of either bread or cheese, or ale, then the word was given, the ploughshare driven into the ground before the door or window, the whole twenty men yoked pulling like one, and in a minute or two the ground before the house was as brown, barren and ridgy as a newly ploughed field. But this was rarely done, for everybody gave something.[55]

In his study of Christmas-time revels in seventeenth-century New England, Steven Nissenbaum gives a further example of how the failure of the wealthy to provide hospitality during this season might result in violence. When a band of four young men from Salem village invaded the house of one John Rowden on Christmas night in 1679, they were refused a drink in return for their song. As a consequence,

> [T]hey threw stones, bones and other things ... against the house. They beat down much of the daubing in several places and continued to throw stones for an hour and a half with little intermission. They also broke down about a pole and a half of fence, being stone

wall, and a cellar ... was broken open through the door, and five or six pecks of apples were stolen.[56]

Two points emerge from these examples. First, we can see that a common feature of festival revelry in pre-modern societies is the symbolic inversion of the relation between social superiors and inferiors. As Nissenbaum writes: "At other times of the year it was the poor who owed goods, labor, and deference to the rich. But on this occasion the tables were turned—literally. The poor—most often bands of boys and young men—claimed the right to march into the houses of the well-to-do, enter their halls, and receive gifts of food, drink and sometimes money as well. And the rich had to let them in—essentially to hold 'open house.'"[57] Anthropologists and historians have commonly viewed the function of these inversions as a "safety valve" whereby the poor let off steam and released tensions created by the hierarchical social order.[58] These symbolic inversions reminded the elite of their obligation to ensure the fundamental well-being of the poor while they simultaneously extracted labor and goods from them.

As Nissenbaum writes, "[this] kind of misrule ... did not really challenge the authority of the gentry ... The gentry were in fact widely tolerant of these episodes of misrule, viewing them as an opportunity to make up for a year of exploitation by giving a generous handout at Christmas."[59] This attitude of tolerance is well reflected in the comments of the wealthy Roman Pliny (first century CE) concerning his withdrawal to remote rooms in his house while his slaves celebrate the Saturnalia: "When I retreat to these rooms, I feel that I am really quite away from my own house; and I take great pleasure in this—particularly at the Saturnalia, when the rest of the place resounds with merry shouts in the free spirit of the holiday. For in this way I do not interrupt my household's amusements, nor they my work."[60]

Yet a second point also emerges from the examples of ritual hospitality cited above, and that is the potential of such ritual revelry to result in violence. As we shall see in the final section of this chapter, the frequency throughout history with which festival revelry has escalated into real riot and protest has led historians to recognize that the license and reversals of festivals not only serve as a safety valve but can also be used by the lower orders to express discontent. Before I address the revolutionary potential of revelry, I want to point to two further features of festival ritual that seem to be reflected in the anecdotes about Megara.

So far I have established that festival revelry from ancient to early modern times included the right of the poor to be feasted by the rich and the license to abuse the rich both physically and verbally. The second feature of festival revelry has already been implied, though its relation to the anecdotes about Megara is worth spelling out. Here I am referring to the license to transgress norms of behavior, for example by cross-dressing, openly sexual/ribald behavior, reversal of roles between genders ("women on top"), or excessive public drunkenness. These features of festival revelry have been eloquently discussed by Natalie Zemon Davis and others in relation to Early Modern Europe, as I shall discuss in more detail below. At this point, it is simply worth noting that these reversals and transgressions are well-known features of a number of Greek festivals, and may have been part of the festivities in Megara at which the events recalled by Plutarch took place.

For example, at the festival of the Thesmophoria and other celebrations of the goddess Demeter, women took control by conducting the rite themselves and by excluding men. As Jack Winkler has observed, the festival featured an imitation by the women of the official procedures for the election of magistrates. The women elected their own magistrates who held titles parallel to those of the official male magistrates.[61] The practices of the festival therefore inverted the normal hierarchy of male domination.[62] The women further broke the customary norms of female behavior by using vulgar language and by making obscene jokes as they handled and ate cakes shaped in the form of male genitals. At another festival of Demeter, the Adonia, women gathered on rooftops at night for drinking, feasting, dancing, and ribald laughter. According to Winkler's ingenious interpretation of the symbolism of the wilted shoots which the women carried to the rooftop gardens, part of the women's laughter is based on a sexual joke about the brevity of male sexual powers in contrast to the enduring role of women in human and agricultural production.[63]

A more obscure but perhaps even more striking example of gender role reversal is an Argive festival known as the Festival of Insolence (*ta hubristika*). At this festival, men and women exchanged clothes and fought one another.[64]

Most prominent of all ancient festivals of inversion are of course the Dionysiac festivals, where parades with huge phalluses (fig. 11), obscenity, sexuality, cross-dressing, excessive drinking and feasting accompanied the performance of tragedy and comedy.[65] Tragedy, of course, put the most transgressive behavior of all on stage for the community to witness: fathers killing daughters, brothers killing one another, patricide, matricide and incest.[66] Comedy, in turn, not only ridiculed those in authority (both particular elite politicians and the ordinary citizens as a whole), but featured role reversals, obscenity, and ribald sexuality.[67]

In this regard, it is significant that Aristotle mentions in his *Poetics* that the Megarians claim to have invented comedy long before the Athenians "during the time of their democracy."[68] Whatever the truth of the matter, it is striking that the Megarians could plausibly make this claim. At a minimum, we may infer that the Megarians had festivals involving some form of comic performances (and hence traditions of comic ritual reversals) in Aristotle's time (the fourth century BCE). It is likely that these comic traditions went quite far back, possibly as far back as the early sixth century. An observation made by Antony Edwards is relevant to this question. Edwards noted the similarity of several lines in the poetry of the Megarian Theognis to rituals of comic reversal.[69]

> Cyrnus, the city is still the city, but the people are different.
> Those who before knew neither justice or law
> But wore goatskins on their backs
> And grazed like deer outside the city
> These are now respected, and those who before were respected,
> are now base. Who can bear to look upon this?
> And they deceive one another and laugh at each other
> Not knowing how to distinguish between the opinions of the
>   respectable and the base.[70]

Conventionally, these lines have been interpreted as the exaggerated reaction of the traditional ruling elite to social and economic changes that were bringing new groups to power.[71] Yet one might wonder, instead, whether these lines reflect the disgust of the elite at the reversals, insult, and obscenities typical of certain festivals. Could this be a comic festival?

The last feature of the transgressive behavior of festival revelry mentioned above, namely excessive public drunkenness, is amply attested in the Megarian anecdotes. Plutarch writes that the Megarians who rolled the wagons of the sacred ambassadors into the lake were drunk (*methusthentes*). Less directly, Plutarch's use of the analogy of the corrupting effects of the drinking of unmixed wine to describe the unruly behavior of the poor may be inspired by a detail in the original Megarian oral tradition— not mentioned by Plutarch and hence lost to us—that the poor were actually drunk when they invaded the houses of the rich. In other words, while Plutarch (and Plato before him) suggests that the masses, when given too much freedom, are as unruly as drunkards, drunkenness may have been an actual feature of the ritual behavior of the Megarians in the events described by Plutarch.

If we turn now from transgressions against informal social norms of behavior to transgressions of formal laws, we may examine the third feature of festival revelry attested in Plutarch's anecdotes about Megara: temple robbery (*hierosulia*).[72] While Plutarch takes such sacrilege as yet another example of the crimes that took place during the time of unbridled democracy (*akolastos dēmokratia*), it is possible that this too was a feature of festival revelry. At a festival of Hermes Charidotes ("Giver of Joy") on Samos, it was permitted to steal (*kleptein*) and rob (*lōpodutein*).[73]

In Early Modern Europe, moreover, food rioters made use of the ritual forms of hospitality when they plundered not only the homes of the wealthy, but also public and private granaries, local mills, wagons on their way to market, and, in one case, a Franciscan monastery.[74] In the medieval period, finally, assaults committed during Carnival were not subject to prosecution.[75] In each of these cases, therefore, actions normally subject to sanction under the law were permissible during festival times. It is possible, therefore, that plunder of sacred property (*hierosulia*) was an aspect of the license of festival revelry.

It is perhaps worth noting, in this regard, that temples were not only the places where valuable objects were dedicated to the gods, but were also public enterprises deeply invested in agricultural production. Temples owned lands and drew rents in coin and in kind from the working of these sacred lands. In addition, tithes were sometimes collected in grain. Since some of this agricultural produce was stored in sacred precincts, temples were analogous to granaries and were appropriate targets for the aggressive actions of the hungry poor.[76]

So far I have argued that invasion of the houses of the rich, drunken and disorderly behavior, and temple robbery can all be explained as features of festival revelry. But what about the drowning of sacred ambassadors? Surely such a sacrilegious and murderous act was not an accepted part of festival revelry? Indeed, Plutarch tells us that, when the Megarians failed to punish the offenders, the league of states responsible for maintaining the cult at Delphi (known as the Delphic Amphictiony) took the matter into their own hands and punished some offenders with death and others with exile. Certainly for the Greeks represented by the Amphictionic League, festival license was *not* an excuse for the drowning of sacred ambassadors.[77] We might conclude, therefore, that this incident was an extraordinary act of brutality, and for that reason, presumably, was remembered in Megarian historical traditions. Like the "Return of Interest" legislation or *Palintokia*, the perpetrators of this outrage were memorialized through a specialized term, "the Wagon Rollers" (*hoi hamaxokulistai*) —a term whose obscurity in later ages was the impetus for Plutarch's brief exposition of the incident.

Plutarch's explanation of this term, however, is deeply influenced by the anti-democratic tradition. As we have seen already, Plutarch associates the event with the insolence (*hubris*) and savagery (*ōmotes*) that flourished under the unbridled democracy (*akolastos dēmokratia*). Similarly, he attributes the failure to punish the crime to the disorder (*ataxia*) of the Megarian government. The failure to check lawlessness, as we have seen, is a key feature of Plato's analysis of the flaws of democracy in Book 8 of the *Republic*.[78] In one of the most pointed formulations of this claim, Plato writes with his customary irony:

Is not the ease (*praotes*) of some convicted criminals a fine thing?
Or have you never seen how in such political system [i.e., democ-
racy], those who have been sentenced to death or exile remain [in the
city] none the less, and go around in public, as if they were heroized
spirits of the dead, without anyone paying attention or seeing them?
(558a)

Plato's claim that democracy is lenient toward criminals represents a skillful negation of one of the qualities of democracy championed by its pro-
ponents. While democrats used the term "mildness/gentleness" (*praotes*)
to refer to their moderation toward their political opponents in contrast
to non-democratic regimes, the oligarchs spun this term much more neg-
atively as part of the lack of discipline (*akolasia*) which they viewed as
characteristic of democratic rule.[79]

With this ideological context in mind it is easy to see how Plutarch, or
fourth-century writers such as Aristotle, might have made the connection
between the criminal act against the sacred ambassadors and democracy
in sixth-century Megara. If we remove this anti-democratic inference
from the anecdote, how else can we explain the incident?

In answering this question, we are both hindered and helped by the
nature of the oral traditions in which it was remembered. We are hindered by the fact that these oral traditions were not interested in recalling
the historical context of the event, which may relate to quarrels between
Peloponnesian states (the ambassadors were "from the Peloponnesus")
or may have been retribution for some sacred offense. We are helped,
however, by the fact that the incident was remembered in part because
it was associated with a particular descent group (*genos*) which became
known by the moniker "Wagon Rollers" (*hoi amaxokulistai*). This detail
is important because it demonstrates that the incident was not a product
of mob violence, as Plutarch suggests, but was a more limited act of aggression perpetrated by a particular family. The fact that Plutarch refers
to this family as a *genos* suggests that it may have been an elite family, not
unlike the Alcmeonidae of Athens, who became similarly polluted (*enages*)
after an act of sacrilege relating to an attempted tyranny known as the
Cylonian affair.[80] In sum, there is much we do not know about the events
that led to the drowning of sacred ambassadors in archaic Megara. What
we can say, however, is that the incident bears no necessary connection to
a democratic regime.

From Revel to Riot

So far I have suggested that many of the features of unruly behavior
attributed by Plutarch to a democracy at Megara can be explained as

examples of typical forms of festival revelry. Yet, as I have already noted in regard to the drowning of the sacred ambassadors, this explanation is insufficient since it does not explain why these incidents were so memorable that they were preserved in Megarian oral traditions. If these incidents were simply typical instances of the reversals and transgressions of festival revelry, why did the Megarians bother to remember them? Clearly there was something in these incidents that went beyond the norm.

I argue in the final section of this chapter that the events recorded by Plutarch reflect the escalation of the symbolic inversions and license of festival revelry into real riot and protest. The cause of this escalation of violence was the particularly strained conditions of the poor in Megara in the sixth century BCE. A variety of types of evidence demonstrate that relations of reciprocity between rich and poor were breaking down as a result of population growth and economic expansion. The poor were becoming increasingly indebted to the rich and found it more difficult to make ends meet.[81] Under these conditions, the poor resorted to cultural mechanisms for symbolically representing the obligation of the rich to ensure the well-being of the poor—namely festivals in which the rich feasted the poor—to express their discontent with the changing social and economic conditions.

Historians of Early Modern Europe have long noted that festivals were frequently occasions for expression of discontent with the ruling classes. They argue that festivals function not only to reinforce the social order by temporarily reversing it, but also serve as a mechanism for criticizing and even rebelling against the social order. Emmanuel Le Roy Ladurie, for example, observed that the peasant insurrection of 1580 in Languedoc was instigated by the youth societies in charge of popular festivals. On this occasion, the youths used their customary license to mock authorities to incite the peasants and artisans to revolt. According to contemporary sources, the leader of the artisans was a "coarse and clownish fellow" who was "insolent" before respected authorities. In accord with the reversal of the social hierarchy, the revelers/rebels threatened the nobility "with dirty and wicked words 'to turn their houses upside down' ... and there was not a yokel who did not behave as if he were as great a lord as his lord." In this case, the rich perceived the threat posed by the peasants as so grave that they responded by massacring the peasants over the course of three days.[82]

In her studies of culture and society in sixteenth- and seventeenth-century France, Natalie Zemon Davis has observed the same tendency of festivals to serve as a mechanism for expressing discontent. Davis argues that the reversal of the social hierarchy and the license to criticize authority afforded by festivals provided occasions and models for rebellious behavior and protest for the lower classes who otherwise had no official institutional means to express discontent. For example, the youth groups known as the "Abbeys of Misrule" frequently used their license to mock authorities during Carnival as a means to criticize the greed of local magistrates or "the high cost of bread and the empty stalls of the merchants." On a number of occasions, Davis notes, festival protest escalated into real uprising and rebellion.[83] Davis's most striking claim in this regard is her argument that the license afforded to women, or men dressed as women, during festivals provided images and behavioral models which inspired some women to actions which went far beyond the normative roles for women in this patriarchal society.[84]

Peter Burke similarly has observed that the authorities in seventeenth-century Sicily and Naples recognized the potential of Carnival festivities to escalate into rebellion. As Burke puts it, the officials were aware that if they did not take preventative action by, for instance, banning the carrying of arms during Carnival, "there might be a 'switching' of codes, from the language of ritual to the language of rebellion."[85] Finally, Robert Darnton has brilliantly demonstrated how a group of printer's apprentices in a Paris printing shop in the 1730s made use of the cultural forms of popular revelry to ridicule and threaten their master.[86]

These early modern examples of the relation between revelry and riot, symbolic inversion and real rebellion, are useful for interpreting events in sixth-century Megara. First of all, they demonstrate how ritual forms could serve as the basis for protest or rebellion. That is to say that the incidents of revelry, riot, and violence reported by Plutarch may reflect the escalation of ritual license into rebellion, or the borrowing of ritual forms in order to voice real protest.

Even more important than the recognition of the potential for revelry to serve as a mechanism for protest, however, are the implications of the early modern examples for our understanding of the causes and consequences of riotous behavior in Megara. It is striking that the occasions for festive rebellions in the early modern period were often the worsening economic conditions of the laboring poor, usually as a result of famine, high prices, or oppressive taxation.[87] In the case of Darnton's printer's apprentices, moreover, the workers were responding to the outsourcing of work to cheap day laborers. This development was undermining the apprentices' status and contributing to the breakdown of the relationship of mutual dependence between shop owners and journeymen. In the words of Darnton, the cheap day laborers "personified the tendency of labor to become a commodity instead of a partnership."[88] In other words, the workers were responding to the breakdown of patriarchal relationships between rich and poor, not trying to undermine this traditional form of reciprocity.

In his study of food riots in eighteenth-century England, E. P. Thompson shows how the forms of protest adopted by crowds imitated official procedures for setting a fair price on corn, but also drew from traditional rituals of hospitality involving the feasting of the poor by the rich.[89] Thompson concludes, moreover, that worsening economic conditions and, even more important, the breakdown of traditional notions of reciprocity between rich and poor ("the moral economy") were the root causes of the food riots: "It is of course true that riots were triggered off by soaring prices, by malpractices among dealers or by hunger. But these grievances operated within a popular consensus as to what were legitimate and what were illegitimate practices in marketing, milling, baking etc. This in its turn was grounded upon a consistent traditional view of social norms and obligations, of the proper economic functions of several parties within the community, which, taken together, can be said to constitute a moral economy of the poor."[90]

In another study, Thompson shows how peasants borrowed from cultural rituals involving cross-dressing, black-face, and incursions onto the properties of the rich to protest their exclusion by the Crown from the forests in eighteenth-century England.[91] The peasants had traditionally used the forests as sources of timber, turf (for fuel), and wild game, and therefore viewed the king's action as a violation of their customary rights. Interestingly, the meticulous attention paid by the king to the well-being of the royal red deer was a glaring symbol of his indifference to conditions of the poor, just as in Darnton's account of the Paris printing shop, the good life enjoyed by the mistresses' favorite cat (la grise) highlighted the misery of the printer's apprentices and provoked them to riot.

Building on Thompson's work on the relation between popular culture and protest in early modern England, David Underdown has argued that incidents of revelry and riot in seventeenth-century England not only borrowed from widespread social rituals involving the inversion of norms, but became particularly violent when changing economic conditions threatened traditional village life and the reciprocal relation between wealthy landowners and laboring peasants.[92] Underdown's analysis suggests that revelry and riot were aimed at the enforcement of the traditional order. As Underdown writes, "[The intention of riot] was usually to compel authority to maintain a traditional order, rather than overturn it. Food rioters were inspired by the values of a vaguely sensed 'moral economy' in contrast to the values of a market economy now being adopted."[93] Similarly, Kirkpatrick Sale has shown how the Luddite revolt of 1811–12 utilized blackface to protest the changes of the Industrial Revolution which were undermining the traditional economy.[94]

Through these early modern comparisons, I do not intend to suggest that ancient Megara was undergoing economic changes of the nature and scale of, for example, the Industrial Revolution. Rather, I suggest a much more general similarity with the Megarian case, namely that the poor used cultural rituals of revelry to protest changing economic conditions and their worsening situation. More specifically, I suggest that changes in society and the economy (discussed below) threatened the mutual dependence between rich and poor. Whereas previously, the rich had ensured the basic economic well-being of the poor in return for "labor, goods and deference," the poor now found themselves subject to more formally enforced debt mechanisms and increasing economic hardship.[95]

The most striking evidence for these conditions in Megara is the "Return of Interest" legislation (*Palintokia*), which, as Plutarch attests, was passed as a result of the riotous behavior of the poor.[96] Under this law, the interest that the poor had given to their creditors was returned to them. As mentioned already, similar legislation is attested for early sixth-century Athens, and it is therefore likely that increasing debt and worsening economic conditions for the poor were experienced in many regions of Greece at this time. As we have seen, the sixth-century Athenian lawgiver Solon enacted measures known as the "Lifting of the Burdens" (*Seisachtheia*). These reforms involved even more radical new regulations than the "Return of Interest" legislation at Megara. In Athens, debts were cancelled altogether, and the practice of enslaving individuals for debt was abolished.[97] The latter practice had apparently led not only to the reduction of the poor to "unseemly slavery" (*doulien aeikea*) in Athens, but also to the sale of debtors into slavery abroad.[98] We can imagine that the laboring poor of archaic Megara faced similar prospects of enslavement and sale abroad when they rose in riot, and conversely, that poor Athenians used ritual forms of revelry to provoke Solon (and his elite supporters) to "lift their burdens."

This last suggestion puts a comment made by W. R. Connor into a new perspective. Connor observed that the word *Seisachtheia* echoes the names of festivals ending in –eia, and, furthermore, that Plutarch mentions that the term was the name given to a public sacrifice (*thusia*) made to celebrate Solon's reforms.[99] Connor argues therefore that Solon's reforms should not be conceived simply as legislative or legal measures but also as "a festival, perhaps a procession through the countryside or a ritualized destruction of the boundary markers [which marked mortgaged property]."[100] If we accept my suggestion that the poor used ritual revelry to force Solon and his fellow elites to enact economic reform, then the creation of a festival and rituals to commemorate these events makes even more sense. One can imagine indeed that the ritualized destruction of the boundary stones echoed the ritual violence meted out against the property of the rich in the events that led up to the reforms.

One more comment about Solon's reforms is significant in this regard. Solon's economic legislation included a ban on the export of all agricultural produce except olive oil.[101] If we follow the logic of Thompson's observation that protest in eighteenth-century England was provoked in particular by the export of grain during times of dearth, we might imagine that Solon's ban on exports was a response to riots over the export of grain by the wealthy while the poor were suffering starvation, debt, and enslavement.[102]

But what were the root causes of the dire conditions of the poor in Athens and Megara? Here we may adduce two interrelated factors: population growth and increased production for market trade. Recent demographic studies have shown that while earlier models of explosive population growth in early Greece are untenable, steady population growth of up to 1 percent per annum beginning in the eighth century would have resulted in considerable strains on the economy by the sixth century.[103] On the one hand, population growth meant that there were "more mouths to feed." On the other hand, there was more labor available to work the land, and as a result the value of land outstripped the value of those available to work it.[104] As Ian Morris puts it:

> [T]he most likely situation is that population growth produced a situation where landowners would actually want to get rid of some of their sharecroppers, or else renegotiate the terms of dependency. No doubt most landowners felt constrained by custom and by patriarchal obligations towards "their" *hektemoroi* [sixth-parters = "share-croppers"]. But ... [t]he implication of much of Solon's poetry is that new market opportunities were transforming the ideology of gain.[105]

While Morris draws these inferences on the basis of Athenian evidence, the parallels with Megara at this time are strong. Besides the comparable evidence for economic reforms (*Palintokia/Seisachtheia*), a similar transformation of "the ideology of gain" is detectable in Megarian poetry. If we take the poetry of Theognis of Megara (Solon's contemporary) as representative of ideological conflicts in early Megara, then the vitriolic condemnations of selfish pursuit of gain echo those in Solon's poetry.[106]

> Good men have never yet destroyed the city
> But whenever it is pleasing to evil men to act outrageously
> And destroy the people and claim that unjust deeds are just
> For the sake of private gain and power
> Don't expect that city to remain quiet for long
> Even if now it is at peace
> When these things are dear to evil men
> The gains bring public misfortune.[107]

> Take counsel with yourself about leading a reverent life with modest means rather than growing rich by seeking money unjustly.[108]

Theognis' poetry, as Solon's, seems to reflect the attempt of the ruling elite to check the tendencies toward the rampant pursuit of personal gain which was undermining the relation between rich and poor and threatening the stability of the community.[109] In Athens, we can be fairly certain that the export of grain, wine, and olive oil was one mechanism by which the wealthy sought to increase their personal profits at the expense of the poor.[110] Besides Solon's ban on agricultural exports, Athenian transport amphorae and pottery attest to widespread Athenian trade links throughout the Mediterranean.[111] Evidence for Megarian trade is more elusive, but indicative nonetheless. First, Megarians were on the forefront of the movement to found new settlements overseas. Recent research suggests that these early settlements abroad were not state-sponsored responses to overpopulation, but often the result of individual adventurism in pursuit of gain.[112]

In the fifth century, moreover, Megara was well known for its export of woolen garments, and it is likely that the seeds of this trade go back at least as far as the sixth century.[113] Indeed, Aristotle reports that the late seventh-century tyrant Theagenes won the support of the poor by "slaughtering the cattle of the rich."[114] While we may reasonably doubt Aristotle's claim that Theagenes gained tyrannical power through this act, the anecdote does reflect the basis of elite wealth in Megara, namely sheep and grazing land.[115] Indeed we may suspect that one cause of the sixth-century crisis was that the wealthy sought to increase the size of their herds and their control over land in their pursuit for profit.[116]

It is important to emphasize that neither population growth nor production for market trade were new phenomena in the sixth century. Indeed, these trends go back to the eighth century at least.[117] Furthermore, it must be stressed that the surplus production must have been rather small given the increased needs of the growing population.[118] Nevertheless, the poetry of Solon and Theognis, as well as the emergency economic measures taken to respond to the situation, suggest that these two trends together contributed to a crisis in the early to mid-sixth century. Interestingly, the response of the ruling elite to the crisis is paralleled in the early modern examples. The comparative examples suggest, moreover, that elites sought to address the economic plight of the poor in order to *contain* violent protest and *prevent* rebellion against their rule. In other words, the ruling elite recognized the potential for the economic crisis to lead to a more serious threat to their rule, and took steps to prevent this.

In her study of food riots in sixteenth-century France, for example, Natalie Zemon Davis shows that one response to riot was the creation of a new public institution (the Aûmone Générale) to replace traditional mechanisms for poor relief such as "handing out alms at the door," "handouts at funerals and other anniversaries, doles from monasteries and ...

cathedrals" and "sporadic action" by municipal authorities.[119] These new measures were devised by "a coalition of notables" "so there would be no cause for the people to get stirred up."[120] Similarly, Thompson observes that municipal authorities in eighteenth-century England occasionally engaged in symbolic enforcement of the traditional paternalist model of the market when the gap between this model and the realities of the market grew too great. The authorities acted sporadically to ensure that the poor had access to grain at a reasonable price in order to demonstrate "to the poor that the authorities were acting vigilantly in their interests."[121] Later, the authorities took more concrete action through the creation of charities and subsidies designed "to buy off riot."[122]

The comparative examples suggest that the *Palintokia* and *Seisachtheia* represent measures to address the economic problems of the poor in order that they might not lead to more serious challenges to elite rule. In other words, these measures were mechanisms for preserving elite rule, not an indication of the overturning of elite rule in favor of democracy. But what do I mean by "elite rule"? I suggest that the political system of sixth-century Megara was not so different from other sixth-century city-states at this time: a relatively small group of wealthy families managed public affairs through rotating public offices and a council.[123] It is of course possible that access to public office (including the Council) was extended during this time to a broader group of well-off citizens who were not among the traditional ruling elite, as apparently happened in Solonian Athens.[124] But even if we posit similar reforms at Megara, few scholars would call this political system a democracy.[125] Even in Eric Robinson's insightful analysis of the full range of ancient forms of democracy, Solonian Athens does not qualify as a democracy.[126]

That said, it is important not to underestimate the long-term consequences of the riotous action of the poor in archaic Megara (and Athens). Despite the general success of the *Palintokia* (*Seisachtheia*) in checking rebellion, the symbolic implications of the action of the poor could not be erased. The poor had demonstrated their ability to force the rich to act on their behalf, and gained stature and self-consciousness in the process. As Thompson has noted, it is only at this point in historical investigation into popular riots that really interesting questions get asked. That is, "granted that the primary stimulus of [economic] 'distress' is present, does their behavior [that is the behavior of the poor] contribute towards any more complex, culturally mediated function, which cannot be reduced ... back to stimulus once again?"[127] In the case of Megara, we may surmise, the efficacy of the ritualized forms of protest adopted by the poor was an expression of non-elite self-awareness of their collective identity and potential to influence the affairs of the community. To quote Thompson once again,

> While [the] moral economy [of the poor] cannot be described as
> "political" in any advanced sense, nevertheless it cannot be described
> as unpolitical either, since it supposed definite, and passionately
> held, notions of the common weal—notions which, indeed, found
> some support in the paternalist tradition of the authorities; notions
> which the people re-echoed so loudly in their turn that the authori-
> ties were, in some measure, the prisoners of the people.[128]

Though the political consciousness of the Megarian poor is a long
shot from democracy, we must recognize that this kind of collective self-
awareness was an essential pre-condition for the creation of more egalitarian forms of political organization. While we can be relatively certain
that the main features of a democratic government were instituted in
Athens in 508/7 BCE, we are less certain of the institutional trajectory of
the Megarian political system. Some scholars posit the existence of a democratic regime in Megara c. 427–424 BCE on the basis of the historian
Thucydides' references to a group of exiles banished by the masses (*to
plēthos*) at this time.[129] An ostrakon discovered in Megara may reflect the
existence of a democracy, but as I have argued elsewhere, need not necessarily do so.[130] In general, the sources suggest that Megara remained oligarchic for much of the fifth and fourth centuries.[131] If so, the success of
the *Palintokia*—and most likely other unpreserved legislation—in fending
off "democratic" political revolution in Megara is remarkable.

Conclusion

I have argued that the anecdotes of social disorder reported in Plutarch
reflect the escalation of ritual forms of revelry into riot and protest. I suggested that although the Megarian poor made skillful use of cultural
forms to express discontent, they were prompted to act neither by the
desire for nor the realization of a democracy. Indeed, the poor were concerned to assert a patriarchal relation between rich and poor in the face
of rapid social and economic change, not to overturn it. Finally, I argued
that the "Return of Interest" legislation (*Palintokia*) provided temporary
economic relief, and was designed to preserve the power of the elite in
response to potentially destabilizing discontent by the lower orders of
society. Though this measure was successful in preventing more serious
revolution, the long-term implications of popular protest for non-elite
political self-consciousness were important preconditions for the later
development of more egalitarian forms of political organization in particular places in later Greek history.

In conclusion, I would like to pose an additional answer to a more
general theoretical question of why subordinate groups use ritual forms

to express discontent with the status quo. Indeed, the lengths to which the poor went to borrow from ritual forms in engaging in protest strikes the modern mind as an extraordinary and unnecessary expenditure of effort.[132] Scholars have adduced numerous plausible reasons for the use of ritual, including the lack of availability of formal mechanisms for protest, the role of rituals of reversal in providing occasions and models for the expression of discontent, and the importance of the socially sanctioned license to criticize authorities in facilitating popular protest.

There are, I believe, several additional reasons for the frequency of ritual forms of protest in the pre-modern world. First and most obviously, the practices of ritual were useful as an organizing principle for the masses. By borrowing from traditional cultural forms of revelry, the crowd of protesters were able to coordinate their actions and speech in a way which otherwise was not possible without elaborate preparation—an impossibility among groups which must earn a living through constant toil. Second, the use of ritual forms lent a certain symbolic clarity to the protests. Ritual forms of hospitality between rich and poor, for example, were ideal mechanisms for signaling discontent with changes in the reciprocal relations between these two classes. By engaging in symbolic forms of ritual reversal, moreover, the rich were made to understand that an extreme consequence of their inaction would be violent uprising and the overturning of their superior position in the community.

Perhaps even more important than the symbolic clarity of ritual protest was the restraint that the language of ritual imposed on the actions of rioters. By articulating their protest at least in part through symbolic forms, the rioters actually refrained from more widespread and disruptive forms of protest. Although many of the examples surveyed above do involve violent actions, the relatively limited level of destruction is striking. These limitations were important for the poor, who, after all, might suffer most from the disruptive effects of widespread violence. The rich also benefited from the restraint imposed by ritual, since they were spared the potentially devastating effects of rampant violence against their property, but still gained a powerful warning to uphold their side of the "social contract." It was a warning which they readily heeded.[133]

Finally, I would like to offer a few thoughts on what the case of ancient Megara can offer to models of peasant protest in historical scholarship generally. E. P. Thompson and James Scott have produced studies of peasant protest and resistance in eighteenth-century England and contemporary Malaysia respectively. Crucial to the work of both scholars is the idea that specific changes in economic relations between rich and poor in each historical period were the material causes of peasant resistance and rebellion. The case of ancient Megara provides further support for this claim, yet it also provides an historical example very remote in time from the momentous changes set into motion by the Industrial Revolution in nineteenth-century Europe or the Green Revolution in South East Asia in the twentieth century.

Against this deep historical backdrop, it becomes particularly clear that the drive of the rich to increase their profits and of the poor to secure their well-being was an ongoing process that was more or less a continuous feature of social life in pre-modern agrarian societies. While there may have been periods of relative tranquility and, conversely, times of violent strife, there was never a time when the poor could rely on the rich to live up to the obligations of the "moral economy" without a struggle. What I have tried to demonstrate in this chapter is that cultural mechanisms such as festival revelry played a crucial role in regulating relations between rich and poor, and that although legislation was sometimes a result, it was not the formal political and legal institutions but informal social practices that were the primary "weapons of the weak" in archaic Greece.[134] Popular culture, moreover, continued to play a crucial role in the regulation of the social order in classical Greece, as I show in the next chapter. In what follows, we will see how popular practices existed alongside (and sometimes within) the formal institutions of the classical city-state and were an equally vital arena for politics as the political assembly and the law courts.

5

Street Theater and Popular Justice in Ancient Greece

IN HIS ESSAY, *Greek Questions*, Plutarch records that the people of Aeolian Cyme addressed women caught in adultery as "donkey-riders."[1] This moniker was applied, Plutarch tells us, because the people of Cyme paraded these women around the city mounted on a donkey, after first making them stand on display on a stone in the public marketplace for all to see. According to a fragment of Aristotle, the people of Lepreum in the Peloponnesus bound adulterers and led them around the city for three days.[2] Adulteresses at Lepreum were made to stand in the marketplace for eleven days in a transparent tunic with no belt.[3] According to Nicolaus of Damascus, adulterers and adulteresses in the region of Pisidia were mounted together on a donkey and paraded around the city for a fixed number of days.[4]

It might seem easy to dismiss these episodes as bizarre practices representative of less advanced Greek city-states or regions lacking the benefits of Greek civilization. Indeed, since such practices are not attested in classical Athens, previous generations of scholars of Greek law tended to see popular rituals of public humiliation as characteristic of a pre-law stage of development before the advent of the formal judicial structures of the state.[5] More recent scholarship, both in classical studies and anthropology, has shown that there is no predictable linear development from informal popular practices to formal state institutions, and that in fact the two systems of social organization and control tend to develop and exist alongside one another.[6] For example, the anthropologist Julian Pitt-Rivers, in his classic 1954 study of the people of a town in Andalusia in southern Spain, concluded that

> [o]ne personality may stand closer to the sanctions of the law than those of the community or vice versa, but every member of the pueblo participates to a lesser or greater extent both in the formal but also in the infra-structure.[7]

Pitt-Rivers provides several examples of the coexistence of popular and formal institutions. For instance, members of the pueblo have both formal names used in official state contexts and nicknames used in everyday informal interaction. Similarly, the services of state-trained medical practitioners are utilized alongside those of *sabias* or "wise women," who were thought to possess supernatural powers. Moreover, formal laws against adultery coexist with popular practices such as the *cencerrada* ("the ringing of the cow-bells") or the *vito*, a mocking, satirical, and frequently obscene traditional song and dance designed to humiliate persons guilty of flagrant breaches of social norms.

Mikhail Bakhtin, in his brilliant analysis of the folk traditions that inspired Rabelais, has similarly observed that the popular culture of the Middle Ages constituted a "second world and a second life outside officialdom ... in which all medieval persons participated more or less."[8] Significantly, Bakhtin equates this "second life" with popular festivity and in particular the social rituals surrounding Carnival: "The men of the Middle Ages participated in two lives: the official and the carnival life. Two aspects of the world, the serious and the laughing aspect, coexisted in their consciousness."[9]

In this chapter, I build on recent work that shows that informal social practices continued to play a vital role in the regulation of the social order in classical Greece.[10] While some scholars have recognized the importance of informal social mechanisms like gossip in the regulation of the social order, others continue to privilege institutions in their analysis of the classical Greek city-state.[11] Such underestimation of the role of popular culture is in part a natural consequence of the nature of our sources, which mostly take for granted the operation of informal collective practices in the regulation of social life. By gathering disparate anecdotes and interpreting them in light of comparative evidence, however, one can recover considerable evidence for extra-legal collective action against social offenders.[12]

In this chapter, I argue that not only was popular justice frequently used alongside more "official" forms of punishment, but that the Greeks made much more flexible use of the various modes of social control than is recognized by modern scholarship emphasizing the "rule of law" in the Greek city-state.[13] My study of popular justice shows that the classical Athenians (for example) showed no hesitation in punishing particular offenders through informal, yet highly public, forms of popular justice. Moreover, I demonstrate that even the "formal" institutions of the Athenian democracy incorporated various forms of popular justice within the "official" frame. Indeed, one of the major conclusions of this chapter is that the boundary between civic institutions and popular culture was much more fuzzy than currently recognized, and indeed that the categories "formal" and "informal" or "official" and "popular" are highly misleading when applied to classical Athens.

A second major aim of this chapter is to demonstrate that methods of popular justice were not simply a practical means of punishing offenders against social norms. Rather, they were crucial contexts for the symbolic interaction of elites and masses.[14] As Josiah Ober has shown, the democratic law courts of classical Athens not only served to resolve conflicts and reach just verdicts but were also arenas for symbolic communication between elite litigants and mass juries.[15] I demonstrate that episodes of "popular" justice reveal many of the same structural and symbolic features as the "formal" law courts. In particular, careful consideration of the evidence shows that "informal" collective justice in ancient Greece often targeted elite offenders. This fact suggests that rituals of popular justice were not only concerned with specific criminal offenses but also with *relations of power*.

I argue that the masses, including ordinary farmers and craftsmen, used rituals of popular justice to make highly public symbolic statements about their role in the community. On such occasions, the masses reminded the powerful of their shortcomings and thereby reduced the elite symbolically to their own level, or even reversed their positions. The masses now upheld the norms of the community while the powerful were shown to have transgressed them. In this sense, informal collective justice enacted a reversal of the social hierarchy just like the rituals of hospitality and popular festivity discussed in the previous chapter. Like those rituals, and like the theme of reversal in the folktales and fables examined in chapters 2 and 3, episodes of popular justice were an important mechanism for ordinary citizens, as well as women and even slaves, to assert their power. As in the earlier discussion of rituals of hospitality, moreover, I suggest that, by utilizing forms of popular festivity, the masses were not only able to coordinate their action and its symbolism effectively, but gained additional legitimacy and license for punishing the powerful.[16]

This chapter will examine three types of popular justice in particular: public shaming, the razing of houses, and stoning. In each case, we will see that, in addition to being highly public communal events, these punishments operated alongside, within, and sometimes in opposition to the formal institutions of the Greek city-state.

Street Theater and Adultery: Ritualized Public Humiliation

In contrast to the institutional perspective of some modern scholars of Greek law, David Cohen emphasizes the dynamic interplay between formal laws and informal social mechanisms (for example, gossip) in articulating sexual norms and controlling sexuality in classical Athens.[17] Yet despite this perspective, Cohen does not emphasize that even in classical Athens, collective rituals of public humiliation—both in the courts and outside them—were the primary means of punishing adulterers and affirming social norms.[18] Indeed, Cohen has cast doubt on the historicity of our sources for ritualized public humiliation of adulterers.[19] In response, others have argued convincingly that the fact that comic plays are our principal source for this sort of public humiliation does not diminish the probability that it occurred.[20] On the contrary, since brief comic allusions were enough to evoke these modes of popular justice for the average Athenian theater audience, they were undoubtedly well known and widely practiced.

Unfortunately, those scholars who accept the validity of our evidence for public humiliation of adulterers either conceptualize these practices solely as formal legal penalties or consider them to be individual rather than collective practices.[21] By contrast, I will argue that the public humiliation of adulterers in Athens (and elsewhere in Greece) was not only primarily an extra-legal practice but one that was performed in the presence of and with the active participation of the community at large. As we shall see, both ancient and comparative evidence shows that men and women, adults and children—and perhaps even non-citizens and slaves—took part in these rituals.

The importance of "informal" collective modes of punishing adulterers is partly confirmed by the fact that what survives of the "formal" laws relating to adultery deal primarily with resolving disputes over whether the informal practices were properly followed, rather than with meting out punishment for the offense itself.[22] As long as the treatment of the adulterer fell within certain generally accepted practices, however, cases of adultery probably rarely reached the courts.[23] It is important to emphasize, therefore, that although our knowledge of popular practices often derives from legal provisions, we must not assume that formal legal procedures were the primary route for dealing with such offenses. Indeed, while public humiliation of adulterers was apparently included among the penalties imposed by the law courts in certain circumstances, this is an example of the overlap between institutional and popular justice, as we shall see, not evidence that formal law suppressed popular justice and that ritual humiliation could only take place through institutional channels, as some have assumed.[24]

With this proviso in mind, we can now examine the formal laws for what they tell us about the extra-legal treatment of adulterers. Modern scholars generally agree that while the law allowed that adulterers caught in the act could be killed with impunity, the right to exact this extreme penalty was seldom exercised.[25] The more usual practice was that adulterers were apprehended by the offended husband, publicly subjected to abuse, and ransomed.[26] Indeed, the public abuse and ransoming of adulterers seems to go back to Homeric times (the eighth century BCE). In the song of Demodocus in Book 8 of the *Odyssey*, the god Ares is physically bound, made an object of ridicule, and required to pay compensation for his adulterous affair with the goddess Aphrodite.[27] In this case, the lovers are trapped *in flagrante delicto* by an invisible cage devised by the offended husband, Hephaistos. The god of fire then calls upon the other Olympian gods to witness the outrage to his bed and marriage.[28] The gods gather in the forecourt of Hephaistos' house and laugh at Ares' predicament:

> Unquenchable laughter arose among the immortal gods
> As they looked upon the device of clever Hephaistos.
> And they were saying to the one next to them as they looked,
> "Evil deeds do not prosper. Indeed, the slow one has surpassed the quick,
> since Hephaistos, who is slow and lame, has caught with his craft, Ares,
> who is the swiftest of the Gods who dwell on Olympus.
> And he owes compensation for adultery (*moichagria*)."[29]

We will return at the end of the chapter to the ideological significance of the theme of the mighty Ares brought low by the lame blacksmith Hephaistos. The important point now is that Ares and Aphrodite are put on display with their hands and feet trapped by Hephaistos' unbreakable bonds (*desmous arrektous*). Although this form of punishment is well suited to the skills of the divine master craftsman, the public display of criminals with their heads, hands, and feet bound in the stocks is attested for historical Athens.[30] According to Demosthenes, an early Athenian law on theft, mistreatment of parents, and draft dodging, allowed that convicted offenders not only be fined, but also bound up in stocks for five days and five nights.[31] As Demosthenes explains:

> The lawgiver imposed being bound in the stocks in addition to the fine in order that all might see [the convicted criminal] bound up (*dedemenon*) ... for the lawgiver thought that the one who had done such shameful deeds ought to live in shame for the rest of his life (*en aischunēi zein ... ton allon bion*), since he had been bound in the stocks in addition to this fine (*dethenta de pros toutōi tōi timēmati*).[32]

It is noteworthy that Demosthenes explicitly observes that being held in the stocks entails public shaming, and that this punishment is imposed in addition to the monetary fine.[33] Moreover, the public humiliation of a

bound criminal requires community participation over a period of time—
according to Demosthenes, for the rest of the criminal's life!—and takes
place outside the confines of a formal institutional structure. The penalty
therefore incorporates a form of popular justice along with a formal penalty (a monetary fine paid to the public treasury). This is the first example
of many in which "formal" legal procedures and "informal" collective
sanctions operate side-by-side as modes of punishing offenders against
social norms.

The more important point for our present purposes is that the law on
theft shows that public display in the stocks as an object of ridicule is
attested in classical Athens and therefore that similar types of punishment
could have been used against adulterers, as the Homeric example suggests.
Indeed, a variation on this practice is attested for historical Lepreum, as
we saw at the beginning of this chapter. There, bound (*dedemenous*) adulterers were led around the city for three days, presumably on a cart or
donkey, or walking with only their hands bound.

The public witnessing of bound offenders, however, was only one of a
variety of modes of public humiliation attested in the ancient sources.
Indeed, in classical Athens, the laws allowed someone who had apprehended an adulterer to "use [the adulterer] in whatever way he wishes,"
specifying only that the victim be neither maimed nor killed in the process.[34] Despite the apparent open-endedness of the law in regard to the
treatment of the adulterer, comic sources suggest that the abuse of adulterers often fell into certain customary forms, as I shall discuss shortly.
What needs stressing at the moment is that these customary rituals of
humiliation—in order to be effective—must have taken place in public
before an onlooking and verbally or physically participating crowd.[35] As
E. P. Thompson writes in his study of popular justice in eighteenth-century
England: "Until the nineteenth century, publicity was the essence of the
punishment. It was intended ... to humiliate the offender before his or her
neighbors."[36]

The very public nature of the rituals cited at the beginning of the chapter is obvious. In each case, the offenders were paraded around the city,
sometimes for several days.[37] We must imagine a jeering crowd lining the
streets of the city as the procession passed. Perhaps it was on this occasion,
in particular, that spectators in Cyme addressed adulteresses as "donkey
riders," and we can easily imagine other terms of abuse being hurled at
the offenders.[38] Representations of similar rituals in Early Modern Europe
provide some indication of the potential for widespread participation by
men, women, and children (fig. 9).[39] Indeed, as in other popular rituals
such as Carnival, in forms of popular justice "there was no sharp distinction between actors and spectators."[40] I shall argue later in the chapter that

Figure 9.
Dr Syntax with the Skimmerton Riders. Thomas Rowlandson's illustration
to William Coombe's *The Tour of Dr Syntax*, 1813. In this popular ritual, a
hen-pecked husband and his wife are ridiculed by being mounted together on
a donkey and paraded through the town. Note the prominence of women and
children both in the procession itself and in the crowd lining the streets.

popular justice in ancient Greece shared features with popular festivity,
including not only widespread crowd participation, but also processions,
verbal abuse, and a reversal of roles between the powerful and the lowly.[41]

The potential for active crowd participation in rituals of popular justice in ancient Greece is evident from several of the examples of the treatment of adulterers described at the beginning of the chapter. In addition
to being paraded through the streets of the city, at Cyme and Lepreum
offenders were made to stand, sometimes for many days, in the central
public space of the city, the marketplace (*agora*). As the legal, political,
commercial heart of the ancient city, the *agora* was the most frequented
public place in the whole city. Citizens from all walks of life came to the
agora to buy and sell, read public notices, gossip, serve on juries, get a
shave or haircut, serve on the council and as magistrates, worship the gods,
get news about the latest events, and so on. In short, almost everything to
do with life in the polis took place in the *agora*.[42] As Demosthenes says of
the ordinary Athenian citizen: "Each one of you frequents the *agora* for
public or private business."[43]

It was not just male citizens, however, who frequented the *agora*. As David Cohen has persuasively argued, most Athenian women were not confined to their homes, despite the frequent articulation of this ideal in literary sources.[44] In addition to their participation in religious rituals and other social rites, many women worked in the fields alongside their husbands and even sold products of their labor in the marketplace.[45] In comedy and other literary sources, women are represented selling wool, bread, vegetables, garlands, ribbons, and perfume in the *agora*. We must imagine, therefore, that Athenian women were important witnesses to rituals of public humiliation, and possibly even played an active role in the shaming of an adulterer in the same way as women at Sparta are represented in our sources as reinforcing social norms among the men.[46]

Slaves were also present in the streets and marketplaces of Athens, and would therefore also have been potential witnesses and participants in rituals of social shaming of adulterers. Greek comedy and oratory depicts household slaves running errands both between houses and in the public spaces of the city, most importantly, the *agora*.[47] Publicly owned slaves, such as the ones employed to test coinage, worked in the marketplace in the city and the Piraeus, as did banking slaves and slaves working in workshops and shops.[48] Many of these slaves operated independently, some even living separately and paying over a portion of their income to their masters.[49] Slaves were so ubiquitous in the public spaces of the city, and sometimes so difficult to distinguish from Athenian citizens, that, as we saw in chapter 1, certain disgruntled Athenians were inclined to grumble that the arrogance of slaves was becoming intolerable.[50] Even accounting for the exaggeration and hostility of these writers to the Athenian democracy, it is clear that slaves in Athens were a prominent part of the civic landscape, and that they moved about the streets and marketplaces of the city with considerable freedom. Citizens, women, and slaves, we must conclude, would therefore all have been witnesses to rituals of public humiliation.

The choice of the *agora* as the place for display of adulteresses, then, corresponds well with the aim of this ritual to humiliate the offender publicly and expose her to the violence of the crowd.[51] It is not surprising, moreover, given the bustle of this busy place, that adulteresses at Cyme were required to stand on an elevated stone. In this way, they were "visible to all" (*emphanē pasi*). In other places, length of exposure—up to eleven days at Lepreum—presumably served the same function of ensuring that the adulteresses were put on display before the widest possible audience.[52]

In Athens, the public character of ritual humiliation is less obvious but implicit in many sources. In a law against the unjust apprehension of a person as an adulterer, for example, a provision allows that if the man filing a suit for unjust apprehension actually proves to be an adulterer, he may be abused, without a knife, *in the presence of the court*:

> If [the one filing suit for unjust apprehension as an adulterer] is judged to be an adulterer, the law orders him to hand over sureties to the one who convicts him, and *in the presence of the court*, the [offended husband] may use (*chresthai*) [the adulterer] however he wishes without a knife, on the grounds that he is an adulterer. (Dem. 59.66)

In the rather peculiar (but apparently not uncommon) situation of a failed suit for unjust seizure as an adulterer, Athenian law allows for both the payment of a fine and public humiliation. Like the law on theft discussed above, this law incorporates a formal penalty (fine) and a mode of popular justice (ritualized public humiliation). The overlap between institutional and popular justice is especially clear in this example, since the mass jury in an Athenian court roughly parallels the crowd of participants in informal collective rituals of justice.[53] We must observe, moreover, that the participants in this striking instance of popular justice within the courts would have included not only the jurors proper, but also the potentially even larger crowd of bystanders who stood outside the fenced off area of the courts and watched the proceedings.[54] This crowd could have included citizen men, women, and children, free non-citizen residents, and even slaves. As we have seen, all of these groups frequented the *agora* where the courts were located and might be attracted by the prospect of the spectacle of public humiliation of an adulterer.[55] We know from numerous sources that Athenian popular juries—and bystanders—could be very vocal about expressing their approval or disapproval during a trial.[56] It is likely, similarly, that in the context of a failed attempt to claim that one had been unjustly apprehended as an adulterer, both official jurors and informal spectators participated in the humiliation of the offender by hurling verbal abuse at him. The interconnections and interchangeability between official and popular forms of justice in classical Athens can scarcely be better illustrated.

Yet Herodotus preserves an even more striking example of joint participation in an instance of popular justice by the members of an official body and a crowd of bystanders. In 479 BCE, toward the end of the Greco-Persian wars, a member of the Athenian Council named Lycides suggested that the Athenians entertain a proposal of surrender from the Persians. In response,

> The Athenians—both those inside the Council House and those outside (*hoi te ek tes boules kai hoi exothen*) immediately became outraged and, surrounding Lycides, they stoned him to death.[57]

Herodotus' account suggests spontaneous joint collective action against Lycides both by members of the Council and bystanders. It is perhaps significant, moreover, that Herodotus employs the same term used of heckling in the courts and other civic contexts to describe the noise that attended Lycides' stoning: "A commotion (*thorubos*) arose ... around the person of Lycides."[58] Herodotus' use of this term indicates that he viewed the collective uproar against Lycides as conceptually analogous to collective verbal ridiculing of speakers in civic contexts, another indication of the overlap between "formal" and "informal" justice.

As we have seen, Athenian law granted the offended husband very wide latitude in devising forms of public humiliation for the adulterer: he may treat him however he likes without a knife. Commentators have generally assumed that the prohibition against using a knife prevents permanent disabling or death, as the provisions for the treatment of adulteresses in Athens seem to confirm (see below).[59] Notwithstanding this restriction, we can imagine a very wide range of symbolic rituals of public humiliation. Some of these rituals may have been similar to those attested for Cymae, Lepreum, and Pisidia mentioned earlier. Others are alluded to in comedy and elsewhere and may be fleshed out through imaginative historical reconstruction. Such reconstruction is necessary because the public and extra-judicial nature of these rituals is insufficiently emphasized by scholars viewing classical Athens from a strictly legal perspective.[60]

In his comedy *Clouds*, Aristophanes mentions two forms of ritual abuse of adulterers. The context is a parody of the clever arguments devised by contemporary rhetoricians. Aristophanes satirically suggests, through his character "Wrong Argument," that an adulterer should defend himself by noting that even Zeus was defeated by desire, and therefore he, the adulterer, a mere mortal, cannot be expected to be stronger than a god. In response, Wrong Argument's opponent, "Better Argument," asks: "But what if [the adulterer], trusting you, has a radish stuffed up his ass or has his pubic hair plucked out with hot ash?" (1083). In the first form of abuse, referred to in modern scholarship as "radishing," a large vegetable (the ancient radish was much larger than its modern namesake), or sometimes a spiny fish, was forced into the anus of the adulterer (fig. 10).[61] Most scholars agree that, while this treatment was obviously painful, it was primarily aimed at humiliating the adulterer by assimilating him to the passive partner of a sexual relationship, thereby giving him an inferior, female role.[62] Similarly, the subjection of the adulterer to genital depilation put him symbolically in the position of a woman, since the plucking of pubic hair was a common feature of female personal grooming.[63]

Indeed, the symbolic representation of men as women was a common form of ridicule in ancient Greece, used not only in the treatment of adulterers, but also in the humiliation of cowards.[64] As Pauline Schmitt-Pantel

Figure 10.
Spiny Fish and Radish (from J. Roy, "Traditional jokes about the punishment of adulterers in ancient Greek literature," *Liverpool Classical Monthly* 1991: 76).

has noted, according to Aelian, adulterers in the city-state of Gortyn were crowned with wool as a mark that they were "unmanly" (*anandros*) and "womanish" (*gunnis*).[65] Similarly, in the laws of Charondas of Catana, cowards were made to sit in the *agora* for three days in woman's dress.[66] More broadly speaking, military cowardice is often associated with women (and conversely bravery with men), as the very etymology of the words for courage (*andreia*, "manliness") and cowardice (*anandria*, "lack of manliness") suggests.[67]

It is noteworthy that the ritual humiliation of adulterers with vegetables and hot ash left no permanent outward marks on them.[68] As we have seen, in fact, several laws affirm that permanently disabling an adulterer or adulteress was not permissible, thereby attesting to the primarily symbolic nature of the punishment. In the absence of lasting physical signs of their apprehension as adulterers, moreover, public witnessing of these rituals must have been crucial to the effectiveness of this form of humiliation.[69] It is likely, therefore, that this form of abuse was conducted in the street or even in the *agora* before a crowd of jeering spectators. Even if the adulterer was caught in the act in the house of the offended husband, he might have been hauled out into the street or dragged to the *agora* (probably naked) before being subjected to ritual abuse.[70]

This reconstruction highlights another possible overlap between the extra-legal treatment of an adulterer and "official" justice: the legal procedure of *apagōgē* ("conducting away") allowed ordinary Athenians to seize certain types of criminals (*kakourgoi*, "evildoers") and bring them before a magistrate. According to Virginia Hunter's reconstruction of the official procedure, "one presumed guilty or caught in flagrante was seized in the street, perhaps surrounded by neighbors and demesmen [residents of the same district] ... There followed a parade to the office of the Eleven through the streets of Athens and probably across the Agora. This kind of violent seizure was meant to be deeply humiliating to the arrested."[71] Hunter's view of this procedure as a "parade" and her emphasis on public humiliation among a crowd of bystanders again points to the blurred lines between "formal" and "informal" justice.

The knowledge that a person had been subject to a form of popular justice must have circulated widely and was possibly remembered by addressing the offender as "the wide-assed one" (*ho eurupr\u014dktos*), or "woman" (*gun\u0113*), much as adulterous women at Cyme were addressed as "donkey-riders." The habitual labeling of social offenders is attested at Sparta, where a man thought to be cowardly was cut off from all normal social interaction and was called "The Trembler" (*ho tresas*).[72] Comparable labeling of adulterers in Athens is perhaps implied in Right Argument's question in the *Clouds*: "What argument [will the adulterer] be able to make that he is not 'wide-assed' (*eurupr\u014dktos*)?"

It is also possible, however, that some rituals of humiliation resulted in the creation of outward marks that identified the adulterer at least for a period of time. A few lines in Aristophanes' comedy *Acharnians* have led some scholars to posit that adulterers could have their head shaved, thus marking them publicly as adulterers at least until their hair grew in (849):

> nor does Kratinos, who is always shaved with one blade adulterer-style, approach you in the agora.[73]

Similar lengthy periods of public humiliation are attested elsewhere. Most strikingly, at Lepreum adulterers were ritually humiliated for three days, and adulteresses for *eleven days*. In early modern England, ritual humiliation or "rough music" could go on for days.[74]

The evidence for the treatment of adulteresses in ancient Athens is relatively clear and well known. Yet it is worth expanding on the features that align these practices with popular justice. The law dictates that the husband must divorce his wife, and that she must not attend public sacrifices or wear ornamentation.[75] Once again formal law here probably borrows from popular practices, and certainly ones that had to be enforced through extra-legal communal actions.[76] As is well-recognized, the barring of the adulteress from the most important public events open to women was a form of symbolic disenfranchisement, and the ban on adornment also set her apart in a public and visible way from other citizen women. If the adulteress ignored these prohibitions, moreover, the law allowed her to be symbolically stripped naked: her outer cloak (*himation*) could be torn off, leaving her in only her tunic (*chiton*). With this treatment, we may compare the display of adulteresses at Lepreum who were made to stand in the *agora* for eleven days in a transparent tunic with no belt.[77] Similarly, cowards and celibate men at Sparta were made to walk around the *agora* naked in winter.[78] In each case, informal collective viewing and mockery would be required to achieve the aim of public humiliation.

Some laws go so far as to encourage the active participation of the bystander in the humiliation of the adulteress. For example, adulteresses who refused to refrain from public life or personal ornamentation could be physically abused, short of any permanent disabling or death. This last provision puts the adulteress on a par with the adulterer since both are subject to symbolic physical abuse (a form of *hubris*) that diminished their honor.[79] The sources make clear, moreover, that both the ritual stripping and physical abuse of adulteresses took place in the street or in public places: whoever encounters her may do what he wishes without penalty. While Aeschines' version of the law suggests that males would have been the ones inflicting these penalties (as is clear from the masculine article and participle, *ton entuchonta*: "the man who encounters her"), Demosthenes' version is more open-ended: "Let the adulteress suffer whatever she suffers." We should imagine that women might also participate in the ritual abuse of adulteresses, particularly since women attended and played important roles in public religious life and therefore might be expected to be present when a known adulteress tried to enter a public temple or attend a sacrifice.[80] It is noteworthy in this regard that in eighteenth-century accounts and illustrations of rituals of popular justice, women often play a prominent role (fig. 9).[81] Indeed, in Early Modern Europe, women were sometimes disproportionately represented among the participants in popular revelry because of the relative immunity they were allowed due to their gender.[82]

A striking example of the participation of women in popular justice in ancient Greece is the stoning of Lycides in 479 BCE. As we have seen, Lycides was stoned by his fellow councilors and the crowd outside the council house for his suggestion that the Athenians submit to Persia. In addition, Herodotus tells us that the Athenian women, when they heard what had happened to Lycides, went on their own accord to the house of Lycides and stoned both his wife and their children:

> When a commotion arose in Salamis around the person of Lycides, the women learned what was happening. Of their own accord, the women, encouraging one another and taking one another as partners in the enterprise, went to the house of Lycides and stoned both his wife and his children.[83]

This episode illustrates not only the role of women in rituals of popular justice, but also the extra-legal and collective nature of such rituals.[84] The women learned of the stoning of Lycides through informal channels (the shouting crowd) and responded instantaneously and collectively. They gathered and coordinated their action through word of mouth, and their behavior replicated, in the manner of ritual, the actions of the men.[85]

Modern horror at this ghastly violence against an innocent woman and her children prevents us from recognizing the relative restraint of both men and women in this episode. Despite what elite critics say about such episodes, they do not represent random "mob violence."[86] Rituals of popular justice follow established forms and tend to target particular individuals. They do not involve widespread violence and destruction. As E. P. Thompson writes, such rituals "not only give expression to a conflict within a community, [they] also regulated that conflict within forms which established limits and imposed restraints."[87] In the next section, I shall further explore the importance of the first part of Thompson's statement, namely the ways that the masses use ritual forms of popular justice to give "expression to a conflict within a community."

Popular Justice and Politics: Mass versus Elite

So far I have argued—through the example of adultery—that rituals of popular justice not only were practiced alongside and within the formal institutions of the state but that they played an important role in the articulation of social norms and the control of social deviation, even in relatively complex states like classical Athens. In the next section, I turn to my second argument, namely that such rituals were crucial mechanisms for the negotiation of relations between mass and elite in many Greek communities.

Three factors are important to my argument. First, comparative evidence suggests that not every social infraction in pre-modern societies was punished through rituals of popular justice. Rather, prominent or powerful figures were particularly targeted. Although it is likely that episodes involving elite offenders are overrepresented in our sources for ancient Greek popular justice, it is nevertheless significant that the ancient evidence reveals that elites were in fact targets of this form of social regulation.[88] Third, rituals of popular justice not only display an inversion of roles between elites and masses similar to that common in other social rituals, but also share specific practices with other collective rituals. In particular, parades on donkeys, verbal abuse, obscenity, and the hurling of objects were common both to rituals of popular justice and occasions of popular festivity. These facts taken together suggest that popular justice, like other social rituals, sometimes served as a context for the symbolic disciplining of the elite by the masses and the assertion of non-elite control over the moral and political boundaries of the community.

In his study of eighteenth-century English forms of popular justice, Thompson argues that not every instance of social transgression was punished through collective rituals of informal justice.[89]

> Because certain adulterers were rough musicked, it cannot be assumed that we are observing a community of pagan puritans, for whom marital fidelity was an imperative ... On the contrary, I suspect that each occasion when adulterers and similar offenders were subjected to rough music had a known history; that more evidence would lead us to particular aggravations of an offence, which, in other cases, might pass unnoticed—or noticed only by gossip.[90]

Thompson suggests that "[t]he decisive factor may be whether offenders are already unpopular for other reasons" and goes on to observe that among the many causes of dislike, the following were prominent: "disapproval of a magisterial decision ... an officious or severe prosecution ... tithe collection ... the overzealous extending of fishing rights by landlords, enclosure ... in short, any person riding rough-shod over local custom."[91]

A similar argument can be made about forms of popular justice in ancient Greece, namely that they were used selectively to express and negotiate tensions between elites and masses. I will first discuss two prominent forms of popular justice—house-razing and stoning—in this light, and then turn back to the evidence for ritualized humiliation of adulterers.

In his important article, W. R. Connor discusses the evidence for the ritual destruction (*kataskaphē*) of houses in ancient Greece.[92] In addition to numerous references to this practice in Greek tragedy, there are eleven instances (in sources of varying historical reliability) of its use in ancient Greece. Connor notes that the evidence he gathers "is likely to represent only a small portion of the instances of this punishment in antiquity."[93] While Connor is mainly concerned with the symbolic significance of ritual destruction in relation to notions of the household and pollution, he does observe that at least four of his eleven cases imply that the action was undertaken "without formal legal sanction."[94] Furthermore, in drawing attention to the use of the term *kataskaphē* to describe destructions of city walls, and even whole cities, Connor suggests that "we should be cautious ... about assuming that *kataskaphē* was regularly a cut and dried legal procedure, carried out without emotion and ceremony by a government official or board."[95] Citing the example of the destruction of Athens' city walls after its defeat in the Peloponnesian War, he notes that according to our sources, this destruction took the form of an informal collective festival, complete with "flutes, prostitutes and revelry and the shared joy at the extirpation of the offender."[96]

Connor's incidental comments can be taken much further to show that the razing of houses was primarily a form of popular justice, despite its occasional incorporation in formal law. Furthermore, this form of popular justice was often enacted against elite offenders (particularly, tyrants, traitors, and military commanders thought guilty of misconduct). Ritual destruction of houses therefore constitutes one of the best examples, along with stoning, of the role of popular justice as a symbolic medium for mass-elite interaction.

Our sources reveal much by their failure to be specific about whether house-razing was a penalty imposed through formal legal channels. For example, the Athenian historian Thucydides reports that after the conclusion of a treaty between Sparta and Argos in 418 BCE, the Spartans blamed King Agis for failing to capture Argos when it would have been easy to do so. Moreover, when the Spartans heard that the city of Orchomenus had also been captured,

> they were even more aggrieved and straightaway out of anger and contrary to their character they resolved to raze [King Agis'] house and fine him ten thousand drachmae. He persuaded them not to do this, saying that he would remove the blame by some good deed on campaign. [If he did not do so], they could do with him what they wished. The Spartans abstained from imposing a fine and razing his house.[97]

Thucydides' description of the emotions of the Spartans, particularly their anger and the hastiness of their response, suggests that the Spartans' desire to impose these penalties was spontaneous, a product of their immediate collective emotions rather than a formal legal process.[98] Thucydides' claim that the Spartans acted "uncharacteristically," however, must be read against the idealizing view of Sparta popular among critics of Athenian democracy.[99] If we remove these critical overtones, it appears that the Spartans reacted to their perception of a failure of leadership with a plan to engage in a traditional form of popular justice: razing of the house.[100] Yet the addition of a monetary fine that would have been exacted through formal institutional channels (the magistrates known as Ephors) suggests that the Spartans, like the Athenians, did not consider spontaneous collective action incompatible with institutionalized justice.[101]

Comparison of this episode with a similar one that allegedly took place in Argos at the same time confirms that an initial response to perceived failures by Greek commanders could entail spontaneous, even violent, collective action.[102] According to Diodorus, the Argives were as angry with their commanders as the Spartans were with theirs.

Because [of their anger], the Argives undertook to kill their leaders by pelting them with stones. Only with difficulty and after much entreaty did [the Argives] agree to allow [the generals] to live. Nevertheless, [the Argives] confiscated their property and razed their houses. (12.78.5)

The Argives' initial desire to stone their leaders strongly suggests spontaneous ritualized collective action, typical of popular justice, as we have already seen in the case of Lycides. Moreover, Diodorus emphasizes the narrowness of the generals' escape from death. As in the case of Thucydides' Spartans, the commanders were spared as a result of emotional appeal (*deēsis*) rather than a formal defense (*apologia*). The final outcome in this instance, moreover, again combines two forms of punishment: the razing of the house and the confiscation of property. This duality, I suggest, illustrates not simply that modes of popular justice coexisted with formal justice in the ancient Greek state. Further examples will show that for certain types of offenses—particularly those involving an elite leader's betrayal of the collective interest—the impersonal exaction of formal penalties was insufficient to express collective anger against the offender. In these cases, outlets for the active communal punishment of the offender were needed.[103]

When the Spartan King Leotychides was caught red-handed sitting on a glove stuffed with silver while on campaign in Thessaly in the 470s, he was brought back for trial in Sparta. The charge was that he had accepted bribes rather than conquer Sparta's enemies. Herodotus reports that Leotychides was sentenced to exile *and* that his house was razed (6.72.2).[104] Similarly, in an Athenian decree of 411/10 BCE, the traitors Antiphon and Archeptolemus were not only sentenced to death and their property confiscated, but it was specified that their houses were to be razed, and that the convicted traitors be denied burial in lands controlled by the Athenians.[105]

The ban on burial in territory controlled by the Athenians is a typical penalty imposed on traitors and could be accompanied by the digging up and hurling of the body or bones of the traitor (and possibly his ancestors) over the borders of Attica.[106] This action, like that of razing of the house itself, would most likely be accomplished by a large group of citizenry, possibly in a festive mood, as they ritually removed all traces of the offender from their community.[107] By performing this ritual action, participants not only removed pollution, but created a visual spectacle that was enacted and witnessed by the entire community. Such forms of ritual expulsion—like ostracism and the annual expulsion of a scapegoat—were important occasions for collective participation in a ritual that defined the political and moral boundaries of the community.[108]

An account of the overthrow of the tyranny of the Cypselid family in Corinth in the mid-sixth century reflects how such collective rituals as razing the house and the hurling of bones across borders could play an important role in the articulation of the political unity and identity of a community.[109]

> Cypselus was tyrant of Corinth until some Corinthians, after form-ing a conspiracy, killed him and liberated the city. The people then razed the houses of the tyrants and confiscated their property and cast Cypselus, unburied, over their border. And they dug up the tombs of his ancestors and hurled the bones away. Then the people themselves immediately established the following constitution.[110]

In this passage, there is a clear distinction between the small group of conspirators who actually overthrew the tyrant and the ritual action of the people in symbolically expelling the tyrant from the community. Simi-larly, after Timoleon overthrew the tyranny of Dionysios II in Syracuse in 343/2, he invited the people to come and help destroy the defensive struc-tures of the tyrant. According to Plutarch, the people responded to their newfound freedom not only by participating in the ritual destruction of the fortifications associated with the tyrant, but also by razing the tyrants' houses and tombs:

> [Timoleon] made a proclamation that anyone who wished should come with iron tools and help with the destruction of the fortifica-tions of the tyrant. And when they all came, considering the decree and that day to be the surest beginning of their freedom, they over-turned and razed not only the citadel, but also the houses and tombs of the tyrants.[111]

This example of house destruction does not begin as a spontaneous pop-ular act, but rather in response to a formal decree. Nevertheless, what began as an invitation to destroy public buildings associated with the tyrant, became in the hands of the mass of Syracusans a ritualized collec-tive act of destruction of the private homes and tombs of the tyrant. The people took affairs into their own hands and imposed their own sort of justice on the fallen tyrant. It is as if the people themselves needed to participate actively in extirpating tyranny from their community in order to constitute themselves politically. Moreover, Timoleon leveled off the ground and built popular courts in place of the tyrant's buildings, thereby "gratifying the citizens and making democracy superior to tyranny."[112] In this case, the construction of popular courts on the ruins of the tyrants' buildings echoes the symbolic meaning of the collective act of destruc-tion, namely that the people not only were the rightful holders of supreme political power, but that they would actively punish any transgressions against their prerogative.[113]

This account of the participation of the masses in the overthrow of the Syracusan tyranny also hints at the sheer physical labor involved in razing the house.[114] Timoleon called on anyone who wished to participate, and apparently "all" (*pantes*) came. Moreover, they came equipped with iron implements, presumably because a great deal of force was required to tear down such buildings.[115] Connor notes that the word *kataskaphē* is etymologically related to the verb *skaptein*, "to dig," and that therefore "we should probably imagine the actual removal of some or all of the foundation of the house."[116] It is also likely that the house was set on fire as part of the ritual destruction.[117] In sum, it is clear that such ritual destructions were spectacular communal events in which elite transgressors against collective values (tyrants, traitors, and military commanders who failed in their duties) were symbolically exterminated.

In popular rituals of social control, the entire community acted collectively in a highly physical and visible way to punish an elite offender. Active collective participation increased the cohesion of the community, which engaged in an act of self-definition by punishing an "Other." Perhaps even more important, the gathering of the masses and their collective punishment of an elite offender sent a message to elites not only that transgression against the wider community would not be tolerated, but that the wider community itself, not the elites, were the ultimate power holders in the community.[118]

As James C. Scott has observed, the mere gathering of the masses affects elites and non-elites alike through visual spectacle and symbolism. Describing the reaction of high-caste observers of mass meetings of untouchables in the Punjab, Scott writes: "What was said was less important than the stunning show of force that the mere congregation of untouchables as untouchables had on all concerned. If untouchables could show such coordination, discipline, and collective strength, what prevented them from turning those skills to collective struggle against domination?" Of non-elites, Scott writes that they were "emboldened by the act of massing itself" because of the "visual impact of collective power," the anonymity and hence lessened risk, and finally the "collective exhilaration of ... declaring oneself in the face of power."[119]

In classical Athens, the "visual spectacle and symbolism" of mass action was certainly a factor within the formal legal system.[120] As already noted, in the popular law courts the masses rendered judgment on elite leaders and thereby expressed their control over the norms by which the community was ordered.[121] I suggest that this symbolism was even more powerful in the context of acts of popular justice, where the masses not only sat in judgment of elite offenders but actively participated in the execution of the penalty.[122] In classical Athens, and other democratic states like Argos, the formal law courts and—even more directly—informal practices of popular justice worked in tandem to negotiate collective values and articulate popular power. In non-democratic states, such as Sparta and Corinth, however, it was primarily through popular rituals that the masses asserted their control over the norms of the community and negotiated their relations with their leaders.

My argument about the symbolic and political nature of acts of popular justice against elites raises questions about a notorious event in Athenian political history, the trial and execution of the generals who won the battle of Arginusae in 406 BCE.[123] These generals won a great naval victory for the Athenians against Sparta, but, because they failed to rescue shipwrecked Athenians in the aftermath of the battle, they faced the ire of the Athenians when they returned to Athens. The generals argued that a storm had made it impossible to rescue the men. The Athenians, however, were unrelenting and, contrary to their laws, they sentenced the generals to death without a proper trial. Several features of this event suggest parallels with forms of popular justice. First, the Athenians acted passionately in response to their grief and anger over the massive loss of life. Their emotions were brought to a fever pitch, moreover, by a clever bit of political theater: the mourning relatives of the dead were presented at the assembly meeting, and a man who survived by floating in a meal tub claimed that he had been enjoined by those who had not survived to report the failure of the generals to the people. On hearing this testimony, the crowd (*ochlos*) shouted down (*eboa, ethorubēse*) the proposals of a few to follow due process in granting each general an individual trial.

Despite the representation of the mass of Athenians acting as an unrestrained mob (and we must note that our source, Xenophon, is no friend of popular rule), this event is to be distinguished from forms of popular justice. First, the events took place in a formal political context, namely, several successive assembly meetings. Moreover, despite some unrestrained voicing of popular sentiment, the assembled Athenians acted through formal political and legal channels: they listened to proposals and counterproposals, they cast votes, and they handed the convicted offenders over to official magistrates (the Eleven) for punishment (execution). The fact that the Athenians violated the legal principle of individual trials, therefore, does not turn this episode into an instance of popular justice.

Ironically, however, an event that does qualify as popular justice occurred several years later against the one who had proposed the collective trial of the generals, a councilor named Callixeinus. Callixeinus and four of his supporters were apprehended shortly after the execution of the generals on the grounds that they had deceived the people. Owing to the political turmoil of these years, however, the accused were able to flee into exile and escape punishment. When political order was restored in 403, Callixeinus returned to Athens, apparently thinking that the affairs of 406 would be forgotten after all that the city had been through since then. He was wrong. According to Xenophon, Callixeinus "was hated by all and died of starvation."[124] Implicit in this terse line is a collective shunning so extreme and so effective that Callixeinus was unable to secure food for survival.[125] Scholars are accustomed to interpreting Sparta as an extreme culture of shame, but are less used to viewing classical Athens in this light.[126] Yet the fact that an Athenian citizen could be shunned to such a degree that he died of starvation is a striking example that informal popular justice was a powerful and active mode of social control even at the height of Athens' political development.

Indeed, this is the principal insight that can be gained from the juxtaposition of these two events, namely the execution of the Arginusae generals and the death of Callixeinus. These episodes show that the Athenians were perfectly comfortable with the use of popular justice and did not hold dogmatically to the principle of due process in cases where they deemed more "informal" practices were in order.[127] The events in the aftermath of the Battle of Arginusae illustrate that the Athenians had a much more flexible attitude to justice than some scholars suppose.[128] The Athenians, like other Greeks, participated simultaneously in two systems of justice—the official and the popular—and used these systems interchangeably and in ways that implicated one with the other. In justice, as in other areas of life, the Athenians held contradictory norms that were equally valid, but applicable in different contexts.[129]

The examples of house razing discussed above illustrate both its popular character and the fact that elites were the primary victims of such rituals. The evidence for the most clearly attested form of popular justice, namely stoning, confirms this pattern.[130] As we have seen in the famous case of the stoning of Lycides, as well as the near-stoning of the Argive generals just discussed, this punishment was an extra-legal collective form of popular justice.[131] Indeed, stoning as a form of execution requires a large crowd in order to be effective, a feature that clearly distinguishes it from the official modes of execution in ancient Greece, namely throwing the offender into a pit, exposure by being hung from a plank or pole (*apotympanismos*), and poison.[132] Stoning is also a very controlled form of popular justice: particular offenders were targeted, and there was no widespread violence and destruction.

The elite status of those subject to stoning is generally apparent from the main types of offense that elicited this punishment: tyrants, traitors, and commanders judged guilty of failures of leadership.[133] The fact that Lycides was not only a councilor but also was active in making proposals does not prove that he was a member of the elite definitively, but it in-

creases the likelihood.[134] As M. H. Hansen has shown, elites were disproportionately represented on the Council, and even more so in the record
of speakers in public contexts.[135] Herodotus' conjecture that Lycides was
bribed by the Persians, moreover, suggests that he was a prominent leader,
whom the Persians expected to be able to influence public opinion.[136]

In a second historical case of stoning in classical Athens, the offender
was definitely of elite status. In 409 BCE, the Athenians captured a cousin
of the flamboyant politician Alcibiades on board an enemy ship. Although
the other captives were sent back to Athens, this Alcibiades (he shared a
name with his more famous cousin) was stoned to death.[137] Unfortunately Xenophon does not describe this event in any detail. We can, however, surmise that both the evidence of treason (capture aboard an enemy
ship) and his membership in one of the most prominent of Athenian families, the Alcmeonidae, were principal factors in determining his summary
treatment. Furthermore, we may infer that the Athenian sailors played an
active part in meting out this punishment, although Xenophon says only
that the Athenian commander "had him stoned" (*kateleusen*).[138]

Other examples of stoning confirm that they were usually performed
by the masses against elite transgressors of social and political norms.
Herodotus tells us that when Aristagoras of Miletus captured the tyrant
Coes of Mytilene and handed him over to his people, the Mytilenean people "immediately took hold of him, led him out [of the city] and stoned
him to death."[139] Alcaeus' suggestion that Pittacus, tyrant of Mytilene,
was "fit to be stoned" (*labolio*) therefore expresses a real possibility.[140]
Furthermore, if we accept Daniel Ogden's arguments that the epithet
leustēr can mean both "stone-thrower" and "one who is fit to be stoned,"
then its application to the tyrant Cleisthenes of Sicyon makes a great deal
of sense.[141] Though not all tyrants were guilty of transgressions against
the community—indeed despite Alcaeus' suggestion, Pittacus seems to have
been a popular and fair leader—single rulers who showed insufficient
regard for the common good could find themselves subject to stoning at
the hands of the people.[142]

So entrenched was the connection between betrayal of the collective
interest and stoning, that, by the fourth century, the suggestion that a
particular leader ought to be stoned became a commonplace of political
oratory.[143] Demosthenes argued that his rival Aeschines deserved to be
stoned for his role in the destruction of Phocis.[144] Lycurgus similarly suggested that Leocrates should be stoned for selfishly abandoning the city
following Athens' defeat at the battle of Charonaea in 338.[145] Dinarchus,
in turn, argued that Lycurgus deserved to be stoned, and apparently alluded to the historical exemplum of Lycides' stoning for treason.[146] Hyperides also drew on the example of Lycides in accusing one Autolycus of
treason for his poor performance as a general in Thrace in 361.[147] These

rhetorical uses of the topos of stoning are not to be confused with actual instances of popular justice. Nevertheless, the orators' allusions indicate how this form of punishment was associated in the popular imagination with failures of leadership.[148]

A final example of a stoning illustrates both its nature as a collective ritual and its customary function of punishing elite transgressions against the common good.[149] Following the Greek victory in the Persian wars, the Persian governor of the Chersonesus, a man named Artayctes, was captured by the Athenians. Artayctes had previously robbed the sacred precinct of the Greek hero Protesilaus in the territory of Elaeus. Although Artayctes offered monetary compensation to the people of Elaeus, they wanted revenge and urged the Athenian commander, Xanthippus, to put Artayctes to death. Xanthippus consented and "[the people of Elaeus] led Artayctes out to a promontory ... and hung him up by fastening him to a plank. Then they stoned Artayctes' son to death before his eyes."[150] Once again, the brutal punishment of the presumably innocent son prevents us from recognizing the treatment of Artayctes and his son as a form of controlled popular justice. Nevertheless, the collective action of the people of Elaeus follows the pattern of the stoning of Lycides: the offender is a powerful figure; he and his family are targeted; and the punishment is exacted collectively and publicly in a spectacular (albeit gruesome) fashion.

If we turn now back to adultery, we must note that the evidence for the social status of victims of ritual humiliation is scant. In the one historical case of adultery that has survived in our sources, there is reasonable evidence that the offender, Eratosthenes of the district of Oa, was notorious and that he belonged to prominent circles. Indeed, J. K. Davies proposes that he was related to the Eratosthenes who was one of the Thirty Tyrants in 404/3.[151] By contrast, the cuckolded husband appears to be of middling status.[152] While we cannot hope to recover the exact historical context of the conflict between these two individuals as we can in many early modern examples, it is not unlikely that there were other, possibly political, tensions besides the fact of adultery that led to the confrontation between this elite offender and the middling citizen whose wife was seduced.[153]

It is perhaps noteworthy in this regard that a ballot (*ostrakon*) against the notoriously wealthy and powerful politician Megacles accuses him of being an adulterer.[154] Indeed, sexual offenses feature among the accusations against several other candidates for ostracism.[155] If ostracism—as I have argued elsewhere—was another symbolic ritual through which Athenians collectively expressed and negotiated tensions within their community, then it provides indirect support for the political functions of the ritual humiliation of elite adulterers by the Athenian masses.[156] If we consider, finally, the myth with which I began my discussion of the treatment of adulterers, one might detect some class tension in the Homeric story of the affair of Ares and Aphrodite. Hephaistos, the offended husband, is after all lame and slow, while he is cuckolded by the swift and strong Ares.[157] If myth borrows structures from historical relationships and conflicts, then this story may lend further support to the theory that popular justice (here specifically the ritual abuse and humiliation of adulterers) was a forum for mass-elite interaction and negotiation.

Violence and Popular Festivity

I would like to conclude with a caveat and several final observations. First, the caveat. I do not intend to idealize popular justice or suggest that it was a better mechanism of social control than formal institutions. As in Samuel Walker's assessment of popular justice in colonial America, informal rituals of social control in ancient Greece represented "the best and the worst" impulses, and could be at different times either just or oppressive.[158] On the other hand, my interpretation of classical Athens as a society that used "informal" and "formal" modes of justice interchangeably—and indeed embedded forms of popular justice within their "official" institutions—constitutes a challenge to certain recent approaches to justice in classical Athens.

Gabriel Herman has recently argued that classical Athens was a remarkably non-violent society in which the individual's desire for retaliation had been curtailed in favor of "punishment administered by the state's coercive agencies."[159] While Herman correctly identifies one strain in Athenian norms and behavior, my study suggests that he pushes his claims too far.[160] Indeed, Herman's insistence on a strict distinction between state-inflicted punishment as "communally sanctioned and deemed legitimate," and private "violence" causes him to overlook much of the revealing overlap between these two spheres.[161] Specifically, Herman's approach allows him to ignore both the ways that the community could engage in spectacular cruelty within the formal legal system (e.g., the physical abuse of the adulterer in the courts with a verbally abusive crowd looking on) and also the ways that the community acted in cruel but "legitimate" (i.e., "communally sanctioned") ways outside the courts (e.g., the social exclusion of Callixeinus and his death by starvation).[162]

Finally, let us turn to the connections between popular mechanisms of social control and various types of festival rituals. In Early Modern Europe, the parading of individuals mounted (sometimes backwards) on asses or donkeys was a central feature of a number of popular festivals and modes of informal collective justice, most notably Carnival in Continental Europe and a ritual of popular justice known as Rough Music in

Figure 11.
Phallus procession. Unattributed mid-sixth-century BCE Attic black-figure cup.
Museo Archeologico, Florence, 3897. Photo courtesy of the Soprintendenza per
i Beni Archeologici della Toscana, Firenze.

England.[163] Peter Burke, furthermore, has noted that there was a tendency for elements of one festival or ritual to "wander" to other festivals
or rituals, and more specifically that rituals of popular justice adopted
features of Carnival and vice versa.[164] In other words, popular justice
became "carnivalesque"—that is, an occasion when normal roles were
reversed—and Carnival became, in addition to its other functions, an occasion for popular protest against anyone who transgressed the norms of
the community.[165]

A similar argument can be made about the forms of popular justice
discussed in this chapter, since they share features with other collective
rituals in ancient Greece. For example, in addition to the features of the
festivals of Dionysus discussed in the previous chapter, the god was
mounted on a donkey and paraded through the town accompanied by a
group of drunken revelers who hurled verbal abuse, voiced obscenities,
and displayed huge model phalluses (figs. 7, 8, and 11).[166] With these
features of Dionysiac ritual we may compare the treatment of adulterers,
who, as we have seen, were mounted on donkeys in some places, paraded
around the city and subject to verbal and sexual abuse in Athens and
elsewhere.[167] The common association of Dionysus, donkeys, and adulterers with excessive or transgressive sexual desire was undoubtedly part
of the reason for the shared practices.[168]

Given the apparent similarities of the two rituals, moreover, one might
well wonder if they shared other features, such as the large crowd of rev-

elers, music, and excessive drinking and eating. The practice of effeminizing adulterers, moreover, would be well-suited to the atmosphere of cross-dressing attested at the Dionysia.[169] As we saw in the previous chapter, Dionysiac ritual, like Carnival, featured a reversal of ordinary norms of behavior, a symbolism that I have suggested imbued rituals of popular justice insofar as the mass of ordinary citizens took upon themselves the role of disciplining the powerful.[170] Indeed, comparative evidence from Early Modern Europe shows that rituals of popular justice were often postponed until Carnival when ordinary rules against insult and public defamation of the powerful were lifted.[171] If a similar case is true of ancient Greece, then we may imagine that at least some of the rituals of popular justice described above (particularly the ritual humiliation of adulterers) took place during festivals and/or featured a carnivalesque atmosphere of drunkenness, sexuality, obscenity, and other forms of popular revelry. House-razings and the digging up of the bones of traitors could also borrow these festival elements, as I have already suggested.[172]

The case of stoning may also borrow from ritual forms of festival behavior. Intriguingly, Pausanias reports that a festival in Troezen was called "the Stoning" (*Lithobolia*).[173] While the central ritual event of this festival must certainly have involved some form of collective throwing of stones, our evidence is insufficient to uncover the symbolism of this practice.[174] Similarly, a festival of Demeter at Eleusis, known as the "The Throwing" (*Ballētus*), apparently featured a ritual battle in which stones were thrown.[175] Perhaps most significantly, at the festival of the Thargelia in Athens and at other festivals in other cities, scapegoats were driven out of the city by throwing stones and other objects, and it is even possible that in some places scapegoats were stoned to death.[176] The ambiguity of myths and rituals relating to scapegoating is especially intriguing. While in myth powerful men—particularly kings—were victims of scapegoating, in ritual practice it was lowly criminals and vagabonds who were chosen to serve as scapegoats.[177] This dual symbolism of king/criminal may have made stoning a particularly appropriate ritual form for popular action against elite transgressors of communal norms.

The instances of stoning discussed in this chapter differ from these festival rituals in that the stonings appear to be spontaneous actions, whereas the festivals took place once a year at a set time. Nevertheless, it is still likely that this form of popular justice borrowed some of its practices and symbolism from festival rituals (and vice versa). In regard to scapegoating rituals, the symbolism of collective elimination of pollution, as well as the purification and renewal of the city, is especially relevant.[178] The other festival rituals involving stoning—the *Lithobolia* and the *Ballētus*—have many parallels in other cultures and cannot be reduced to a single symbolic meaning.[179] Nevertheless, both festivals also featured verbal obscenities (*aischrologia*), a practice which connects them with other rituals of popular justice, not to mention a wide array of festivals, as we have seen in the previous chapter.[180] We may therefore conjecture that stoning as a form of popular justice, like the other forms of popular justice discussed above, shared multiple features with popular festival revelry.

The similarities between collective acts of extra-legal justice and festival rituals should not be surprising.[181] In ancient Greece, as in Bakhtin's Middle Ages, popular festivity was a crucial medium for the expression of the people's view of the world and, in particular, their opposition to the official order.[182] On a more practical level, moreover, the overlap between festive practices and rituals of popular justice allowed the masses to coordinate their actions with minimal preparation and organization. Once informal channels of knowledge transfer (e.g., gossip) had done their work of identifying a social offender, all members of the community would have known exactly what to do. Furthermore, the symbolism of ritual acts of justice—whether it be the identification of a particular type of offender against collective norms or a more general statement of the power of the masses to regulate elite behavior—would have been communicated more effectively by its very similarity, for example, to religious rituals used to remove pollution from the community (as in scapegoating) or to reverse customary hierarchies (as in Dionysiac rituals). Finally, the importance of the customary license of festival time must have played a significant role in conferring legitimacy on collective acts of physical and verbal violence toward elite individuals.[183] Indeed, the festive features of popular justice go some way toward "formalizing" popular justice in a way that supports the central argument of this chapter, namely the inextricability of formal and informal modes of justice in ancient Greece.

EPILOGUE

6

Conclusion

THROUGH THE CASE STUDIES presented in this book, I have explored some manifestations of the culture of ordinary Greeks and their slaves and have attempted to explain their significance. In some cases, I have focused on telling details in familiar works of literature. In others, I have hunted down obscure anecdotes that shed light on a wider world of popular practices and discourses. In doing so, I hope to have revealed glimpses of a dynamic sphere of culture that is unfamiliar to those who view ancient Greece solely from the perspective of its formal political institutions or "high" literature. In this world, fantasies of magical abundance, feasting, and lording it over one's superiors were more prominent than didactic poems about the value of hard work and moderation. In this world, political leaders were imagined as ineffective buffoons and their acts were ridiculed through obscene double entendres. In this world, masters made sacrifices at the tomb of a dead runaway slave where slaves also dedicated a portion of what they stole from their masters. And finally, in this world, ordinary citizens, women, and slaves actively resisted domination by using forms of festival ritual as a symbolic (and sometimes violent) reminder to the powerful of their obligations toward those lower on the social scale.

Most crucially, I have argued that these exuberant forms of popular culture were far from frivolous occasions when ordinary farmers, craftsmen, and slaves "let off steam." Rather, I have suggested that these "living" forms of culture—largely lost in the textual and archeological remains—were vital to the ways that ordinary Greeks and their slaves made sense of the world, created a distinctive identity for themselves, and negotiated their relations with those around them. Although I have emphasized that these forms of popular culture typically did not overturn the social order, I have argued that they were a vital counterbalance to the power of the wealthy, and played a crucial role in the construction of a social equilibrium through which the basic needs of all members of the community were met.

In the first case study (chapter 2), I analyzed the curious story of a runaway slave to show how it reveals the ways that masters and slaves on the island of Chios negotiated a *modus vivendi* that made it possible for both groups to live in a (reasonably) stable state of mutual dependence. I suggested that the story was formulated to explain the origins of a cult through which the Chian masters and their slaves worked out the terms of their relationship. The basic premises of this relationship were that slaves were to render loyal service to their masters, while masters were obligated to provide sufficient livelihood for slaves and treat them humanely. Crucial to the argument of this chapter was the idea that slaves, not just masters, actively negotiated for and enforced this agreement, and that they did so largely through the informal social mechanism of story-telling in the context of their joint worship of a dead slave. This chapter, therefore, provides an illustration of the role of folktales in the negotiation of social relations in the Greek city-state.

Chapter 3 provides a second example of the role of popular discourses in ancient Greek politics. This time, however, it is the storytelling of ordinary Greek citizens, rather than their slaves, that is at center stage. Analysis of the story of Cleisthenes, tyrant of Sicyon, shows that it is influenced not simply by official anti-tyrannical discourses, but also by the themes of popular culture, particularly obscenity, grotesque bodily images, and the debasement of the "high" through association with the "low." In these popular traditions, the political reforms of the tyrant are ridiculed through allusions to lowly animals, particularly those with obscene connotations and gross bodily features. By engaging in playful but false etymologies, and by contaminating the high with the low, popular traditions not only engaged in veiled critique of the official order, but articulated a pattern of destruction and renewal that, according to Bakhtin, is characteristic of the festive outlook of popular culture. In this case study, therefore, we caught a glimpse of popular non-literary culture as it is refracted through Greek literature. While it is important to distinguish between the literary articulation of popular themes and living forms of non-elite culture, this chapter shows that comparison with other types of Greek literature (especially comic drama and satire) as well as literary and non-literary texts of later historical eras (especially medieval Europe) reveals patterns that allow one to identify the key themes and their significations for popular audiences.

Chapters 4 and 5 turn from "discourses" to "practices." Chapter 4 argued that social rituals of hospitality played an important role in articulating the principle that the powerful were obliged to ensure the well-being of the poor in ancient Greek communities. Comparison of the ancient Greek evidence for these rituals with similar practices in Early Modern Europe showed that such rituals were a typical cultural mechanism for the maintenance of the ideal of balanced reciprocity between elites and masses, but could turn violent when certain minimal conditions of living for the poor were not met. Such was the case in archaic Megara, where the poor broke into the houses of the rich, demanded hospitality, and abused the rich physically and verbally if their demands were not met. In Megara and Athens, such episodes of protest resulted in the enactment of formal legislation (remembered as the "Return of Interest" and "Lifting of Burdens"). The close association of episodes of popular protest and legislation is a clear sign that these informal social rituals were effective political tools. Finally, I argued that it was not simply adult male citizens who were active in such rituals, but women, children, and potentially even non-citizens and slaves. This example, therefore, demonstrates the inclusive nature of popular culture and the ways that those marginal to the institutional structures of the state participated in the political development of the Greek city-state.

Chapter 5 examines the sphere of justice and argues that popular forms of social control such as shaming, stoning, and the razing of the house not only operated alongside and sometimes within the formal legal institutions, but could also serve as a mechanism for the symbolic disciplining of elites by the masses. While scholars have recognized that the formal law courts of classical Athens had an important role in negotiating relations between elites and masses, I argue that episodes of popular justice were often a much more spectacular and powerful format for such political communication. Against the idea that episodes of popular justice are mere relics of an older legal system, I show that the treatment of adulterers, tyrants, traitors, and military commanders who betrayed the collective interest illustrates the still vital role of popular justice as well as its unproblematic (to the Greeks) use even in the fully developed classical Greek city-state. Once again, moreover, the whole community—including women, children, non-citizens, and slaves—could participate in these rituals, thereby making popular justice a more inclusive form of political action than the formal institutions that restricted participation to adult males.

By emphasizing the role of popular culture in political relations in the Greek city-state, I do not intend to deny that ordinary farmers and craftsmen also had access to and made vigorous use of formal political institutions. Already in the time of Homer, ordinary Greeks gathered in the assembly, made decisions concerning war and peace, and sometimes even criticized their leaders.[1] By the seventh century, formal written laws played an important role in regulating the political order. Seventh-century laws, furthermore, reveal that popular assemblies and councils were vital organs in the institutional structure of the community. By the sixth century, moreover, popular unrest led to the passage of laws affirming the basic political and legal rights of the mass of ordinary citizens in Athens (and probably other city-states that are less well attested). By the fifth century, Greek communities—most notably, again, Athens—were equipped with remarkably sophisticated political and legal institutions. It is undeniable that many of these developments were the result of political action taken individually and collectively in formal institutional contexts.

Yet a central argument of this book has been that to focus on these institutional contexts of political action obscures what was a parallel and equally vital realm of political relations. Ordinary Greeks were not constrained to act solely through formal political and legal channels. Their worldviews and ideals were not articulated exclusively—or even primarily—in formal public speech in the political assembly. Rather, ordinary citizens expressed themselves through a range of popular practices and discourses including festival revelry, storytelling, and the spontaneous collective punishment of social offenders. Ordinary citizens, moreover, used "formal" and "informal" modes of action interchangeably and flexibly—neither getting upset about breeches of the "rule of law" when communal consensus called for summary action, nor divorcing popular practices from formal institutions where the two might work in tandem. While I would not deny that the remarkable sophistication of the institutions of Athenian democracy is one of the great achievements of the ancient Greeks, I contend that this achievement must be examined realistically in its historical context and not artificially divorced from other aspects of the life of the ancient Greeks.

A final example will help to illustrate this point vividly. Scholars have recently paid considerable attention to a decree passed by the Athenian democracy in 410, shortly after it was restored following the brutal one-year rule of the Oligarchy of the Four Hundred.[2] This decree, named after its proposer, Demophantos, declared that anyone who overthrew the democracy or held office when the democracy had been overthrown was an enemy of the Athenians and could be killed with impunity. In addition, the decree gives the text of an oath, sworn collectively by the Athenians, obligating themselves to kill any person who overthrew the democracy or held office when the democracy had been overthrown, as well as anyone who set himself up as tyrant or helped in establishing someone else as tyrant.

On the most generous reading, the decree authorizes individual Athenians to take patriotic action in defense of the democracy. The decree sanctions violence on behalf of democracy by proclaiming that one who kills an opponent of democracy is exempt from legal prosecution. The decree, moreover, explicitly limits the scope of permissible violence by specifying precisely against which types of political actors such acts may be perpetrated, namely, those who overthrow democracy and those who hold office when democracy has been overthrown, including tyrants and those who help establish a tyrant in power.

It is tempting to interpret this decree in idealizing terms both as encouraging patriotic acts in defense of democracy and as memorializing the enactment of an official political ritual (an oath) articulating the political identity of the Athenians. By gathering together in the chief civic divisions of the democracy, moreover, the Athenians collectively affirmed their democratic institutions and ideals. This reading is not false, but it is partial. By swearing to rise up and kill anyone who might overthrow the democracy, the Athenians were also authorizing extra-judicial action against the enemies of democracy. Such action did not have to be pursued through formal institutional means, i.e., summons before a court, a trial, and acquittal or condemnation to a punishment exacted by state officials. Moreover, unless a family member contested the identification of the victim as anti-democratic, the killer was not required to defend his action judicially. In other words, this decree authorizes the performance of the most violent act—murder—without recourse to judicial process. Like the law on adultery that authorized the murder or physical abuse of an adulterer discussed in chapter 5, this law allows for the performance of "justice" against an enemy of the democracy by citizen or citizens acting outside the formal institutions of the state.

While the active role required of private citizens in bringing cases to court has long been recognized as a defining feature of a legal system that lacked a public prosecutor or any substantial police force, less emphasis has been placed on the ways that the laws operate flexibly to authorize punishment of social offenders entirely outside the judicial frame. In this regard, the Decree of Demophantos, like the laws on adultery, illustrates how extra-institutional action and formal laws could operate in tandem to regulate the social order. I suggest that it is only by recognizing the wide scope for "private," yet communally sanctioned, action—even under the fully developed Athenian democracy—that a balanced perspective on the politics of the ancient Greek city-state can be achieved.

Even more vitally important for the argument of this book is the fact that recognition of the extra-institutional sphere of politics allows the historian to capture more concretely the political life of (institutionally) marginal groups in Greek society—namely, women, free non-citizens, and even slaves. While male citizens made flexible use of institutions and informal social practices, women, non-citizens, and slaves were compelled to operate through the latter since they had no direct access to political and legal institutions. By considering the role of popular culture in politics, therefore, one gains access to the ways that these groups contributed to the social and political life of the ancient Greek city-state.

In addition to illustrating the role of popular culture in the political life of Greek city-states, a further major aim of this book has been to demonstrate some of the ways that comparative history and anthropological studies can illuminate aspects of Greek culture that are only faintly visible in our surviving sources. I have drawn from studies of peasants in sixteenth-century France and contemporary South East Asia, from studies of popular culture in eighteenth-century England and of slaves in the American South. The aim of these comparisons has not been to equate ancient Greece with any of these other times and places, but to illuminate patterns of discourse and practice that transcend the historical specificities of time and place. Several important conclusions have emerged. First of all, it has become clear that ordinary farmers, craftsmen, and slaves in ancient Greece made use of culture in ways that are similar to their counterparts in other time periods. Not only were folktales, fables, and festival ritual a medium for imagining a different social order, but they served as a crucial mechanism for the articulation of non-elite collective identity and opposition to those above them.

Second, the study of popular culture in ancient Greece puts studies of peasant and slave culture in more recent periods in deeper historical perspective. Given that ancient Greek farmers, craftsmen, and slaves employed similar themes and cultural mechanisms to articulate their ideals and negotiate their relationship with those more powerful than themselves, we see that the social and political tensions and the responses to it by peasants and slaves in more recent eras were not unique to their particular historical circumstances. The rise of modern forms of slavery, the Industrial Revolution, and the more recent "Green Revolution" in South East Asia were only the most dramatic challenges in a whole series of developments affecting social and political relations in historical communities. The deep historical perspective offered by the ancient evidence further illustrates that there never was a perfectly balanced "moral economy" or an older agrarian order in which the powerful engaged in harmonious reciprocity with the weak. In particular, the evidence of ancient Greece shows that the social equilibrium reached between the rich and the poor or between master and slave was always a fragile one that had to be continually constructed and reconstructed in the face of changing social, political, and economic conditions. The concept of the "moral economy" was articulated as a reference point and a (fictional) traditional ideal to which elites were exhorted to conform. Alongside the fantasy of a world of plenty and a world in which slaves were on top, these imaginary constructs were the tools by which ordinary farmers, craftsmen, women, and slaves—both in ancient Greece and in more recent times— waged war against those more powerful than themselves. While ancient Greek farmers and Malaysian peasants, to name just two examples, also made use of formal state institutions in their fight for social justice, the sphere of popular culture remained a powerful force in the negotiation of relations between rich and poor. To borrow a phrase from James Scott, popular culture was, and continues to be, "a weapon of the weak."

Notes

Chapter 1. Peasants, Politics, and Popular Culture

1. Hobsbawm 1988, 21.

2. By using a better documented historical period to construct a model for understanding a less well documented one, my use of the comparative method differs from the standard typologies constructed by theorists of the comparative method (e.g., Skocpol and Somers 1980; Tilly 1984). Current debate about the strengths and weaknesses of the comparative method is usually framed from the perspective of those comparing modern nation-states (see, for example, Cohen and O'Connor 2004). My approach shares something with the "modular" method proposed by Roehner and Syme 2002. These scholars suggest that complex historical events such as the French Revolution should be broken down into smaller "modules" (e.g., unrest in the countryside, insurrection of the Paris population) which can then be compared with similar phenomena in other times and places. In a sense, each of the essays in this book examines one "module" or aspect of Greek civilization (oral storytelling, popular festivity, popular justice) and compares it to these phenomena in other societies.

3. For this and other criticisms of the comparative method, see Cohen and O'Connor 2004, who also supply a useful bibliography of scholarship on the methodology of comparative history.

4. This method is similar to the third major method of comparative history identified by Skocpol and Somers 1980, 181–82, namely "macro-causal analysis" by which the comparative approach is used to disprove traditional causal explanations of particular historical trajectories and to construct new historical generalizations. On the use of models in ancient history, see Finley 1985; Ober 1996. Recent uses of comparative approaches in ancient history include Hansen 2000, 2002; Dal Lago and Katsari 2008a; and Scheidel 2009.

5. Historians of ancient Greece generally agree that ancient Greece (by which is usually meant classical Athens) was exceptional compared to other contemporaneous civilizations for its stable institutions and material prosperity. See, for example, Ober 2008. More controversially, some scholars argue that Athens was exceptional in its adherence to the rule of law and non-violence (Herman 2006; Harris 2006). The arguments of this book refute these claims.

6. Athenian politicians (*rhetores*); see Hansen 1983a, 1983b, 1984, and 1999, 266–74. Although originally these men belonged to a select few established Athenian families of wealth and property, by the second half of the fifth century a more diverse group of men, including those whose wealth was relatively recently acquired through manufacturing and other enterprises, emerged as leaders. Cf. Connor 1971; Mossé 1995, 131–53. For elite values in Athenian political oratory, see Loraux 1986; Ober 1989.

7. Ober 1989.

8. On the importance of chapbooks in popular culture of Early Modern Europe, see Kunzle 1973. But also see Burke 1994, 71–74 for skepticism about the value of chapbooks and broadsides for recovering the attitudes of peasants.

9. The collections gathered by folklorists, however, cannot be assumed to be exactly replicas of popular oral forms. However, by cross-checking them against popular tales preserved in medieval literature, some reasonable approximation of their popular form can be reached (Darnton 1984, 20–23). Scholars of ancient Greek popular culture, by contrast, have only literature written by elites, though more could be done to explore connections between this literature and modern Greek folk culture.

10. Even in this latter case, much has been lost, and scholars often rely on post-bellum accounts for antebellum culture.

11. More could be done, however, in examining modern Greek folktales and popular culture as a refracted source for ancient popular culture. Alexiou 2002 does some work in this direction.

12. Burke 1994 similarly characterizes the elites who drew on popular culture as "brokers" or "mediators" and advocates an "oblique approach to popular culture via these mediators." (78).

13. Forsdyke 2005b and chapter 4 below.

14. Surviving ancient literature bearing greater or lesser relation to popular cultural forms includes: fragmentary mimes (see, e.g., Hordern 2004 on Sophron's mimes); iambic poetry (see chapter 2 below on Archilochus); comedy (see, e.g., Rösler 1986; Reckford 1987, 441–98; and Edwards 1993 on Aristophanes); satire (e.g., Lucian, who preserves some elements of lost Menippean satire); and the ancient novel (see, e.g., Reardon 1989). Hansen 1998 provides a translation of some novels, fables, and a few other examples of popular culture. See also Bremmer 1997, who uncovers evidence for ancient collections of jokes, among which feature the witty sayings of the third century BC poet Machon. On Machon, see Gow 1965; Kurke 2003. Collections of proverbs similarly derive, at least in part, from popular culture (see e.g., the collection by Zenobius, second century CE and generally Lazardis 2007).

15. See, e.g., Aly 1921; Murray 1987, 2001; Luraghi 2005; Griffiths 2006.

16. Rösler 1986; DuBois 2003, 181–82; Kurke 2006, 2011.

17. Burke 1994.

18. Stallybrass and White 1986.

19. Ibid., 61. A parallel example from ancient Greece of this sort of construction of "authorship" and the "high" in opposition to the "low" can be observed in Aristophanes' claims about himself and his comic poetry in opposition to that of his rivals. Whereas his rivals engage in low buffoonery (*bomolocheumata*), Aristophanes asserts, his comedies are sophisticated and do not partake of "marketplace humor" (*skommasi agoraiois*) (e.g., *Peace* 729–816). As commentators have noted, Aristophanes in fact employs precisely the kinds of low humor that he derides. It is also noteworthy that Aristophanes claims that he attacks the powerful in his poetry, whereas his rivals make fun of ordinary people and women (*Peace*,

751–52). Of course, Aristophanes ridicules ordinary people and women too, and it appears that other comic poets ridiculed the powerful. Olson 2007 usefully presents the comic fragments by theme (including ridicule of politicians), and Storey 2003 presents the comic art of Eupolis, one of Aristophanes' rivals.

20. Stallybrass and White 1986, 61.

21. Ibid. For further criticism of Bakhtin's reading of Rabalais as a direct mirror of peasant culture as well as his rigid distinction between high and low culture, see Burke 1994; Bremmer and Roodenburg 1997. Gurevich 1997 attributes Bakhtin's views on official and unofficial culture to his experience in Stalinist Russia. It should be noted, however, that Stallybrass and White argue that although Ben Jonson tried to establish his identity as author above and against that of popular improvisory theater of his time, he was not successful. According to these scholars, Jonson was not fully able to free himself from the theater and the fair, and his literary text was "haunted" by the suppressions of the low (1986, 75–77). Popular culture "appear[s] as negated or denied elements, taking on a new and different form under the sign of their negation" (76). By taking into account this use of popular culture as a negative pole for the ideological self-fashioning of the "author," it seems that Stallybrass and White allow some hope of recovering the more positive manifestations and symbolisms of popular culture. Cf. Burke 1994, 58–64. Burke speaks of a "two-way traffic" between learned culture and popular culture (58) and provides many examples of cultural movement in both directions.

22. See especially the debate in the *American Historical Review* 97 (1992) between L. W. Levine, T. J. Jackson Lears, Robin D. G. Kelley, and N. Z. Davis.

23. Davis 1992, 1410.

24. This methodology of looking for vestiges of earlier versions of oral tales has been used successfully by scholars of oral history (Vansina 1985; cf. Thomas 1989). In the context of ancient history, Jonathan Hall has used this method to analyze the inconsistencies, ruptures, and "suturing" of breaks in mythical genealogies as a way of understanding how the early Greeks constructed and reconstructed their ethnic identities (Hall 1997). Similarly, I have attempted to recover earlier versions of some of the narratives in Herodotus' *Histories* by examining elements that do not quite fit their Herodotean context (Forsdyke 1999 and chapter 3 below).

25. On the performance context of tragedy and comedy, see Goldhill 1990; Csapo and Slater 1994; and Wilson 2000.

26. See chapter 2, with discussion and further references in n.47.

27. Hopkins 1993 notes this possibility in relation to the anonymous biography of Aesop. For further discussion, see chapter 2 below.

28. Homer, *Iliad* 1.231.

29. Hesiod, *Works and Days* 264.

30. Alcaeus, fr.129; Diogenes Laertius 1.81.

31. Similarly, Bresson 2007, 75 observes: "Ce n'est pas pour rien que le vocabulaire de la Grèce ancienne désigne les riches comme 'les gras' [hoi pachees]."

32. Camporesi 1989, 37. Cf. Bakhtin 1984 passim.

33. Scott 1985, 187.

34. Ibid.

35. Ibid.

36. Since the 1950s and '60s, historians have been concerned with "history from below." A founding father of this field is George Rudé, "whose work has been dedicated not to the study of dominant social groups or classes, of 'elites' or their agents, but to ordinary pre-industrial urban and rural laborers and artisans" (Krantz 1988, 3). Rudé's most important works, for the purposes of this study, are Rudé 1964, 1980. Antecedents to Rudé include Michelet, Lefebvre, Bloch, though "grassroots history" only really advanced starting in the 1950s (Hobsbawm 1988, 15).

37. McLellen 1995, 30; Thompson 1991. See, however, Arnold 2000, who shows how Gramsci's negative view of the peasantry also contained the seeds of a more positive understanding of the ways that peasants manipulated dominant cultural constructions (e.g., Catholicism) toward non-hegemonic ends. These aspects of Gramscian thought played a major role in the emergence of subaltern studies in India (see below).

38. Rudé 1980, 22.

39. Ibid., 21–31.

40. Hobsbawm 1959, 2000; Thompson 1993.

41. Le Roy Ladurie's "micro-historical approach" is only one strand of the influence of the "Annales School." For a fuller account of this intellectual movement, see Burguière 2009.

42. Le Roy Ladurie 1978, 1980.

43. Ginzburg 1992; Sabean 1984.

44. Davis 1975. For the anthropology, see Gluckman 1963, 1965; and Turner 1969.

45. Darnton 1984; Geertz 1973.

46. Burke 1994 (originally published 1978); Trexler 1980; Muir 1997.

47. Foucault 1977; Hunt 1984; Wilenz 1985; Kertzer 1988. For critical discussion of some of this work, see Hunt 1989; Burke 1997, 2001; and Bonnell and Hunt 1999.

48. Work on civic ritual, especially in classical Athens, includes Winkler and Zeitlin 1990; Neils 1992; Osborne 1994a, 1994b; de Polignac 1995; Wohl 1996; Maurizio 1998; Goldhill and Osborne 1999; Wilson 2000; Bers 2000; Goff 2004; Cole 2004; Yatromanolakis and Roilos 2004; Ober 2008, 194–99.

49. For overviews of the Subaltern Studies project, now covering subordinate groups worldwide, see Chaturvedi 2000 and Ludden 2002. A seminal study is Guha 1983.

50. Scott 1985.

51. Ibid., 193–94.

52. Vlassopoulos 2007a.

53. Notable exceptions include Jones 2004; Schmitz 2004; Osborne 1985a, 1987; Cohen 2000.

54. For an overview of recent debates, see Cohen and O'Connor 2004.

55. For an argument along these lines in relation to contemporary peasant societies, see Kerkvliet 2009.

56. A major criticism of studies of popular culture is that they tend to homogenize "the people" and fail to recognize both the diverse makeup of the mass of ordinary citizens, but also the wide range of other ways of dividing society. Cf. Desan 1989; Chandavarkar 1994, 1998.

57. Bresson (2007, 151, 206) suggests that in Athens, less than 50 percent of the population was engaged in agriculture. For the wide range of non-agricultural occupations attested in classical Athens, see Harris 2002.

58. Foxhall 2007, 4. See Jameson 1994 for further discussion of this problem.

59. Athens: Osborne 1992; Foxhall 1992, 2007, 31; Bresson 2007, 151–55. Sparta: Hodkinson 2000; Bresson 2007, 151, 155. Greece, generally: Bresson 2007, 155. Bresson does, however, note (151) that land-ownership was less inegalitarian than in the Near East. Scholars emphasizing the relative equality of landownership in ancient Greece include Hanson 1999; Morris 2000.

60. Bresson 2007, 150.

61. Osborne 1991, 1992, 1996b; Foxhall 2007, 38–50; Moreno 2007, 37–76.

62. The fifth-century politician Cleon, for example, gained his living from ownership of a leather processing facility (Aristoph, *Knights* 44). Hyperbolus, a late-fifth-century politician, owned a lamp factory (Aristoph, *Peace* 690). Demosthenes, the fourth-century politician, owned both a couch and a knife factory (Dem. 27.9). For discussion, see Connor 1971 and Mossé 1995.

63. For example, the wealthy fifth-century politician Nicias is reported to have owned one thousand slaves and rented them out at the rate of an obol per day per man (Xen., *Por.* 4.14–15). Xenophon also mentions two other men, Hipponicus and Philemonides, owning six hundred and three hundred slaves respectively, and states explicitly that there were others who rented out their slaves in this way.

64. Slaves widely used in agriculture: Burford 1993, 208–22; Jameson 1977, 1992, 2001; Cartledge 2001; Bresson 2007, 128, 130. Wood 1988 argues against widespread slaveholding among ordinary Athenians, but is refuted by Burford 1993, 264–65, n.69. Morris and Papadopoulos 2005 propose that the numerous towers found in the Greek landscape were for slave agricultural laborers. Osborne 1995 suggests that slaves were primarily used in manufacturing and trade. On slave agents in trade and banking, see Cohen 1992, 2000.

65. Finley 1998, 145–60.

66. See most recently, Dal Lago and Katsari 2008. See also Bradley 1987, 1989, 1994; and Patterson 1982.

67. Cartledge 1985; Rosivach 1993.

68. Hunter 1994; Cartledge 1985.

69. While scholars still debate the extent of slave labor on non-elite lands, the current consensus seems to be that a farmer with an average amount of land (e.g., 4.5 hectaires or 50 plethra) made use of a slave or two. On Bresson's estimate of Attic landholdings (2007, 150), this would equate to 9,200 slave-owning citizens out of a population of 25,000 citizens. Cartledge 2001, 163 suggests that "at least half of the 25,000–50,000 adult male Athenian citizens owned at least one slave," and Jameson 1977, 2001 would even allow for the poorest citizens (thetes) to have owned slaves. Both Cartledge 2001 and Jameson 2001 draw attention to the significance of the appearance of masters and their slaves on the naval lists (*IG* I[3]

1032 with Graham 1992, 1998; and Hunt 1998). Scheidel (2008, 107), on the other hand, considers the scale of "sub-elite" slave-owning unknowable, and like Osborne 1991 and Foxhall 2007, confines his study to elite slave-owners.

70. Foxhall 2007, 36. Cf. Bresson 150–55.

71. For Greek democracies beyond Athens, see Robinson 1997.

72. For a popular council counterbalancing a more restrictive council, compare the evidence for Chios (discussed by Robinson 1997, 90–101, though I would not agree with Robinson's judgment that Chios was a "functioning democracy").

73. For an overview of the practical and ideological distinctions between slave and free in classical Athens, see Fisher 1993; Hunter 1994; DuBois 2003. A key source for ancient Greek concepts of citizen and slave is Aristotle's *Politics*.

74. For the blurring of lines between legal statuses in classical Athens, see Jameson 1997; Cohen 2000; Vlassopoulos 2007b, 2009.

75. *IG* 1^2 374 with Rihll 2008, 127.

76. For discussion of these slaves, see Cohen 2000, 130–54; Kazakévich 2008; and Fisher 2008.

77. On ancient banking and the employment of slaves as bankers, see Cohen 1992, 2000.

78. On public slaves, see Jacob 1979 and Cohen 2000, 136–37.

79. Graham 1992, 1998; Hunt 1998.

80. Bäbler 1998, 22–32, however, points out that female slaves on grave monuments usually wear a distinctive long-sleeved dress.

81. Pseudo-Xenophon, *Constitution of the Athenians* 1.10.

82. For example, Plato, *Republic* 563b. For further discussion, see Jameson 1997; Cohen 2000; Vlassopoulos 2009; and Forsdyke forthcoming.

83. Foxhall 2007, 126 provides a chart of the agricultural labor required in each period of the year.

84. As Bresson puts it (2007, 165), a primary characteristic of agriculture in Greece is "un environnement climatique très incertain," particularly in levels of rainfall. Bresson argues (70–76) that although there were no major famines in classical Greece affecting hundreds of thousands of people in vast areas, as in medieval and Early Modern Europe, Japan, and China, nevertheless there were regular smaller famines affecting one or two cities. For classical Athens, Bresson estimates that there was a "deficit of rainfall" every third year, and a major catastrophe (less than 200 millimeters rainfall per year) six times every century.

85. Gallant 1991; Sallares 1991.

86. For the debate, compare Osborne (1985a, 142–44; 1987, 195–97); Burford (1993, 85–86); Jameson (1992, 136), who deny the applicability of the term, to Wood (1988, 54–56, 104–22); Gallant (1991, 4); and Cartledge (1993, 132), who accept the term. Ste. Croix observes the utility of the concept of a peasant economy for understanding Greek and Roman society in comparative perspective, and provides a useful discussion of different types of peasants (1981, 208–26).

87. Cartledge 1993, 132.

88. Gallant 1991, 4 with further references.

89. *OED*, 2nd edition; Cf. Wolf 1966, 9–10. See Osborne 1987, 194–96 for a catalogue of some of the differences between ancient and early modern city-states,

notably the lack of a strong divide between city and country (also noted by Cartledge 1993, 134; contra: Jones 2004). On the other hand, Mohlo, Raaflaub, and Emlen 1991 engage in productive comparative studies between ancient and medieval Italian city-states.

90. The quotation comes from Ste. Croix (1981, 33) and the full context is as follows: "[A] large part of production in antiquity was always carried on … by small free producers, mainly peasants, but also artisans and traders … [T]hese numerous individuals neither exploited the labor of others … nor were themselves exploited to any marked degree, but lived not far above subsistence level, producing little surplus beyond what they themselves consumed, they formed an intermediate class between exploiters and exploited. *In practice, however, they were only too likely to be exploited.*" Emphasis added.

91. The very fact of unequal distribution of land in ancient Greece, discussed above, is probably at least partly due to the loss of land to rich creditors by poor subsistence farmers who had been unable to repay their debts.

92. For discussion, see Forsdyke 2005b, 2006, and chapter 4 below.

93. Cartledge 1993, 133.

94. Ste. Croix 1981, Lintott 1982; Fuks 1984; Gehrke 1985.

95. As Bresson 2007, 133 notes, the rich oligarchs were indicted for cutting down some wood on sacred land in order to make stakes for vines as part of their wine-making enterprises. The prosperity of these wine-exporting Corcyran landowners must have aggravated the sense of injustice among the indebted ordinary farmers and the slaves whose labor was exploited for the production of wine (see Bresson 2007, 130). In this context, the infringement on sacred lands was the spark that set off popular opposition to the rich landowners and led to the legal indictment by the popular leader Peithias.

96. Thucydides, 3.70 and 3.81.

97. Thucydides, 8.21.

98. Aelian, *Historical Miscellany* 14. 24, quoted by Fuks 1984, 182. For the date, see Fuks 1984, 183, with bibliography cited therin. The translation given is Fuk's.

99. Aristotle, *Constitution of the Athenians* 27.3; Plutarch, *Life of Cimon* 3.3, 10.

100. Plato, *Republic* 566A, 566E; *Laws* 684E, 736C; cf. Isocrates, *Panathenaia* 259. The quotation is from Cartledge 1993, 133. See also Gallant 1991, 186–87; Ste. Croix 1981, 215. Rosivach 1992 argues that the demand to redistribute land represents only the fears of opponents of democracy, and that in classical Athens democratic leaders never actually proposed such measures.

101. Foxhall 2007, 32.

102. Thucydides, 3.73. It is noteworthy that the slaves are approached "in the fields," suggesting that these slaves were agricultural.

103. Thucydides, 8.38, 8.40 and chapter 2. The parallel with the flight of Athenian slaves who deserted when the Spartans established a base in Attica (Thuc. 7.27.5) is striking, and suggests that flight was only possible when the masters were under duress resulting from the presence of a foreign enemy. This interpretation corresponds to a pattern observed in slave rebellions in the modern

period, which are more likely in the context of a war (cf. Genovese 1979; Cartledge 1985).

104. Herodotus, 7.155.2. Cf. Timaeus, fr.56; *FGrHist* I 204; *FGrHist* I 170; Diodorus, 8.11; Aristotle, *Politics* 1303b20, 1302b32; Dionysios Hal. 6.62.

105. It should be noted, however, that although Herodotus uses the term *douloi* for the slaves at Syracuse, he also notes that they had a common ethic identity as "Kyllyrians." Aristotle, furthermore, in his lost *Constitution of the Syracusans* (F 586 (Rose)); cf. How and Wells 1928, 194–95; van Wees 2003, 45–46) compared the Kyllyrians to the Spartan helots, and therefore scholars consider them to be native Sicils reduced to slavery by Greek colonists at the time of the foundation of Syracuse in 733 BCE. The "ethnic homogeneity" of the slaves in Syracuse would then explain their ability to unify and resist their Greek masters. But the fact that these slaves or serfs joined with the free Greek citizens of Syracuse against the wealthy landowners suggests that ethnic identity was not the only basis of the collective consciousness of this group of slaves.

106. One might add the examples of Syracuse under Dionysios I (405–367 BCE) and Sicyon under the tyrant Euphron (368–66 BCE). Both these leaders enfranchised slaves as part of a generally popular political program, thereby gaining the support of the free demos and the slaves in their struggle against the wealthy landowners. Plato and Aristotle, moreover, clearly associate tyrannical rule with the enfranchisement of slaves: Plato, *Rep.* 9.571–80; Aristotle, *Politics* 1314a29–1315b11. For discussion of Dionysios and Euphron, see Lewis 2009.

107. Bresson 2007, 133. See also Gomme et al. 1970, 86–87.

108. Scott 1985, 28–36. A concern with theft of the master's property, for example, seems to motivate much of the advice offered to slave-owners in Xenophon's treatise on household management, *Oeconomicus*. Similarly, implicit in Xenophon's discussion of the various incentives and punishments necessary to motivate slaves to work hard is the idea that slaves are inclined to work slowly or inefficiently unless such techniques are applied. See chapter 2 for further discussion.

109. Aristoph., *Knights* 25–26; Plato, *Prot.* 310c.

110. Thuc., 1.139.2.

111. Thuc., 7.27.5.

112. The structural conditions leading to the revolt of the Spartan helots are analyzed in comparative perspective by Cartledge 1985.

113. This explanation for the absence of slave revolt is articulated explicitly in Ste. Croix 1981, 146, who drew on ancient discussions of the difficulties of managing slaves (such as the Spartan helots) who come from the same place and speak the same language (Plato, *Laws* 777b4–d5; pseudo-Aristotle, *Oeconomica* 1344b18; Athenaeus, *The Learned Banqueters* 264f–265a). See also Cartledge 1985, 17–22; Garlan 1988, 191.

114. For pidgin Greek, see Aristophanes, *Thes.* 1001–1225.

115. Vogt 1973, 136–42.

116. See Harris 1989, 111 and Harris 2004, 160 for examples of slaves literate in Greek.

117. Eur. *Ion* 194–200.

118. Examples of Hellenized Greek slaves include Bäbler 1998, 94–97, 159–63.

119. For example, Bäbler 1998, 131–42 (stele of Antipatros). Similarly, the Painter Lydos, a mid-sixth-century vase-painter, who was likely a slave of Lydian origins, left a signature with a mistake: *ho ludos egrsen* (instead of *egraphsen*); this could indicate imperfect grasp of Greek by a Lydian slave, though Tsetskhladze 2008 observes that this could simply be a mistake made by a Greek. This explanation is excessively skeptical in my view.

120. Bäbler 1998, 142–47.

121. For example, names containing the name of the Near Eastern divinity Men are formed according to Greek syntax for an adjective: Apollonios, Manes. Similarly, Peter Hunt has suggested (via personal communication) that Pasion's son, Apollodorus, was named by translating a Phoenician theophoric name (Apollo = Men), as in the case of Pythodorus (Isocr.17.33). Cf. Trevett 1992, 17.

122. I owe the observation of the significance of the cosmopolitan nature of big commercial cities like Athens to Peter Hunt, personal communication.

123. On slave names, see Masson 1972; and Robertson 2008.

124. Masson 1972, 17.

125. Lauffer 1979, 124–28. I owe this observation to P. Hunt (personal communication).

126. Plato, *Republic* 327a on the Thracian cult of Bendis. Interestingly, Plato attests that there were separate processions of Thracians and Athenians, suggesting that the Thracians had opportunities to mix independently of citizens. Cf. SEG 39: 210 dedication of Daos, winner of the Torch race, to Bendis (late fourth–early third century). See also Garland 1987, 1992.

127. Lysias, 23.3, 23.6 with Lewis 1996, 13–19.

128. Hunter 1994, 70–91.

129. Harris 2002; Bresson 2007.

130. Bresson 2007, 150.

131. Xenophon, *Memorabilia* 3.7.6.

132. Athenaeus, 269c–e = Kassel and Austin fr. 137. The translation is from Olson 2008, 239, 241.

133. See Wilson 2000 for the organization of festival liturgies (*chorēgia*). The principal other liturgies were the trierarchy (financing and commanding a war ship) and the gymnasiarchy (paying for the training and maintenance of a tribal contingent preparing to compete in the athletic competition of the Panathenaia).

134. The claim (Millett 1989; Arnaoutoglou 1994) that the democratic state rendered private patron-client relations unnecessary in classical Athens, therefore, needs to be revised, as some scholars have begun to do (Gallant 1991; Mossé 1994; Jones 2004). State patronage was neither impersonal, nor did it wholly replace non-state forms of reciprocity between elites and masses.

135. E.g., Dem.18.268.

136. Jones 2004, 81. On honorary decrees to elites for their services to the city, see Whitehead 1983, 1993 and Veligianni-Terzi 1997.

137. As Thomas Gallant 1991 has observed, the norm of reciprocity between rich and poor was not only central to the ancient Greek experience but also pro-

vides a point of contact with later periods of agrarian history. Indeed, Gallant proposes three central facts of the ancient Greek economy that place ancient Greece in line with other peasant societies:

1. "The average ancient peasant household existed on the very edge of viability" (p. xi).
2. "There was a communally held belief that members of the upper class should provide subsistence insurance for the remainder of the community" (p.xi 3). By the Hellenistic period [mid-fourth-century BCE onward], wealthy elites were no longer upholding their obligations to the poor, and "dependency, chronic indebtedness and immiseration" was the result (p. xii).

While Gallant probably overemphasizes the extent of bare subsistence farming and neglects a class of better off ("middling") farmers, his observation that the Greeks ascribed to a widely held tenet of pre-modern and modern agricultural societies—the obligation of the rich to ensure the basic well-being of the lower orders—is well grounded in the ancient evidence, as I demonstrate below and in the chapters that follow. Indeed, a large part of the present study aims to illuminate the informal ("extra-institutional") discourses and practices by which peasants and slaves in ancient Greece asserted this principle as their primary defense against the predatory tendencies of the wealthy.

138. Ober 1989.

139. On naturalization in Athens, see Osborne 1981–82.

140. On metics, see Whitehead 1977; Adak 2003. There is some debate over whether metics could represent themselves in court: see Todd 2007, 13–14, with references cited therein.

141. Hunt 1998, 126.

142. Cohen 2000, 17–22 provides a catalogue of influential metics, from the architect Hippodamus of Miletus, to the philosopher Aristotle and the historian Theopompus. Lysias' family is frequently noted for its easy sociability with Plato and his circle, as depicted in Plato's *Republic*.

143. As is the case of Neaira, an ex-slave prostitute from Corinth: Pseudo-Demosthenes 59.

144. Plutarch, *Life of Pericles* 24, 32, 37.

145. Cohen 2000 makes a similar argument, though pushes his claim much further to suggest that Pericles' Citizenship Law itself allowed for the granting of citizenship to the children of permanently residing metics and foreigners. See also Vlassopoulos 2009.

146. Pasion, on whom see Trevett 1992. Pasion and his ex-slave Phormion seem to have identified not just with citizens over slaves, but wealthy citizens over non-elites insofar as they competed with the leading citizens in their financial donations to the city. Cf. Cohen 2000, 20.

147. The employment of slaves in banking, however, may also be related to the Athenian prejudice against working in the permanent employ of others (e.g., Aristotle *Rhetoric* 1367a32) with Cohen 2000, 142–43. Some texts show that

even this prejudice could be overcome in cases of pressing financial need: e.g., Isaeus 5.39, Dem. 57.35–36.

148. Aristotle *Politics* 1253–1260. Aristotle does, of course, make some distinctions between slaves, children, and women (as does Schaps 1998), but in general, his conception is that each of these groups lack the full rationality of the adult male.

149. See, for example, the evidence discussed by Hunter 1994, 9–42; Foxhall 1989, 1996; Schaps 1998; Cohen 2000, 30–48.

150. For the role of women in civic cult, see Dillon 2002; Goff 2004; Cole 2004; Connelly 2007.

151. Tragedy frequently transgressed gender norms, from the masculine Clytemnestra of Aeschylus' *Agamemnon* to the strong female heroines of Sophocles' *Antigone* and Euripides' *Medea*. Aristophanic comedy frequently featured women on top (*Lysistrata, Women of the Assembly*), and it is an open debate whether the transgressive behaviors of women in Greek drama reinforced normative gender relations or questioned them. For discussion and further bibliography, see Zeitlin 1996. For an example of women challenging male authority, see Winkler 1990.

152. There is some controversy, however, over whether slaves were actually tortured. See for example, Gagarin 1996; and Mirhady 2000.

Chapter 2. Slaves Tell Tales: The Culture of Subordinate Groups in Ancient Greece

1. My title is inspired by Robert Darnton's chapter, "Peasants Tell Tales: The Meaning of Mother Goose," in his book, *The Great Cat Massacre and Other Episodes in French Cultural History* (New York, 1984).

2. Athenaios, *The Learned Banqueters* 265d–266e. The translation is my own, though I have borrowed at a few points from the translation given in Olson 2008.

3. Briggs, *Dictionary of British Folk-Tales* 1, 391–93, quoted in Darnton 1984, 43.

4. Dio 77.10.2. Translation E. Cary (Loeb 1927).

5. Drimakos' name is possibly significant. The name is derived from the adjective "drimus" which means "fierce" and is used, for example, to describe the furious rage of Achilles in the *Iliad*, or the keenness of battle itself. Homer, *Iliad* 18. 322; 15.696: "Once again keen battle (δριμεῖα μάχη) arose around the ships." I am not suggesting here that the second element of Driamakos' name comes from the word for battle (μάχη) which has a chi instead of a kappa.

6. For ancient slave rebellions: Shaw 2001 with bibliography. For slave rebellions in more modern times, see Genovese 1979. For betrayal as the means by which slave-leaders were captured, cf. Shaw 1984, 16, 46.

7. Aly 1921, 1. Aly was writing under the influence of the nineteenth-century celebration of "das Volk" as the ancient root of the national cultures, as well as the growth of folklore research into an academic discipline. More recent research has problematized the concept of "the people," arguing that it is a rhetorical construction that never corresponds in any clear-cut way to a definite section of the

populace (Burke 1994, 3–64). Furthermore, as Darnton points out, folktales change according to historical time and place (French and German versions of Little Red Riding Hood are radically different, as are sixteenth-century and modern versions). Folktales, then, do not express "the unchanging operations of man's inner being" (Darnton 1984, 13).

8. Scott 1990, 19. Of course Scott's typology of peasant speech is a heuristic model. Real peasant speech rarely falls neatly into these categories. For example, peasants may tell tales (fables, folktales) among themselves as well as in the presence of their superiors. Presumably, the subversive meanings are more directly acknowledged (e.g., through gesture, tone of voice, facial expression, or even direct articulation) in in-group performances.

9. Scott 1990, 19.

10. Levine 2007, 113. Cf. 105: slave trickster tales were a "mechanism … by means of which psychic relief from arbitrary authority could be secured, symbolic assaults upon the powerful could be waged, and important lessons about authority relationships could be imparted."

11. Ibid., 105.

12. Ibid., 113–14, 125. Levine also emphasizes that slave trickster tales were not just about fantasy of triumph over one's oppressors; they were much more complex and diverse than this. Specifically, these stories also inculcated lessons concerning prudent behavior in the unchangeable conditions of slavery (Levine 2007, 115 and below) and even sometimes represented the duplicity and moral corruptness of the whites in the figure of the trickster (118). It should also be noted that Levine is careful to survey the entire spectrum of traditional slave tales, including not just trickster tales, but "moralistic tales" which inculcate the very values that tricksters sometimes seem to undermine—e.g., friendship, hardwork and sincerity (Levine 2007, 90–101; 120). It is worth quoting Levine's conclusion: "The trickster served as agent of the world's irrationality and of man's fundamental helplessness. Whenever animals became too bloated with their power or importance or sense of control, the trickster was on hand to remind them of how things really were. No animal escaped these lessens; not Wolf, not Lion, not Elephant, indeed, not the trickster himself. Throughout there is a latent yearning for structure, for justice, for reason, but they are not to be had, in this world at least. If the strong are not to prevail over the weak, neither shall the weak dominate the strong. Their eternal and inconclusive battle served as proof that man is part of a larger order which he scarcely understands and certainly does not control" (120).

13. Drimakos' name, if it is Greek, as the etymology proposed above suggests, is perhaps further evidence of the fact that the story derives from the Chians and not their slaves. On the other hand, we must assume that slaves on Chios learned Greek (see chapter 1 above) and were given Greek names. Sometimes slave names reflected their ethnicity. On slave names, see note 123 above.

14. Levine 2007, 106–7; 117.

15. The storyteller employs the same rhetorical device of paradox that Herodotus employs in telling the story of a Spartan encounter with the Persian king: "Law is their [the Spartans'] master, and they fear [law] much more than your men fear you" (7.104.4).

16. *Pace* Robin Osborne, who responded to an earlier oral version of this essay by arguing that the story of Drimakos offered nothing for slaves. Even Brent Shaw (see discussion below), who draws a sharp distinction between the myth of the social bandit and the reality of violent anti-social men, does not doubt that stories about social bandits relate to the popular desire for a "figure of protest": "There can be no doubt that the stories themselves mirror popular aspirations attached to an ideal figure of the bandit" (Shaw 1984, 44).

17. It should be noted, however, that peasant and slave tricksters often seem to be rewarded only with a good meal (Darnton 1984, 32–34; Levine 2007, 126–29). Afro-American tales of animal tricksters place more emphasis on vindicating themselves and humiliating their adversaries. In Afro-American slave tales, animal tricksters gain total revenge, human tricksters only a meal and/or the pleasure of outwitting their masters (Levine 2007, 131–32). For these points, see further discussion below.

18. I owe this observation to Franco Basso. Yet one could argue, of course, that Drimakos' lover gets the hero's reward—wealth and freedom—just like the hero of the French folktale.

19. It should be noted, however, that the rewards for the successful trickster in French folktales are usually limited to a transformation of circumstance for the hero himself, not an overturning of the social order (Darnton 1984, 58–59).

20. Levine argues that human tricksters differed from animal tricksters in that they were more bound by the conditions of slavery (2007, 131–32).

21. Darnton 1984, 33–34.

22. Finley 1998, 191 notes this parallel, though emphasizes the distinction between banditry of free men and slaves.

23. Hobsbawm 1959, 13–29; 2000, 19–33.

24. Hobsbawm 2000, 29–30.

25. Blok, 1971, 1972; Lewin 1979a, 1979b; Shaw 1984, 34, 37, 38, 40, 41; Fentress and Wickham 1992, 173–99; Grünewald 1999.

26. Shaw 1984.

27. Ibid., 50.

28. Ibid., 48.

29. For role reversal in symbolic anthropology, see, for example, Babcock 1978; Stallybrass and White 1986.

30. Shaw 1984, 49.

31. Ibid., 51.

32. Dio 77.10.

33. Dio 77.10.2. This quotation is also highlighted by Shaw 1984, 47.

34. Dio 77.10.5.

35. Almond and Pollard 2001, 55. For a review of the scholarship and references, see Almond and Pollard 2001.

36. Ibid., 77.

37. One answer to this question is the symbolic power of marginal figures and role reversals (see n.28 above). This answer certainly provides a rationale for elite appropriation of a popular figure, but does not fully explain the many features of popular ideology remaining in the tale.

38. Although Cincinnatus could also be a construction of Roman peasants, in much the same way as Russian peasants imagined the Tsar as a defender of their interests against wealthy landowners (cf. Burke 1978/1994, 150–55).

39. Hdt. 5.92a. For a similar theme, compare the image of "rivers flowing backwards" in the Greek proverbial tradition (e.g., Aeschylus fr. 335, Euripides, *Medea* 410 and Dem.19.287 with Santini 1997). As MacDowell 2000, 330 comments, the phrase *anō potamōn* ("rivers flowing upwards") was "a proverbial expression for what is topsy-turvy."

40. This rhetorical figure became known in ancient rhetorical theory as "comparison from what is impossible" or, for short, "the impossible" (*adynaton*). For discussion of this figure in Greek and Latin rhetoric and literature, see Rowe 1965. I thank my colleague Ruth Caston for this reference.

41. Scott 1990,167.

42. Kunzle 1978, 89.

43. Compare Phaedrus' interpretation of fables as a genre invented by slaves as a medium for talking secretly with each other (Phaedrus iii.pr.33–44); and Aesop Vita W 75–76, where Aesop tells the story about his sexual liaison with the wife of his master in the disguised form of a fable.

44. Although I am suggesting here that Aesop and his fables were an invention of the subordinate classes, the ambiguity of the form led to its adaptation to a variety of ideologies. The most famous post-classical re-writing of Aesop's Fables is that of the seventeenth-century French noble, La Fontaine, whose versions clearly reflect the morality of his own social circles.

45. Compare Hopkins 1993, who acknowledges that the story could be understood by different members of the social order in different ways, but focuses in his essay on the meaning it had for Roman citizens. In other words, he does not explore what it might have meant for slaves or other subordinate groups such as the poor.

46. The genre of "Aesopic Fables" proved a flexible genre in which a wide variety of themes appear, including the natural right of the strong to dominate the weak (e.g., Hesiod *W&D* 203–12). It would be wrong, therefore, to claim that fables or analogies with the animal world were solely a feature of the culture of subordinate groups.

47. Both the genre of iambic poetry and Archilochus himself seem to have connections with cultic worship of this sort. For discussion of the origins and nature of iambic poetry, see West 1974; Richardson 1974, 214; O'Higgins 2003; Rosen 1988; Brown 1997; and Gerber 1999. For a convenient catalogue of the evidence for ritual obscenity, see Fluck 1931. For Archilochus' connection to the cults of Demeter and Dionysus on Paros and Thasos, see Brown 1997, 44–49. Popular themes in Archilochus include not only obscenity and sexuality, but also animal fables (fr. 172–80; 185, 187) and abusive speech (e.g., fr. 196a).

48. Kunzle 1978, 85 makes a similar case for nineteenth-century WUD images, which are reinterpreted in ways that support the status quo, thus downplaying their revolutionary essence. Whereas earlier renditions of the fish in the sky motif leave the birds in freedom, these later versions "twist and reverse the traditional motif" by suggesting that the fish will be quickly devoured by birds.

49. Forsdyke 1999.

50. Kunzle 1978, 82. Cf. Burke 1978/1994, 189–91, who similarly emphasizes the multiple, and sometimes conflicting, meanings of Carnival and the carnivalesque theme of WUD for elites and masses.

51. It is possible that early modern versions of the WUD articulate slightly more explicitly a critique of social hierarchy insofar as they represent at least one example of reversal of human relations (children spank parents). Greek examples, by contrast, stay within the realm of reversals of the natural order (e.g., land and sea, fish and birds) and thus avoid direct allusion to human social hierarchies. I do not believe that this is a significant difference, since the inversion of roles between children and parents hardly represents a very direct allusion to social hierarchies of human communities.

52. For this theme in the Homeric epics, see *Odyssey* Book 7 (Land of the Phaeacians) and Book 9 (Land of the Cyclops). In Athenian traditions, the rule of the tyrant Peisistratus, as well as the period of political ascendancy of the politician Cimon, were compared to the age of Kronos: Aristotle, *Constitution of Athens*, 16.7, Plutarch, *Life of Cimon* 10.6.

53. The same theme occurs in Hesiod's version of the story of Prometheus and Pandora. In this tale (logos/ainos), Prometheus stole fire from the gods and gave it to mankind. In revenge, Zeus sent Pandora (womenkind) among them and she became the source of all evils for men. Cf. 90–91: "But before [Prometheus' trick and Zeus' revenge], the races of men lived on the earth/Without any troubles, neither harsh toil nor sickness."

54. Festivity (*thalia*: abundance, good cheer – *Od*.11.603) is central to popular culture and is therefore a key aspect of popular conceptions of the Age of Kronos.

55. Hesiod, *Works and Days* 109–20. Compare also the fourth race, the race of Heroes, who are more than just the third Race of Bronze. Though some of the generation of heroes die in war, Zeus settled the rest in the islands of the blessed where the earth bears fruit for them without toil (160–69). As Paul Cartledge has reminded me, this fourth race interrupts the otherwise degenerate sequence of Hesiod's Myth of the Ages, and therefore seems like an intrusion.

56. For a good overview of Hesiod and Hesiodic poetry, as well as contemporary Hesiodic scholarship, see Most 2006, xi–lxxiv. West (1978, 179) notes that the myth of a "Golden race" that lived in the time of Kronos is independent of the "Myth of the Ages" into which it is inserted in Hesiod's *Works and Days*. The latter myth seems to be an import from the Near East (West 1978, 28), whereas the former is native to Greece. Specifically, the idea of a "Golden race" was probably a popular mythical explanation of the harvest festival of the Kronia at which masters and slaves feasted together in celebration of the harvest. Cf. Baldry 1952, who shows that before Hesiod, the notion of a time of plentiful abundance was a traditional idea associated with the reign of Kronos, not with a Golden Age.

57. Burke 1994, 40.

58. Ibid., 40.

59. Ibid., 190.

60. "Big Rock Candy Mountain" is believed to be a hobo song, and was recorded in 1928 by Harry McClintock.

61. Hesiod, *Works and Days* 176–78.

62. Cf. Baldry 1952, 85: "The 'traditional picture' [of a Golden Race] is one that must have grown up and been kept alive among the country-folk, and it is no accident that our chief early sources for it are the farmer-poet Hesiod and the writers of Attic comedy. It was the hard-worked peasant, the weary harvester, who longed for nature to produce her fruits without ploughing or reaping and dreamed of a time when 'the wheat-bearing field brought forth on her own accord plentiful and unstinting harvest.'" Jones 2004, 227–72 similarly credits the concept of a Reign of Kronos to a "rural" perspective that is then appropriated and developed by Greek philosophers such as Plato. Cf. Most 2006 xxxviii–xlii, who emphasizes the theme of work (and justice) as defining the human condition in the *Works and Days*.

63. Cartledge 1993, 135.

64. Reckford 1987, 97 recognizes these elements and, following Zielinski 1885, interprets them as a key element in his theory of Aristophanic comedy as fairytale-plays (89–104). Reckford interprets these passages not merely as *adunata*, but as "a way of thinking clearly and creatively about the future" which "implies possibilities of political and social revolution" (326). For Reckford, the comic theme of a magical Golden Age is a form of utopian thinking that explores "possibilities of social change that ordinarily seem unthinkable" (325). Reckford, then, allows for revolutionary as well as conservative interpretations of comic reversals and transgressions. Note also the connections between unnatural fertility/abundance and the figure of Dionysus in myth and ritual (see, e.g., Euripides' *Bacchae* and Greek vase-painting in which Dionysus is surrounded by abundant growth of vines); Reckford 1987, 100–101, 324. On the theme of Cockaigne in Aristophanes, see Sutton 1980, 55–67, who notes comedy's dependence on Hesiod for this theme, emphasizes the importance of lack of work (*apragmosunē*) in these images of the ideal life, and the "strong resemblance to medieval fables about the Land of Cockaigne" (Sutton 1980, 58, with earlier bibliography cited therein). Further recent discussion of this theme includes Versnel 1993; Ceccarelli 1996; and Wilkins 2000, 110–23.

65. Athenaeus 268b–d = Kassel and Austin fr. 1. The translation is from Olson 2008, 235. This play, and those discussed below, date to the fifth century. See also the even more elaborate rendition of this theme from Pherecrates *The Miners* (Athenaeus 268d–269c = Kassel and Austin fr. 113).

66. Athenaeus 267e–f = Kassel and Austin fr. 16. Translation is from Olson 2008, 231. Aristotle, *Politics* 1253b33–40 similarly draws the connection between the fantasy of objects that can do their own work and the fantasy of no slave labor.

67. Athenaeus 269c–e = Kassel and Austin fr. 137. The translation is from Olson 2008, 239, 241.

68. For the myth of Prometheus and Pandora, see Hesiod, *Works and Days*, 42–105.

69. Ancient sources for the festivals of Kronos and Saturn include Accuis, *Annales* 2–7 (Warmington) and Macrobius, *Saturnalia* 1.24.22–23. For further discussion, see Versnel 1993, and below (this chapter), and chapter 4.

70. On the "burden" of slavery for masters, see Genovese 1974; Bradley 1994. The recognition of the burden of slavery on masters in no way minimizes, of course, the much greater suffering of the slaves themselves.

71. McCarthy 2000.

72. For this interpretation of the function of Greek fables, see Cascajero 1991.

73. Scholars who argue for Greek fables as articulating peasant or slave perspectives include: Crusius 1913; Meuli 1954; La Penna 1961; Ste. Croix 1981; Cascajero 1991; and Rothwell 1995. La Penna's study is problematic for its synchronic approach that does not distinguish between early Greek fables and those that appear in later collections. Meuli and Cascajero are much more sensitive to the ways that elites appropriated and adapted fables to their own ideologies. Cascajero is particularly valuable in this regard, and anticipates many of the arguments made in this section. Meuli (1954, 80) notes that the fable is considered a form of lower-class entertainment in Aristophanes' *Wasps* (e.g., 566–67), and Rothwell develops this argument in full.

74. Holzberg 2002, 16–17.

75. See, e.g., van Dijk 1997, 379.

76. The Greeks do not seem to have associated the fable with a specific individual or even genre in the first centuries after its adoption. For example, the seventh-century iambic poet Archilochus, who also made use of the fable, introduces the fable of the Eagle and the Fox as "a story (*ainos*) that men tell." Sometimes the fable is associated with particular cities (Sybaris) or regions (Libya, Phrygia, Cilicia, Caria, and Egypt), but it is clear that this is shorthand for "an anonymous story from far away." By the fifth century, however, the fable is firmly associated with the slave Aesop.

77. For the Near Eastern origins of the fable see, e.g., West 1984; Holzberg 2002.

78. West 1984, 128. Some scholars contest West's claim that Aesop's fables and his life circulated in book form in the fifth century, since the chief evidence, the verb πεπάτακας (lit. "to have walked over", i.e., "to be familiar with") in Aristoph. *Birds* 471 ("nor have you made yourself familiar with Aesop") does not necessarily imply a book (Dunbar 1995, 326; Kurke 2011, 19–21). It is immaterial to my argument whether the Aesop story circulated only orally or also in book form.

79. Holzberg 2002, 13–17 provides a similar reconstruction.

80. Hansen (1998, 109) does not recognize the significance of this shift when he writes that the story is "transferred with little change from the Assyrian sage Ahikar to the Phrygian sage Aesop." To call Aesop a sage, tout court, is to gloss over a key difference. Hanson is more on track when he writes (1998, 109) that "for most of the biography [Aesop] is a man of lowly origins enjoying a superiority of wit to the powerful persons of the world. The fantasy is certainly akin to that of the lowly peasant lad who by means of wit, luck and a good heart wins the princess and half the kingdom." Hanson also notes (1998, 109) that Aesop is the "successor to the stock character of the clever slave in ancient comedy and a predecessor of the clever slave of modern [Afro-American] folktales."

81. Holzberg 2002, 15.

82. Oddly, Holzberg is firmly opposed however to the idea that fables were a medium of resistance for slaves and other subordinate groups (see above). The origins of many slaves in the Near East is often indicated by the standard names given to them by their Greek owners: e.g., Syra ("Syrian girl"), Phryx ("Phrygian"), Dardanis ("Dardanian girl," from Dardania in the Troad), Aristoph. *Peace*, 1138, 1146; *Wasps* 433, 1371.

83. For instance, a basic element of the plot, namely Aesop's death at Delphi, is clearly present already in the fifth century: Hdt 2.134.4; Aristoph. *Wasps* 1446–49. On the Second Sophistic, see below.

84. Even Meuli (1954), the principal proponent of the "sociological explanation" of fables (see also Crusius 1913), does not deny that they were also used by the strong against the weak (cf. van Dijk 1997, 4). In addition, it should be noted that even among a particular group, fables do not articulate a single message. As Levine (2007) shows, and I demonstrate below, slave folktales express a wide variety of slave needs, ranging, for example, from the straightforward desire for violent revenge against masters to the need for caution in interacting with superiors.

85. Van Dijk recognizes this point when he sums up his survey of ancient and modern theories of the fable by stating "neither the functions nor the characters of the genre should be restricted" (1997, 112). The bulk of van Dijk's large book is devoted to describing the wide range of functions of the fable in Greek literature. Van Dijk does not consider the question of the pre-literary origins of the fable in popular and/or slave culture.

86. The diverse linguistic backgrounds of slaves are not an obstacle to the idea of a slave culture. Knowledge of Greek was crucial to the effectiveness of slaves in Greece, and therefore, masters had no choice but to encourage the rapid acquisition of Greek language by their slaves. The use of Greek presumably made it easier for these particular slave cultural products to enter and interact with the culture of free Greeks. For slave-owner anxiety about the potential for a common language to facilitate rebellion among slaves, see Athenaeus 264f–265a, paraphrasing Plato's *Laws* (see discussion below).

87. Perry 1 = van Dijk 4F1a–h. Archilochus' version (fr.172–81 West) is the oldest surviving version of the fable, though Aristophanes also alludes to the fable in *Birds* 650–53.

88. Translation is from Gerber 1999, 185.

89. Van Dijk 1997, 142–44 with bibliography cited therein.

90. This idea is already proverbial by the time of Homer. At *Iliad*, 22.261–65, Hector suggests that Achilles make an agreement with him that the victor in their combat hand over the corpse of the vanquished for burial. Achilles rejects this proposal by citing the proverbial hostility of lions and men and wolves and sheep. For the fluid relation between fables and proverbs in popular culture, see below.

91. Fr.177. Translation is from Gerber 1999, 192. The idea that there is justice among animals is central to the parallelism between human and animal worlds demanded by fables. Yet Hesiod contrasts beasts with men on the basis that there is no justice among the former (*Works and Days*, 276–77), cited below.

92. Genovese 1974; Levine 2007.

93. Genovese 1974; Levine 2007.

94. Though note La Penna 1961, who observes that the number of fables featuring divine justice is very small; usually the conflict between the strong and weak is decided either by the rule of force, or by the cunning of the weaker party. La Penna, however, considers the entire corpus of fables from Hesiod through the late Roman period, an approach that does not distinguish between the themes of early fables and those preserved in rhetorical collections.

95. Scott 1985, 177–78.

96. Van Dijk 1997, 173–76 with bibliography cited therein.

97. For masters, on the other hand, the fable could serve to warn of the dangers lurking in their own homes.

98. Tacitus, *Annales* 14.42.3; with Bradley 1994, 107–31. For some Greek examples, cf. Antiphon 5.69, 5.48, 1.14–20.

99. Perry 3 = van Dijk 17F5, 17A2, 17A5.

100. *Peace* 129–30; cf. *Wasps* 1446–48 and Lys.695; *Life of Aesop* 135–39.

101. La Penna 1961 even suggests that this fable contains a critique of conventional Greek religion insofar as it depicts Zeus as outwitted by a dung beetle.

102. *Peace* 133–34.

103. Cf. Olson 1998, xxxiv, for this interpretation. For Aesop as a turnip, *Life of Aesop* 14.

104. Achaeus, *Omphale Trag.GrF* I (Snell) 20 F34 = van Dijk 15A1 = Diogenes Laertius 2.17.

105. Homer, *Odyssey* 8.329–32. For further discussion of this scene, see chapter 5 below.

106. For another echo of fable in Homer, see n.90 above. No fables in Homer: Meuli 1954, 73; van Dijk 1997, 124. Homer does represent Odysseus telling an *ainos* (a term that sometimes signifies a fable, see n.108 below), when, disguised as a beggar, he tells a tale to the swineherd Eumaios in order to get him to lend him a cloak for warmth during the night. Odysseus' story bears little resemblance to animal fables, however. Cf. Meuli 1954, 73–76.

107. Perry 4a = van Dijk 2F1. Perry pairs this fable with 4b, a version of the "bird in the hand is better than a bird in the bush." In Perry 4b, the nightingale tries to persuade the Hawk that she is too small to fill his belly and he would be better off trying to catch a bigger bird. The Hawk responds that he would be foolish to give up a small piece of food in his claws in the hopes of a bigger meal that is not yet found. Why does Perry put these two together? Each fable probably had many versions in living oral culture. The use of the nightingale is well suited to both versions. Since the nightingale was conceptualized as a lamenting singing bird (cf. tale of Procne, Aristoph., *Birds*), it is well employed as futilely decrying its fate. On the other hand, the nightingale is a small bird, and therefore well suits the attempt to get free on the grounds of hope of better nourishment. In both, the nightingale's pleas fail to convince the hawk.

108. For the use of the term *ainos* of the animal fable, see for example, Hesiod, *Works and Days* 207, Archilochus fr. 174 (West), and Aristophanes, *Peace* 45–48. For discussion of this term, see Nagy 1979, 237–40; Rosen 1988, 30–31. Other terms frequently used to describe the fable include *logos* (e.g., Aristophanes, *Peace* 129; *Birds* 651; Herodotus 1.141) and *muthos* (Aeschylus fr.139 Radt). For

discussion of this terminology, see van Dijk 1997, 79–90; and Holzberg 2002, 20. Satirical analogies between men and animals are common in Aristophanes. In Aristophanes' *Wealth* (47, 756), the politician Cleon is equated first with a dung beetle, and then with a dog.

109. Hesiod, *Works and Days* 207–211.

110. West 1978, 205.

111. Ibid.

112. Hesiod, *Works and Days*, 276–77.

113. For the parallel between beasts and men in fable, see e.g., Archil.fr.177 cited above.

114. See also van Dijk 1997, 127–34 who also suggests other meanings of the fable, even within the Hesiodic context.

115. DuBois 2003, 170–88, fails to distinguish between this obvious meaning and the hidden meaning, and therefore argues that fables do not articulate the point of view of slaves but of masters. DuBois' conclusion is surprising since she cites (albeit briefly) and is thus aware of the work of James Scott on the relation between folktale, fable, and proverbs, hidden speech and popular resistance.

116. The idea that the weak should not contend directly with the strong also lurks in a fable that Herodotus puts in the mouth of Cyrus, King of Persia. After the Ionians and Aeolians had been conquered by Persia, they sent envoys to Cyrus asking to be subjects on the same terms by which they had previously been subject to Lydia. In response, Cyrus told the story of a flute player who had hoped to entice some fish to jump up onto land by playing some music for them. When his tactic failed, he threw out a net and trapped a large number. When he saw the fish jumping up and down on the shore he said to them: "Stop dancing, since you did not jump to shore and dance when I was playing the flute." Herodotus follows the story with the explanation that the Ionians and Aolians had not rebelled from the Lydians when requested by Cyrus, but only when he had conquered them by force were they ready to obey. The analogy suggests that it is better to submit to greater powers in the hopes of being treated better than if one futilely resists.

117. Aristotle, *Politics* 1284a15–18. Aristotle attributes the story to Antisthenes, a fifth-century philosopher and a student of Socrates. Given the connections between Socrates and popular culture—and Aesop's fables in particular (see chapter 1, n.16 above)—it is not unlikely that Antisthenes was drawing on popular culture in telling this fable.

118. Cf. Aristophanes, *Birds* 375–76, where the Hoopoe trots out a series of proverbs as advice to his fellow birds in their dealings with Pisthetairos and humans generally: "Caution saves everything" and "Wise men can learn even from their enemies." Interestingly, the context here is the natural hostility of birds and men (the Greeks ate a wide variety of birds), a variation on the familiar theme of the impossibility of friendship between natural enemies in animal fables and proverbs, as is emphasized by the allusion to an animal proverb concerning wolves in *Birds* 369.

119. For the close relation between fable and proverb, see van Dijk 1997, 113, though van Dijk does not include proverbs in his study. For recent discussion of Greek proverbs, see Lardinois 1997.

120. Aristoph., *Peace* 1083, 1086; 1114.

121. Aristoph., *Peace* 1076, 1112. For a Homeric example of a similar proverb, see *Iliad* 22.262–64, cited in n.90 above. On the ancient rhetorical figure of *adunata*, see n.40 above.

122. Levine 2007, 115.

123. Aristotle, *Rhetoric* 1393b8–22.

124. Phalaris became tyrant of Acragas in Sicily and ruled from approximately 570–554 BCE.

125. Compare the use of this image of the bridled horse to signify political enslavement in Aeschylus *Persians* and Herodotus' *Histories*, as discussed in Forsdyke 2001.

126. Archilochus fr. 237 = van Dijk 4F3.

127. DuBois 2003 is particularly insightful on the symbolic and practical roles of the slave's body in ancient Greece. See also Hunter 1994.

128. Aristotle *Rhetoric* 1393b22–a1 = van Dijk 39F2.

129. Scholars of ancient slavery provide a full exegesis: Finley 1998 (originally published 1980); Garlan 1988; Bradley 1994; Hunter 1994; Garnsey 1996; DuBois 2003; Andreau and Descat 2006.

130. Aristotle, *Politics* 1253b–1255b. There are echoes of this theory in other works by Aristotle, for instance, the following passage from the *Nicomachean Ethics* 1161b which boldly states the paradoxical idea that slaves benefit from being used by the masters, not the other way round: "Where there is nothing in common between ruler and ruled, there can be no friendship between them either, any more than there can be justice. It is like the relation between a craftsman and his tool, or between the soul and the body or between master and slave: all these instruments it is true are benefited by the persons who use them, but there can be no friendship, nor justice, towards inanimate things; indeed not even towards a horse or an ox, nor yet towards a slave as a slave. For master and slave have nothing in common: a slave is a living tool, just as a tool is an inanimate slave."

131. Recent discussion of Aristotle's theory of natural slavery includes Cartledge 2002; Garnsey1996; DuBois 2003, 189–205.

132. Genovese 1974; Dal Lago and Katsari 2008b.

133. Seneca, *Letter* 47.

134. On Athenaeus and his immense work, *The Sophists at Dinner*, see Braund and Wilkins 2000.

135. For the Greek text and an English translation of this work (also sometimes called *The Sophists at Dinner*), see Olson 2008. Unfortunately, we know very little about Nymphodorus, the itinerant geographer who first recorded the tale, according to Athenaeus. Nymphodorus lived in the third century BCE and his work survives only in fragments: see Jacoby *FGrHist* 572.

136. For the importance of displays of learning as well as morality in Athenaeus' *The Learned Banqueters*, see Wilkins 2000, 9–11 and Braund and Wilkins 2000, 27.

137. As Wilkins notes (2000, 23), this fictive frame to the dinner conversation is modeled on Plato's *Symposium* and other Platonic dialogues.

138. 224b. On luxury and particularly the symbolic associations of fish in Greek culture, see Davidson 1997.

139. For luxury as a key theme of Athenaeus' work, see Braund 2000, 10–11; Wilkins 2000, 27. Braund rightly emphasizes that while scholars have conventionally taken Athenaeus as a mere antiquarian whose work can be mined for fragments of earlier authors, in fact the work is "deeply concerned with contemporary Roman and imperial society" (Braund 2000, 18).

140. 228c–d.

141. For the theme of the harmful effects of luxury, see 228c.

142. For the explicit condemnation, see e.g., 255d, 256f, 258b, 259f, 260f.

143. 239e.

144. 249f–250a.

145. 256d and 257e–f.

146. 253b.

147. 262b.

148. 263b.

149. The phrase "poison of slavery," is borrowed from Cartledge 1985, 19.

150. 264b.

151. 264b. The speaker does acknowledge, however, that even this type of slavery has some difficulties. These arise from the fact that the slaves all speak the same language and therefore can better organize rebellions. This was the case with the Messenians, among other states (264e–f).

152. The fourth-century Chian historian Theopompus is cited as the source of the claim that the Chians were the first to use chattel slaves (=Theopompus *FGrHist* 115 F122). For discussion see Vidal-Naquet 1986, and "Something to Do with Chios?" below.

153. 266f.

154. 265a–b. The quotation is from Plato, *Laws* 776–78. Interestingly, Athenaeus quotes selectively from this passage in the *Laws*, leaving out some sections like 777b5, where Plato admits that slaves are not just property but human beings (*anthrōpoi*) and that, as such, the distinction between slave and master is not easily accepted by men. Athenaeus sums this up with the simple statement: "this form of property is difficult as is shown by the insurrections of the Messenians." On Athenaeus' use of his sources, see Pelling 2000; and Gorman and Gorman 2007.

155. I owe this idea to Josine Blok, who pressed me to think more about the role of the hero shrine in the story. I take this opportunity to thank Josine and other members of the ancient history group at the University of Utrecht who offered many insightful suggestions in response to an earlier oral version of this chapter.

156. 266d. It is perhaps noteworthy that, according to some traditions, a hero-cult was established in honor of the slave Aesop after his unjust conviction and death at the hands of the Delphians (Vita W; P.Oxy.1800). Thus the story of Drimakos may be influenced by the narrative pattern of an offense leading to a propitiatory cult that we see in numerous stories of the origins of cults (e.g., the cult of Hera and Medea's children at Corinth as described in Euripides, *Medea* 1378–83; the cult of Neoptolemus at Delphi as mentioned in Pindar, *Nemean* 7.44–47). More important, however, the stories of Drimakos and Aesop adapt

this narrative pattern to the common theme of fables and other forms of popular storytelling, namely the revenge of the weak against the strong. In both stories, free Greek citizens, after mistreating a slave, are forced by subsequent misfortune (caused either by divine or human agents) to propitiate a slave. This dramatic reversal of status, though figured in religious terms in these two stories, is a staple pattern of a wide variety of popular forms of culture, as I argue throughout this book. While we cannot be certain that the propitiatory cult was part of the Aesop tradition already in classical Greece, the fact that Herodotus in the fifth-century BCE knows of Aesop's unjust death at the hands of the Delphians is suggestive (2.134; cf. Aristophanes, *Wasps* 1446–48).

157. Compare Graf 1985, 123–24, whose interpretation is similar to mine. Graf notes both the double dimensions of the cult and the correspondences between the cult and the treaty worked out by Drimakos. Graf situates the cult in the historical context of ongoing conflict between the Chians and their slaves (on which see below), and suggests that the cult served to mediate between these two parties. Finally, Graf does not rule out either the existence of an historical slave leader who was heroized as the Kindly One, nor the idea that an even older heroic cult lies behind the aetiological legend of Drimakos.

158. The bibliography on hero-cult is vast. Good starting points are Hägg 1999 and the bibliography cited therein, and Ekroth 2007.

159. Morris 1988.

160. Boedeker 1998; Auffarth 1999. Others have interpreted this boom as a product of competition between city-states for the cultural capital of panhellenic heroes. See Hall 1999, and chapter 3 below.

161. Connor 1993; Kearns 1989.

162. The festival of Kronos in Greece and Saturn in Rome was also a cultic context for the interaction between slaves and masters (see below). Yet these cults were not hero-cults, let alone cults in which a slave was the focus of the worshipping community.

163. Cf. Graf 1985, 123–25.

164. On monuments as a source of oral traditions in Herodotus, see Griffiths 2006, 139. On monuments and memory generally in ancient Greece, see Alcock 2002.

165. The fact that, according to the story, the shrine is dedicated to a formerly hostile figure who is neutralized and even transformed into a protecting force is parallel to other hero-cults. For example, hero shrines were dedicated at Thebes to the Seven Against Thebes, and at least one of the Seven (Amphiareus) is claimed as a protecting deity for Thebes: Pindar N.9.21–27; O.6.12–17; Hdt. 8.134. Compare also the story of Oedipus, whose hero-cult at Coloneus in Attica served as a protecting force for Athens.

166. The only historical figures given shrines are usually founders of cities (*oikistai*), and even the highly unusual case of the heroization of Brasidas at Amphipolis may be classified in this category (cf. Malkin 1987). On hero-cults to the Seven Against Thebes, cf. chapter 3.

167. This suggestion is also made by Jacoby and is admitted as possible by Graf 1985, 125.

168. Genovese 1974. Compare Finley's comments on the relative absence of major slave revolts in antiquity: "the vast majority of slaves in antiquity somehow accommodated themselves to their condition, whether passively and sullenly or positively, or perhaps most commonly, by a combination of both ... How else could the slaves have survived except by compromise and accommodation?" (1998, 182–84).

169. Thompson 1993, 224.

170. Ibid., 230. For more discussion of how peasants protest oppressive practices through rituals, see chapter 4 below.

171. Rabelais, *Gargantua* Chapter 23. An English translation may be found in Screech 2006, 288–89.

172. The translation is from Screech 2006, 288–89.

173. Genovese 1979. Garlan 1988, 183 observes this parallel, as does Finley 1998, 181–82.

174. Genovese 1979, 51. It is possible, on the basis of these historical parallels, that the cases of "willing subordination" of certain groups to others cited approvingly by Athenaeus 263d (the Mariandynians strike a bargain with the Heraclots) and 264b (the Penestae make a deal with the Thessalians) are a result of similar such agreements.

175. Genovese 1979, xiv.

176. Vita G, 26.

177. Genovese 1974, 147; cf. 222–23.

178. Vita G 38–43.

179. Hopkins 1993, 24.

180. Hopkins 1993, 19 entertains the possibility that the story was read aloud by slaves, but does not develop the implications for slave understandings of the story.

181. Genovese 1979.

182. Cartledge 1985. Athenaeus himself, in a passage that immediately follows his account of Drimakos, reports that slaves in Samos used the same tactic of forming a maroon community on a mountain during their successful rebellion against their masters. Athenaeus 267a: "Malacus, in his Annals of Siphnos, records that Ephesus was settled by slaves of the Samians, to the number of a thousand, who at first had retired to the mountain of the island and done much mischief to the Samians. Five years after this the Samians, in obedience to an oracle, made a conditional treaty with the slaves, and they departed unharmed from the island, sailing forth to Ephesus, where they landed. The Ephesians sprang from them." While elements of this story are clearly mythical, it still reveals knowledge of the slave strategy of creating maroon communities.

183. Shaw 2001. One might also compare Genovese 1974 on the religious authority of slave preachers and their role in slave resistance and rebellion.

184. Shaw 1984, 46–48. As Shaw very succinctly puts the problem of our sources: "The historical possible and the ideologically necessary ... intermingle and merge to form the story" (46).

185. Vansina 1985; Thomas 1989; Fentress and Wickham 1992.

186. Austin and Kassel (fr. 296 = Athenaeus 266f). On Eupolis, see Storey 2003. Cf. *Life of Aesop* 28, where Xanthos observes, shortly after purchasing

Aesop, that: "I didn't realize that I bought a master for myself." This idea is echoed in 32, when, after Aesop divines her illicit designs on a good-looking slave, Xanthos tells his wife (jokingly) that Aesop is now master over her; and in 39, when Aesop teaches Xanthos correct speech. Clearly, by the second century CE, the idea that slaves dominated their masters was a well-worn comic topos. Compare also the slave character Karion in Aristophanes' *Wealth*.

187. L. Gibbs (review of van Dijk (*BMCR* 1998: 98.5.18)) points out that the proverb should not be separated artificially from the fable as a form of popular culture, since there was clearly a fluid relation between the two. See "Animal Fables" above, with references in n.118 above for some examples from comedy.

188. On the connections between comedy and popular culture, see chapter 1, "Popular Culture: How to Recover It?" with references in n.14.

189. Theopompus, *FGrHist* 115 F122 with Vidal-Naquet 1986. Vidal-Naquet contests the validity of this claim and relates Theopompus' interest in and claims about the origins of chattel slavery to contemporary fourth-century debates and anxieties, especially regarding the growth of profit-driven economic activity. Epigraphy: Robert 1938, 118–26. Robert suggests that these slaves were manumitted for service in the navy, a point accepted by Hunt 1998, 86. For the use of slaves in the Chian navy, see Thuc. 8.15.2.

190. Thuc. 8.40.2. Paul Cartledge suggests to me that Thucydides must mean the largest number of slaves in relation to the free.

191. Jameson 1992, 140. Morris and Papadopoulos (2005, 204), however, note that Chios is an exception to their theory that stone towers in the Greek countryside represent slave quarters. The absence of such towers is not a negation of the importance of chattel slavery in Chios; rather, this gap can be explained, according to the authors, by architectural norms in Ionia, which differed from those of mainland Greece.

192. For a summary of the archaeological evidence, see Roebuck 1986 and Yalouris 1986. Aristotle, *Pol.* 1291b24 attests to the large number of Chian merchants, and wine from the Chian colony Maroneia in Thrace is already noted by both Homer (*Il*.9.71–2; *Od*.9.196–8) and by Archilochus fr. 2 (West).

193. Hdt. 6.8.2.

194. Hdt. 9.106.4; Thuc. 3.10.5, 7.57.4. For an overview of Chios' role in the Athenian Empire, see Barron 1986.

195. Thuc. 8.24.4.

196. Thuc. 8.39.3, 8.40.2. It is noteworthy that Thucydides uses the word *lēisteia* ("banditry") to describe the plundering of the Chian fields at the hands of the Athenians and the runaway Chian slaves.

197. Graf 1985, 122–23 summarizes the examples.

198. Polyaenus 3.9.23.

199. Plut., *On the Virtue of Women* 3.245b. Plutarch claims that the Chian slave women were just as insulted by this proposal as their mistresses were, and fought heroically on behalf of Chios. We may well suspect that ideology, not history, lies behind this statement as well as Plutarch's claim that not a single slave deserted to the side of Philip. Yet comparative examples (including ancient Sparta and modern slave societies) show that it is not uncommon for slaves to fight for their masters. See Hunt 1998 and Brown and Morgan 2006.

200. Poseidonius, *FGrHist* 87 F 38, and Nic.Dam., *FrGrHist* 90 F 1, 33.

201. Robert 1938, 117–26.

202. For the exploitation of the slaves in other states, see for example the role of slaves in the civil war at Corcyra, Thucydides' paradigmatic example of the conflicts that broke out between oligarchs and democrats throughout Greece during the Peloponnesian War (Thuc.3.80). In general, see Hunt 1998 for the use of slaves in Greek warfare, and Serghidou 2007.

203. Kowalzig 2007.

204. On the Kronia, see Versnel 1993; Mactoux 1994; Parker 2005, 202–3, and chapter 4 below. Slaves were also accorded a place in the Anthesteria, as Mactoux notes (1994, 113): *IG* II² 1672.204; Callim.fr.178.2; Athenaeus 437e.

205. I thank Matthew Christ for pointing out the significance of this cult for my discussion. For the slave refuge in Athens, see Christensen 1984. Christensen suggests that such refuges were much more widespread in Greece than our sources suggest.

206. *Et.Mag.* s.v. *thesiotrips*.

207. Although it should be noted that this comic tradition conflicts with Thucydides' claim that the Chians punished their slaves especially harshly (see above). Cultural ties between Athens and Chios were close from at least the fifth century onward. Besides the bond of Ionian kinship, Chios was a close ally of Athens during the periods of the Delian League, the Athenian Empire, and through most of the Peloponnesian War (see above). According to Thrasymachus (*DK* fr.3) and Theopompus (*FGrHist* 115 F 104), the Athenians included Chios in all their official prayers for the city's prosperity. Indeed, the formula "and for the Chians" had already become the topic of comic parody by the late fifth century (Aristoph., *Birds* 877–79; Eupolis, *Poleis* fr.246). Finally, the familiarity with Athenian culture and history of Chian poets and histographers such as Ion and Theopompus attests to the close relations between these states. On Ion, see Jennings and Katsaros 2007. On Theopompus, see Flower 1994.

Chapter 3. Pigs, Asses, and Swine: Obscenity and the Popular Imagination in Ancient Sicyon

1. Scholars recognizing problems with Herodotus' account include: Jeffery 1976, 164; Parker 1994, 406–7; Osborne 1999, 283; van Wees 1999, 39. On archaic tyranny, see Forsdyke 2005a; Anderson 2005; Hall 2006; Lavelle 2005. Anderson 2005 provides an excellent survey of earlier scholarship.

2. Bakhtin's conception of folk culture, particularly carnival and the popular grotesque, cannot of course be applied uncritically to the ancient world. For critical discussion, see recently the essays in Branham 2002; and Rösler 1986. This critical discussion shows, however, that the basic elements of popular humor identified by Bakhtin, including especially obscenity, the grotesque body, and reversals of hierarchy—all of which are the focus of my inquiry—are central to both the ancient and medieval popular culture (see, e.g., Rösler 1986; Edwards 1993). For more critical discussion of Bakhtin's concept of humor, and particularly Bakhtin's argument that it characterized non-elite rather than elite culture, see the essays in

Bremmer and Roodenburg 1997. While I agree that Bakhtin's contrast between high and low culture is overdrawn, I suspect that much of the overlap between spheres is due to elite appropriation of motifs that make best sense as articulations of non-elite perspectives (see chapter 1 and below). For the validity of the concepts of popular and official tradition (though sometimes overlapping) in relation to Greek history, see Thomas 1989 and chapter 1 above.

3. On humor in Herodotus generally, cf. Dewald 2006 and earlier bibliography cited therein. Though none of these studies is particularly concerned with the relation between Herodotean humor and non-elite sources, Dewald (154) notes the connection in Herodotus between humor and "trickster figures, often marginal underdogs themselves, who regard those with power over them with a jaundiced but cunning eye." She also mentions, but does not elaborate on, the element of carnival and ritualized grotesque in Herodotean humor (n.27).

4. For discussion of the ways that literary texts absorb and adapt themes from popular culture, see chapter 2.

5. Festival forms of ridicule of authorities, cf. Bakhtin 1984, 196–277; Davis 1975; Burke 1994 and, for some Greek examples, chapters 4 and 5 below. For similar ridicule in popular oral tradition, or literature partaking of popular themes, the works of Rabelais (*Gargantua* and *Pantagruel*) are exemplary: the Church, the legal profession, and scholarly world all come in for mocking. In Greek traditions, the iambic poems of Archilochus (e.g., fr. 114), and the parodies of official assembly procedures in Aristophanic comedy (e.g., in *Acharnians, Women of the Thesmophoria*, and *Women of the Assembly*) are good examples of popular ridicule of officials and official institutions.

6. Homeric epic achieved official status as high literature by the sixth century, when rhapsodes, or professional performers of Homer, competed in public festivals. Cf., e.g., Neils 1992; and Nagy 2002.

7. Bakhtin 1984, 13–14, 284–88, 304–5.

8. For an example of the exaggeration of the high style, see the activities of a certain Hegemon of Thasos (late fifth century) who, according to Athenaeus' report (10.406d–407d), was famous at Athens in the late fifth century for his parodies of epic poetry; cf. Athenaeus 449b–c, a parody of the high-blown literary style not dissimilar to the parody of Aeschylean style found in Aristophanes' *Frogs*.

9. The pseudo-Homeric *Margites* dates to the late sixth century BCE and *Batrachomyomachia* to the first century CE, but reflecting a tradition that went back as far as the fourteenth century BCE. See West 2003, 224–37, for discussion. Compare also the satyr play, of which only one example survives, namely, Euripides' *Cyclops*. The fundamental comic move of these parodies is to associate the high with the low, a move similar to the "extraordinary realism" of the comic grotesque, as described by Bakhtin, in which literary characters depicted performing mundane tasks, e.g., Hecuba washing diapers (Bakhtin 1984, 304, 309).

10. Murray 1987 identified this element of Herodotean narratives central to what he called "Eastern moralizing traditions" as opposed to the political traditions of mainland Greece that Herodotus also used. Despite Murray's groundbreaking work on oral tradition in Herodotus, this is a false distinction, as Luraghi 2005 has convincingly demonstrated. See Murray's further thoughts in Murray 2001.

11. Genovese 1974; Darnton 1984; Scott 1990, all discussed in chapter 2 above, and below.

12. The remainder of this paragraph is a summary of Hdt.6.86.

13. Compare the uses of Christianity by slaves in the American South as described by Genovese 1974, 163–83.

14. Jeffery 1976, 164; Griffin 1982, 80.

15. *Moralia* 157e.

16. Rabelais, *Pantagruel* Ch.20 = Screech 2006, 147–48.

17. For Lucian's *Descent into Hades*, see Sidwell 2004, 93–109.

18. Bakhtin 1984, 370. This theme, called by Bakhtin "grotesque realism," is also known as "World Upside Down," or "WUD." On the "World Upside Down," see chapter 2 above.

19. Bakhtin 1984, e.g., 11–12, 75, 250, 290–96, 370–407. According to Bakhtin, popular festive imagery is fundamentally positive, yet often harnessed for satirical and hence (negative) critical purposes. There is, according to Bakhtin, an "inner contradiction and tension" (291) in the symbolism of this imagery and "it is difficult to say where praise ends and where condemnation starts" (294). Whereas in Herodotus, the tyrant is the focus of this imagery, in medieval culture it was often the cleric or monk. Both are "the contradictory symbol of procreative force and material bodily superabundance" (295).

20. Ogden 1993, 1997, 101–4.

21. As Ogden 1997, 206, notes, he was not the first to notice the association with scapegoating ritual. On the stoning of scapegoats, cf. Bremmer 1983.

22. Bremmer 1983.

23. Ogden 1997, 101.

24. For the story of Polycrates and his ring, see Hdt. 3.39–43. Polycrates tries to avoid his inevitable fall from prosperity by throwing away his most prized possession. The story of Polycrates is a variation of a common folktale (Aarne-Thompson 1961, 763A; Versnel 1977; Hansen 2002, 190 n.13). For this folk wisdom in Rabelais, where it is directed at Picrochole, who is called a "perfidious tyrant," cf. Book 1 (Gargantua) 158: "Thus do all things have a period and a close; and when they have reached a certain superlative point they fall in ruins, for they cannot long remain at such a point. Such is the end of those who have not learned by reason and temperance to moderate their own good fortune and prosperity." This theme is often expressed using imagery from the natural world, perhaps a sign of its relation to the rural world of peasants. The theme of rise and fall in Herodotus' *Histories*, and indeed in tragedy, though transformed into a higher literary style may indeed be derived from a form of popular fantasy in which the inevitable fall from prosperity of the high and mighty is imagined.

25. The trickster theme appears clearly in the late source Nicolaus of Damascus (Augustan Age). Nicolaus' version (*FGrHist.* 90 F61.4–5) of how Cleisthenes became king—a typical example of fratricidal violence and deception within the tyrant-family.

26. A similarly comic account of the transfer of cult from one god to another may be found in Aristoph., *Peace*, 418–20, a satirical distortion of the granting of favors that was central to Greek cultic worship.

27. Pausanias 2.5.6–2.6.7. It is curious, however, that the Roman-era tourist makes no mention of the cults of Adrastus and Melanippus. Indeed, although Pausanias gives an extended account of the deeds of the third-century leader Aratus, to whom a hero-cult was dedicated, he apparently did not observe cults to these legendary heroes in the Sicyonian marketplace (*agora*). Furthermore, although Pausanias mentions the tyranny of Cleisthenes twice in his account of the Sicyonian agora, and even notes that the council-house and stoa were built by the tyrant, he does not tell the story of Cleisthenes' cultic manipulations.

28. Parker 1994, 411 makes the same point ("and so was yet another myth of tyrannical cruelty born"), and also argues that the labelling of Cleisthenes as a "stone-thrower" is a fabrication dating to a later period when Delphi was hostile to tyrants. The theme of tyranny as detrimental to the polis goes back to the archaic period and originated among elites (see n.31 below). Solon rejects tyrannical power for himself partly on the grounds that it would entail accumulation of wealth for himself at the expense of violence toward the community (Solon fr. 32–35). Similarly, Alcaeus reviles Pittacus as a "devourer of the polis" and claims that he himself was protector of the people (fr.129).

29. See references in n.31 below. Of course, not all members of the state welcomed a tyrant. In particular, rivals of the tyrant from wealthy aristocratic families often fought violently among themselves for exclusive power (cf. Forsdyke 2005a).

30. Aristot., *Pol.* 1315b15.

31. Aristotle's rationale for the stability of the Orthagorids is that they ruled moderately. An anecdote told by Aristotle, namely that Cleisthenes crowned a judge for awarding a victory to his opponent, is probably a false aetiology for a statue in the Sicyonian agora. It nevertheless may reflect traditions concerning Cleisthenes' moderate rule. For positive traditions about archaic tyrants underlying negative fifth-century ones, see Osborne 1996, 192–97; Forsdyke 1999, 2005a. Periander is an interesting example, since he is almost universally reviled as the most brutal of archaic tyrants, yet there is also a more positive tradition that he served as arbitrator (Hdt.5.95.2) and that he numbered among the Seven Sages (Nic.Dam. *FGrHist* 90 F 58.4, D.L.1.98).

32. Cf. Schmitt-Pantel 1992, 39–42, 53–60.

33. Jeffery 1976, 164 (quoted above) observes that the names are "insulting" and probably derive from "some anti-Kleisthenic lampoon," but does not explore the source or meanings of this "lampoon." Parker 1994, 408 briefly notes that if Herodotus had been more critical, "he would surely have seen that the popular tradition had misrepresented grotesquely the intentions of the Tyrant of Sicyon," but again does not explore the meaning of the tribes in popular tradition and why he (correctly, in my view) thinks that they are "grotesque."

34. Parker 1994, 407: "the correct adjectival forms from these words [would be] ... Ὕειοι, Ὄνειοι ... Χοίρειοι inter alia."

35. Bakhtin 1984, 32, 63. The satyr is perhaps the figure par excellence exemplifying the breakdown of boundaries and the "hyperbolism of bodily images" in Greek popular culture. Another striking example can be found in Semonides' notorious poem abusing women, where the characters of women are compared to

various types of animals, including, notably, the sow and the ass (see below). Semonides' poem, in fact, is a form of iambic poetry, a genre associated not only
with abuse and obscenity, but also with popular festivity (West 1974; O'Higgins
2003). On fables and proverbs, see chapter 2 above.

36. Bicknell 1982, 196 observes the obscene connotation of the word *choiros*
and on this basis argues that *choireatai* was not one of the tribal names. Bicknell,
however, fails to note that obscene double meanings are also present in the other
two tribes and therefore on this reasoning these are false tribal names too. As
Bakhtin has observed, 1984, 460: "the formation of proper names from abusive
terms is one of the methods used most frequently by Rabelais as well as by folk
humor in general."

37. Translation by West 1994, adapted.

38. Of the two dominant interpretations of iambic poetry, the ritual model
views iambic poetry as closely connected with festival performances of obscene
speech (see, e.g., West 1974; Halliwell 2000; O'Higgins 2003). The secular or
sympotic model, however, views literary iambic as having developed out of cultic
performances, but by the time of Archilochus it was already a distinct literary
genre that was no longer confined only to abusive or obscene speech (see, e.g.,
Pellizer and Tedeschi 1990 xxix–xxx; Bowie 2001; Kantzios 2005). For my purposes, one needs only to accept that the obscenity and abuse of women in Semonides bears some relation to the obscene speech that was characteristic of
popular festivity.

39. For the grotesque body as a feature of abuse in popular tradition, cf. Aristophanes *Thesm.* 815: "you men are greater gluttons (γάστριδες) than us women."
Occasionally abusive popular speech creeps into high literature, as in Achilles'
critique of Agamemnon as "devourer of his people" (*Il.*1.231) and, similarly, in
Alcaeus' critique of his rival Pittacus as "pot-bellied" and a "devourer of the community" (Alcaeus fr.129).

40. See, e.g., *Ach.* 739–817 passim; *Wasps* 573, 1353, 1364; *Ec.* 724; *Thesm.*
289–90; 538–40, with Austin and Olson's (2004) comment. "The emphatic repetition of χοῖρον from 538 must reflect the fact that Aristophanes' audience found
public use of the obscenity funny" (212). Henderson 1991, 131–32. On the connection between Aristophanic comedy and cultic obscenity see, e.g., Edwards
1993; and Halliwell 2000.

41. Ancient sources for the Thesmophoria include Aristophanes' *Women of
the Thesmophoria* and a scholion to Lucian, *Dialogues of Courtesans* ii.1. For
recent discussion, see O'Higgins 2003 with bibliography.

42. Ancient commentary (scholion) on Lucian, *Dialogues of the Courtesans*, 2.1.

43. For this theme in the cult of Demeter, see Winkler 1990; and O'Higgins
2003.

44. Translation from West 1994. While West translates παλιντριβής as "obstinate," as in "resisting all blows" (*LSJ*), this word possibly had its own obscene
double meaning in popular language, since its primary meaning is "rubbed all
over" (*LSJ*). See also Archil.fr.43.

45. Hedreen 2004; on phallic processions at the Dionysia, see Csapo 1997.

46. See Schmit-Pantel 1981 and chapter 5 below.

47. Bakhtin 1984 78, 109.

48. Ibid., 78, 81–82.

49. von Blumenthal 1940, 127.

50. One could also compare the debasement of Cleisthenes with the use of scatological and sexual humor to ridicule Athenian politicians in Old Comedy. For example, *Peace* 45–48, where Cleon is compared to a dung beetle since both "eat shit." Rosen (1988, 28–31) uses this passage as an example of the roots of comedy in Ionian iambic poetry, especially in its abusive obscene speech (*aischrologia*).

51. Bakhtin 1984, 81.

52. See further chapter 2 above.

53. Jeffery 1976, 164–65; Parker 1994, 409–10, citing Plutarch, *Mor.* 401d. For Choireai as a place name, see Hdt. 6. 101, which mentions a region of Eretria on Euboia, which is also attested epigraphically (Knoepfler 1997, 373, 379).

54. Osborne 1996, 183.

55. Van Wees 2003, 38–41. Andrewes 1956, 59 similarly views the names as originally negative (see below), but suggests that they were designed to characterize Dorians within Sicyon itself, as opposed to non-Dorians like himself.

56. Hobsbawm and Ranger 1992; Anderson 2006.

57. Thomas 1989.

58. Lycurgus and Solon are good examples of this phenomenon. On legends of the Greek lawgivers, see Szegedy-Maszak 1978. On the attribution of laws to Solon, see: Hansen 1990 and Scafuro 2006.

59. Scott 2005, 420 on Hdt. 6.126.3. For example, the herdsman Titormos, who beat the legendary Milon of Croton in a wrestling match, is said to have been the brother of one of the suitors. While there are no reliable dates for Titormos, Milon of Croton was a figure from the latter half of the sixth century. Similarly, a son of Pheidon of Argos is mentioned, seemingly because Pheidon himself was legendary for his introduction of a system of weights and measures and his hubristic usurpation of authority over the Olympic Games, as Herodotus mentions. Despite the difficulties of dating Pheidon, his appearance in this narrative is clearly a product of his status as the most famous historical figure from Argos. Though the tradition seems to be aware that Pheidon lived earlier than Cleisthenes of Sicyon insofar as it is Pheidon's son and not Pheidon himself who was a suitor, this adjustment does not resolve the real chronological difficulties. Pheidon himself was a sort of culture hero, as the attribution of coins and other innovations demonstrates. Other legendary figures appearing in this narrative include Smindyrides of Sybaris, renowned for his extravagant luxury, and Euphorion of Paion in Arcadia, who was said to have offered hospitality to the Dioscouroi in his own home and who provided accommodation for travelers. Scott 2005, 421–23. Cf. also here Bakhtin's discussion of *Coena Cypriani* ("Cyprian's Supper"), a comic travesty of sacred texts dating from the fifth to the eighth centuries CE, which "brings together persons from the most diverse periods of Biblical history," "from Adam and Eve to Christ" (287–88). "It is, as it were, the gathering together of all history, represented by the protagonists seated around the festive table" (288).

60. Boedeker 1998, 170.

61. Hall 1999, 52.

62. Ibid., 55.
63. Pariente 1992, 218.
64. Paus. 1.43.1, 1.30.1.
65. Euripides *Suppliants*; Hdt 9.27.
66. Hdt. 9.27, Paus.1.39.2; Pariente 1992, 208.
67. Hdt. 9.27.
68. Vansina 1985; Hall 1997, 2002.
69. Paus. 2.6.6.
70. Renfrew and Cherry 1986.
71. Snodgrass 1986.
72. It should be stressed that while we know of these developments best in Athens, it is not unlikely that similar cultural programs were introduced in other city-states at around this time.
73. Neils 1992; Nagy 2002.
74. West 1989.
75. For the relation of tragedy to Athenian civic ideology, see Winkler and Zeitlin 1990.
76. On "telescoping" in oral traditions, see Thomas 1989.
77. Olympic victories (576/572): Hdt. 6.126; Pythian victory (582): Paus. 10.7.3.
78. Foundation of Pythian games in Sicyon: Scholion to Pindar, *Nem.* 9. For the foundation of the other games of the "circuit," see Golden 1998, 10–11. For the Panthanaia, see Neils 1992.
79. Compare Figueira 1999 and Luraghi 2009 on the ways that the Messenians "positioned themselves on the cultural map of Greece" through the construction of conspicuous monuments at panhellenic sanctuaries. On the politics of construction of treasuries at Delphi, see Neer 2003.
80. Tholos: Coste-Messalière 1950, 50–54; Monopteros: Coste-Messaliere, 19–233; Szeliga 1986. My discussion of the archaeology is indebted to the synthesis of Parker 1994. Parker notes that though some scholars dispute that the building is Sicyonian (e.g., Szeliga 1986), the common consensus is that it is.
81. If the two mounted figures do indeed represent Castor and Pollux, Spartan heroes, then this may attest to good relations between Sparta and Sicyon, a piece of evidence that may strengthen my reconstruction of the tribal changes below.
82. It perhaps should be noted that we know very little about the physical structures of ancient Sicyon (cf. Griffin 1982).
83. Connor 1993.
84. On the heroes of Attica, see Kearns 1989.
85. Hall 1997, 2002.
86. Ulf 1996, 2009.
87. Luraghi 2009.
88. Luraghi 2001; Hall 2003; Funke and Luraghi 2009.
89. Compare the popular etymology of the Ozalian Locrians as the "smelly Locrians," a false derivation of the place name from the verb ὄζειν "smell" (Strabo 9.4.8). Again, the humor is based on the attribution of a base bodily function (sweating, stinking) to a people/place.

90. Hdt. 5.67.1, 5.69.1.

91. See, however, Ogden 1997, 115–18, who argues that Ἀρχέλαοι was a title of a cultic official.

Chapter 4. Revelry and Riot in Ancient Megara: Democratic Disorder or Ritual Reversal?

1. Hobsbawm 1988, 23.

2. Plutarch, *Moralia* 295d and 304 e–f (= *Greek Questions* 18 and 59).

3. Robinson 1997, 114. Oost 1973, however, is skeptical of a sixth-century Megarian democracy in the form that we know it from the fifth and fourth centuries. Robinson dismisses this criticism on the grounds of its narrow conception of ancient democracy and argues instead that the archaic Megarian democracy need not have had the full-blown institutional apparatus of classical Athenian democracy. While I certainly agree with this latter point, I will argue that the evidence does not even support the existence of a more moderate form of democracy. For the variety of ancient conceptions of democracy, see Robinson 1997, 35–64.

4. The term "moral economy" is borrowed from Thompson 1993, 188, cited below. Thompson discusses his definition further at 1993, 336–51, where he specifies that in his groundbreaking study, *The Making of the English Working Class*, he used it to describe the food riots of 1795 as an attempt to "re-impose the 'old paternalist moral economy' as against the economy of the free market" (337). Thompson's use of the adjectives "old" and "customary" to describe the "moral economy," and his placement of the moral economy in opposition to the free market, suggest that the moral economy was in fact rooted in older social relations. I will suggest, by contrast, that the moral economy is an ideological construct aimed at legitimizing the normative outlook of the poor, and that it never corresponded very precisely with an older social order. For this reason, I place the word "customary" in quotations.

5. Robinson 1997, 115; Okin 1985, 14; Legon 1981, 104–5. Aristotle, in turn, probably relied on local Megarian historical traditions, known to us through fragments of four authors (Praxion, Dieuchidas, Hereas, and Heragoras) dating to the fourth and third centuries BCE (Okin 1985, 20–21). See Jacoby *FGrHist* 484–86 and Piccirilli 1975 for the fragments.

6. In what follows, I highlight only a few key concepts which are relevant to the present discussion. For fuller treatment of the anti-democratic tradition see Ober 1998.

7. Hdt. 3.80–80, a famous passage known as the "Constitutional Debate." It is generally accepted that this debate reflects contemporary (fifth-century BCE) Greek political theory, and not an historical debate between Persian nobles. For recent discussion see Pelling 2002.

8. Hdt. 3.81.1. The equation between tyranny and democracy is of course a commonplace in late-fifth- and fourth-century thought (cf. Raaflaub 1979; Forsdyke 2005a; and below).

9. Hdt. 3.81.2.

10. Hdt. 3.81.1.

11. See for example, Thucydides 6.54, 2.65, 3.36–49, 6.1, 6.8–26, 6.60–61.

12. 6.55–61. For further discussion, see Forsdyke 2005a, 267–77.

13. Since this work is preserved among the works of Xenophon, its author is sometimes referred to as Pseudo-Xenophon, or [Xenophon]. This passage is from Pseudo-Xenophon 1.5. Cf. Pseudo-Xen. *Ath.Pol.*1.9 for the idea that in an oligarchy the valuable citizens (*hoi chrestoi*) keep the lower classes (*tous ponerous*) in check (*kolasousin*); see 1.10 for the lack of restraint (*akolasia*) of slaves and resident foreigners at Athens. Note also that at 1.9 the masses are conceived of as crazy (*mainomenous*)!

14. Compare also Euripides' description of the behavior of the Greek army in his *Hecuba* of c. 424 BCE: "The unrestrained mob (*akolastos ochlos*) and the anarchy of the sailors (*nautikē anarchia*) is stronger than fire." The critique of democracy as "unrestrained" (*akolastos*) is the ideological counterpart to the concept of "holding the masses in check" (*katechein to plēthos*, Thuc. 2.65.8) which was characteristic of the oppressive rule of the tyrant in Athenian fifth-century democratic ideology (see Forsdyke 2001, 332–41).

15. Plato uses various words derivative of the noun *akolasia*: *akolastainein*, 555d; *akolastoi*, 555c.

16. Plato, *Rep.* 557b. For the tyrant's ability to do whatever he likes without legal restraint, see Hdt. 3.80.3. Democrats, on the other hand, viewed the ability to do as one likes as a crucial aspect of democratic freedom (cf., e.g., Aristotle *Pol.* 1317a40–b17, with discussion by Hansen 1996).

17. Plato, *Rep.* 560e.

18. For Thucydides on civil war: 3.82. For Plato see *Rep.* 558c, 561d.

19. *Moralia* 295d (= *Greek Questions* 18).

20. Ibid.

21. Hansen 1990, 78. For further discussion of the eclipse of Cleisthenes as founder of the democracy in Athenian civic traditions, see now Anderson 2007.

22. For this debate see Aristot., *Ath.Pol.* 29.3 and 34.3 with Rhodes 1981, 115, 376–77, 416, 420, 427–34, 440–41.

23. *Pol.* 1273b36–39.

24. *Ath.Pol.* 5–11.

25. *Ath.Pol.* 6.1.

26. *Ath.Pol.* 8.4, *Ath.Pol.*8.1 and *Ath.Pol.* 9.1–2; *Pol.* 1274a1–6. See Hansen 1990 78–79 for a list of all of the constitutional reforms ascribed to Solon by fourth-century sources. Among the reforms, the Council of Four Hundred has the best claim for historicity (Raaflaub 1996, 1065).

27. *Ath.Pol.* 8.4.

28. For Aristotle and other ancient critics of democracy, a basic injustice of democratic rule was its plunder of the wealth of the elites and the redistribution of this wealth among the masses (cf. Aristot., *Pol.* 1305a 4–5; 1309a14–20; 1320b2–4; 1321a31–5). For democrats, the system for the redistribution of wealth (or liturgy system) was a legitimate device for ensuring that elites used their wealth for the common good. Critics of democracy viewed this system as a clever ruse for unfairly depriving the rich of their rightful possessions. As Pseudo-Xenophon writes: "The demos thinks it right to receive pay for singing, running, dancing and

sailing in the ships in order that they may have money and the rich become poorer" (1.13). On this reasoning, legislation that forced the wealthy to return interest on their loans could only be the product of the extreme kind of democracy of which Athens was the principal example. For further discussion of the liturgy system and the institutionalization of this sort of reciprocity between elites and masses, see Wilson 2000; and Forsdyke forthcoming.

29. Eric Robinson points out to me that Aristotle had more information on early Megara than what Plutarch preserves for us in his *Greek Questions*. In response to this point, I make the following observations: Aristotle relied on local Megarian historians of the later classical period (n.4 above), who in turn presumably relied on the evidence of Megarian oral traditions, as well as local monuments and inscriptions. Oral tradition tends to preserve the remarkable and the shocking, not the mundane details of early constitutions. It is striking, in this regard, that—granting that the extant fragments of the local Megarian historians are extremely few—they tend to contain information on myth and cult, not archaic or classical political development. For comparison, it is noteworthy that Aristotle's *Constitution of Athens*—the only surviving example of the 158 constitutional histories written by his school—has little reliable constitutional detail for the archaic period. Solon's *Seisachtheia* and some of his laws are striking exceptions. The details of the *Seisachtheia* were probably preserved because of the festival established to commemorate it (see below). Solon's laws were remembered because they were inscribed on wooden tablets which survived until Aristotle's time and beyond (see Rhodes 1981, 131–34).

30. Cf. Robinson 1997, 116–17: "The *palintokia* sounds like far too drastic a measure to impose unless the people who benefited had played a powerful role in its enactment." For modern views on Solonian Athens, see n.93 below.

31. There is one more piece of ancient testimony which could be seen as indirect evidence of a democracy in Megara, namely, Aristotle's claim that the settlement of Heraclea Pontica was briefly ruled by a democracy shortly after its foundation by Megarians and Boeotians c. 560 (*Pol.* 1304b31–4). Yet there are several reasons for rejecting the idea that this testimony supports the existence of democracy in sixth-century Megara. First, given that Heraclea Pontica was founded not only by Megarians, but by a "substantial" number of Boeotians (Graham 1982, 123), there is no reason to assume that the political system of the new settlement reflected that of Megara. Second, it is highly likely that Aristotle understood the various episodes of civil war in archaic Heraclea Pontica (*Pol.* 1305b2–10, 33–39; 1306a31–b2) in anachronistic fourth-century terms of struggles between democrats and oligarchs. I argue in Forsdyke 2005a that most episodes of civil war in archaic Greece can be viewed as instances of intra-elite competition for power.

32. For the Saturnalia, see Versnel 1993, 136–227. The bibliography on Carnival is enormous. For orientation see Abrahams and Bauman 1978; Davis 1975 97–123; Burke 1994, 178–204; Le Goff and Schmitt 1981.

33. 22.1.20.

34. 5.13.5–8. The translation is from Beard, North, and Price 1998, 130.

35. Macrobius' *Saturnalia* 1.11.1, 24.22–3, Accius, *Ann.*2–7 (cited below). As Versnel 1993, 149 notes, the sources differ as to whether masters and slaves dined together, or whether slaves dined before their masters (a reversal of usual custom),

or whether masters actually served their slaves. These distinctions are unimportant for my purposes since all cases illustrate the breakdown or reversal of the social hierarchy.

36. *Ann.* 2–7. The translation is from Warmington 1961. Cf. Philochorus, *FGH* 328 F97 = Macrobius, *Saturnalia* 1.10.22; Plutarch, *Mor.* 1098b.

37. Athenaeus 14.639. Versnel 1993, 103 suggests that the ritual at Troezen occurred during a festival of Poseidon.

38. 14.639–40 = Baton (*FGH* 268) F 5.

39. Athenaeus 3.110B.

40. This paragraph is a paraphrase of Athenaeus 4.139 = Polykrates *FGH* 588 F1. It is tempting to reinterpret the reports about Cimon's daily hosting of all comers at his estate (Aristot., *Ath.Pol.* 27.3; Plutarch, *Life of Cimon* 10) as a politically powerful extension of the ritual practices of the Kronia. Or have Aristotle and Plutarch once again misinterpreted an earlier event? One can see how Cimon's exemplary fulfillment of the ritual on one occasion might be remembered in the oral tradition and then misinterpreted as a political gesture.

41. Versnel 1993, 95. Note the comparison of Peisistratus' rule to the reign of Kronos in Aristot., *Ath.Pol.* 16.7. For further discussion of the myth of the Golden Age, see chapter 2 above.

42. For ritual abuse of authorities during Carnival in the early modern period, see Davis 1975, 138–39; Burke 1994, 187–88; assaults exempt from prosecution: Coulton 1925, 27, cited by Thomas 1964, 53.

43. Horace, *Satires* 2.7 is read by Versnel 1993, 149 as an allusion to the license to criticize masters during the Saturnalia. For ritual abuse (αἰσχρολογία/ τωθασμός/τὰ ἐκ τῶν ἀμαξῶν σκώμματα/γεφυρισμός) at the Dionysia and festivals of Demeter, see Fluck 1931; Winkler 1990; Cole 1993; Edwards 1993; and O'Higgins 2001. An important text for verbal abuse at festivals is Aristot., *Pol.* 1336b14.

44. Ephorus, *FGH* 70 fr. 29 with Versnel 1993, 104.

45. For these rituals, see Burkert 1985, 101–2; Parke 1977, 76–77; Smyth 1906, 493–95, 507–8.

46. Smyth 1906, 507 suggests that the boys also carried the image of a swallow around with them.

47. Theognis, *FGH* 526 F1 = *PMG* 848 = Athenaeus 8.360. The translation is from Trypanis 1971. For modern parallels to the Swallow Song, see Passow 1860, numbers 306–8, and Smyth 1906, 507–8. For an illustration, see the vase mentioned by Smyth 1906, 508.

48. Compare also the song preserved in Plut. *Theseus* 22 and Suda: s.v. *diakonion*. For the bough in Aristophanes' comedies, see *Knights* 729, *Women of the Assembly* 1053.

49. Pseudo-Herodotus, *Life of Homer* 2.33. Translation is from West 2003.

50. Athenaeus 359–60. The translation is from Gulick 1930. The festival of St. Basil in modern Greece preserves some elements of this ritual (Smyth 1906, 494). I thank my colleague Artemis Leontis for pointing out this modern parallel.

51. I thank my colleague Ruth Scodel for making me aware of this ritual.

52. Bradtke 2000, 7.

53. Ibid., 16, 17.

54. Ibid., 7, 9–10.

55. Dyer 1876, 41 quoted by Bradtke 2000, 22.

56. *Essex Quarterly Courts*, VII, 331–32, cited by Nissenbaum 1996, 17.

57. Nissenbaum 1996, 8.

58. For anthropological interpretations of rituals of reversal as safety valves, see Gluckman 1965, 109–36; 1963, 110–36; and Turner 1969, 166–203. For this approach in historical studies, see Darnton 1984, 75–104. Davis (1975, 97–151), and Burke (1994, 201–2) both accept the validity of this principle, but also modify it in important ways (see below).

59. Interestingly, the term used by authorities to characterize the revelry of Christmas was "disorder" (Nissenbaum 1996, 14–15); cf. Burke's characterization of the authorities' attitude to Carnival as "chaos, disorder and misrule" (1994, 189)).

60. Pliny, *Letters* II.17.23–4. The translation is from Beard, North, and Price 1998 (vol. II), 126.

61. Parker 2005, 276.

62. Winkler 1990, 194; Foley 1994, 72.

63. Winkler 1990, 198–206.

64. Plut. *Mor.* 245e–f; Paus. 2.20.7–8.

65. On obscenity at the Dionysia, see Cole 1993.

66. On tragedy and reversal see, for example, Zeitlin 1996, 341–74.

67. On comedy, ridicule and reversal, see: Edwards 1993; Zeitlin 1996, 375–416; and Halliwell 2000.

68. Aristotle *Poetics* 1448a29–b4.

69. Edwards 1993, 99. On the question of the nature of the poetry preserved under the name of Theognis, see n.106 below.

70. Theognis 53–60.

71. E.g., Robinson 1997, 116.

72. *Mor.* 304e = *Greek Questions* 59.

73. Plut. *Mor.* 303d. The verb *lōpodutein* specifically refers to clothes-stealing, but can refer more generally to robbery of any kind (*LSJ*).

74. Thompson 1993, 227–29; Davis 1975, 27–28.

75. Coulton 1925, 27 cited by Thomas 1964.

76. For example, the sanctuary of Demeter at Eleusis collected tithes in barley and wheat, which was stored in a temple precinct: *IG*³ 78 with Cavanaugh 1996.

77. One might note, nevertheless, that wagons (*hamaxai*) are associated with one form of ritual revelry, namely the "ritual abuse from wagons" (*ta ek tōn hamaxōn skōmmata*) which took place during the Dionysia and involved revelers processing on wagons and abusing anyone whom they encountered. See Fluck 1931, 34–51 for the sources.

78. I thank Ryan Balot for pointing out to me Plato's condemnation of the laxity of democracy in punishing criminals.

79. In Forsdyke 2005a, 231–70, I demonstrate that "mildness/gentleness/toleration" (*praotēs*) became an important term of positive self-evaluation for the democracy following the repressive rule of the oligarchs of 403. Representative

passages include: Isoc. 7.67, Aristot., *Ath.Pol.* 22.4. The claim that criminals roam free in democratic Athens, moreover, is contradicted by the frequent representation of the Athenians as litigious to the extreme. This feature of the Athenian democracy is ridiculed most famously in Aristophanes' *Wasps*, but is evident in many other sources. For example, Pseudo-Xenophon observes that the Athenians handle more public and private lawsuits and judicial inquiries than all of mankind (3.2). In 3.4–5, the author lists some of the many disputes dealt with by the courts, including crimes of insolence (*hubris*). Nevertheless, the author admits that even if the courts sat year round, they could not deal with all the crimes because of the large population of Athens. This last comment presumably is the basis of the elite critique of democracy as "soft on crime," though the idea of deliberate negligence in the pursuit of injustice is an inflammatory misrepresentation, just as in American politics today.

80. For the Cylonian affair, see Hdt. 5.70; 1.61. I owe the observation of the possible elite connotations of the term *genos* to Adam Rabinowitz. On the privileged status of members of *genē* in Athens, see Parker 1996, 56–66.

81. van Wees 1999, 34–35 similarly relates Plutarch's anecdote to the breakdown of patronage relations between rich and poor in archaic Megara and even briefly notes the parallel with riots in later European history. Van Wees does not, however, observe the relation of this anecdote to festival rituals, and therefore does not discuss the full cultural context and sociopolitical implications of the action of the poor.

82. Le Roy Ladurie 1974, 192–97.

83. Davis 1975, 118–19; 147–50.

84. Ibid., 124–51.

85. Burke 1994, 203–4.

86. Darnton 1984, 75–104. Lincoln 1985 similarly explores the potential of religion to serve as the basis for rebellion. Lincoln, however, is less motivated by anthropological approaches to festivity than he is reacting to Marxist views of religion as the tool of the elite, as in Hobsbawm 1959.

87. Thompson 1993, 188.

88. Darnton 1984, 80.

89. Thompson 1993, 224–8; cf. 239–40. Thompson also notes (234–35) that rioters made use of "ritualised hooting or groaning outside retailers' shops" as well as popular recreations such as football to gather a crowd.

90. Thompson 1993, 188–89. For a similar example of moral economy of the poor and its breakdown in a contemporary peasant society, see Scott 1985, who describes the effect of the "green revolution" (the introduction of modern irrigation and fertilization techniques as well as the use of the combine harvester) on the previously existing mutual dependence between rich and poor in a Malaysian village in the 1970s. Interestingly, one symptom of the breakdown of the previously existing order was the refusal of the rich to feast the poor or give them gifts in return for their labor, as they had previously done (see 169–78).

91. Thompson 1975.

92. Underdown 1985.

93. Ibid., 118.

94. Sale 1995.

95. For a similar development in a modern peasant society, see Scott 1985, where the introduction of double-cropping in Malaysia in the late 1960s opened up new opportunities for profit for large landowners. As a result, the desire of the rich for further profit "led them to repudiate their obligations to their poorer neighbors" (176). Malaysian peasants similarly experienced a formalization and increasingly onerous exaction of their debts. For example, whereas traditionally Malaysian peasant tenants paid their rents to large landowners in kind after the harvest and in proportion to the success of the actual crop, now they had to pay a fixed amount in cash before the harvest, regardless of fluctuations in crop yield.

96. Plut., *Mor.* 295d.

97. *Ath.Pol.* 6 and 9.

98. Solon fr.36.8–15.

99. Plutarch, *Life of Solon* 16.

100. Connor 1987, 49.

101. Plutarch, *Life of Solon* 24.1.

102. Thompson 1993, 212–15.

103. Morris 2002; Scheidel 2003.

104. Morris 2002, 36.

105. Ibid.

106. For the controversy over the relation of the poetry preserved under the name of Theognis to an actual historical poet from Megara, see essays in Figueira and Nagy 1985; Bowie 1997; and Lane Fox 2000. My formulation reflects the position of Cobb-Stevens, Figueira, and Nagy 1985, who view the corpus as "the crystallization of archaic and early classical poetic traditions emanating from Megara" (2).

107. Theognis 43–50.

108. Theognis 145–46.

109. Compare van Wees 1999, who uses the terms "aggressive acquisitiveness" and "spiraling acquisitiveness" to describe this phenomenon in Megara.

110. This claim is fully argued in Forsdyke 2006.

111. For transport amphorae, see Johnston and Jones 1978. For pottery and its implications for regular and widespread trade, see Osborne 1996.

112. Foxhall 1997 uses the evidence of survey archaeology to demonstrate that the land had not reached its carrying capacity in the sixth century BCE. Cf. de Angelis 1994. For new settlements abroad as a product of individual adventurism and profit-seeking, see Osborne 1998, 257–59, 268. For a list of early settlements abroad with Megarian involvement, see Graham 1982, 160–62.

113. Aristoph., *Acharnians* 519, *Peace* 1003, Xen. *Mem.* 2.7.6, Diog.Laert. 6.41.

114. *Politics* 1305a8–28.

115. In Forsdyke 2005a, I interpret the slaughter of the cattle of the rich as part of the struggle between elites over power and prestige, rather than a product of tensions between elites and masses. Cf. van Wees 2000, 66. It is also possible that this episode represents a particularly striking instance of symbolic hospitality between rich and poor. In other words, Theagenes sacrificed the cattle of his

opponents and offered a feast to the poor, a ritual of hospitality that underlies most Greek festivals (cf. Schmitt-Pantel 1992).

116. Compare van Wees 1999 for a similar interpretation of the Megarian crisis.

117. See the archaeological evidence cited in n.79 above.

118. Frier 2000.

119. Davis 1975, 37. Doxis Doxiadis (personal communication) informs me that wills from early nineteenth-century Greece contain provisions for the support or feasting of the poor of the village or town.

120. Davis 1975, 28–29.

121. Thompson 1993, 199–200.

122. Ibid., 243–44; 300–301, 303.

123. Formal public offices appear throughout Greece during the seventh century and are commonly interpreted as a device for regulating competition between elites for power (Foxhall 1997, 119). The following magistracies are attested for Megarian colonies in inscriptions dating to the Hellenistic period (323–31 BCE): *basileus, aisymnatae, dāmiourgoi, stratēgoi and grammateus* (see Legon 1981, 55–58).

124. For this change in Solonian Athens, see *Ath.Pol.*7 and Raaflaub 1996, 1064–65. Foxhall 1997 argues that Solon's property classes did not extend significant political rights beyond those who had very considerable wealth. The only evidence for a similar change in archaic Megara would be Theognis 53–60 (cited above), though these lines are "constitutionally unspecific" (Robinson 1997, 116).

125. Compare scholarly assessments of Solonian Athens: Rhodes 1981, 118–20; Raaflaub 1996, 1062–71; Robinson 1997, 39; Foxhall 1997. Wallace 2007 represents a dissenting voice.

126. Robinson 1997, 39: "We may safely eliminate Solonian Athens as a candidate for democracy, for while important measures were taken to create or enhance the participation of the demos, such as the admission of thetes (for the first time?) into the assembly, the assembly itself still played a meager role, and the power of the aristocratic Areopagus continued to dominate."

127. Thompson 1993,187.

128. Ibid., 188–89; cf. 293–94.

129. Thuc. 4.66.1; cf.3.68.3 with Legon 1981, 235–37. Hornblower 2004, 231–32 summarizes competing scholarly views, but ultimately accepts that Megara was democratic at this time.

130. I argue in Forsdyke 2005 that ostracism-like procedures attested outside of Athens (e.g., at Argos, Miletus, Megara, Syracuse, Cyrene, and the Chersonesus) are local versions of a general Greek practice of using written ballots (leaves or potsherds) as a means of determining a penalty (removal from public office or exile). As such, they are not necessarily direct imitations of Athenian ostracism or necessarily democratic.

131. Legon 1981, 276–79, 289–94 discusses two unsuccessful attempts to overthrow the oligarchy in 375/4 and 340s BCE.

132. Note especially Thompson's demonstration (1993, 185–258) of the striking restraint of food rioters in enforcing the price of grain. Rather than plunder

and steal from those who produced or sold the grain, the rioters went to great lengths to give such persons what they thought ought to be the right price for their grain.

133. Thompson 1993, 289–93 makes a similar point by stressing the restraint of rioters and the general success of the riots in moderating the conflict between the marketers and the consumers of grain.

134. The phrase "weapons of the weak" is borrowed from the title of Scott 1985.

Chapter 5. Street Theater and Popular Justice in Ancient Greece

1. Plutarch, *Moralia* 291F–292A (= *Greek Questions* 2): "Who was 'the woman who rode on a donkey' among the people of Cyme? A woman caught in adultery was led into the marketplace and placed on a certain stone for all to see. Then she was mounted on a donkey and led around the city. After this, she was made to stand again on the same stone. She lived the rest of her life without honor [or "without citizen rights"], bearing the name 'donkey-rider.' As a result of this ceremony, they considered the stone unclean and ritually purified it." (Τίς ἡ παρὰ Κυμαίοις ὀνοβάτις; τῶν γυναικῶν τὴν ἐπὶ μοιχείᾳ ληφθεῖσαν ἀγαγόντες εἰς ἀγορὰν ἐπὶ λίθου τινὸς ἐμφανῆ πᾶσι καθίστασαν· εἶθ' οὕτως ἀνεβίβαζον ἐπ' ὄνον, καὶ τὴν πόλιν κύκλῳ περιαχθεῖσαν ἔδει πάλιν ἐπὶ τὸν αὐτὸν λίθον κατασταθῆναι καὶ τὸ λοιπὸν ἄτιμον διατελεῖν, 'ὀνοβάτιν' προσαγορευομένην. τὸν δὲ λίθον ἀπὸ τούτου καθαρὸν οὐ νομίζοντες ἀφωσιοῦντο). Cf. Hesychius s.v. ὀνοβάτιδες.

2. Aristotle, fr. 611–42 (ed. Rose): "The people of Lepreum bound whomever they caught in adultery and led them around the city for three days. And they held them in dishonor [or "disenfranchised them"] for the rest of their lives. Women caught in adultery were made to stand in the marketplace for eleven days in a translucent tunic without a girdle. In addition, they held them in dishonor [or "disenfranchised them"]."(Λεπρεεῖς οὓς ἂν λάβωσι μοιχοὺς περιάγουσι τρεῖς ἡμέρας τὴν πόλιν δεδεμένους καὶ ἀτιμοῦσι διὰ βίου, τὴν δὲ γυναῖκα ια ἐπ' ἀγορᾶς ἄζωστον ἐν χιτῶνι διαφανεῖ ἱστᾶσι καὶ ἀτιμοῦσι).

3. Both adulterer and adulteresses at Cyme and Lepreum were also subject to lifelong ἀτιμία ("loss of honor"), presumably in this context, entailing loss of citizen rights. On the meaning of ἀτιμία, see Harrison 1971, 169–76.

4. Nicolaus of Damascus, *FGrHist* 90 fr.130: Ἐὰν δὲ μοιχὸς ἁλῷ, περιάγεται τὴν πόλιν ἐπὶ ὄνου μετὰ γυναικὸς ἐπὶ ἡμέρας τακτάς.

5. Latte 1931; cf. Gernet 1981, 143–276; 1984, 21. Cf. Herman 2006, discussed below. For the development of the evolutionary perspective on ancient law beginning in the second half of the nineteenth century, see Thomas 1984, 3–5. This perspective is usually framed in terms of a development from private vengeance to public punishment or from family or clan to state. While I would certainly not deny that there was some development of Greek law along these lines, I suggest that scholars have overestimated the degree to which formal state institutions replaced informal (or what these scholars misleadingly call "private") practices. See, for example, Gernet 1984, 21–22, who argues that public humiliation survived

only in relation to a few offenses (theft, calumny, and adultery) where they were incorporated into law as formal penalties.

6. David Cohen (1991, 1995) has drawn on comparative anthropological and historical studies in order to critique evolutionary approaches to the development of the law. Cohen argues for an approach to Greek law that recognizes that law is embedded in society, not a separate structure, as in "rule of law" approaches. While Cohen's work (along with Hunter 1994) has been inspirational for my own study, I am concerned in this chapter with a specific area of informal social practices—spontaneous collective actions designed to punish transgressors of social norms—which Cohen curiously neglects. Cohen's main emphasis is on how law fits into a wider system of social norms and practices, especially concerning sexuality, feuding, and violence. Compare Walker's 1998 discussion of crime and social control in colonial America, where he notes that despite the existence of "sheriff, constables, judges, courts, jail and gallows," "they played a relatively minor role in maintaining law and order" compared to informal methods of popular justice (13).

7. Pitt-Rivers 1971, 201. Pitt-Rivers notes that his use of the term "infrastructure" to describe informal popular practices is rather unsatisfactory (161). Elsewhere he uses the phrase "popular institutions" (189).

8. Bakhtin 1984, 6. Bakhtin has been criticized for assuming that literary texts like Rabelais's *Gargantua* and *Pantagruel* are direct reflections of popular culture, and for drawing too much of his analysis of medieval Europe from his own experiences in Stalinist Russia. Bakhtin's basic claim, however, of the existence of two spheres of culture is still valid, if modified to allow for interaction and cross-pollination between them. For discussion, see chapter 1.

9. Bakhtin 1984, 96.

10. Some scholars have posited a decline in the importance of popular culture since the early modern period. Burke (1994, 207–86) discusses the reasons for this decline. Compare also Bakhtin 1984, 33. See, however, Pitt-Rivers 1971 and Bradtke 2000 for twentieth-century examples of popular justice, as well as n.100 for a contemporary example.

11. Compare the comments of Thomas 1984, 5–6 on the predominantly "formalist" nature of current research into ancient forms of punishment. More broadly, Connor (1996, 218) exhorts historians of Athenian democracy to "look not only at constitutional and legal changes but also at 'civil society,' that is, the network of shared activities, voluntary associations, religious and commercial undertakings, indeed *all communal action not initiated by the state*" [my emphasis]. There are some notable exceptions, of course, to the "formalist" study of Greek law, including Cohen 1991 (discussed below); Hunter 1994; Allen 2000, as well as the essays in the volume which Thomas 1984 introduces. The essays in the recent *Cambridge Companion to Greek Law* (Gagarin and Cohen 2005) recognize the embedded nature of Greek law, but do not discuss popular rituals of social control at any length. Gernet 1981 should also be mentioned for its pioneering exploration of the relation between religious and penal ritual. Gernet even makes brief mention (262–63) of the public character of the procedure of ἐπαγωγή ("leading away [to a magistrate]") i.e., summary arrest by a private citizen. After

noting that as a response to a flagrant offense, "*apagōgē* of necessity requires publicity, for such publicity suits the glaring quality of the crime," he concludes: "*Apagōgē*, then, involves popular justice." Cf. Hunter, p. 22 below. Finally, Schmitz 2004 should be mentioned. In chapter 4 of a monumental study, Schmitz examines informal, collective methods of shaming social offenders at the village and neighborhood level in ancient Greece. Although Schmitz makes many important observations, he argues that formal state institutions in Greece took over older customs of informal shaming and private vengeance (402–9). He therefore supports a more evolutionary scheme of historical development (e.g., 402) than I do. Furthermore, he does not recognize the persistence of extra-legal justice in classical Greece, nor does he emphasize its collective dimension.

12. Comparative material, of course, should never be used as primary evidence for practices and conditions in the ancient world. Such material can, however, be used cautiously to support ancient evidence or provide possible models and interpretations. For discussion of the comparative method, see chapter 1 above.

13. For the "rule of law" in classical Athens, see especially Herman 2006; and Harris 2006.

14. My use of the categories elite and masses is of course a crude binary division that elides many possible sub-groupings and identities within ancient Greek communities, as I discuss in chapter 1. Nevertheless, for my specific interests in this chapter, this categorization is the most useful. I use the term elite in the very narrow sense of those who formed the wealthiest 5 percent of the population and provided the political leadership of Greek states. Political leadership in ancient Greece was determined by a combination of wealth, good birth, divine favor, and excellence in a variety of socially recognized skills, particularly prowess in battle and public speaking. The masses were comprised of all those who did not form the leadership, but who participated in politics to a lesser (oligarchic states) or greater extent (democratic states). The masses, therefore, included a large number of middling as well as poor citizens, as I discussed in chapter 1. Moreover, for many of the rituals that I discuss in this chapter, the mass of ordinary citizens may have been accompanied by resident non-citizens (metics) and slaves, women (citizen and non-citizen), and youths or children. Popular justice is then one of the spheres of everyday life in which the political and legal divisions of the community are less important. For further discussion of the lines between political and legal statuses, see chapter 1 above. For further discussion of the utility of the modern concepts of mass and elite for understanding Athenian society, see Ober 1989, 11–17.

15. Ober 1989. Similarly, the essays in Hunter and Edmondson 2000 examine how formal law and legal practice serve to create symbolic status distinctions between different groups within the community (e.g., citizens, metics, slaves).

16. My approach is indebted to the theoretical, anthropological, and comparative-historical work of Gluckman 1965; Turner 1969; Foucault 1977; Burke 1978/1994; Babcock 1978; Le Roy Ladurie 1979; Bakhtin 1984; Davis 1975; Muir 1997, who see collective rituals (political, legal, religious, and popular) as occasions for articulation, contestation, and negotiation of collective values. For the influence of this work on Greek history, see Osborne 1985b; Goldhill 1990,

1991; and Connor 1987. Goldhill has explored this theme again under the rubric of "performance culture" (1999). Goldhill's aim is to draw connections between different areas of Athenian life by examining the performative aspects of a wide variety of Athenian practices. Goldhill's approach shares much in common with my own, especially in its theoretical emphasis on the overlap between practices inside and outside the formal institutions of the state. Nevertheless, none of the essays in Goldhill's volume examines popular justice, and indeed most focus on institutional contexts (theater, lawcourts, civic festivals).

17. Cohen 1991. On gossip as a mechanism for social control, see also Hunter 1994.

18. Even Cantarella 2005, who recognizes ritual humiliation as an informal social practice, emphasizes formal trials as the primary means of dealing with adultery.

19. Cohen 1985.

20. Roy 1991; and Carey 1993.

21. Carey (1995, 412) argues that the law on adultery mentioned by Aristotle explicitly prescribed public humiliation of the adulterer (see next note). Cantarella 2005, on the other hand, recognizes that humiliation was primarily an informal practice, but views it as a matter of honor between two individuals.

22. Although we know that there was a law on adultery (*Ath.Pol.*59.3), the law itself has not survived. Carey 1995, 412, however, proposes that the law cited in Lysias 1.28 is the law on adultery, and argues partially on this basis that this law specified death, if the adulterer was caught in the act and admitted his guilt; otherwise, the law allowed for abuse and ransom of the adulterer. If Carey is correct, then the law explicitly allowed for ritualized humiliation and abuse of the adulterer. My point, however, is that in most cases these practices would have been implemented without recourse to the law. It was primarily in cases in which informal practices were exploited unjustly (e.g., the adulterer was lured into an act of adultery in order that he might be killed, as is apparently alleged by the prosecution in Lysias 1) or a person was unjustly detained and abused as an adulterer (as is alleged in Dem. 59.66) that there was recourse to legal process. Cantarella 2005, 244 is an exception among modern scholars in recognizing that the modes of public humiliation of the adulterers "were not legal penalties" but "common practices." Cantarella, however, places these practices in the realm of modes of individual revenge of male honor, not in the context of communal rituals of public humiliation, as I do.

23. Cf. Kapparis 1995, 111–13.

24. So Carey (see n.21 above).

25. E.g., Cohen 1991; Carey 1995; Kapparis 1995, 110; Cantarella 2005, 244. For the provision giving immunity to a husband who kills an adulterer caught in the act, see Demosthenes 23.53: Ἐάν τις ἀποκτείνῃ ἐν ἄθλοις ἄκων, ἢ ἐν ὁδῷ καθελὼν ἢ ἐν πολέμῳ ἀγνοήσας, ἢ ἐπὶ δάμαρτι ἢ ἐπὶ μητρὶ ἢ ἐπ' ἀδελφῇ ἢ ἐπὶ θυγατρί, ἢ ἐπὶ παλλακῇ ἣν ἂν ἐπ' ἐλευθέροις παισὶν ἔχῃ, τούτων ἕνεκα μὴ φεύγειν κτείναντα. Cf. Lysias 1.30.

26. As noted already, scholars differ only as to whether these penalties were part of formal law. The principal classical sources for abuse and ransoming are:

Lysias 1.25, 1.29; 1.49, Dem. 59.65–66, as well as the passages from Aristophanes discussed below.

27. For an excellent discussion of this episode, see Brown 1989. Brown not only observes the relation of this episode to the treatment of adulterers in historical Greek city-states, but emphasizes the public nature of the mockery of the gods and the parallels with such rituals of humiliation in Rome and Early Modern and Modern Europe.

28. O'Higgins (2003, 45) notes that only the male gods come to observe the humiliation of Ares and Aphrodite. The goddesses are explicitly noted to have stayed at home out of modesty (*Od.* 8.324). O'Higgins classifies the laughter represented in this passage as typical of epic: it is performed by males and has the function of excluding or creating a distinction (here the community against the social offender). Women's laughter, according to O'Higgins, was a characteristic feature of women's cult and had an inclusive, community-bonding, function. The comparative evidence I present in this chapter would seem to support a broader role for women in the humiliation of social offenders than O'Higgins' theory allows for.

29. Homer, *Odyssey* 326–32. For the theme of the weak overcoming the strong in Greek popular culture, see chapter 2 above.

30. Compare Hephaistos' use of an invisible cage to pin Hera to her throne in the myth about his return to Olympus told in the now fragmentary *Homeric Hymn to Dionysus* and preserved for us only in late sources (Paus.1.20.3; pseudo-Libanius, *Narr.* 30.1 viii 38f. Foerster; cf. Aristid., *Or.* 41.6 ii.331 (Keil); Hyg. *Fab.*166; Serv. *Auct.Ecl.* 4.62). For discussion, see West 2001.

31. Dem. 24.105; cf. Lysias 10.16. Compare also the decree of Cannonus, cited by Xenophon (*Hell.*1.7.20), where anyone suspected of wronging the people must plead his case in fetters (δεδεμένον). This latter law is comparable to another attributed to Charondas of Catana, according to which proposers of revisions to laws must place their head in a noose while the assembly discussed and voted on the new law (Diod.Sic. 12.17)

32. Dem. 24.114. The use of the archaic term for stocks (ποδοκάκκη) suggests that the law goes back to early times. Nevertheless, penalties of public humiliation of social offenders (both free and slave) through exposure in wooden devices (e.g., ξύλον, κύφων) were still practiced in the classical period. The evidence is collected and discussed in Gernet 1981, 252–57 and Hunter 1994, 176–81. Demosthenes' interpretation of the intent of the use of the stocks (to induce shame by being seen by all) suggests that the stocks would have been in a public place, probably the agora, as is attested for other Greek states (Aristot., *Pol.* 1306b; cf. Gernet 1981, 265; Hunter 1994, 181). It is interesting to note that Aristotle's mention of the penalty of public display in the stocks concerns at least one case of adultery.

33. There has been a great deal of recent debate about the role of shame in ancient Greece, particularly concerning the utility of the modern distinction between shame and guilt (cf. Dodds 1964 for the classic statement of this distinction in relation to Greek culture and, more recently, Fisher 1992). Some scholars such as Cairns 1993 and Williams 1993 have argued that this distinction is oversimplified

and that shame involves both the views of society and the self regarding one's individual identity. For the purposes of this chapter, I accept that the shame is a product of both self and society, but that rituals of popular justice are directed more at one's social self than individual self insofar as publicity is extremely important. On popular justice as a form of *hubris* affecting the honor of individuals, see n.64 below.

34. For adulterers: Lysias 1.49; Xen. *Mem.* 2.1.5; Dem.59.66. For adulteresses: Dem. 59.85–87; Aeschines 1.183.

35. As Carey 1995, 414 notes: "This would always be done in front of witnesses, and therefore involve public humiliation." Cf. Carey 1993, 54 cites Xen. *Mem.* 2.1.5 where the captured adulterer is said to suffer hubris and shameful things. Carey writes: "The emphasis here is on humiliation." It is important to note that Carey's emphasis is on legal witnesses, not on a large crowd of people of the community, as I am suggesting.

36. Thompson 1993, 480. Publicity was also a key feature of official forms of punishment. As Dr. Johnson said with regard to public hangings, "executions are intended to draw spectators. If they do not draw spectators, then they do not answer their purpose" (Johnson cited by Burke 1978, 197). Compare Foucault 1977, 34: "[Public torture and execution] ... is intended, either by the scar it leaves on the body or the spectacle that accompanies it, to brand the victim with infamy ... public torture and execution must be spectacular." Cf. p. 57: "In ceremonies of public execution, the main character was the people." Similarly, Samuel Walker observes of colonial America that "the central feature of punishments, which sets them apart from modern practice, was their public character" (Walker 1998, 32). Walker notes that the most common forms of punishment were whipping in the public square and "the public humiliation of an hour in the stocks or pillory." Both Walker and Foucault are concerned with official forms of punishment, but their observations on the ritual nature of punishment and its relation to political power are also relevant to the analysis of popular forms of justice.

37. Schmitt-Pantel (1981, 118) takes the phrase "around the city" (περιάγουσι ... τὴν πόλιν) literally, suggesting that the offenders were led around the territory of the city in the manner of scapegoats. While this may be possible, it is clear that the offenders are also led through the streets of the city, not least to and from the agora. See below on the parallels with official procedure of *apagōgē*. Ogden 1997, 21 also sees a parallel between the scapegoat and the adulteress on the grounds that scapegoats at Abdera were stood on a grey block and then led around the perimeter of the city (Callimachus F90 (Pf.), with *Diegesis* ii.29–40).

38. See below, this section, on the habitual labeling of social offenders according to their offense.

39. William Coombe's representation of a skimmington ritual in his epic poem *The Tour of Dr Syntax* explicitly mentions that "men and boys" as well as "female voices" joined the action.

40. Burke 1978, 182. Burke draws here on Bakhtin's observation (1984, 7) that Carnival "is not a spectacle seen by the people; they live in it, and everyone participates." Compare William Coombe's account of a skimmington in his epic poem *The Tour of Dr Syntax* where members of the crowd are pelted with filth,

just as are the offenders themselves. Compare Foucault 1977, 57–59, who shows that the crowd (including women) participated actively in rituals of official punishment in eighteenth-century France. This participation involved both verbal abuse (either of the condemned or of the officials) and sometimes physical attacks.

41. It is perhaps significant that Plutarch (*Mor*.519B) records a law from Thurii (an Athenian colony) that banned comic ridicule of citizens except for adulterers and busy-bodies: εὖ δὲ καὶ ὁ τῶν Θουρίων νομοθέτης· κωμῳδεῖσθαι γὰρ ἐκώλυσε τοὺς πολίτας πλὴν μοιχοὺς καὶ πολυπράγμονας. Cf. [Xen.] *Ath.Pol.* 2.18 with discussion by Henderson 1990b, and the scolium to Aristoph., *Birds* 1297 ("the decree of Syracosius") with discussion by Halliwell 1991b and Trevett 2000. Since the term κωμῳδεῖν is always used in the restricted sense of ridicule in a performance of comedy (so Henderson 1990b, 307), rather than the more general sense of any form of ridicule, this passage suggests an interesting link between the ritualized humiliation of adulterers and the genre of comedy. At the end of the chapter, I suggest that forms of popular justice share some features with certain types of popular festivity, including the verbal abuse that formed part of Dionysiac ritual and the dramatic performances that took place during this festival.

42. On agora as legal, political, and religious center, see Camp 2001. For agora as center for exchange of information and gossip, cf. Hunter 1994 and Lewis 1996, 13–19. For the "blending of formal and informal, public and private" activities that took place in the agora, see Millett 1998, 215. Millett's focus is on the agora as "the major zone of personal interaction in Athens" (211) and his list of activities that took place there (215) does not include the public display of social offenders. Millett does, however, observe that exclusion from the agora (e.g., of cowards) was a "way of making a formal and public statement about a man's reputation" (224) and that agora was a place where elites like Meidias (Dem. 21.158) could put themselves on display. It is noteworthy, moreover, that Millett uses the term "street theater" to describe public rituals of buying and selling that took place in the agora (222; Millett 1990, 193–94), and therefore is well aware of the performative dimensions of action before spectators in the marketplace.

43. Demosthenes 25.51.

44. Cohen 1991.

45. For women's participation in religious rites, see Dillon 2002; Connelly 2007. For women's work, see Scheidel 1995, 1996; Brock 1994.

46. For Spartan women enforcing social norms see, for example, Herodotus 5.51 (on Gorgo) and the many sayings of Spartan women preserved in Plutarch *Moralia* 240c –242d.

47. Hunter 1994; Vlassopoulos 2007, 2009.

48. For public slaves, see Jacob 1979; Cohen 2000. For banking slaves, see Cohen 1992.

49. Fisher 2008, 124–25.

50. [Xen.], *Ath.Pol.* 1.10–12; Plato, *Rep.* 563b. For further discussion, see chapter 1.

51. Compare Burke's observation (1978, 198) that the point of the stocks and the pillory in Early Modern Europe was "part public shaming, part the exposure of the offender to the violence of the crowd."

52. Schmitt-Pantel (1981, 118) notes that it was only adulteresses who were put on display in the agora, not adulterers. She explains this difference by suggesting that exposure in the agora is more humiliating for women than for men, since women are ideally supposed to remain inside the house. But both men and women were paraded through the streets, also a humiliating public place for ideally sequestered women. It is also noteworthy that men were displayed in the agora for other crimes (e.g., theft, see above).

53. Juries in classical Athens typically ranged from 201 to 2,501 citizens, depending on the importance of the case. See Hansen 1999, 187.

54. See e.g., Dem. 18.196, Din.1.30. See Lanni 1997 for a full discussion of the evidence for bystanders as well as for the rope or wicker that separated jurors from bystanders. Lanni notes that the presence of bystanders at formal legal proceedings constitutes a form of "informal social control" (189), and is thus in itself a good example of the juxtaposition of formal and informal practices in classical Athens.

55. For citizen women in the marketplace (despite the Athenian ideal of seclusion within the household), cf. Brock 1994. For punishment as public entertainment in the early modern period, see "Violence and Popular Festivity" below.

56. Bers (1985) discusses the evidence for heckling of litigants by jurors. Bers suggests, moreover, that "the presence of spectators within the *dikastērion* may have promoted *thorubos* [heckling]" and notes that "when *thorubos* [heckling] erupted, a member of the jury panel would not often have been able to tell whether the author of a shout or murmur was a fellow dikast or a man standing in the half-circle ... of bystanders" (8). On the effect of this sort of crowd participation on free speech in Athens, see Wallace 2004; Roisman 2004; and Tacon 2001.

57. Herodotus 9.5.

58. Ibid.

59. Harrison 1968, 33; MacDowell 1978, 125; Carey 1995, 414.

60. Cantarella 2005, 244 is a partial exception to this statement. She recognizes that the forms of public humiliation were not formal legal practices, but "customary" ones. She does not, however, view them as collective rituals, but rather the practices of aggrieved male individuals seeking revenge for slights to their honor.

61. Cf. the scholia on Aristophanes, *Clouds* 1083; Lucian, *Peregrinus* 9 (which also attests to beating and monetary compensation as responses to adultery). Semonides 7.12–18 envisions a husband knocking out his adulterous wife's teeth with a stone.

62. E.g., Dover 1989, 105–6; Schmitt-Pantel 1981, 120; Carey 1993, 54. Anal penetration also assimilates the adulterer to a male prostitute, a profession which disqualified one from citizenship (cf. Aeschines 1.29–32, with Dover 1989, 19–39). For recent discussion of Greek homosexuality and modification of the active-passive distinction made famous by Foucault 1985, see Halperin 1990; Winkler 1990; and Davidson 1997, 2001. Davidson, in particular, argues that men who were penetrated in anal sex were womanish not because they were passive and subordinate, but because they enjoyed sex in the manner of women. Furthermore,

according to Davidson, the construction of ancient female sexuality was morally problematic not because it was passive and subordinate, but because it was insatiable (Davidson 1997, 167–82).

63. Schmitt-Pantel 1981, 119–20; Carey 1993, 53. See also Aristoph. *Wealth* 168, with discussion by Sommerstein 2001, 144–46. For genital depilation with hot ash as characteristic of women, see Aristoph. *Lys.* 88–89, 151; *Frogs* 516, *Assembly Women*, 724, and the discussions of Bain 1982 and Kilmer 1982.

64. Schmitt-Pantel 1981, 120. On the association between adulterers and effeminacy, see also Davidson 1997, 167–68.

65. *Var.Hist.* 12.12. Schmitt-Pantel 1981, 120. The fifth-century law code from Gortyn, however, makes no mention of this treatment. Willetts (1967, 28) suggests that the crowning of adulterers with wool is part of "a later stage of development, when the state had taken over, wholly or in part, the punishment of adultery from the family." On my argument, however, this form of public humiliation may have been a product of informal collective, rather than official state action. This would explain why it is not featured in formal written law, which specifies only that compensation is due, and that the captor may "do whatever he wishes" if the captive is not ransomed within five days (Col.II.33–36).

66. Did.Sic.12.16, a parallel also noted by Schmitt-Pantel 1981, 120.

67. For recent discussion of the construction of courage in ancient Greece, see the essays in Rosen and Sluiter 2003.

68. By comparison, in colonial America, adulteresses wore a scarlet letter "A" and burglars had their hands branded with the letter "B," or sometimes "T" for "thief." Repeat offenders could have their foreheads branded with the letter "R." Cf. Walker 1998, 32–33.

69. On the need for the creation of social knowledge or social memories of a wrongdoing as a key feature of punishment, see above and Allen 2000, 202–5.

70. Compare Kapparis 1995, 112: "The place where the punishment took place was the house of the insulted man in most occasions. Some people would have felt the desire to make the humiliation worse by making it more public, either by leaving the door wide-open, or even by dragging the adulterer into the middle of the market and inflicting the punishment in full view of the public." Kapparis cites two ancient sources for the public nature of these rituals of humiliation: a scholiast to Tzetz. *Plu*.168 and Catullus 15.17–19. These sources are late, and of marginal value as witnesses to classical Greek practices. The lack of more mainstream testimonies is due to the fact (mentioned above) that classical authors assume widespread familiarity with these practices and therefore do not mention them for the most part, let alone explain them in any detail.

71. Hunter 1994, 177 (my emphasis). Cohen argues that adulterers were classed as κακοῦργοι (1991, 110–22), though his argument is refuted by Carey 1995.

72. Hdt.7.231.

73. For this interpretation, see Olson 2002, 284.

74. Thompson 1993, 487. The prolonged abuse of adulterers and adulteresses in Lepreum and Pisidia raises some questions. Were the offenders given food and water? When and how were they permitted to urinate?

75. Dem.59.85–87: Ἐπειδὰν δὲ ἕλῃ τὸν μοιχόν, μὴ ἐξέστω τῷ ἑλόντι συνοικεῖν τῇ γυναικί· ἐὰν δὲ συνοικῇ, ἄτιμος ἔστω. μηδὲ τῇ γυναικὶ ἐξέστω εἰσιέναι εἰς τὰ ἱερὰ τὰ δημοτελῆ, ἐφ᾽ ᾗ ἂν μοιχὸς ἁλῷ· ἐὰν δ᾽εἰσίῃ, νηποινεὶ πασχέτω ὅ τι ἂν πάσχῃ, πλὴν θανάτου. Aesch.1.183: Τὴν γὰρ γυναῖκα ἐφ᾽ ᾗ ἂν ἁλῷ μοιχὸς οὐκ ἐᾷ κοσμεῖσθαι, οὐδὲ εἰς τὰ δημοτελῆ ἱερὰ εἰσιέναι, ἵνα μὴ τὰς ἀναμαρτήτους τῶν γυναικῶν ἀναμειγνυμένη διαφθείρῃ· ἐὰν δ᾽εἰσίῃ ἢ κοσμῆται, τὸν ἐντυχόντα κελεύει καταρρηγνύναι τὰ ἱμάτια καὶ τὸν κόσμον ἀφαιρεῖσθαι καὶ τύπτειν, εἰργόμενον θανάτου καὶ τοῦ ἀνάπηρον ποιῆσαι, ἀτιμῶν τὴν τοιαύτην γυναῖκα καὶ τὸν βίον ἀβίωτον αὐτῇ παρασκευάζων.

76. Cf. Latte 1932, who notes that divorce of adulteresses seems customary already in Homer, *Od.* 8.318, where Hephaistos expects to have the bride-price or marriage gifts (ἔεδνα) back for his unfaithful wife Aphrodite.

77. Schmitt-Pantel 1981, 120–21.

78. Plut., *Lyc.*15.1–2; Xen. *Lac.Pol.* 9.5. Schmitt-Pantel makes this comparison and notes that Sparta and Athens oppose each other thus in the matter of procreation.

79. Fisher 1992 identifies the diminishment of honor and the production of shame as key features of the Greek concept of hubris (cf. Arist., *Rhet.*1378b23–30). For recent discussion of the meaning of *hubris* and its relation to shame, see Cairns 1996 and n.30 above. Carey (1995, 413–14) writes of the provision allowing physical abuse of adulterers: "[I]t was not a light penalty. In a society like our own which places less premium on public face it is difficult to grasp the severity of this sanction. But the effect of this clause in the law was to deprive the *moichos* [adulterer] of the sanction of the *graphē hubreōs* [the right to prosecute for outrage] when subject to acts which normally would be classed as hybris and which were normally actionable even when committed against slaves." Despite the limited legal framework in which Carey places ritual abuse of adulterers, he does nevertheless capture some features of the public humiliation that such treatment entailed. Cf. also Lucian, *On the Death of Peregrinus* 9, where the adulterer is subject to beating or whipping (πολλὰς πληγὰς) in addition to being radished.

80. Compare the evidence that Athenian women restricted access to the Thesmophoria by keeping out prostitutes and slaves (Dillon 2002, 112). For a recent overview of girls and women in Greek religion, see Dillon 2002.

81. See especially Davis 1975, 124–51. Women play an important role in instigating, planning, and carrying out the skimmington in Hardy's *Mayor of Casterbridge* and in the Groaning ritual described in Rollison 1981, 92. William Coombe's account of a skimmington in his epic poem *The Tour of Dr Syntax* shows women playing a prominent role.

82. Davis 1975 124–51.

83. Hdt. 9.5.3.

84. Gras 1984, 77 includes another instance of spontaneous action by women as a case of stoning, even though no stones are used. Herodotus reports that after a battle in which the Athenian forces had been eliminated except for one man, the Athenian women surrounded the sole Athenian survivor and killed him by poking him with the pins that held their clothes in place (5.87). The historicity of this episode is doubtful since it serves as an aetiology for the adoption of Ionian dress.

If we remove the story from the clearly fictive aetiological context in which it is deployed (and therefore eliminate the idea that the women's act was in some way unjust and necessitated a change of dress to remove these potential weapons from the hands of women), we are still left with the presumably historically valid belief that women might spontaneously engage in collective punishment of a social offender. On the other hand, for the aetiology to be plausible, there must have been something in the story that transgressed Greek ideas about proper female collective action. I suggest that what was outrageous for the Athenians is not the fact of collective female action, but the use of a stoning-like procedure against someone who was not deserving of this treatment, namely, the presumably innocent survivor of a disastrous military campaign. The use of stoning would have been appropriate against the commander, if it were felt that he did not conduct the campaign well (see Diod. 12.78.5 and Thuc. 5.60.6, discussed above) and indeed the similarity of this episode to cases in which commanders who retreated from battle without accomplishing their mission perhaps explains the women's decision to use a stoning-like ritual.

85. Another example of women's participation in rituals of social control is attested for Sparta, where, according to Plutarch Lyc.14.3, at certain festivals women mocked young men who had committed wrongs, thereby humiliating them in public and preventing further transgressions in the future. This ritual nicely illustrates the overlap between festival revelry and popular justice that I explore in the final part of the chapter.

86. Rosivach 1987 characterizes the stoning of Lycides in this way. But Gras 1984, 76 emphasizes that stoning is "not an uncontrolled act by an uncontrollable people ... but a ritual which allows to the throwing of stones an escape from its banal essence and its placement at the heart of the functioning of the Greek city." Cf. also p. 83. Yet Gras also distinguishes (86) between stonings performed by male citizens, which he classes as "political acts," and stonings by women, which he classifies as "passionate, hysterical" insofar as they harm innocents.

87. Thompson 1993, 486. Note also Thompson's work on food riots (same volume) and Forsdyke 2005b and chapter 4 above, where I suggest some reasons for this restraint.

88. It is noteworthy, however, that Christ 2006 argues that prominent individuals were magnets for charges of draft-dodging and cowardice.

89. Thompson 1993, 513–21.

90. Ibid., 513–14.

91. Ibid., 515–16, 519. See also Rollison 1981, and Thomas Hardy's fictional account of a skimmington—a type of ritual humiliation of social offenders in eighteenth-century England—in his 1885 novel *The Mayor of Casterbridge* (both cited by Thompson). This is not to deny that there were many other causes, not directly related to mass-elite tensions, and not involving an elite offender. For example, rituals of popular justice were often used to mock second marriages, couples who were ill-matched in age, unfaithful partners, and quarrelsome couples regardless of the social status of those involved: Davis 1975, 104–9; Pitt-Rivers 1971, 169–77; Thompson 1993, 482. Indeed, popular rituals are tremendously flexible in their uses and occasions, as Thompson himself and many others

(e.g., Davis 1975) have shown. My point is that they can be used as a medium for mass-elite interaction and communication, and that the ancient Greek evidence suggests that they often were. Gilmore 1987, 89 nicely sums up the various uses of popular justice when he notes that Carnival was used by subordinate classes "to express ... resentments against the rich and powerful, to indict social injustice, as well as to chastise peasant offenders against the moral traditions of the pueblo, its ethics, its norms of honesty." Scott 1990, 174, however, comments on this passage as follows: "It is useful to recall that during carnival the use of social sanctions against members of one's own class may have the purpose of disciplining those who are trying to curry favor with elites at the expense of their peers."

92. Connor 1985.

93. Ibid., 84.

94. Ibid., 83.

95. Ibid., 98.

96. Ibid. Sources: Xen. *Hell.* 2.2.23 and Plut. *Lys.*15.

97. Thucydides 5.63.2.

98. The Council of Elders (Gerousia), along with the Ephors, would have been the magistrates responsible for a formal trial of one of the Spartan kings (Xen. *Spartan Constitution* 8.3; 10.3; Plut. *Lyc.* 26.2). Nevertheless, the Spartan assembly did play a role in foreign policy, and it is conceivable that it could have been the context in which a failed campaign was debated and judged (cf. Kennell 2010, 113–14).

99. See Ober 1998, 52–121; and Forsdyke 2005a, 267–70.

100. For a recent example of house-razing as a mode of popular justice, compare the reaction of the relatives of those who died aboard the Egyptian ferry boat when it sank in the Red Sea in February 2006. Frustrated by the slow response of the Egyptian government and aware of the close ties between the government and the owner of the shipping line, the relatives went to the headquarters of the shipping company and burned them down (*New York Times*, February 12, 2006).

101. Thucydides' use of the verb βουλεύω, to describe the Spartans' initial decision implies a formal context, which Gomme, Andrewes, and Dover (1970, 89) suggest was the assembly.

102. It is possible, as Connor notes (p. 82, n.9), that Thucydides' representation of the Spartan episode has colored Diodorus' account of events in Argos. Thucydides himself reports (5.60.6) that the Argives undertook to stone one of the generals, Thrasylus, but that when he escaped to an altar, he survived. The Argives, according to Thucydides, nevertheless confiscated Thrasylus' property. It is noteworthy that Thucydides presents this episode as a formal legal process, and uses the technical legal terms for a trial (δίκη) and judicial decision-making (κρίνειν). On the basis of this and other parallels, Schmitz suggests that stoning was part of a formal legal process (2004, 393–94). I would not dispute that sometimes such punishments are incorporated into the formal legal process, but would suggest, along with Connor 1985, that they need not always have been. It is perhaps noteworthy in this regard that, according to Thucydides (5.60.6), the customary place for cases involving conduct on compaign was in the bed of the River Charandros outside the city of Argos. Thus, the "trial" took place in an open spot,

not in the political assembly or other formal public space such as the lawcourts. For a similar example, see the case of the tyrant Coes of Mytilene, who was taken outside the city before being stoned (Hdt. 5.37.2).

103. Studies by social psychologists show that subjects who are mistreated only experience a reduction in anger and frustration if they are allowed to injure directly the one who mistreated them: Scott 1990, 186, citing Berkowitz 1962. Danielle Allen's work on Athenian tragedy and legal reasoning shows that the Athenians understood that acts of violence could cure anger (see Allen 2005, 380–85).

104. It is unclear whether Leotychides' exile was the formal penalty or merely a result of his attempt to avoid the formal penalty of death. For the difficulty of distinguishing penalties of death from penalties of exile, cf. Forsdyke 2005a, 11.

105. Plut., *Mor.* 833d–834b. In addition, it was decreed that stones be set up on the site of the razed house inscribed with the words "of Archeptolemus and Antiphon, the traitors." Official memorials ensured that the offender and his offense were inserted into the social memory of the Athenians (cf. Allen 2000, 203). It was also decreed that the offenders and their descendants (both legitimate and illegitimate) be denied civic rights and hence became outlaws from the city.

106. Xen.*Hell.* 1.7.22, Lyc. *Leoc.* 113.

107. Compare Connor 1987, 49 who argues that Solon's reforms, the "Lifting of Burdens" (*Seisachtheia*), would have been celebrated with "a festival, perhaps a procession through the countryside or a ritualized destruction of boundary markers [which marked encumbered property]." For discussion of this interpretation, see chapter 4 above. Note that Gernet 1984, 28 suggests that refusal of burial and razing of the house are relics of primitive forms of punishment which survived into later times to accompany formal legal penalties of death.

108. See Forsdyke 2005a on ostracism; Bremmer 1983 on scapegoating; and Faraone 2004 on other forms of ritual expulsion. The hurling of bones over borders should be seen as the ritual equivalent (albeit in inverse) of the escorting of bones of mythical heroes back into the territory of the state. In the latter case, the community participates in the return of heroic bones and founds a hero-cult which symbolizes some of the positive qualities that they wish to identify with their community.

109. Nicalaus of Damascus (first century BCE) is, of course, not a very reliable source for archaic Greek history. Nevertheless, his account shares patterns with similar episodes in, if not of archaic, at least classical Greek history (see below). Nicolaus' testimony, therefore, may reveal genuine Greek collective practices.

110. Nic.Dam., *FrGrH* 90 F60.

111. Plut., *Tim.* 22.1–2.

112. Plut., *Tim.* 22.3. By contrast, the razed houses of Antiphon and Archeptolomus were marked by stone inscriptions that identified the ruins as belonging to the traitors—a powerful symbolic reminder of the consequences of treason for the rest of the citizenry.

113. It is significant that, at the beginning of each assembly and council meeting in Athens, the herald recited a curse against traitors which apparently called down destruction not only on the traitor and his family, but his "house." In some

versions of the curse, "house" clearly stands for family (e.g., the parody at Aristoph.*Thesm.* 349). In other versions, however, the house is specified in addition to
individual and family, and therefore seems to indicate house-razing (e.g., Dem.
19.71). If so, then this is another example of popular justice within the formal
institutional context. This example is also significant for the role of house-razing
in articulating a political identity (this time, of the Athenian democracy).

114. This point is made by Connor 1985, 85.

115. Compare Strepsiades in the *Clouds* (1485–92) who brings a mattock
and firebrands to destroy Socrates' Thinkery (see n.117 below).

116. Connor 1985, 85.

117. Ibid. See, e.g., Soph.*OC* 1318, Eur. *Helen* 196ff., *Rhesus* 391, and Pausanias 8.27.16. One might also add the evidence of the destruction of Socrates'
Thinkery at the end of Aristophanes' *Clouds*, an act which is called a κατασκαφή
(1488), and burning clearly takes place (1490–97). For discussion, see Kopff 1977,
who notes the parallel with the burning of the house of the Pythagoreans at
Croton.

118. My argument is the converse of Foucault's argument about the relation
between political power and official forms of punishment. Foucault suggests that
the most important aspect of the ritual of public execution in eighteenth-century
France was its political symbolism in demonstrating the power of the sovereign,
though he also shows that the spectating crowd could subvert this power relation
if it deemed the punishment unjust (1977, 48–57). I suggest that rituals of popular justice played a similar role in articulating *popular* power. Our interpretations
share emphasis on the spectacular, theatrical, public, ritual, symbolic, and political nature of punishment.

119. Scott 1990, 65–66.

120. For the visual spectacle of the elaborate procedures of the courts, see
Bers 2000.

121. Ober 1989.

122. In classical Athens, the most serious penalties (death, imprisonment, exile,
disenfranchisement) arising from public suits (the class of action used to deal with
the type of offenses discussed in this chapter) were executed by the Eleven (the
latter two through the procedures of ἀπαγωγή or ἔνδειξις). Financial penalties
such as fines or confiscation of property were exacted by financial officers known
as πράκτορες or πωληταί. See Harrison 1971, 185–87.

123. Xen., *Hell.* 1.7.1–35.

124. Xenophon, *Hellenika* 1.7.35.

125. Callixeinus' situation may be illuminated by comparison of social shunning in peasant villages in contemporary South East Asia: "A peasant household
held in contempt by their fellow villagers will find it impossible to exchange harvest labor, to borrow a draft animal, to raise a small loan, to marry their children
off, to prevent petty thefts of their grain or livestock, or even to bury their dead
with any dignity" (Scott 1990, 131). Though Callixeinus presumably belonged to
the wealthiest class of Athenians, his conviction on the charge of deception of the
people will have resulted in the confiscation of his property, leaving him little or no
resources to buffer him against this sort of social shunning. One might ask why
Callixeinus preferred to die rather than go into exile again. Comparison with

examples of shunning in Sparta (see next note), as well as numerous literary evocations of the misfortune of exile (e.g., Andocides 1.5; Hyperides 1.20), suggests that for the ancient Greeks, death was often preferable to wandering without a community.

126. Cf., e.g., Hdt. 7.231–232, where he describes the treatment that the sole survivors of the Battle of Thermopylae received when they returned to Sparta: one endured such disgrace that no one would give him a light to kindle his fire or talk to him, and he was called "the Trembler"; another was so dishonored that he hanged himself. With the first Spartan, one could compare the story of Lycophron (Hdt. 3.50–52) which serves as a negative exemplum of Athenian political culture (cf. Forsdyke 2005a, 253–57). A Spartan parallel for the treatment of Callixeinus perhaps can be found in the story of King Pausanias' treason and subsequent death by starvation (Thuc. 128–34; Lyc., *Leocr.* 128–29). Lyc. *Leocr.* 129 notes that at Sparta, death was the penalty for cowardice, and that therefore the salvation of the city was made dependent on courage in battle and shame.

127. There is no sign in our sources that the Athenians felt any remorse after Callixeinus' death, or felt that he should have been granted a trial. Callixeinus' death shows that the Athenians had no problem with extra-legal popular justice so long as it was directed at a communally agreed upon deserving offender. Conversely, these episodes show that the Athenians were not so much distressed that they had transgressed their legal principle of the right to individual trials in executing the generals, but that they had been deceived by Callixeinus into executing them unjustly (i.e., the Athenians judged in retrospect that the generals did not deserve to die).

128. For example, Harris 2006; Herman 2006 argue that the Athenians held strongly to the principle of "rule of law."

129. For the coexistence of contradictory norms in classical Athens, see Humphreys 1985; Cohen 1991, 31 (both of whom draw on Bourdieu 1977). The story of Callixeinus also has implications for recent arguments about Athenian compassion and non-violence (Sternberg 2006; Herman 2006), some of which I will address at the end of this chapter.

130. Modern discussions of stoning in ancient Greece include Hirzel 1909; Glotz 1877–1919; Latte 1932; Gernet 1984, 10–11; Gras 1984; Rosivach 1987; Ogden 1997, 19, who explores the connections between stoning and scapegoating (see chapter 3 above) and Schmitz 2004, 393–400. We will return to the overlap between these two practices at the end of this chapter.

131. Cf. Gras 1984, 83: "La lapidation ... est l'une des manifestations fondimentales d'une justice populaire." Contra Schmitz (2004, 393–400), who argues that the stonings of Lycides and others discussed below (e.g., the tyrant Coes of Mytilene, Alcibiades of Athens) resulted from a formal conviction (for treason, adultery, or sacrilege) by an assembly of the people. Schmitz, I suggest, undervalues the evidence for extra-judicial settings of this punishment, as well as Herodotus and Thucydides' descriptions of the spontaneity of the crowd action. Again, while I would not deny that such punishments could result from formal judicial proceedings, as seems to be the case in Hipponax fragment 128 West, I do not think that they always needed to have formal sanction. Schmitz, by contrast, emphasizes that stoning is primarily a legal penalty and argues (398) that the law

allowed for the spontaneous execution of the punishment of stoning only in cases where the offender was caught in the act, or when he might otherwise flee and escape trial.

132. On the three official methods of execution, see Gernet 1981, 252–76; MacDowell 1978, 254–55; Hunter 1994, 176–81; Todd 2000; Allen 2000, 200–201. MacDowell assimilates ἀποτυμπανισμός with crucifixion, but as Gernet 1981, 252–54 (following Keramopoullos 1923) shows, it differed in that offenders were bound to the pole or plank with clamps, not nails, and hence did not die from loss of blood, but from exposure.

133. Gras 1984, 83 similarly observes that stoning was practiced by the people against "the Prince" and "by the army against their leader." There are some exceptions to this generalization. For example, Thucydides describes how the Athenians stoned to death a group of Corinthian soldiers who accidently became entrapped in an enclosure as they retreated from battle (1.106). See also Hdt. 1.167, who reports that the Carthaginians and the Etruscans stoned to death a group of Phocaean prisoners after the battle of Alalia. In myth, moreover, particularly as expressed in tragedy, stonings result from a much wider array of offences: sacrilege, murder, parricide, incest, and adultery. See Rosivach 1987 for discussion of the tragic evidence and n.143 below.

134. The only other Lycides attested in Athens is a miller mentioned in [Dem.] 53.14. Unfortunately, little is known about the social status of millers, although this one is clearly a citizen, since he brought a case against the speaker. Another miller attested in ancient sources (Din. 1.23) owned slaves and presumably land and buildings, i.e., had considerable wealth. For attestations of millers, see Harris 2002, 94.

135. Hansen 1999, 267–77.

136. Hdt. 9.5.2.

137. Xen.*Hell.* 1.2.13.

138. Compare the active participation of Athenian hoplites in the stoning of a large group of Corinthians who found themselves trapped inside an enclosure during a retreat (Thuc. 1.106). Stonings of enemy combatants should, however, be distinguished from stonings of members of one's own community. Andrewes 1956 finds this instance of stoning incredible, and therefore amends *kateleusen* to *kateleēsas apelusen*, "taking pity on him, released him." The evidence collected in this chapter shows that stoning was not as incredible as Andrewes thought.

139. Hdt. 5.37.2.

140. Fr. 298.

141. Hdt. 5.67.2. Ogden 1993, 1997, 100–104; cf. Gras 1984, 83. Ogden also relates this epithet to the ritual of scapegoating, arguing that the ambiguity of the epithet reflects Cleisthenes' attempt to get rid of Adrastus, in the manner of a scapegoat, as well as the suitability of Cleisthenes himself for expulsion by stoning. For further discussion, see chapter 3 above.

142. On Pittacus, see Forsdyke 2005a, 43–48. For other historical tyrants subject to stoning, see Gras 1984, 83.

143. The frequent occurrence of this topos in oratory suggests that stoning—though an extreme and unusual form of punishment—was not considered a bar-

baric or primitive form of punishment, as Rosivach 1987 argues. When used in the appropriate contexts (i.e., by the people against tyrants or traitors) it was considered an entirely legitimate punishment. Stoning only gets a negative connotation when it is used by tyrannical leaders in tragedy (e.g., Pentheus, Creon, Eurystheus, and Aegisthus) without the support of the people. See Allen 2005, 388–90 for the distinction in tragedy between the illegitimacy of laws created by and for individuals verses the legitimacy of laws that arise from the community as a whole. The case of the Furies in Aeschylus' *Eumenides* fits this paradigm. These gods are unrelenting in their pursuit of Orestes, and support penalties (including stoning) that were much more severe than popularly supported against him.

144. 19.66.

145. *Leocr.*122; cf. 71.

146. Din. Fr. 33 (Mueller) = Photius and Suidas s.v. *kataleusimon*.

147. Hyperides fr.59 (Blass) = Harpocrat. s.v. *kataleusan*.

148. For other examples of stoning of military commanders by their soldiers, see Gras 1984, 84. Compare also Plut. *Phocion* 34.3–4 where the assembly calls out for the stoning of oligarchs and other opponents of democracy.

149. Several legendary episodes replicate the pattern of elite targets of stoning and suggest that, at least in myth, sexual offenses such as rape could be punished by stoning: a companion of Odysseus was stoned for raping a young girl (Paus. 6.6.7); two Arcadian kings were stoned by their subjects, one for rape of a priestess, the other for treason.

150. Hdt. 9.120.4.

151. Davies (1971, 185). Todd (2007, 59–60) accepts Davies' suggestion. Eratosthenes of Oa, was apparently a repeat offender, since he allegedly had seduced the wives of many others (Lysias 1.16). If this accusation is true, and is not simply character assassination, it suggests that Eratosthenes was a man of considerable leisure who could afford to spend time on such intrigues. Carey 1989, 72, however, notes that there is no attempt in the speech to prove the allegation that Eratosthenes was a repeat offender. On the other hand, the witness quoted in the speech ironically suggests that adultery is Eratosthenes' profession, confirming the impression that this is how he spends his time.

152. Carey 1989, 69 presents the evidence: Euphiletus describes his house using a diminutive, and mentions that his wife breastfeeds her own baby. Moreover, Euphiletus does not describe any liturgical activities (a common tactic to win the sympathy of the jury), which suggests that he is outside the liturgical class. On the other hand, Euphiletus has a farm and a town house and he can afford the services of a professional speech-writer. As Carey reasons, this evidence together suggests a man of moderate means, neither elite nor poor. Todd (2007, 57–59) argues that Euphiletus was in fact not well off at all. Todd explains Euphiletus' ability to pay for the speech by Lysias' willingness to offer his services cheaply in return for the opportunity to gain vengeance on a relative of the Eratosthenes who had killed his brother (2007, 60).

153. There is considerable evidence for legal charges being used as grounds for attacks on political opponents (e.g., Dem.21, [Dem.] 59 and, most famously the ongoing litigation between Aeschines and Demosthenes (Aesch.1,2,3 and Dem.

18 and 19). Cohen 1995 has interpreted the ongoing litigation between political rivals as a form of feud.

154. Brenne 2002, ostrakon number 106.

155. Forsdyke 2005a, 156.

156. Forsdyke 2005a.

157. For Hephaistos' lower class status, see now Griffith 2006, 351.

158. Walker 1998, 6.

159. Herman 2006, 411. Other scholars share this view, at least for fourth-century Athens: Harris 2006, Hansen 1999.

160. Herman 2006, 413. Herman's claim that there is no "shred of evidence for crowds gathering to watch executions in Athens" (292) is vitiated by its focus solely on official executions by public officials rather than extra-legal practices. The physical and verbal abuse of adulterers, stonings, and social exclusion leading to death by starvation are arguably customs "suffused with cruelty and bloodshed."

161. For this distinction, see especially Herman 2006, 205.

162. Given the comparative nature of this study, some may wonder whether my interpretation of popular justice implies that I view Athens—or Greek culture generally—as fitting the model of a "Mediterranean society." My emphasis on the collective aspect of popular rituals of social control is quite distinct from David Cohen's focus on individual honor (Cohen 1991, 1995). It is this aspect of Cohen's model, moreover, that is the focus of Herman's attack on the "Mediterranean anthropology" approach to Greek culture (Herman 2006, 95–118). By contrast, I stress the role of popular justice in policing the community and am particularly concerned with the way these rituals mediate relations between *groups* (not *individuals*) within the community. Second, popular justice viewed in these terms is not particularly Mediterranean. Such forms of justice are attested in a wide variety of cultures from Northern Europe to Africa and the Americas. See for example, Gluckman 1963; Turner 1969; Babcock 1978; Hill 1972; Davis 1975; Burke 1978; Le Goff and Schmitt 1981; Sabean 1984; Darnton 1984; Bakhtin 1984; Stallybrass and White 1986; Kertzer 1988; Scott 1990; Thompson 1993; Nissenbaum 1996; Bradtke 2000; and Forsdyke 2005b. I certainly would not deny that the Greeks share some distinctive cultural assumptions and practices with other Mediterranean societies. Indeed, Cohen's identification of individual male honor as one area of overlap seems valid, if allowances are made for different articulations of this core value within different historical cultures. In my view, Herman (2006, 184–203) draws too simple a binary contrast between "feuding societies" where the principle of "a head for an eye" is dominant and centralized states in which offenses are punished through moderate state-imposed penalties. Athens does not fit neatly into either of these categories, but somewhere in between.

163. Davis 1975, 140–41; Burke 1978, 192–201; Thompson 1993, 469–77.

164. Burke 1978, 192.

165. Foucault similarly observes that public executions took on aspects of carnival not only insofar as the condemned man had nothing to lose if he cursed the authorities, but also because "work stopped, taverns were full, the authorities were abused, insults or stones were thrown at the executioner, the guards and the soldiers" (1977, 63). Foucault also shows how popular rioting could result from

official punishments against those with whom the crowd could identify (the poor, vagabonds, thieves, and especially those condemned for rioting) (1977, 61–62). Bakhtin 1984, 200–203, provides another example: the festive form of ritual blows at a mock wedding is used to punish a social offender.

166. For the mounting of the god on a donkey and the phallic parade, cf. Csapo 1997; Hedreen 2004; Parker 2005, 318–26. For other features of Dionysiac ritual, including drunken revelry, ribald sexuality, and obscene speech, see Henderson 1991; Edwards 1993; Cole 1993; Parker 2005, 290–326.

167. Parker 2005, 317 notes that "one of the two Greek verbs for 'to insult in a ritual context' was in fact πομπεύω, literally 'I process.'" For obscenity at the festivals of Demeter see n.180 below. For verbal insults in failed rituals of hospitality between elites and masses, see Forsdyke 2005b and chapter 4 above.

168. For the associations between Dionysus and excessive sexuality, see Parker 2005, 319–21. For donkeys as symbols of excessive sexuality, see Semonides 7; Schmitt-Pantel 1981; Ogden 1997, 21, 116.

169. For cross-dressing at the Dionysia, see Csapo 1997; Parker 2005, 321–23; and chapter 4.

170. For Dionysus and ritual reversal see, for example, Edwards 1993; Zeitlin 1996; Halliwell 1991, 2000; and Parker 2005, 313–14. For other festivals featuring reversal, see Vernsel 1993; and Forsdyke 2005b.

171. Burke 1978, 198 and chapter 4.

172. Burke (1978, 200) cites an example from the city of Palermo in 1647, where a crowd burned the house of an unpopular official when the price of bread was increased.

173. Pausanias 2.32.2. Cf. Hdt.5.82. This connection is noted by Gras 1984, 78; see also Ogden 1997, 19.

174. The connection with the cult of Damia and Auxesia ("Increase/Growth"), however, does suggest that the ritual may have had something to do with agricultural and human fertility.

175. Homeric *Hymn to Demeter*, 265 with Richardson comm.; Hesychius s.v. Βαλλητύς; Athenaeus 406d–407c; Parker 2005, 329.

176. The parallel between stoning and scapegoating ritual is noted by Gernet 1981, 265–67; Gras 1984, 78; and Ogden 1997, 19. The connection is denied by Rosivach 1987 on the grounds that the evidence for stoning of scapegoats to death is not strong. For my argument, it is only necessary to accept (as does Rosivach) that "*something* was thrown." On the Thargelia generally, see Parker 2005, 203–6, 481–83.

177. Bremmer 1983.

178. Gernet (1981, 266) argued for precisely this sort of shared symbolism between stoning and scapegoating. Cf. Gras 1984, 86: "Le citoyen … en frappant le pharmakos il fait renaitre la cité, a chaque printemps, et éloigne d'elle les catastrophes; en frappant le tyran, il fait renaitre la vie démocratique." See also Ogden 1997, 19–23. Gras, following Gernet and Vernant, argues that ostracism also shares this symbolism, and that in the classical city ostracism and the voting pebble replace the archaic and barbaric practice of stoning. This equation ignores the fact that several historical cases of stoning took place after the introduction

of ostracism and the democracy. Moreover, the ostracized person is not "dead for the city," as Gras claims (87). Those who were ostracized retained their property and were allowed to return, often to positions of prestige and honor. Cf. Forsdyke 2005a. For pollution and purification in Greek culture generally, see Parker 1983. On scapegoating, see Bremmer 1983; Ogden 1997.

179. Richardson 1974, 246. Richardson notes that ritual battles involving stoning take place on various occasions, including funeral ceremonies, marriages, and seasonal festivities. Contemporary Islamic festivals still feature stoning rituals. The *New York Times* reported (page A3) on January 11, 2006, that 2.5 million Muslims in Indonesia took part "in the first of three days of a stoning ritual to cleanse sins, throwing pebbles at Jamarat, stone pillars symbolizing the devil" during the Feast of Sacrifice.

180. For obscene speech at festivals of Dionysus, see n.166 above. For obscene speech at other festivals, especially of Demeter, see Fluck 1931; Winkler 1990, 188–209; and O'Higgins 2001, 2003, 15–36.

181. Kertzer 1988, 102–73 explores the reasons for this overlap in a wide variety of past and present cultures. See also Scott 1990, 227.

182. Bakhtin 1984, 81, 92 and chapters 3 and 4 below.

183. Compare Halliwell 1991a and 1991b, on the relation between comic verbal abuse and festival license.

Chapter 6. Epilogue

1. For recent discussion of the historical developments described in this paragraph, see Raaflaub, Ober, and Wallace 2007, with further bibliography cited therein.

2. The text of the decree, although originally inscribed on stone and set up in the marketplace, is preserved for us in Andocides *On the Mysteries* 96–98. Recent discussions include: Ober 2003; Shear 2007.

Bibliography

Aarne, A. and S. Thompson. 1961. *The Types of the Folktale: A Classification and Bibliography*. 2nd rev. ed. Helsinki.

Abrahams, R. D. and R. Bauman. 1978. "Ranges of Festival Behavior," in B. A. Babcock, ed., 193–208.

Adak, M. 2003. *Metöken als Wohltäter Athens: Untersuchungen zum sozialen Austausch zwischen ortsansässigen Fremden und der Bürgergemeinde in klassischer und hellenistischer Zeit (ca. 500–150 v. Chr.)*. Munich.

Adrados, F. R. 1999. *History of the Graeco-Latin Fable*. Translated by Leslie A. Ray. *Mnemosyne*. Supplementum Vols. 201, 207. Leiden: Brill.

———, ed. 1984. *La Fable: huit exposés suivis de discussions*. Entretiens sur l'antiquité classique 30. Vandoeuvres-Geneva.

Alcock, S. E. 2002. *Archaeologies of the Greek Past. Landscape, Monuments and Memories*. Cambridge.

Alexiou, M. 2002. *The Ritual Lament in Greek Tradition*. 2nd ed. Revised by D. Yatromanilakis and P. Roilos. Lanham, MD. First ed., 1974.

Allen, D. 2000. *The World of Prometheus. The Politics of Punishing in Democratic Athens*. Princeton.

———. 2005. "Greek Tragedy and Law," in M. Gagarin and D. Cohen, eds., 374–93.

Almond, R. and A. J. Pollard. 2001. "The Yeomanry of Robin Hood and Social Terminology in Fifteenth Century England." *Past and Present* 170: 52–77.

Aly, W. 1921. *Volksmärchen, sage und novelle bei Herodot und zeitgenossen; eine untersuchung über die volkstümlichen elemente der altgriechischen proserzählung*. Göttingen.

Anderson, B. 2006. *Imagined Communities: Reflections on the Origin and Spread of Nationalism*. Rev. ed. London.

Anderson, G. 2005. "Before Turannoi Were Tyrants: Rethinking a Chapter of Early Greek History." *Classical Antiquity* 24: 173–222.

———. 2007. "Why the Athenians Forgot Cleisthenes: Literacy and the Politics of Remembrance in Ancient Athens," in C. Cooper, ed., *Politics of Orality*. Leiden. 103–27.

Andreau, J. and R. Descat. 2006. *Esclave en Grèce et à Rome*. Paris.

Andrewes, A. 1956. *The Greek Tyrants*. London.

Arnaoutoglou, I. 1994. "Associations and Patronage in Ancient Athens." *Ancient Society* 25: 5–17.

Arnold, D. 2000. "Gramsci and Peasant Subalternity in India," in V. Chaturvedi, ed., 24–49.

Auffarth, C. 1999. "Constructing the Identity of the Polis: The Danaides as 'Ancestors'." in R. Hägg, ed., 39–48.

Austin, C. and S. Douglas Olson, eds. 2004. *Aristophanes Thesmophoriazusae*. Oxford.

Babcock, B. A. 1978. *The Reversible World. Symbolic Inversion in Art and Society*. Ithaca.

Bäbler, B. 1998. *Fleissige Thrakerinnen und Wehrhafte Skythen. Nichtgriechen im klassischen Athen und ihre archäologische Hinterlassenschaft*. Stuttgart.

Bain, D. M. 1982. "κατωνάκην τὸν χοῖρον ἀποτετιλμένας (Aristophanes, *Ekklesiazousai* 724)" *LCM* 7: 7–10.

Bakhtin, M. 1984. *Rabelais and His World*. Indiana. Translated by Helene Iswolsky. Originally published as *Tvorchestvo Fransua Rable*. Moscow Khudozhestvennia literatura, 1965.

Baldry, H. C. 1952. "Who Invented the Golden Age?" *CQ* 2: 83–92.

Balot, R. K. 2001. *Greed and Injustice in Classical Athens*. Princeton.

Barron, J. P. 1986. "Chios in the Athenian Empire," in J. Boardman and C. E. Vaphopoulou, eds., 89–103.

Beard, M., J. North, and S. Price. 1998. *Religions of Rome 2: A Sourcebook*. Cambridge.

Berkowitz, L. 1962. *Aggression: A Social Psychological Analysis*. New York.

Bers, V. 1985. "Dikastic Thorubos," in P. A. Cartledge and F. D. Harvey, eds., *Crux: Essays in Greek History Presented to G.E.M. de Ste. Croix*. London. 1–15.

———. 2000. "Just Rituals: Why the Rigmarole of the Fourth-Century Athenian Lawcourts?" in P. Flensted-Jensen, T. H. Nielsen, and L. Rubenstein, eds., *Polis and Politics: Studies in the Ancient Greek History Presented to M. H. Hansen*. Copenhagen. 553–59.

Bicknell, P. J. 1982. "Herodotus 5.68 and the Racial Policy of Kleisthenes of Sikyon." *GRBS* 23: 193–201.

Blok, A. 1971. "On Brigandage with Special Reference to Peasant Mobilization." *Sociologische Gids* 18: 208–16.

———. 1972. "The Peasant and the Brigand: Social Banditry Reconsidered." *Comparative Studies in Society and History* 14: 494–503.

Boardman, J. and C. E. Vaphopoulou, eds. 1986. *Chios: A Conference at the Homereion in Chios*. Oxford.

Boedeker, D. 1998. "Hero Cult and Politics in Herodotus," in C. Dougherty and L. Kurke, eds. *Cultural Poetics in Archaic Greece*. 2nd ed. New York, 164–77.

Boedeker, D. and K. A. Raaflaub, eds. 1998. *Democracy, Empire and the Arts in Fifth-Century Athens*. Cambridge, MA.

Bonnell, V. and L. Hunt, eds. 1999. *Beyond the Cultural Turn: New Directions in the Study of Society and Culture*. Berkeley.

Bourdieu, P. 1977. *Outline of a Theory of Practice*. Cambridge.

Bowie, E. L. 1997. "The Theognidea: A Step Towards a Collection of Fragments?" in G. W. Most, ed., *Collecting Fragments/Fragmente sammeln*. Göttingen, 53–66.

———. 2001. "Early Greek Iambic Poetry: The Importance of Narrative," in A. Cavarzere et al., eds., *Iambic Ideas: Essays on a Poetic Tradition from Archaic Greece to the Late Roman Empire*. Lanham, MD, 1–27.

Bradley, K. R. 1987. *Slaves and Masters in the Roman Empire*. Oxford.

————. 1989. *Slavery and Rebellion in the Roman World, 140 B.C.–70 B.C.* Indiana.

————. 1994. *Slavery and Society at Rome.* Cambridge.

Bradtke, E. 2000. *Truculent Rustics. Molly Dancing in East Anglia before 1940.* London.

Branham, R. B. 2002. *Bakhtin and the Classics.* Evanston, IL.

Braund, D. 2000. "Learning, Luxury and Empire: Athenaeus' Roman Patron," in Braund and Wilkins, eds., 2000. 1–22.

Braund, D. and J. Wilkins, eds. 2000. *Athenaeus and His World: Reading Greek Culture in the Roman Empire.* Exeter.

Bremmer, J. 1983. "Scapegoat Rituals in Ancient Greece." *Harvard Studies in Classical Philology* 87: 299–320.

————. 1997. "Jokes, Jokers and Jokebooks in Ancient Greek Culture," in J. Bremmer and H. Roodenburg, eds., 11–28.

Bremmer, J. and H. Roodenburg, eds. 1997. *A Cultural History of Humour. From Antiquity to the Present Day.* Oxford.

————. 1997. "Introduction: Humour and History," in Bremmer and Roodenburg, eds., 1–10.

Brenne, S. 2002. "Teil II. Die Ostraka (487–ca.416 v.Chr) als Testimonien," in P. Siewert, S. Brenne, B. Eder, H. Heftner, and W. Scheidel, eds., *Ostrakismos-Testimonien.* Vol. I. *Historia Einzelschriften* 155. Stuttgart.

Bresson, A. 2007. *L'économie de la Grèce des cités.* Paris.

Briggs, K. 2002. *British Folk Tales and Legends: A Sampler.* London. Originally published 1977.

Brock, R. 1994. "The Labour of Women in Classical Athens." *CQ* 44: 336–46.

Brock, R. and S. Hodkinson, eds. 2000. *Alternatives to Athens. Varieties of Political Organization and Community in Ancient Greece.* Oxford. Corrected reprint, 2002.

Brown, C. G. 1989. "Ares, Aphrodite and the Laughter of the Gods." *Phoenix* 43: 283–93.

————. 1997. "Iambic Poetry," in D. E. Gerber, ed., *A Companion to the Greek Lyric Poets.* Leiden, 3–88.

Brown, C. L. and P. D. Morgan, eds. 2006. *Arming Slaves. From Classical Times to the Modern Age.* New Haven.

Burford, A. 1993. *Land and Labor in the Greek World.* Baltimore.

Burguière, A. 2009. *The Annales School. An Intellectual History.* Ithaca. Translated by Jane Marie Todd. Originally published in French, Paris 2006.

Burke, P. 1994. *Popular Culture in Early Modern Europe.* Revised reprint, 1994. Burlington, VT. 1st ed., 1978.

————, ed. 1997. *Varieties of Cultural History.* Ithaca.

————, ed. 2001. *New Perspectives on Historical Writing.* 2nd ed. Cambridge.

Burkert, W. 1985. *Greek Religion.* Translated by John Raffan. Cambridge, MA. Originally published in German as *Griechische Religion der archaischen und klassischen Epoche.* Stuttgart, 1977.

Cairns, D. L. 1993. *Aidos. The Psychology and Ethics of Honour and Shame in Ancient Greek Literature.* Oxford.

———. 1996. "Hybris, Dishonour and Thinking Big." *JHS* 116: 1–32.

Camp, J. M. 2001. *The Archaeology of Athens*. New Haven.

Camporesi, P. 1989. *Bread of Dreams. Food and Fantasy in Early Modern Europe*. Chicago.

Cantarella, E. 2005. "Gender, Sexuality, and the Law," in M. Gagarin and D. Cohen, eds., 236–53.

Carey, C., ed. 1989. *Lysias. Selected Speeches*. Cambridge.

———. 1993. "Return of the Radish or Just When You Thought It Was Safe to Go Back to the Kitchen." *LCM* 18.4: 53–55.

———. 1995. "Rape and Adultery in Athenian Law." *CQ* 45: 407–17.

Cartledge, P. 1985. "Rebels and Sambos in Classical Greece: A Comparative View," in P. Cartledge and F. Harvey, *Crux. Essays in Greek History Presented to G.E.M. de Ste. Croix*. London. 16–46. Reprinted in P. A. Cartledge, *Spartan Reflections*. Berkeley, 2001. 127–52.

———. 1993. "Classical Greek Agriculture: Recent Work and Alternative Views." *Journal of Peasant Studies* 21: 127–36.

———. 1995. "Classical Greek Agriculture II: Two More Alternative Views." *Journal of Peasant Studies* 23: 131–39.

———. 2001. "The Political Economy of Greek Slavery," in Cartledge et al., eds., 2001. *Money, Labour and Land. Approaches to the Economies of Ancient Greece*. London. 156–66.

———. 2002. *The Greeks. A Portrait of Self and Others*. New edition. Oxford.

Cascajero, J. 1991. "Lucha de clases e ideología: introducción al estudio de la fabula esópica como fuente histórica." *Gerión* 9: 11–58.

Cavanaugh, M. B. 1996. *Eleusis and Athens: Documents in Finance, Religion and Politics in the Fifth Century BC*. Atlanta.

Ceccarelli, P. 1996. "L'Athènes de Périclès: un pays de Cocagne? L'idéologie démocratique et l'automatos bios dans la comédie attique" *QUCC* 83: 109–59.

Chandavarkar, R. 1994. *The Origins of Industrial Capitalism in India: Business Strategies and the Working Classes in Bombay, 1900–1940*. Cambridge.

———. 1998. *Imperial Power and Popular Politics. Class, Resistance and the State in India, c. 1850–1950*. Cambridge.

Chaturvedi, V., ed. 2000. *Mapping Subaltern Studies and the Postcolonial*. London.

Cherry, J. F. and C. Renfrew, eds. 1986. *Peer Polity Interaction and Socio-Political Change*. Cambridge.

Christ, M. R. 2006. *The Bad Citizen in Classical Athens*. Cambridge.

Christensen, K. A. 1984. "The Theseion: A Slave Refuge at Athens." *AJAH* 9: 23–32.

Cobb-Stevens, V., T. J. Figueira, and G. Nagy. 1985. "Introduction," in T. J. Figueira and G. Nagy, eds., 1–8.

Cohen, D. 1985. "A Note on Aristophanes and the Punishment for Adultery in Athenian Law." *ZSS* 102: 385–87.

———. 1991. *Law, Sexuality and Society. The Enforcement of Morals in Classical Athens*. Cambridge.

———. 1995. *Law, Violence and Community in Classical Athens*. Cambridge.

Cohen, D. and M. O'Connor, eds. 2004. *Comparison and History*. London.

Cohen, E. E. 1992. *Athenian Economy and Society. A Banking Perspective*. Princeton.

———. 2000. *The Athenian Nation*. Princeton.

Cole, S. G. 1993. "Procession and Celebration at the Dionysia," in R. Scodel, ed. *Theater and Society in the Classical World*. Ann Arbor, 25–38.

———. 2004. *Landscapes, Gender and Ritual Space. The Ancient Greek Experience*. Berkeley.

Connelly, J. B. 2007. *Portrait of a Priestess. Women and Ritual in Ancient Greece*. Princeton.

Connor, W. R. 1971. *The New Politicians of Fifth-Century Athens*. Princeton.

———. 1985. "The Razing of the House in Greek Society." *TAPA* 115: 79–102.

———. 1987. "Tribes, Festivals and Processions in Archaic Greece." *JHS* 107: 40–50.

———. 1993. "The Ionian Era of Athenian Civic Identity." *Proceedings of the American Philosophical Society* 137: 194–206.

———. 1996. "Civil Society, Dionysiac Festival, and the Athenian Democracy," in J. Ober and C. Hedrick, eds., *Demokratia. A Conversation on Democracies Ancient and Modern*. Princeton, 217–26.

Coste-Messelière, P. de la. 1950. *The Treasures of Delphi*. Paris.

Coulton, G. G. 1925. *The Medieval Village*. Cambridge.

Crusius, O. 1913. "Aus der Geschichte der Fabel." In C. H. Kleukens, ed., *Das Buch der Fabeln*. i–lxi. Reprint, Leipzig, 1920.

Csapo, E. 1997. "Riding the Phallus for Dionysos. Iconology, Ritual, and Gender-Role De/construction." *Phoenix* 51: 253–95.

Csapo, E. and W. J. Slater, eds. 1994. *The Context of Ancient Drama*. Ann Arbor.

Dal Lago, E. and C. Katsari, eds. 2008a. *Slave Systems Ancient and Modern*. Cambridge.

———. 2008b. "Ideal Models of Slave Management in the Roman World and in the Ante-bellum American South," in Dal Lago and Katsari, eds., 187–213.

Darnton, R. 1984. *The Great Cat Massacre and Other Episodes in French Cultural History*. New York.

Davidson, J. 1997. *Fishcakes and Courtesans. The Consuming Passions of Classical Athens*. New York.

———. 2001. "Dover, Foucault and Greek Homosexuality: Penetration and the Truth of Sex." *Past and Present* 170: 3–51. Reprinted in R. Osborne, ed., *Studies in Ancient Greek and Roman Society*. Cambridge, 2004, 78–118.

Davies, J. K. 1971. *Athenian Propertied Families, 600–300 BC*. Oxford.

Davis, N. Z. 1975. *Society and Culture in Early Modern France*. Stanford.

———. 1992. "Towards Mixtures and Margins." *American Historical Review* 97: 1409–16.

De Angelis, F. 1994. "The Foundation of Selinous: Overpopulation or Opportunities?" in G. R. Tsetskhladze and F. de Angelis, eds., *The Archaeology of Greek Colonization. Essays Dedicated to Sir John Boardman*. Oxford, 87–110.

De Polignac, F. 1995. *Cults, Territory and the Origins of the Greek City-State*. Translated by J. Lloyd. Chicago.

Demont, P. 2007. "La peur et le rire: la perception de l'esclavage dans les Gre-
    nouilles d'Aristophane," in A. Serghidou, ed., *Fear of Slaves—Fear of Enslave-
    ment in the Ancient Mediterranean*. Franche-Comté, 2007, 179–92.
Desan, S. 1989. "Crowds, Community and Ritual in the Work of E. P. Thompson
    and Natalie Davis," in L. Hunt, ed., 47–71.
Desclos, M. L. 2000. *Le rire des Grecs. Anthropologie du rire en Grèce ancienne*.
    Grenoble.
Dewald, C. 2006. "Humour and Danger in Herodotus," in C. Dewald and J. Marin-
    cola, eds., *The Cambridge Companion to Herodotus*. Cambridge, 145–64.
Dillon, M. 2002. *Girls and Women in Classical Greek Religion*. London.
Dodds, E. R. 1964. *The Greeks and the Irrational*. Berkeley.
Dover, K. J. 1989. *Greek Homosexuality*. Updated with a new postscript. Cam-
    bridge, MA.
DuBois, P. 2003. *Slaves and Other Objects*. Chicago.
Ducat, J. 1976. "Clisthène, le porc et l'âne." *Dialogues d'histoire ancienne* 2:
    359–68.
Dunbar, N. 1995. *Aristophanes Birds*. Oxford.
Edwards, A. T. 1993. "Historicizing the Popular Grotesque: Bakhtin's Rabelais
    and Attic Old Comedy," in R. Scodel, ed., 1993, 89–117. Reprinted in R. Bran-
    ham, ed., 2002, 27–58.
Ekroth, G. 2007. "Heroes and Hero-Cults," in D. Ogden, ed., *A Companion to
    Greek Religion*. Malden MA, 100–114.
Faraone, C. A. 2004. "Hipponax Fragment 128W: Epic Parody or Expulsive In-
    cantation?" *Cl.Ant.* 23: 209–45.
Fentress, J. J. and C. Wickham. 1992. *Social Memory: New Perspectives on the
    Past*. Oxford.
Figueira, T. J. 1999. "The Evolution of Messenian Identity," in S. Hodkinson and
    A. Powell, eds., *Sparta: New Perspectives*. London, 211–44.
Figueira, T. J. and G. Nagy, eds. 1985. *Theognis of Megara. Poetry and the Polis*.
    Baltimore.
Finley, M. I. 1985. *Ancient History. Evidence and Models*. New York.
———. 1998. *Ancient Slavery and Modern Ideology*. Expanded edition, edited by
    Brent Shaw. Princeton. Originally published in 1980.
Fisher, N.R.E. 1992. *Hybris: A Study in the Values of Honour and Shame in An-
    cient Greece*. Warminster.
———. 1993. *Slavery in Classical Athens*. London.
———. 2008. "'Independent' Slaves in Classical Athens and the Ideology of Slav-
    ery," in C. Katsari and E. Dal Lago, eds., *From Captivity to Freedom: Themes
    in Ancient and Modern Slavery*. Leicester, 123–46.
Fisher, N.R.E. and H. van Wees, eds. 1998. *Archaic Greece. New Approaches and
    New Evidence*. Wales.
Flower, M. A. 1994. *Theopompus of Chios. History and Rhetoric in the Fourth
    Century BC*. Oxford.
Fluck, H. 1931. *Skurrile Riten im griechischen Kult*. Endigen.
Foley, H. P. 1994. *The Homeric Hymn to Demeter. Translation, Commentary and
    Interpretive Essays*. Princeton.

Forsdyke, S. 1999. "From Aristocratic to Democratic Ideology and Back Again: the Thrasybulus Anecdote in Herodotus' *Histories* and Aristotle's *Politics*." *CPh* 94: 361–72.

———. 2001. "Athenian Democratic Ideology and Herodotus' *Histories*." *AJP* 122: 333–62.

———. 2005a. *Exile, Ostracism and Democracy: The Politics of Expulsion in Ancient Greece*. Princeton.

———. 2005b. "Riot and Revelry in Archaic Megara: Democratic Disorder or Ritual Reversal?" *Journal of Hellenic Studies* 125: 73–92.

———. 2006. "Land, Labor and Economy in Solonian Athens: Breaking the Impasse between History and Archaeology," in J. Blok and A. Lardinois, eds., *Solon. New Historical and Philological Perspectives*. Leidenm 334–50.

———. Forthcoming. "The Impact of Democracy on Communal Life: Plus ça change, plus c'est la même chose?" in J. P. Arnason, K. Raaflaub, and P. Wagner, eds., *The Greek Polis and the Invention of Democracy: a Politico-cultural Transformation and Its Interpretations*. Malden, MA.

Foucault, M. 1977. *Discipline and Punish. The Birth of the Prison*. Translated by Alan Sheridan. 2nd ed., 1995. New York.

———. 1985. *The Use of Pleasure (History of Sexuality*, vol. 2). Translated by R. Hurley. New York.

Foxhall, L. 1989. "Household, Gender and Property in Classical Athens." *Classical Quarterly* 39: 22–44.

———. 1992. "The Control of the Attic Landscape," in B.Wells, ed., 1992, 155–59.

———. 1996. "Law and the Lady," in L. Foxhall and A.D.E. Lewis, eds., *Greek Law in its Political Setting*. Oxford, 133–52.

———. 1997. "A View from the Top. Evaluating the Solonian Property Classes," in L. G. Mitchell and P. J. Rhodes, eds., *The Development of the Polis in Archaic Greece*. London, 113–36.

———. 2007. *Olive Cultivation in Ancient Greece*. Oxford.

Frank, J. 2005. *A Democracy of Distinction. Aristotle and the Work of Politics*. Chicago.

Frier, B. W. 2000. "More Is Worse: Some Observations on the Population of the Roman Empire," in W. Scheidel, ed., *Debating Roman Demography*. Leiden, 139–59.

Fuks, A. 1968. "Slave War and Slave Troubles in Chios in the Third Century B.C." *Athenaeum* 46: 102–11.

———. 1984. *Social Conflict in Ancient Greece*. Leiden.

Funke, P. and N. Luraghi, eds. 2009. *The Politics of Ethnicity and the Crisis of the Peloponnesian League: Textual and Philosophical Issues*. Washington, DC.

Gagarin, M. 1996. "The Torture of Slaves in Athenian Law" *CPh* 91: 1–18.

Gagarin, M. and D. Cohen, eds. 2005. *The Cambridge Companion to Greek Law*. Cambridge.

Gallant, T. W. 1991. *Risk and Survival in Ancient Greece*. Stanford.

Garlan, Y. 1988. *Slavery in Ancient Greece*. Revised and expanded edition. Translated by Janet Lloyd. Ithaca.

Garland, R. 1987. *The Piraeus. From the First to the Fifth Century BC.* Ithaca.

———. 1992. *Introducing New Gods: The Politics of Athenian Religion.* London.

Garnsey, P. 1996. *Ideas of Slavery from Aristotle to Augustine.* Cambridge.

Geertz, C. 1973. *The Interpretation of Cultures.* New York.

Gehrke, H. J. 1985. *Stasis: Untersuchungen zu den inneren Kriegen in den grie-chischen Staaten des 5. und 4. Jahrhunderts v. Chr.* Munich.

Genovese, E. D. 1974. *Roll, Jordan, Roll. The World the Slaves Made.* New York.

———. 1979. *From Rebellion to Revolution. Afro-American Slave Revolts in the Making of the Modern World.* Baton Rouge.

Gerber, D. E. 1999. *Greek Iambic Poetry.* Cambridge, MA.

Gernet, L. 1981. *The Anthropology of Ancient Greece.* Baltimore.

———. 1984. "Le Droit Pénal de la Grèce ancienne," in *Du châtiment dans la cité. Supplices corporals et peine de mort dans le monde antique.* Rome, 9–35.

Gilmore, D. 1987. *Aggression and Community: Paradoxes of Andalusian Culture.* New Haven.

Ginzburg, C. 1992. *The Cheese and the Worms. The Cosmos of a Sixteenth-Century Miller.* Translated by John and Ann Tedeschi. Originally published in Italian in 1976.

Glotz, G. 1877–1919. "Lapidatio," in C. Daremberg and E. Saglio eds., *Dictionnaire des antiquités grecques et romaines d'après les textes et les monuments.* Paris 1877–1919.

Gluckman, M. 1963. *Order and Rebellion in Tribal Africa.* New York.

———. 1965. *Politics, Law and Ritual in Tribal Society.* Oxford.

Goff, B. 2004. *Citizen Bacchae. Women's Ritual Practice in Ancient Greece.* Berkeley.

Golden, M. 1998. *Sport and Society in Ancient Greece.* Cambridge.

Goldhill, S. 1990. "The Great Dionysia and Civic Ideology," in J. Winkler and F. I. Zeitlin, eds., 1990, 97–129.

———. 1991. *The Poet's Voice. Essays on Poetics and Greek Literature.* Cambridge.

———. 1999. "Programme Notes," in S. Goldhill and R. Osborne, eds., 1999, 1–29.

Goldhill, S. and R. Osborne, eds. 1999. *Performance Culture and Athenian Democracy.* Cambridge.

Gomme, A.W., A. Andrewes, and K. J. Dover. 1970. *A Historical Commentary on Thucydides.* Vol. 4. Oxford.

Gorman, R. J. and V. Gorman. 2007. "The *Tryphe* of the Sybarites: a Historiographical Problem in Athenaeus," *JHS* 127: 38–60.

Gow, A.S.F., ed. 1965. *Machon. The Fragments.* Cambridge.

Graf, F. 1985. *Nordionische Kulte. Religionsgeschichtliche und epigraphische Untersuchungen zu den Kulten von Chios, Erythrai, Klazomenai und Phokaia.* Rome.

Graham, A. J. 1982. "The Colonial Expansion of Greece," in J. Boardman and N.G.L. Hammond, eds., *The Cambridge Ancient History* III.3. 2nd ed. Cambridge, 83–162.

———. 1992. "Thucydides 7.13.2 and the Crews of Athenian Triremes." *TAPA* 122: 257–70.

———. 1998. "An Addendum." *TAPA* 128: 89–114.

Gras, M. 1984. "Cité grecque et lapidation," in *Du châtiment dans la cité. Supplices corporals et peine de mort dans le monde antique*. Rome. 1984, 75–89.

Griffin, A. 1982. *Sicyon*. Oxford.

Griffith, M. 2006. "Horsepower and Donkeywork: Equids and the Greek Imagination." *CP* 101: 307–58.

Griffiths, A. 2006. "Stories and Storytelling in the *Histories*," in C. Dewald and J. Marincola, eds., *The Cambridge Companion to Herodotus*. Cambridge, 130–44.

Grünewald, T. 1999. *Bandits in the Roman Empire. Myth and Reality*. London.

Guha, R. 1983. *Elementary Aspects of Peasant Insurgency in Colonial India*. Oxford.

Gulick, C. B. 1930. Trans. *Athenaeus The Deipnosophists*. Cambridge, MA.

Gurevich, A. 1997. "Bakhtin and His Theory of Carnival," in Bremmer and Roodenburg, eds., 54–60.

Hägg, R., ed. 1999. *Ancient Greek Hero Cult*. Stockholm.

Hall, J. M. 1997. *Ethnic identity in Greek Antiquity*. Cambridge.

———. 1999. "Beyond the Polis: The Multilocality of Heroes," in R. Hägg, ed., 1999. 49–59.

———. 2002. *Hellenicity. Between Ethnicity and Culture*. Chicago.

———. 2003. "The Dorianization of the Messenians," in N. Luraghi and S. Alcock, eds., *Helots and their Masters in Laconia and Messenia. Histories, Ideologies, Structures*. Cambridge, MA, 142–68.

———. 2006. *A History of the Archaic Greek World ca.1200–479 BCE*. Oxford.

Halliwell, S. 1991a. "The Uses of Laughter in Greek Culture." *CQ* 41: 279–96.

———. 1991b. "Comic Satire and Freedom of Speech in Classical Athens." *JHS* 111: 48–70.

———. 1993. "Comedy and Publicity in the Society of the Polis," in A. H. Sommerstein et al., eds., *Tragedy, Comedy and the Polis*. Bari. 321–40.

———. 2000. "Le rire rituel et la nature de l'Ancienne Comédie attique," in M. L. Desclos, ed., *Le rire des Grecs*. Grenoble, 155–68.

———. 2004. "Aischrology, Shame and Comedy," in I. Sluiter and R. M. Rosen, eds., 2004, 115–44.

Halperin, D. M. 1990. *One Hundred Years of Homosexuality and Other Essays on Greek Love*. London.

Hansen, M. H. 1983a. "The Athenian 'Politicians' 403–322." *GRBS* 24: 33–55. Reprinted in Hansen 1989, 1–23.

———. 1983b. "*Rhetores* and *Strategoi* in Fourth-Century Athens." *GRBS* 24: 151–80. Reprinted in Hansen 1989, 25–33.

———. 1984. "The Number of *Rhetores* in the Athenian *Ecclesia*, 355–322 B.C." *GRBS* 25: 123–55. Reprinted in Hansen 1989, 93–125.

———. 1989. *The Athenian Ecclesia II. A Collection of Articles 1983–89*. Copenhagen.

———. 1990. "Solonian Democracy in Fourth Century Athens," in W. R. Connor et al., eds., *Aspects of Athenian Democracy*. Copenhagen, 71–99.

———. 1996. "The Ancient Athenian and the Modern Liberal View of Liberty as a Democratic Ideal," in J. Ober and C. Hedrick, eds., *Demokratia. A Conversation on Democracies Ancient and Modern*. Princeton, 91–104.

————. 1999. *The Athenian Democracy in the Age of Demosthenes*. 2nd ed., Bristol.

————, ed. 2000. *A Comparative Study of Thirty City-State Cultures*. Copenhagen.

————, ed. 2002. *A Comparative Study of Six City-State Cultures*. Copenhagen.

Hansen, W., ed.1998. *Anthology of Ancient Greek Popular Literature*. Indiana.

————. 2002. *Ariadne's Thread. A Guide to International Tales Found in Classical Literature*. Ithaca.

Hanson, V. D. 1999. *The Other Greeks: The Family Farm and the Agrarian Roots of Western Civilization*. 2nd ed. Berkeley. Originally published 1995. New York.

Harris, E. M. 2002. "Workshop, Marketplace and Household. The Nature of Technical Specialization in Classical Athens and Its Influence on Economy and Society," in P. Cartledge et al., eds., *Money, Labour and Land. Approaches to the Economies of Ancient Greece*. London, 67–99.

————. 2004. "Notes on a Lead Letter from the Athenian Agora." *HSCP* 102: 157–70.

————. 2006. *Democracy and Rule of Law in Classical Athens. Essays on Law, Society and Politics*. Cambridge.

Harris, W.V. 1989. *Ancient Literacy*. Cambridge, MA.

Harrison, A.R.W. 1968. *The Law of Athens*. Volume I. Oxford.

————. 1971. *The Law of Athens*. Volume II. Oxford.

Hedreen, G. 2004. "The Return of Hephaistos, Dionysiac Processional Ritual and the Creation of a Visual Narrative." *JHS* 124: 38–64.

Henderson, J. 1990a. "The Demos and Comic Competition," in J. J. Winkler and F. I. Zeitlin, eds., *Nothing to Do with Dionysus? Athenian Drama in Its Social Context*. Princeton, 271–313.

————. 1990b. "Comedy and Publicity in the Society of the Polis," in A. H. Sommerstein, et al., *Tragedy, Comedy and the Polis*. Bari, 307–19.

————. 1991. *The Maculate Muse. Obscene Language in Attic Comedy*. 2nd ed. New York.

Herman, G. 2006. *Morality and Behavior in Democratic Athens. A Social History*. Cambridge.

Hill, C. 1972. *The World Turned Upside Down. Radical Ideas During the English Revolution*. London.

Hirzel, R. 1909. "Die Strafe der Steinigung." *Abhandlungen der Philologisch-Historischen Klasse der Königlich Sächsischen Gesellschaft der Wissenschaften* 27: 223–66.

Hobsbawm, E. J. 1959. *Primitive Rebels. Studies in Archaic Forms of Social Movement in the 19th and 20th centuries*. New York.

————. 1988. "History from Below—Some Reflections," in F. Kranz, ed., 1988, 13–27.

————. 2000. *Bandits*. London. Originally published 1969.

Hobsbawm, E. and T. Ranger, eds. 1992. *The Invention of Tradition*. 2nd ed. Cambridge.

Hodkinson, S. 2000. *Property and Wealth in Classical Sparta*. London.

Hoffmann, G. 1990. *Le Châtiment des Amants dans la Grèce classique*. Paris.

Holzberg, N. 2002. *The Ancient Fable. An Introduction*. Indiana.

Hopkins, K. 1991. "From Violence to Blessing: Symbols and Rituals in Ancient Rome," in A. Mohlo et al., eds., 1991, 479–98.

———. 1993. "Novel Evidence for Roman Slavery." *Past and Present* 138: 3–27. Reprinted in R. Osborne, ed., *Studies in Ancient Greek and Roman Society*. Cambridge, 2004.

Hordern, J. H. 2004. *Sophron's Mimes: Text, Translation, and Commentary*. Oxford.

Hornblower, S. 2004. *A Commentary on Thucydides 2: Books IV–V.24*. Corrected reprint. Oxford.

How, W. W. and J. Wells. 1928. *A Commentary on Herodotus*. Vol. II. Oxford.

Hubbard, T. K. 1992. "Remaking Myth and Rewriting History: Cult Tradition in Pindar's Ninth Nemean." *HSCP* 94: 77–111.

Humphreys, S. 1985. "Law as Discourse." *History and Anthropology* 1: 241–64.

Hunt, L. 1984. *Politics, Culture and Class in the French Revolution*. Berkeley.

———, ed. 1989. *The New Cultural History*. Berkeley.

Hunt, P. 1998. *Slaves, Warfare and Ideology in the Greek Historians*. Cambridge.

Hunter, V. J. 1994. *Policing Athens. Social Control in the Attic Lawsuits, 420–320 B.C.* Princeton.

Hunter, V. and J. Edmondson, eds. 2000. *Law and Social Status in Classical Athens*. Oxford.

Jacob, O. 1979. *Les esclaves publics à Athènes*. New York.

Jacoby, F. 1923–1969. *Die Fragmente der Griechischen Historiker*. Leiden.

Jameson, M. 1977. "Agriculture and Slavery in Classical Athens." *CJ* 73: 122–41.

———. 1992. "Agricultural Labor in Ancient Greece," in B. Wells, ed., *Proceedings of the Seventh International Symposium at the Swedish Institute in Athens*, 135–46.

———. 1994. "Class in the Ancient Greek Countryside," in P. Doukellis and L. Mendoni, eds., *Structures rurales et sociétés antiques*. Paris, 55–63.

———. 1997. "Women and Democracy in Fourth-Century Athens," in P. Brulé and J. Oulhen, eds., *Esclavage, guerre, économie en Grèce ancienne. Hommages à Yvon Garlan*. Rennes, 95–107.

———. 2001. "On Paul Cartledge, 'The Political Economy of Greek Slavery'," in Cartledge et al., eds., 167–74.

Jeffery, L. 1976. *Archaic Greece*. London.

Jennings, V. and A. Katsaros, eds. 2007. *The World of Ion of Chios*. Leiden.

Johnston, A.W. and R. E. Jones. 1978. "The SOS Amphora." *ABSA* 73: 103–41.

Jones, N. F. 2004. *Rural Athens Under the Democracy*. Philadelphia.

Kantzios, I. 2005. *The Trajectory of Archaic Greek Trimeters*. Mnemosune Supplement, 265. Leiden.

Kapparis, K. 1995. "When Were the Athenian Adultery Laws Introduced?" *Revue internationale des Droits de L'Antiquité* 42: 97–122.

Kazakévich, E. G. 2008. "Were the χωρὶς οἰκοῦντες Slaves?" *Greek, Roman and Byzantine Studies* 48: 343–80.

Kearns, E. 1989. *The Heroes of Attica*. Bulletin of the Institute of Classical Studies Suppl. 57. London.

Kelley, R.D.G. "Notes on Deconstructing 'The Folk'." *American Historical Review* 97: 1400–408.

Kennell, N. M. 2010. *Spartans. A New History*. Malden, MA.

Keramopoullos, A. 1923. *Ho apotympanismos: Sumbole arkhaiologike eis ten historian tou poinikou dikaiou kai ten laographian*. Athens.

Kerkvliet, B.J.T. 2009. "Everyday Politics in Peasant Societies (and Ours)." *Journal of Peasant Studies* 36: 227–43.

Kertzer, D. I. 1988. *Ritual, Politics and Power*. New Haven.

Kilmer, M. 1982. "Genital Phobia and Depilation." *JHS* 102: 104–12.

Knoepfler, D. 1997. "Le territoire d'Erétrie et l'organisation politique de la cité," in M. H. Hansen, ed., 1997. *The Polis as an Urban Center. Acts of the Copenhagen Polis Center* 4. Copenhagen. 352–449.

Kopff, E. C. 1977. "Nubes 1493ff: Was Socrates Murdered?" *GRBS* 18: 113–22.

Kowalzig, B. 2007. *Singing for the Gods: Performances of Myth and Ritual in Archaic and Classical Greece*. Oxford.

Krantz, F. 1988. *History from Below. Studies in Popular Protest and Popular Ideology*. Oxford.

Kunzle, D. 1973. *History of the Comic Strip*. Berkeley.

———. 1978. "World Upside Down: The Iconography of a European Broadsheet Type," in B. Babcock, ed., 1978, 39–94.

Kurke, L. 2003. "Gender, Politics and Subversion in the *Chreiai* of Machon." *PCPS* 48: 20–65.

———. 2006. "Plato, Aesop, and the Beginnings of Mimetic Prose." *Representations* 94: 6–52.

———. 2011. *Aesopic Conversations: Popular Tradition, Cultural Dialogue and the Invention of Greek Prose*. Princeton.

La Penna, A. 1961. "La morale della favola esopica come morale delle classi subalterne nell'antichita." *Societa* 17: 459–537.

Lane Fox, R. 2000. "Theognis: An Alternative to Democracy," in R. Brock and S. Hodkinson, eds., 2000, 35–51.

Lanni, A. M. 1997. "Spectator Sport or Serious Politics? Οἱ Περιεστηκότες and the Athenian Lawcourts." *JHS* 117: 183–89.

Lardinois, A. 1997. "Modern Paroemiology and the Use of *Gnōmai* in Homer's *Iliad*." *Classical Philology* 92: 213–34.

Latte, K. 1931. "Beitrage zum griechischen Strafrecht II." *Hermes* 66: 128–58.

———. 1932a. "Moicheia," in *Paulys Real-Encyclopädie der classischen Altertumswissenschaft*. New edition, edited by Georg Wissowa. 2446–49.

———. 1932b. "Steinigung," in *Paulys Real-Encyclopädie der classischen Altertumswissenschaft*. New edition, edited by Georg Wissowa.

Lauffer, S. 1979. *Die Bergwerkssklaven von Laurion*. 2nd ed. Wiesbaden.

Lavelle, B. 2005. *Fame, Money and Power. The Rise of Peisistratos and "Democratic" Tyranny at Athens*. Ann Arbor.

Lazardis, N. 2007. *Wisdom in Loose Form. The Language of Egyptian and Greek Proverbs in Collections of the Hellenistic and Roman Periods.* Leiden.

Lears, T.J.J. 2002. "Making Fun of Popular Culture." *American Historical Review* 97: 1417–26.

Lefranc, A. 1953. *Rabelais: études sur Gargantua, Pantagruel, le Tiers livre.* Paris.

Le Goff, J. and Schmitt, J.-C. eds. 1981. *Le Charivari.* Paris.

Legon, R. P. 1981. *Megara. The Political History of a Greek City-State to 336 B.C.* Ithaca.

Le Roy Ladurie, E. 1974. *The Peasants of Languedoc.* Illinois.

———. 1978. *Montaillou. The Promised Land of Error.* New York.

———. 1979. *Carnival in Romans.* Translated by Mary Feeney. New York.

Levine, L. W. 2002a. "The Folklore of Industrial Society: Popular Culture and Its Audiences." *American Historical Review* 97: 1369–99.

———. 2002b. "Levine Responds." *American Historical Review* 97: 1427–30.

———. 2007. *Black Culture and Black Consciousness. Afro-American Folk Thought from Slavery to Freedom.* 2nd ed. Oxford. Original edition 1977.

Lewin, L. 1979a. "Oral Tradition and Elite Myth: The Legend of Antonio Silvino in Brazilian Popular Culture." *Journal of Latin American Lore* 5.2: 157–204.

———. 1979b. "The Oligarchical Limitations of Social Banditry in Brazil: The Case of the "Good" Thief Antonio Silvino." *Past and Present* 82: 116–46.

Lewis, S. 1996. *News and Society in the Greek Polis.* London.

———. 2009. *Greek Tyranny.* Exeter.

Lincoln, B., ed. 1985. *Religion, Rebellion, Revolution. An Interdisciplinary and Cross-Cultural Collection of Essays.* London.

Lintott, A. 1982. *Violence, Civil Strife and Revolution in the Classical City.* London.

Loraux, N. 1986. *The Invention of Athens: The Funeral Oration in the Classical City.* Cambridge, MA. Originally published in French in 1981.

Ludden, D. 2002. *Reading Subaltern Studies. Critical History, Contested Meaning and the Globalization of South Asia.* London.

Luraghi, N., ed. 2001. *The Historian's Craft in the Age of Herodotus.* Oxford.

———. 2005. "Le Storie prima delle Storie. Prospettive di Ricerca," in M. Giangiulio, ed., *Erodoto e il 'modello erodoteo.' Formazione e trasmissione delle tradizioni storiche in Grecia.* Trento, 61–90.

———. 2009. "Messenian Ethnicity and the Free Messenians," in Funke and Luraghi, eds., 110–34.

MacDowell, D. M. 1978. *Law in Classical Athens.* London.

———. 2000. *Demosthenes on the False Embassy (Oration 19).* Oxford.

Mactoux, M.-M. 1994. "Logique rituelle et polis esclavagiste: à propos des Kronia," in J. Annequin and M. Garrido-Hory, eds., *Religion et anthropologie de l'esclavage et des formes de dépendance.* Paris, 101–25.

Malkin, I. 1987. *Religion and Colonization in Ancient Greece.* Leiden.

Masson, O. 1972. "Les noms des esclaves dans la Grèce antique," in *Actes du Colloque sur l'esclavage.* Annales littéraires de l'Université de Besançon, 140. Paris, 9–23.

Maurizio, L. 1998. "The Panathenaic Procession: Athens' Participatory Democracy on Display?" in D. Boedeker and K. A. Raaflaub, eds., 297–317.

McCarthy, K. 2000. *Slaves, Masters and the Art of Authority in Plautine Comedy.* Princeton.

McLellen, D. 1995. *Ideology.* 2nd ed. Minneapolis.

Meuli, K. 1954. "Herkunft und Wesen der Fabel. Ein Vortrag," in T. Gelzer, ed., 1975. *Karl Meuli. Gesammelte Schriften* II. Basel and Stuttgart. 731–756. Originally published in *Schweizerisches Archiv für Volkskunde* 50 (1954): 65–88.

Millett, P. 1989. "Patronage and Its Avoidance in Classical Athens," in A. Wallace-Hadrill, ed., *Patronage in Ancient Societies.* London, 15–47.

———. 1990. "Sale, Credit and Exchange in Athenian Law and Society," in P. Cartledge et al., eds., *Nomos. Essays in Athenian Law, Politics and Society.* Cambridge, 167–94.

———. 1998. "Encounters in the Agora," in P. Cartledge et al., *Kosmos. Essays in Order, Conflict and Community in Classical Athens.* Cambridge, 203–28.

Mirhady, D. 2000. "The Athenian Rationale for Torture," in Hunter and Edmonson, eds., 53–74.

Mohlo, A., K. A. Raaflaub, and J. Emlen, eds. 1991. *City-States in Classical Antiquity and Medieval Italy: Athens and Rome, Florence and Venice.* Stuttgart.

Moreno, A. 2007. *Feeding the Democracy. The Athenian Grain Supply in the Fifth and Fourth Centuries BC.* Oxford.

Morris, I. 1987. *Burial and Ancient Society: The Rise of the Greek City-State.* Cambridge.

———. 1988. "Tomb Cult and the 'Greek Renaissance': The Past in the Present in the Eighth Century B.C." *Antiquity* 62: 750–61.

———. 1996. "The Strong Principle of Equality and the Archaic Origins of Greek Democracy," in J. Ober and C. Hedrick, eds., *Demokratia. A Conversation on Democracies, Ancient and Modern.* Princeton, 19–48.

———. 2000. *Archaeology as Cultural History.* Oxford.

———. 2002. "Hard Surfaces," in P. Cartledge et al., eds., *Money, Labour and Land. Approaches to the Economies of Greece.* London, 8–43.

Morris, S. and J. K. Papadopoulos. 2005. "Greek Towers and Slaves: An Archaeology of Exploitation." *American Journal of Archaeology* 109: 155–225.

Mossé, C. 1994. "Peut-on parler de patronage dans l'Athènes archaïque et classique?" in J. Annequin and M. Garrido-Hory, eds., *Religion et Anthropologie de l'esclavage et des formes de dépendance.* Paris, 29–36.

———. 1995. *Politique et Société en Grèce ancienne. Le 'modèle athénian.* Paris.

Most, G. W. 2006. *Hesiod. Theogony. Works and Days. Testimonia.* Cambridge, MA.

Muir, E. 1997. *Ritual in Early Modern Europe.* Cambridge.

Murray, O. 1987. "Herodotus and Oral History," in H. Sancisi-Weerdenburg and A. Kuhrt, eds., *Achaemenid History ii. The Greek Sources.* Leiden, 93–115. Reprinted in N. Luraghi, ed., 2001. 16–44.

———. 2001. "Herodotus and Oral History Reconsidered," in N. Luraghi, ed., 2001, 314–25.

Nagy, G. 1979. *The Best of the Achaeans. Concepts of the Hero in Archaic Greek Poetry.* Baltimore.

————. 2002. *Plato's Rhapsody and Homer's Music: The Poetics of the Panathenaic Festival in Classical Athens*. Cambridge, MA.

Neer, R. T. 2003. "Framing the Gift. The Siphnian Treasury at Delphi and the Politics of Architectural Sculpture," in C. Dougherty and L. Kurke, eds., *The Cultures within Ancient Greek Culture. Contact, Conflict and Collaboration*. Cambridge, 2003, 129–49.

Neils, J. 1992. *Goddess and Polis: The Panathenaic Festival in Classical Athens*. Princeton.

Nissenbaum, S. 1996. *The Battle for Christmas*. New York.

Ober, J. 1989. *Mass and Elite in Democratic Athens. Rhetoric, Ideology, and the Power of the People*. Princeton.

————. 1996. "Models and Paradigms in Ancient History," in J. Ober, *The Athenian Revolution. Essays on Ancient Greek Democracy and Political Theory*. Princeton, 12–17. Originally published in *Ancient History Bulletin* 3 (1989) 134–37.

————. 1998. *Political Dissent in Democratic Athens. Intellectual Critics of Popular Rule*. Princeton.

————. 2003. "Tyrant Killing as Therapeutic Stasis: A Political Debate in Images and Texts," in K. Morgan, ed., *Popular Tyranny. Sovereignty and Its Discontents in Ancient Greece*. TX, 215–50.

————. 2008. *Democracy and Knowledge. Innovation and Learning in Classical Athens*. Princeton.

Ogden, D. 1993. "Cleisthenes of Sicyon, ΛΕΥΣΤΉΡ." *Classical Quarterly* 43: 353–63.

————. 1997. *The Crooked Kings of Ancient Greece*. London.

————. 2004. *Aristomenes of Messene: Legends of Sparta's Nemesis*. Swansea.

O'Higgins, L. 2001. "Women's Cultic Joking and Mockery. Some Perspectives," A. Lardinois and L. McClure, eds., *Making Silence Speak. Women's Voices in Greek Literature and Society*. Princeton, 137–60.

————. 2003. *Women and Humor in Classical Greece*. Cambridge.

Okin, L. A. 1985. "Theognis and the Sources for the History of Archaic Megara," in Figueira and Nagy, eds., 1985, 9–21.

Olson, S. D., ed. 1998. *Aristophanes Peace*. Oxford.

————. 2002. ed. *Aristophanes Acharnians*. Oxford.

————. 2007. *Broken Laughter. Select Fragments of Greek Comedy*. Oxford.

————. 2008. *Athenaeus The Learned Banqueters. Books 6–7*. Cambridge, MA.

Oost, S. I. 1973. "The Megara of Theagenes and Theognis." *CP* 68: 186–96.

Osborne, M. J. 1981–82. *Naturalization in Athens*. 2 vols. Brussels.

Osborne, R. 1985a. *Demos: The Discovery of Classical Attika*. Cambridge.

————. 1985b. "Law in Action in Classical Athens." *JHS* 105: 40–58.

————. 1987. *Classical Landscape with Figures. The Ancient Greek City and its Countryside*. London.

————. 1991. "Pride and Prejudice, Sense and Subsistence: Exchange and Society in the Greek City," in J. Rich and A. Wallace-Hadrill, eds., *City and Country in the Ancient World*. London, 119–45.

————. 1992. "'Is It a Farm?' The Definition of Agricultural Sites and Settlements in Ancient Greece," in B. Wells, ed., 1992, 21–27.

————. 1994a. "Democracy and Imperialism in the Panathenaic Procession: the Parthenon Frieze in Its Context," in W.D.E. Coulson et al., eds.,*The Archaeology of Athens and Attica under the Democracy.* Oxford, 143–50.

————. 1994b. "Introduction: Ritual, Finance and Politics: An Account of Athenian Democracy," in R. Osborne and S. Hornblower, eds., *Ritual, Finance, Politics. Athenian Democratic Accounts Presented to David Lewis.* Oxford. 1–21.

————. 1995. "The Economics and Politics of Slavery at Athens," in A. Powell, ed., *The Greek World.* London, 27–43.

————. 1996. "Pots, Trade and the Archaic Greek Economy." *Antiquity* 70: 31–44.

————. 1998. "Early Greek Colonization? The Nature of Greek Settlement in the West," in Fisher and van Wees, eds., 1998, 251–69.

————. 2001. "The Use of Abuse: Semonides 7." *PCPS* 47: 47–64.

————. 2009. *Greece in the Making 1200–479 BC.* 2nd ed. London.

Ostwald, M. 2000. *Oligarchia. The Development of a Constitutional Form in Ancient Greece.* Stuttgart.

Page, D. 1973. *Folktales in Homer's Odyssey.* Cambridge, MA.

Pariente, A. 1992. 'Le monument argien des "Sept Contre Thèbes",' in M. Piérart, ed., *Polydipsion Argos* (BCH Supplement 22). Paris, 195–229.

Parke, H. W. 1977. *Festivals of the Athenians.* Ithaca.

Parker, R. 1983. *Miasma. Pollution and Purification in Early Greek Religion.* Oxford.

————. 1996. *Athenian Religion. A History.* Oxford.

————. 2005. *Polytheism and Society at Athens.* Oxford.

Parker, V. 1994. "Some Aspects of the Foreign and Domestic Policy of Cleisthenes of Sicyon." *Hermes* 122: 404–25.

Passow, A. 1860. *Popularia carmina graeciae recentioris.* Leipzig.

Patterson, O. 1982. *Slavery and Social Death. A Comparative Study.* Cambridge, MA.

Pelling, C. 2000. "Fun with Fragments …" in Braund and Wilkins, eds., 2000, 171–90.

————. 2002. "Speech and Action: Herodotus' Debate on the Constitutions." *PCPhS* 48: 123–58.

Pellizer, E. and G. Tedeschi, eds. 1990. *Semonide: introduzione, testimonianze, testo critico, traduzione e commento.* Rome.

Perry, B. E. 1952. *Aesopica. A Series of Texts Relating to Aesop or Ascribed to Him or Closely Connected with the Literary Tradition that Bears His Name.* Urbana, IL.

Piccirilli, L. 1975. *Megarika. Testimonianze e frammenti.* Pisa.

Pitt-Rivers, J. A. 1971. *The People of the Sierra.* 2nd ed. Chicago.

Porter, J. I., ed. 1999. *Constructions of the Classical Body.* Ann Arbor.

Raaflaub, K. A. 1979. "*Polis tyrannos*: Zur Entstehung einer politischen Metapher," in G. W. Bowersock et al., eds., *Arktouros. Hellenic Studies Presented to B.M.W. Knox on the Occasion of his 65th Birthday.* Berlin. 237–52.

————. 1996. "Solone, la nuova Atene e l'emergere della politica," in S.Settis, ed., *I Greci. Storia, Cultura, Arte, Societa* II.1. Turin, 1035–81.

Raaflaub, K. A., J. Ober, and R. W. Wallace, eds. 2007. *Origins of Democracy in Ancient Greece*. Berkeley.

Reardon, B. P., ed. 1989. *Collected Ancient Greek Novels*. Berkeley.

Reckford, K. J. 1987. *Aristophanes' Old and New Comedy. Volume I: Six Essays in Perspective*. Chapel Hill.

Renfrew, C. and J. F. Cherry, eds. 1986. *Peer Polity Interaction and Socio-political Change*. Cambridge.

Rhodes, P. 1981. *A Commentary on the Aristotelian* Athenaion Politeia. Oxford. Reprinted with Addenda and Corrigenda, 1993.

Richardson, N. J. 1974. *The Homeric Hymn to Demeter*. Oxford.

Rihll, T. 2008. "Slavery and Technology," in Dal Lago and Katsari, eds., 127–47.

Robert, L. 1938. *Études épigraphiques et philologiques*. Paris.

Robertson, B. 2008. "The Slave Names of *IG* I³ and the Ideology of Slavery at Athens," in C. Cooper, ed., *Epigraphy and the Greek Historian*. Toronto. 79–109.

Robinson, E.W. 1997. *The First Democracies. Early Popular Government Outside Athens*. Stuttgart.

Roebuck, C. A. 1986. "Chios in the Sixth Century BC," in J. Boardman and C. E. Vaphopoulou Richardson, eds., *Chios: A Conference in the Homereion of Chios*, 1984. Oxford. 81–103.

Roehner, B. and T. Syme. 2002. *Pattern and Repertoire in History*. Cambridge, MA.

Roisman, J. 2004. "Speaker-Audience Interaction in Athens: A Power Struggle," in I. Sluiter and R. Rosen, eds., 2004, 261–78.

Rollison, D. 1981. "Property, Ideology and Popular Culture in a Gloucestershire Village 1660–1740." *Past and Present* 93: 70–97.

Rosen, R. M. 1988. *Old Comedy and the Iambographic Tradition*. Atlanta, GA.

Rosen, R. M. and I. Sluiter, eds. 2003. *Andreia: Studies in Manliness and Courage in Classical Antiquity*. Leiden.

————. eds. 2004. *Free Speech in Classical Antiquity*. Leiden.

Rosivach, V. J. 1987. "Execution by Stoning in Athens." *CA* 6: 232–48.

————. 1992. "Redistribution of Land in Solon, Fragment 34 West." *JHS* 112: 153–57.

————. 1993. "Agricultural Slavery in the Northern Colonies and Classical Athens: Some Comparisons." *Comparative Studies in Society and History* 35: 551–67.

Rösler, W. 1986. "Michail Bachtin und die Karnevalskultur im antiken Griechenland." *QUCC* 23: 25–45.

Rothwell, K. S. 1995. "Aristophanes' Wasps and the Sociopolitics of Aesop's Fables." *Classical Journal* 93.4: 233–54.

Roussel, D. 1976. *Tribu et Cité*. Paris.

Rowe, G. 1965. "The *Adynaton* as a Stylistic Device." *American Journal of Philology* 86: 387–96.

Roy, J. 1991. "Traditional Jokes about the Punishment of Adulterers in Ancient Greek Literature." *Liverpool Classical Monthly* 16: 73–76.

Rudé, G. 1964. *The Crowd in History, 1730–1848*. New York.

———. 1980. *Ideology and Popular Protest*. Chapel Hill.

Sabean, D. 1984. *Power in the Blood. Popular Culture and Village Discourse in Early Modern Germany*. Cambridge.

Ste. Croix, G.E.M. de. 1981. *The Class Struggle in the Ancient Greek World*. London.

Sakellariou, M. B. 1990. *Between Memory and Oblivion. The Transmission of Early Greek Historical Traditions*. Athens.

Sale, K. 1995. *Rebels against the Futures. The Luddites and their War on the Industrial Revolution. Lessons for the Computer Age*. Reading, MA.

Sallares, R. 1991. *The Ecology of the Ancient Greek World*. Ithaca.

Santini, L. 1997. "Demosth. or.19,287 e la tradizione paremiografica." *Museum Helveticum* 54: 48–52.

Scafuro, A. 2006. "Identifying Solonian Laws," in J. H. Blok and A.P.M.H. Lardinois, eds., *Solon of Athens: New Historical and Philological Approaches*. Leiden, 165–87.

Schaps, D. M. 1998. "What Was Free about a Free Athenian Woman?" *TAPA* 128: 161–88.

Scheidel, W. 1995. "The Most Silent Women of Greece and Rome: Rural Labour and Women's Life in the Ancient World." *Greece and Rome* 42: 202–17.

———. 1996. "The Most Silent Women of Greece and Rome: Rural Labour and Women's Life in the Ancient World. Part II." 43: 1–10.

———. 2003. "The Greek Demographic Expansion: Models and Comparisons." *JHS* 123: 120–40.

———. 2008. "The Comparative Economics of Slavery in the Greco-Roman world," in Del Lago and Katsari, eds., 2008, 105–26.

———. ed. 2009. *Rome and China. Comparative Perspectives on Ancient World Empires*. Oxford.

Schmitt-Pantel, P. 1981. "L'âne, l'adultère et la cité," in J. Le Goff and J-C. Schmitt, eds., *Le Charivari*. Paris, 117–22.

———. 1992. *La Cité au Banquet. Histoire des repas publics dans les cités grecques*. Rome.

Schmitz, W. 2004. *Nachbarschaft und Dorfgemeinschaft im archaischen und klassischen Griechenland*. Berlin.

Scodel, R. ed. 1993. *Theater and Society in the Classical World*. Ann Arbor.

Scott, J. C. 1985. *Weapons of the Weak. Everyday Forms of Peasant Resistance*. New Haven.

———. 1990. *Domination and the Arts of Resistance. Hidden Transcripts*. New Haven.

Scott, L. 2005. *Historical Commentary on Herodotus Book 6*. Leiden.

Screech, M. A. 2006. *Rabelais. Gargantua and Pantagruel*. London.

Serghidou, A. 2007. *Fear of Slaves—Fear of Enslavement in the Ancient Mediterranean*. Actes du XXIXᵉ Colloque du Groupe International de Recherche sur l'Esclavage dans l'Antiquité (GIREA). Rethymnon 4–7 Novembre 2004. Franche-Compté.

Shaw, B. 1984. "Bandits in the Roman Empire." *Past and Present* 105: 3–52. Reprinted in R. Osborne, ed., *Studies in Ancient Greek and Roman Society*. Cambridge, 2004.

———. 2001. *Spartacus and the Slave Wars. A Brief History with Documents*. Boston.

Shear, J. 2007. "The Oath of Demophantos and the Politics of Athenian Identity," in A. H. Somerstein and J. Fletcher, eds., *Horkos. The Oath in Greek Society*. Bristol, 2007, 148–254.

Sidwell, K. 2004. *Lucian. Chattering Courtesans and Other Sardonic Sketches*. London.

Skocpol, T. and M. Somers. 1980. "The Uses of Comparative History in Macrosocial Inquiry." *Comparative Studies in Society and History* 22: 174–97.

Sluiter, I. and R. M. Rosen, eds. 2004. *Free Speech in Classical Antiquity*. Leiden.

Smyth, H. W. 1906. *Greek Melic Poets*. New York.

Snodgrass, A. 1986. "Interaction by Design: The Greek City-State." in Cherry and Renfrew, eds., 1986, 47–58.

Sommerstein, A. 2001. ed. *Aristophanes Wealth*. Warminster.

Stallybrass, P. and A. White. 1986. *The Politics and Poetics of Transgression*. Ithaca.

Stampp, K. 1956. *The Peculiar Institution. Slavery in the Ante-Bellum South*. New York.

Sternberg, R. 2006. *Tragedy Offstage: Suffering and Sympathy in Ancient Athens*. Austin, TX.

Storey, I. 2003. *Eupolis, Poet of Old Comedy*. Oxford.

Sutton, D. 1980. *Self and Society in Aristophanes*. Washington.

Szegedy-Maszak, A. 1978. "Legends of the Greek Lawgivers." *GRBS* 19: 199–209.

Szeliga, G.N. 1986. "The Composition of the Argo Metopes from the Monopteros at Delphi." *AJA* 90: 297–305.

Tacon, J. 2001. "Ecclesiastic Thorubos: Interventions, Interruptions and Popular Involvement in the Athenian Assembly." *Greece & Rome* 48.2: 173–92.

Thomas, K. 1964. "Work and Leisure." *Past and Present* 29: 50–66.

Thomas, R. 1989. *Oral Tradition and Written Record in Classical Athens*. Cambridge.

Thomas, Y. 1984. "Introduction," in *Du châtiment dans la cité. Supplices corporals et peine de mort dans le monde antique*. Rome, 1–7.

Thompson, E. P. 1975. *Whigs and Hunters. The Origins of the Black Act*. London.

———. 1993. *Customs in Common. Studies in Traditional Popular Culture*. New York.

Tilly, C. 1984. *Big Structures, Large Processes, Huge Comparisons*. New York.

Todd, S. 2000. "How to Execute People in Fourth-Century Athens," in V. Hunter and J. Edmondson, eds., *Law and Social Status in Classical Athens*. Oxford, 31–51.

———. 2007. *A Commentary on Lysias. Speeches 1–11*. Oxford.

Trevett, J. 1992. *Apollodorus, the Son of Pasion*. Oxford.

———. 2000. "Was There a Decree of Syracosios?" *CQ* 50: 598–600.

Trexler, R. C. 1980. *Public Life in Renaissance Florence*. Ithaca.

Trypanis, C. A. ed. 1971. *The Penguin Book of Greek Verse*. Harmondsworth.

Tsetskhladze, G. R. 2008. "Pontic Slaves in Athens: Orthodoxy and Reality," in R. Rollinger and C. Ulf, eds., *Lebenswelten. Konstanz–Wandel–Wirkungsmacht.* Wiesbaden. 309–19.

Turner, V. 1969. *The Ritual Process: Structure and Anti-Structure.* Chicago.

Ulf, C. 1996. "Griechische Ethnogenese versus Wanderungen von Stämmstaaten," in C. Ulf, ed., *Wege zur Genese griechischer Identität: die Bedeutung der früharchaischen Zeit.* Berlin. 240–80.

———. 2009. "Ethnicity and Ethnicization of Greek Ethne in Anthropological Perspective," in P. Funke and N. Luraghi, 215–49.

Underdown, D. 1985. *Revel, Riot and Rebellion. Popular Politics and Culture in England 1603–1660.* Oxford.

Usener, H. 1901. "Italische Volksjustiz." *RhM* 56: 1–28. Reprinted in H. Usener *Kleine Schriften.* Berlin, 1913: 356–82.

Van Dijk, G. J. 1997. Ainoi, Logoi, Mythoi. *Fables in Archaic, Classical and Hellenistic Greek Literature with a Study of the Theory and Terminology of the Genre.* Mnemosune: Supplementum 166. Leiden.

van Wees, H. 1999. "The Mafia of Early Greece. Violent Exploitation in the Seventh and Sixth centuries BC," in K. Hopwood, ed., *Organized Crime in Antiquity.* London, 1–51.

———. 2000. "Megara's Mafiosi: Timocracy and Violence in Theognis," in Brock and Hodkinson, eds., 2000, 52–67.

———. 2003. "Conquerors and Serfs: Wars of Conquest and Forced Labour in Archaic Greece," in N. Luraghi and S. E. Alcock, eds., *Helots and Their Masters in Laconia and Messenia. Histories, Ideologies, Structures.* Cambridge, MA, 33–80.

Vansina, J. 1985. *Oral Tradition as History.* London.

Veligianni-Terzi, C. 1997. *Wertbegriffe in den attischen Ehrendekreten der klassichen Zeit.* Stuttgart.

Versnel, H. 1977. "Polycrates and His Ring." *Studi Storico-Religiosi* 1: 17–46.

———. 1993. *Inconsistencies in Greek and Roman Religion II. Transition and Reversal in Myth and Ritual.* Leiden.

Vidal-Naquet, P. 1986. "Reflections on Greek Historical Writing about Slavery," in *The Black Hunter. Forms of Thought and Forms of Society in the Greek World.* Translated by A. Szegedy-Mazsak. Princeton. 168–80. Originally published in 1973.

Vlassopoulos, K. 2007a. *Unthinking the Greek Polis. Ancient Greek History beyond Eurocentrism.* Cambridge.

———. 2007b. "Free Spaces: Identity, Experience and Democracy in Classical Athens." *Classical Quarterly* 57: 33–52.

———. 2009. "Slavery, Freedom and Citizenship in Classical Athens: Beyond a Legalistic Approach." *European Review of History* 16: 347–63.

Vogt, J. 1973. "Alphabet für Freie und Sklaven." *RhM* 116: 129–42.

Von Blumenthal, A. 1940. "Beobachtungen zu griechischen Texten II." *Hermes* 75: 124–28.

Walker, S. 1998. *Popular Justice.* 2nd ed. Oxford.

Wallace, R.W. 1997. "Solonian Democracy," in I. Morris and K. Raaflaub, eds., *Democracy 2500? Questions and Challenges*. AIA Colloquium and Conference Papers 2. Dubuque, IA, 11–29.

———. 2004. "The Power to Speak—and Not to Listen—in Ancient Athens," in Sluiter and Rosen, eds., 2004, 221–32.

———. 2005. "Law, Attic Comedy, and the Regulation of Comic Speech," in M. Gagarin and D. Cohen, eds., 2005, 357–73.

———. 2007. "Revolutions and a New Order in Solonian Athens and Archaic Greece," in K. A. Raaflaub et al., eds., *Origins of Democracy in Ancient Greece*. Berkeley. 49–82.

Warmington, E. H. ed. 1961. *Remains of Old Latin 1*. Cambridge, MA.

Wells, B. ed. 1992. *Agriculture in Ancient Greece. Proceedings of the Seventh International Symposium at the Swedish Institute at Athens, 16–17 May 1990*. Stockholm.

West, M.L. 1974. *Studies in Greek Elegy and Iambus*. Berlin.

———. 1978. *Hesiod. Works and Days*. Oxford.

———. 1984. "The Ascription of Fables to Aesop in Archaic and Classical Greece," in Adrados, ed., 1984. 105–28.

———. 1989. "The Early Chronology of Attic Tragedy," *CQ* 39: 251–54.

———. 1994. *Greek Lyric Poetry. A New Translation*. Oxford.

———. 2001. "The Fragmentary Homeric Hymn to Dionysus." *ZPE* 134: 1–11.

———. 2003. *Homeric Hymns, Homeric Apocrypha, Lives of Homer*. Cambridge, MA.

Whitehead, D. 1977. *The Ideology of the Athenian Metic*. Cambridge Philological Society, Supplementary Volume 4. Cambridge.

———. 1983. "Competitive Outlay and Community Profit: φιλοτιμία in Democratic Athens." *Classica et Medievalia* 34: 55–74.

———. 1986. *The Demes of Attica 508/7–ca. 250 B.C. A Political Study*. Princeton.

———. 1993. "Cardinal Virtues: The Language of Public Approbation in Democratic Athens." *Classica et Medievalia* 44: 37–75.

Wilenz, S. 1985. *Rites of Power. Symbolism, Ritual and Politics Since the Middle Ages*. Philadelphia.

Wilkins, J. 2000a. "Dialogue and Comedy. The Structure of the Deipnosophistae," in D. Braund and J. Wilkins, eds., 2000, 23–37.

———. 2000b. *The Boastful Chef. The Discourse of Food in Ancient Greek Comedy*. Oxford.

Willetts, R. F. 1967. *The Law Code of Gortyn*. Berlin.

Williams, B. 1993. *Shame and Necessity*. Berkeley.

Wilson, P. 2000. *The Athenian Institution of the Khoregia. The Chorus, The City and the Stage*. Cambridge.

Winkler, J. J. 1990. *The Constraints of Desire. The Anthropology of Sex and Gender in Ancient Greece*. London.

Winkler, J. J. and F. I. Zeitlin, eds. 1990. *Nothing to Do with Dionysus? Athenian Drama in Its Social Context*. Princeton.

Wohl, V. 1996. "εὐεβείας ἕνεκα καὶ φιλτιμίας: Hegemony and Democracy at the Panathenaia." *Classica & Mediaevalia* 47: 25–88.

Wolf, E. 1966. *Peasants*. Upper Saddle River, NJ.
Wood, E. M. 1988. *Peasant-Citizen and Slave. The Foundations of Athenian Democracy*. London.
Yalouris, N. 1986. "Apollo Phanaios and the Cult of Phanes," in J. Boardman and C. E. Vaphopoulou, eds., 39–41.
Yatromanolakis, D. and P. Roilos, eds. 2004. *Greek Ritual Poetics*. Cambridge, MA.
Zeitlin, F. I. 1996. *Playing the Other. Gender and Society in Classical Greek Literature*. Chicago.
Zelnick-Abramovitz, R. 2005. *Not Wholly Free. The Concept of Manumission and the Status of Manumitted Slaves in the Ancient Greek World*. Leiden.
Zielinski, T. 1885. *Die Märchenkomödie in Athen*. St. Petersburg.

Index Locorum

General Index